dBASE III PLUS™ MADE EASY

dBASE III PLUS™ MADE EASY

Miriam Liskin

Osborne **McGraw-Hill**
Berkeley, California

Osborne **McGraw-Hill**
2600 Tenth Street
Berkeley, CA 94710
U.S.A.

For information on translations and book distributors outside of the U.S.A., write to Osborne **McGraw-Hill** at the above address.

A complete list of trademarks appears on page 537.

dBASE III PLUS™ Made Easy

234567890 DODO 898

ISBN 0-07-881294-1

This one's for Peter and for Lisa, not that you guys need it anymore.

Contents

Acknowledgments

I'd like to take this opportunity to thank the people who made direct or indirect contributions to this book.

Thanks to my editors at Osborne/McGraw-Hill — to Cindy Hudson, for twisting my arm just hard enough to convince me to write it (now that she's decided to learn dBASE); to Nancy Carlston, who kept things running smoothly; and to Fran Haselsteiner, for understanding my priorities, and for her appreciation of the language (English, not dBASE) and the impact of the written word.

Thanks to Lisa Biow, whose many helpful suggestions were above and beyond the call of duty in her role as technical reviewer, and who also contributed in large measure to the structure and organization of this book through our collaboration on developing and teaching a beginning dBASE III PLUS class.

Many thanks to all the students who "beta-tested" the material in this book by attending my dBASE classes and reminding me which concepts are important, which are confusing or difficult to grasp, and above all, what the average dBASE user really needs to know.

Finally, I'd like to acknowledge the influence of John Muir, author of one of the best "made easy" books on any subject — *How to Keep Your VW Alive: A Manual of Step by Step Procedures for the Compleat Idiot.* This book taught me a lot about VWs and about how to teach beginners: Don't assume any prior knowledge, and keep going until you've covered everything the reader needs to know, even if it gets complicated.

Introduction

dBASE III PLUS is one of the most powerful and sophisticated data base management programs available today. It also has a reputation for being "unfriendly" and intimidating. In part, this reputation was inherited from dBASE II; and to that extent it is undeserved, because dBASE III PLUS is both easier for a novice to learn and more convenient for an expert to use than its predecessor.

Nevertheless, many users find that getting started with dBASE III PLUS — or, indeed, any data base program — is more difficult than learning to use a word processor or spreadsheet. Some of the concepts are less intuitive, and your work with the computerized data base often does not parallel as closely the way the same tasks are carried out manually. Data base software is frequently used for applications involving calculations, transfers of information, and decision-making processes that would be complicated and difficult even if you did not have to master new concepts at the same time. Finally, as with any high-end software, you may find the sheer volume of commands and functions overwhelming.

This book will help you surmount those barriers and begin doing productive work with dBASE III PLUS almost immediately. The first three chapters introduce the essential data base management concepts that will underlie all of your work with dBASE III PLUS, and they outline a basic approach to application design that can be used effectively by a person with no formal training in systems analysis. Chapters 4 through 12 describe in detail the general strategies and specific commands that you can use to maintain a system composed of one or more related data base files and to extract useful information from the data. Chapter 13 addresses some of the problems involved in transferring data between dBASE III PLUS and other programs, and Chapter 14 presents a brief introduction to writing simple batch-type dBASE III PLUS programs consisting of commands you have already learned.

You do not need any prior experience with dBASE III PLUS or other data base managers to understand any of the material in this book. However, a basic familiarity with the use of an IBM PC, PC XT, PC AT, PS/2, or compatible computer is assumed. You should be comfortable with the keyboard layout, know the location and usage of special keys (in particular, the cursor movement keys, CTRL, ESC, and the programmable function keys), and possess some understanding of the MS-DOS operating system and its intrinsic commands and utility programs.

dBASE III PLUS can be used at three distinctly different levels:

- Through a system of pull-down menus called the ASSIST mode, or the Assistant
- By typing commands one at a time, next to a command prompt called the "dot prompt," much as you do when you execute MS-DOS commands
- By writing programs in the built-in programming language provided with dBASE III PLUS

This book focuses squarely on the middle level. Its aim is to help you attain a level of proficiency that will enable you to use dBASE III PLUS at the dot prompt to solve your business and personal data base problems. The Assistant is introduced in Chapter 2 and Chapter 14 touches on elementary programming concepts, but, for the most part, the emphasis is on working in interactive mode, at the dot prompt, where dBASE III PLUS excels in power and flexibility.

This outlook derives from the expressed needs of many of my students and clients, who have relatively sophisticated applications and who are willing to devote some time and energy to the learning process, but who have neither the time nor the inclination to become programmers. While dBASE III PLUS may not be the easiest program to learn, once you have mastered a basic command repertoire, it is an easy program to use. The command language, which is concise and logical in its structure, is close enough to human languages that typing commands will soon seem natural and intuitive. Once you have mastered a basic command vocabulary, you will appreciate the fact that most commands can be executed as fast as you can type them, without wading through several levels of menus, and with few preparatory steps.

If your application is simple and you have little prior experience with computers, you may want to spend more time working in the menu-driven ASSIST mode before you graduate to the dot prompt. Many of the commands described in this book can be executed from the Assistant, and once you become familiar with the menus and the process of making selections, you will not need explicit instructions to adapt the procedures in this book to the ASSIST mode. Keep in mind, however, that not all of the commands you can use at the dot prompt are available through the menu system, and that in some cases it is actually more cumbersome and confusing to carry out a command sequence through the Assistant than by typing commands directly.

This book is both a tutorial for first-time users and a reference guide for your ongoing work with dBASE III PLUS. The tutorial material is based on a customer and order-tracking data base for an imaginary company called National Widgets, Inc., which is developed and expanded throughout the book. Most of the chapters include one or more Hands-On Practice sections, and you will benefit enormously by entering the sample data and working through all of the tutorials, and by trying at least some of the examples presented in the body of the text. If you are actively involved in a data base project, you might also want to try carrying out the same commands or procedures on copies of your own files.

While it is intended for beginners and does not assume any prior knowledge of dBASE III PLUS or of data base management concepts, this book does take you far beyond the beginning level. Accordingly, a fairly wide range of commands and command options are covered, and you may find as you go through a chapter for the first time that there is too much new material to absorb at one sitting. In addition, you will tend to focus more closely on certain topics, perhaps because they are directly applicable to your own data base projects. Later, you may want to return to the same chapters to pick up the concepts that seemed too difficult or the examples that appeared esoteric the first time through, but that may be more relevant in the light of your greater experience.

You may also feel that some of the examples, especially in the later chapters, concentrate on minute details of the National Widgets sample system. Try not to lose sight of the forest for the trees—each of the examples was chosen to clarify the purpose of a commonly used command or to illustrate typical combinations of commands used to carry out fundamentally similar operations on virtually any data base. Every attempt was made to model the National Widgets system on real-world data processing needs and to make the command sequences as illustrative as possible of typical solutions to real data base management problems.

No matter what your level of experience, the most important assets you can bring to your work with dBASE III PLUS are an assertive attitude and a willingness to experiment. The best way to overcome your initial intimidation is to jump in and begin working right away. Take the time to set up the National Widgets files and enter the sample data, so that you can experiment with unfamiliar commands in a safe setting, without risking your own data bases. Try as many command options and variations as you can think of. If you think you see a viable alternative to one of the strategies or techniques presented here, try it—there is often more than one good way to accomplish any particular goal, and your choices may be guided as much by personal style as by more objective factors.

Above all, try to relax and enjoy yourself—and have some fun with dBASE III PLUS.

—Miriam Liskin

Chapter 1

Introduction to Data Base Management

The term *data base management* is used collectively to describe the diverse operations involved in using a computer to store, manipulate, retrieve, and report on information. What kind of information goes into a data base? That depends entirely on you. A nonprofit organization might have a mailing list data base consisting of names, addresses, and telephone numbers; a small business might want to set up an inventory data base that tracks part numbers, item descriptions, costs, selling prices, and quantities sold, on hand, and on order; and a lawyer might need to categorize and cross-reference documents introduced as evidence in a trial.

None of these information management activities requires a computer; in fact, all the individuals and businesses cited in the aforementioned examples most likely keep track of their data on paper with some kind of manual system. When a data base is small and must be accessed by only a few people who are familiar with the information, even a relatively informal manual system may serve the purpose. With greater volumes of data, however, or in larger organizations where different people may want to access the same information in a variety of ways, computerizing can yield enormous gains, both in processing efficiency and in the utility of the information that can easily be extracted from the mass of raw data.

A FUNCTIONAL DEFINITION OF DATA BASE MANAGEMENT

The easiest way to understand data base management concepts and visualize what you can do with a data base management program like dBASE III PLUS is to work from a functional definition. In general, data base management software allows you to carry out the following operations:

- Define the individual items of data to be maintained
- Design screen layouts for entering and displaying data
- Enter data according to a predefined format
- Retrieve specific data to be viewed or printed
- Change or delete data
- Rearrange data into different orders for screen displays or reports
- Select subsets of the data for specific purposes
- Perform calculations and store, view, or print the results
- Produce printed reports that provide meaningful information to people who are not familiar with computers or data base management software

You may recognize in this definition the computerized analogs of operations that you are currently carrying out manually. For example, defining a screen format for entering or displaying data is equivalent to designing a paper form for recording the same information. Retrieving specific information in order to make changes accomplishes the same goal as taking a particular form out of a file drawer, crossing out an old address, writing in a new one, and returning it to its proper place in the file. Selecting a subset of the data for a special purpose and rearranging the selected data into a different order is not unlike typing mailing labels in ZIP code order for those people on a mailing list whose memberships are due to expire the following month.

Perhaps you are graduating to dBASE III PLUS because you have reached the limits of a less capable file manager, such as PFS, PC-File III, or the Data Query commands in Lotus 1-2-3. If so, you already have some familiarity with these fundamental data base operations, but even if you have never used any software billed as a file manager or data base program, you may already have had some indirect experience with data base management. Anyone who has used an accounting program or specialized software for applications such as medical or law office management, client billing, or job costing has been using a data base manager, since these programs perform the functions that make up the operational definition of data base management.

The difference between these "canned" programs and a general-purpose data base manager like dBASE III PLUS is that the packaged programs are customized for specific applications and cannot readily be adapted to the unique needs of individual users. They operate only on predetermined types of data and produce only the reports deemed necessary by their designers. With a canned client billing package, if you wanted to add the client name to a report that listed only the account number, print a client list grouped by city and state rather than in alphabetical order, or use a nonstandard method for computing hourly charges, you would be out of luck.

With dBASE III PLUS, you can carry out the same types of operations on any type of information, design your own screen and report formats, define your own calculations, and specify any criteria for selecting and rearranging the data. You can use the same software for all the vastly different data base applications enumerated at the beginning of this chapter as well as many others.

Of course, this freedom and flexibility has its price. If you can find a canned program that satisfies most of your requirements and fits within your budget, you will be able to get the system up and running much faster and with less effort and frustration than by doing it yourself with dBASE III PLUS. Be aware also that many data base applications are complex enough to require programming, and although dBASE III PLUS includes a full-fledged programming language, you may not have the time, aptitude, or desire to become a dBASE III PLUS programmer.

Nevertheless, dBASE III PLUS is a powerful and flexible tool well suited for the data base management needs of many individuals, businesses, and non-profit organizations. If you are willing to devote the necessary time to learning to use dBASE III PLUS and setting up your applications, you can accomplish some very sophisticated data base management tasks without programming.

THE BENEFITS OF COMPUTERIZING

As you work through the analysis and planning phase, keep in mind which kinds of operations can benefit most from computerization. You stand to gain the most

- When you can enter information once and then print it in several formats or sorted orders
- When the computer can take over calculations that are complex or tedious by hand
- When the computer enables anyone in the office to perform tasks that would otherwise require special expertise
- When the ability to easily generate reports provides more timely or less expensive access to management information

- When the ability to easily cross-reference information enables you to produce reports that would be far too time-consuming to consider preparing manually

It is equally important to bear in mind that even though computers can perform calculations far more quickly than humans, not every job can be done faster or better with a computer. This is especially true when a great deal of user input is required, since it usually takes about the same amount of time to enter information into a computerized data base as it does to write or type it on paper. If the computer must then sort the data and print a report, producing that final piece of paper may actually take longer than typing the report. On the other hand, if you can enter information once, perform a complex calculation, and then produce three different reports drawing on the results, you have realized a substantial gain over your manual system.

DEFINITIONS OF SOME COMMON TERMS

For the most part, this book avoids using "computerese" and attempts to explain new concepts in familiar, nontechnical language. However, in any specialized field, a certain amount of jargon is not only inevitable but beneficial, since it allows some important concepts to be expressed concisely and unambiguously.

The definitions of data base terminology presented in this section are consistent with the way the terms are used in the dBASE III PLUS manuals and in many other books on the subject. Be aware that this usage is "standard" only within the dBASE III PLUS user community. Other popular data base programs that you may have used in the past or may encounter in the future assign different meanings to some of these words or use different terms to express the same concepts.

In a dBASE III PLUS data base, each item of information is called a *field,* and the set of fields that describe one logical unit of information is called a *record*. For example, in a mailing list data base, the logical storage unit is one person. In each person's record, you might have fields for the name, street address, city, state, ZIP code, and telephone number. In an inventory data base, the logical unit of information is one stocked item, and an inventory record might contain fields for the part number, a brief description, cost, selling price, and quantity on hand.

A collection of records that share the same format—that have the same fields—is called a *file*, or a *data base*. If there were 250 people on the simple mailing list in the previous example, the mailing list data base or file would have 250 records, each of which contained six fields.

These terms may seem natural and intuitive to you, because they are often used in almost exactly the same way to talk about manual filing systems. If you maintained customer records on ledger cards stored in a file folder or file box, you might say, "Go to the accounts receivable file and get me Kelly's records." In another setting, where a file drawer or an

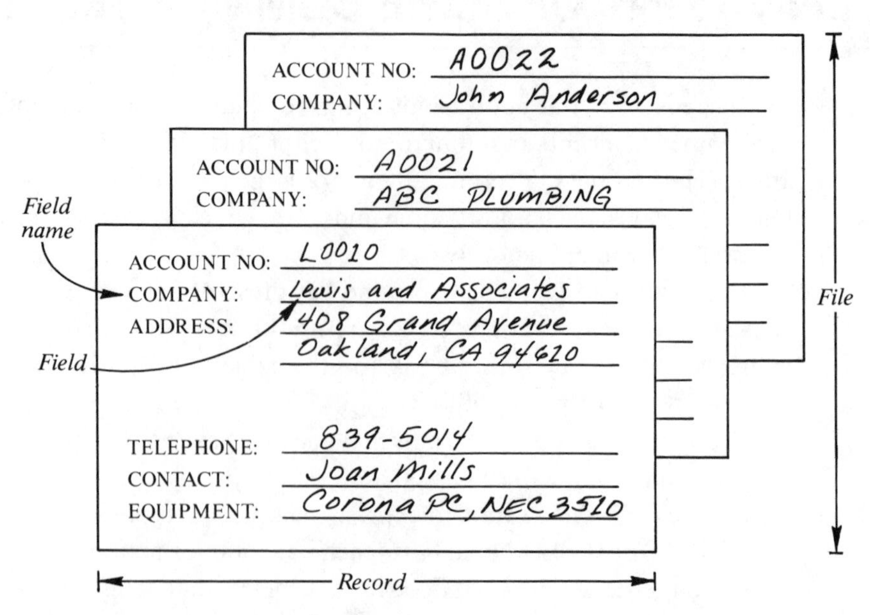

Figure 1-1 *The ledger card model for a data base*

entire filing cabinet were devoted to storing accounts receivable information, each customer might have a separate folder, and you would be more likely to say, "Get me Kelly's file." This discrepancy between data base terminology and colloquial usage can be potentially confusing when you begin working with dBASE III PLUS, or later on when you attempt to communicate with less experienced users about your data bases.

The ledger card, or file card, analogy represents one good way to visualize a dBASE III PLUS data base: You can imagine one paper form representing a record, with the fields in a more or less vertical arrangement on the page. The entire stack of ledger cards (or other paper forms) constitutes a file. This model is illustrated in Figure 1-1.

If you have worked with a spreadsheet program such as Lotus 1-2-3 or SuperCalc (both of which offer some data base management capabilities), you may feel more comfortable visualizing a data base as a table much like a spreadsheet. In this model, the fields are lined up in columns and each record extends horizontally across the page (which might have to be very wide to accommodate all the fields). The table model is illustrated in Figure 1-2.

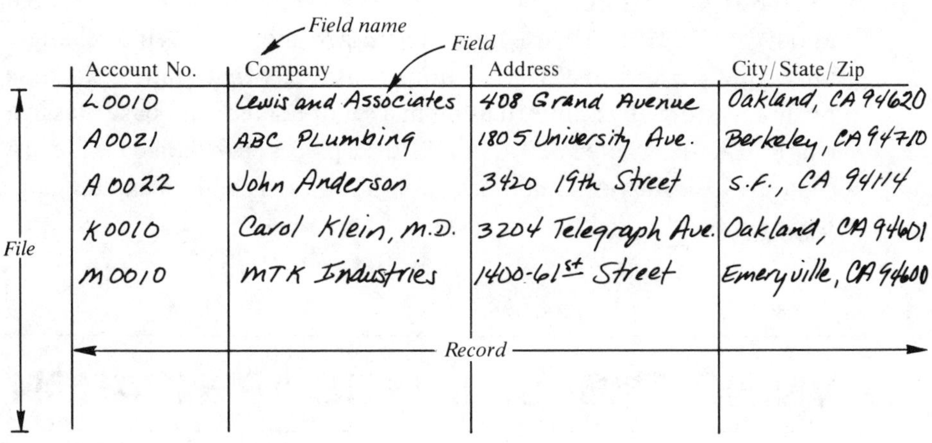

Figure 1-2 *The tabular model for a data base*

As you will see in Chapter 4, dBASE III PLUS allows you to view a data base on the screen in two standard layouts, one of which closely resembles the ledger card model, while the other approximates the tabular arrangement.

A dBASE III PLUS application may consist of a single data base, or it may require two or more discrete files. For example, many mailing list applications need only a single name and address data base, while a client billing data base for a professional office might comprise a dozen interrelated files, including one for client names and addresses, one for hourly charges, one for payments, and so on.

dBASE III PLUS allows you to *relate,* or link, two files based on fields that contain information common to both. For example, in an order-tracking system, each customer might be assigned an account number; a field for this code would be included in both the customer file and the order file. By comparing the contents of the account number field in the two files, dBASE III PLUS can associate an order with the matching customer or find all the orders placed by a given customer. Because of its ability to work with multiple related files, dBASE III PLUS is often described as a *relational* data base (although this usage does not conform to the more technical definition of the term *relational* as originally developed for mainframe data bases).

Some authors use the term *data base* to describe a set of related files, but the dBASE III PLUS documentation and most of the books written about dBASE III PLUS use *file* and *data base* more or less interchangeably. One reason for this variation in usage is that some data base programs store all the information in a set of related data base files in a single disk file, whereas dBASE III PLUS places each data base file in a separate disk file (or sometimes two disk files, as will be explained in Chapter 3).

PLANNING A dBASE III PLUS APPLICATION

Before you can use dBASE III PLUS to set up a data base, you must define what you want the system to accomplish. The functional definition of data base management presented earlier in this chapter suggests the types of questions you will need to ask yourself in order to clarify your goals:

- What items of information must be maintained?
- How should the data be presented on the screen? Must the data entry and inquiry screens emulate existing paper forms?
- What criteria will be used to retrieve records in order to view, change, delete, or print data?
- In what different sequences will data be viewed or printed?
- What subsets of the data (which fields from which records) must be selected for specific purposes?
- What calculations or transformations must be performed on the data?
- What transfers of information must take place between files or within a file? Must data be archived and then deleted from any files?
- What screen output and printed reports must the system produce?

If your dBASE III PLUS data base will replace or augment an existing manual system, your job will be much easier than if you are trying to computerize a new application or bring in house operations that are currently being performed by outside contractors. Even if you intend to completely revamp your present procedures, a careful study of the manual system can provide a valuable framework for your needs analysis. Without a comparable "paper" system, you have no choice but to proceed directly to a description of the functions you anticipate you will need. But since your initial study cannot be as complete, you should be prepared for the eventuality that more extensive revisions will be required as the system grows and evolves.

Undoubtedly, you are already impatient to begin working with dBASE III PLUS, especially if you feel that implementing a new system or improving your old one is long overdue. Yet the process of analyzing your present system and projecting your future needs can be difficult, tedious, and time-consuming. It can also be somewhat traumatic, since you will have to rethink all your familiar manual procedures and examine the workings of your organization in greater detail than you have in years — or perhaps ever.

For all these reasons, the temptation will be strong to abbreviate the planning phase or skip it entirely. Try not to yield to this temptation! Regardless of how much or how little prior experience you have with computers or data base management software, all the time spent on advance planning will pay big dividends later in time saved, because you will not have to make as many changes and additions to the data bases.

STUDYING SAMPLES FROM THE MANUAL SYSTEM

An excellent way to begin your needs analysis is to gather a complete set of the documents that make up your present manual system. For example, an accounts receivable system might include customer ledger cards, order forms, a price list, invoices, monthly statements, bank deposit slips, a cash receipts journal, an invoice register, an aging report, and a quarterly sales tax summary. Carefully studying these paper forms will help you extract a list of the items of information that must be entered into the system, many calculations and transfers of information that must be performed, and the printed reports the system must produce.

If at all possible, the sample documents should contain matching data. With the accounts receivable example, the invoice you select should match the order form, and the invoice data should appear on the customer ledger card, the statement, the invoice register, the aging report, and the sales tax summary. Similarly, the bank deposit slip and the cash receipts journal should include the payment data for the sample invoice. By matching the samples, you will find it easy to trace the flow of information through the system and reconstruct the calculations and data transfers that must be performed.

OUTLINING THE WORK FLOW AND SCHEDULE

Armed with a set of sample documents (or, for a new application, a description of the required documents), you can proceed to outline the present and projected work flow and processing schedule. If you are emulating or replacing a manual system, you can describe the tasks currently being carried out by hand as well as any new capabilities you would like to add. For a new system, you will necessarily be limited to the proposed new operations. For each task, ask yourself these types of questions:

- *What items of information are involved?* Each required item must either be included as a field in one of the data bases or calculated from other fields.

- *How big is each item?* The data base fields must be wide enough to accommodate the required data.

- *Approximately how many of each item are there?* These numbers will help you estimate how large your data bases will be and choose the most efficient ways to manipulate the data.

- *What calculations or transformations are carried out?* Make sure that you know how to carry out all mathematical computations or data transformations that must be performed.

- *What transfers of information are involved?* You will have to design computerized equivalents for such transfers of information as posting transactions or archiving and deleting obsolete data.

- *What prior processing or special preparation is required?* You will have to ensure that any required calculations or transfers of information are carried out before you perform other calculations or print reports that depend on the results.

- *How often is the operation performed?* The frequency of a task influences how important processing speed is and how inconvenient any required special preparations or prior calculations will be.

- *How long does it take to carry out the task manually?* This information will provide the perspective to gauge which operations can gain the most from computerization and which should be given a lower priority.

Your answers to the questions involving sizes and quantities need not be exact. For example, it makes little difference whether you generate 100 invoices per month or 150, but a business that produces 1000 invoices a month might handle posting differently from one having 100. Also, for numeric quantities, the number of items processed is usually more important than their magnitude. A business with gross annual sales of $1 million that sells $10 items will have a much larger transaction file—which will require more storage space and processing time—than a business with the same annual gross that sells products in the $10,000 range.

If you anticipate that your answers to any of these questions will change significantly during the next year or two, you might make two parallel lists: one that describes your present situation and one with future estimates. For example, if there are currently 2000 names on your mailing list, but you have arranged to purchase another organization's 3000-name list at the end of the year, you should plan your data base to comfortably handle 5000 names. If the most expensive item in your inventory sells for $49.95, but you expect to add a new product line next year, you might decide to add an extra digit to the price field to accommodate prices over $100.

Try to be realistic, however. It is easy for an organization with 300 donors and a new fund-raising director to make the optimistic prediction that the roster will increase to 2000 in two years. The resulting data base design may turn out to be unnecessarily complicated or cumbersome if the anticipated growth never materializes.

OUTLINING THE REPORTS

For some people, enumerating the items of information to be maintained in a data base is the most natural approach to the system design process, while others visualize the goals of a system in terms of the printed output it must produce. You can tackle the problem from either perspective, but even if your natural inclination is to begin by specifying the input to the system, it is essential to include in your advance planning a description of the required reports.

In fact, the output of the system is often more helpful than the input documents in pinning down data base structures. Obviously, any information that appears on a report must either be entered directly into a data base or calculated from other fields. In addition, you must include fields for any information you will use either in selection criteria—to decide which records are included on a given report—or to specify the order in which the records should be printed.

Studying the present and proposed reports will also help you avoid a very common pitfall: creating a huge data base with many fields for information that could be maintained just as well by hand or that is already being maintained adequately by hand. There is little point in spending time entering information that already exists on paper if all you ever intend to do is view the data on-screen or print it in more or less the same form.

A field belongs in a data base only if it meets at least one of the following tests:

- Do you always need to see the information on screen?
- Must the data be printed on a report?
- Is the information required for a calculation or statistical summary?
- Will the data be used as the basis for selecting which records should be displayed, processed, or printed?
- Will the data be used to specify the order in which records are displayed or printed?

Be especially careful with data bases that appear to require large amounts of text or numerous fields that are not used in calculations. You would not, for example, want to retype a lengthy description of each of your clients' business activities into a data base if this material were already available on paper in the form of handwritten notes. It might, however, be desirable to include several fields for codes identifying each client's type of business and major products or services so that you could quickly extract the ones that matched a given business profile—and then refer back to the paper files for more detail.

In other cases, deciding what information to include is much less clear-cut. Suppose you were setting up a data base for a doctor who asks all new patients to fill out a four-page medical history questionnaire. Your first inclination might be to enter all the responses into a patient history data base, but depending on how the doctor wanted to use the information, this effort might be unnecessary and inefficient.

For example, the medical history might include questions about allergies. To find out whether a particular patient has hay fever, it would be just as easy to pull the patient's folder from the manual filing system and refer to the original questionnaire as it would be to call up the patient's record in the data base. If, however, the doctor wanted to be able to find out how many patients had allergies, it would be far easier to extract this information from the data base than to thumb through all the patient questionnaires.

Unfortunately, it is easy to weigh the facts, carefully consider your intended usage of the data, and still make the wrong judgment. The doctor in this example might have decided, based on the foregoing analysis, to omit the allergy data, and most of the other items on the questionnaire, from the patient data base. Six months later, a new drug might appear on the market that effectively treats hay fever symptoms with few undesirable side effects, and the doctor might want to send a pamphlet describing this drug to all patients who have pollen allergies — a contingency that would have been difficult to predict in advance.

The point is that whether or not you can accurately foresee all your future requirements, try to identify at the outset the fields you will need, and at the same time carefully evaluate each item of information to determine whether it really belongs in one of your dBASE III PLUS data bases.

AN INTRODUCTION TO THE NATIONAL WIDGETS SYSTEM

The examples and Hands-On Practice sessions in this book are based on a customer- and order-tracking system for an imaginary small business called National Widgets. This firm, located in Berkeley, California, is a mail-order supplier of computer accessories and supplies. National Widgets has been in business for three years and had about $600,000 in gross sales last year. The company is managed by the owner and employs four other people full time: a bookkeeper, two clerk-typists who also answer the telephones, and one person who handles shipping and receiving.

National Widgets has about 350 regular customers who account for about one-third of its monthly volume of 500 orders; the remaining orders come from one-time buyers or people who call so infrequently that their records are dropped between orders. Both the number of customers and the number of orders are expected to double over the next two years.

Eventually National Widgets hopes to purchase a packaged accounting program or develop one internally, but carrying out such an ambitious goal with dBASE III PLUS requires quite a bit of programming, and the bookkeeping is currently manageable on paper. The owner has two overall goals for the initial dBASE III PLUS system:

- To automate and expand the mailing list processing currently being done manually to include more frequent and more selective mailings, and to print letters as well as mailing labels

- To allow the owner and bookkeeper more immediate access to information that is currently difficult and time-consuming to obtain by hand, including customer buying patterns and ordering trends

To satisfy these requirements, the system must contain information on National Widgets' regular customers, inventory items, and orders. Although it would be desirable to maintain some totals, such as a customer's total purchases, the data bases need not duplicate information required for accounting purposes, such as invoice or payment amounts, or the current balance. This information will be maintained in three main data base files:

- A *Customer File,* which stores customer names, addresses, telephone numbers, and year-to-date and overall totals

- An *Order File,* which stores detailed information about each item a customer has ordered, including order date, part number, quantity ordered, selling price, and discount

- An *Inventory File,* which stores information about the company's products, including the part number, description, cost, price, and quantity on hand

The structures of these files are developed more fully in Chapter 3.

Chapter 2

Installing and Running dBASE III PLUS

This chapter outlines the hardware and operating system requirements for running dBASE III PLUS and describes how to install and start up the program. The exact installation procedure you will follow depends on the particulars of your system configuration: the amount of RAM (random access memory) you have in your computer, whether you have floppy disks or a hard disk, and which version of dBASE III PLUS you own—version 1.0, which is copy-protected, or a later version (copy protection was dropped as of version 1.1).

If dBASE III PLUS is already installed on your computer, you may want to skim the installation instructions, but do not skip this section entirely. Optimizing the performance of dBASE III PLUS and making full use of all of the program's capabilities require several preparatory steps to set up the DOS working environment. It would be a mistake to assume that this preparation has been done correctly, or at all.

This chapter also briefly introduces the two modes of operation of dBASE III PLUS: the menu-driven ASSIST mode, also referred to as the Assistant, in which you give commands and select options through a system of pull-down menus, and the command-driven mode, in which you type commands directly next to a "dot prompt" that is equivalent to the MS-DOS "A>" prompt or "C>" prompt. For the most part, this book concentrates on working at command level and helping you overcome the anxiety many people feel when they are confronted with the bare dot prompt rather than a "friendlier" command menu.

Even if you intend to work primarily at the dot prompt, the ASSIST menus can serve as an easy, unintimidating introduction to the use of dBASE III PLUS, since using them does not require that you memorize command syntax. Also, the appearance of the screens and the commands used to navigate through the menu hierarchy and select options are common to all dBASE III PLUS menu-driven commands, including those used to define report and label formats. Practicing with the menus is a good way to familiarize yourself with a command structure that you will use extensively in later work with dBASE III PLUS.

HARDWARE AND OPERATING SYSTEM REQUIREMENTS

dBASE III PLUS runs on the IBM PC, PC XT, PC AT, and PS/2 computers, and on most IBM-compatible computers. You will need either two floppy disk drives of at least 360K capacity each or one floppy drive and a hard disk. dBASE III PLUS works with any combination of video card and monitor, but it uses only text-based graphics and does not make use of any special graphics capabilities of the color/graphics or EGA adapters.

You do not need a printer to run dBASE III PLUS, but a printer is highly recommended. You can use any type—dot-matrix, ink-jet, daisy-wheel, and laser printers—all with no special installation or configuration procedures, since dBASE III PLUS does not directly support any special print features or graphics capabilities.

All versions of dBASE III PLUS work with any printer that uses a parallel interface, but only version 1.1 or later can communicate with printers connected to your computer's serial port. Attempting to send data to a serial printer with version 1.0 will result in a "Printer is not ready" error message, even if the printer is turned on and on-line, and even if you have used the DOS MODE utility to initialize the serial port and redirect output to this port. If you experience this difficulty, contact Ashton-Tate's Technical Support Department for a correction or information about upgrading to a later version.

dBASE III PLUS requires at least 256K of RAM, and it will make use of any additional installed memory, up to 640K (it does not recognize extended or expanded memory) to create more work space so that certain operations, such as sorting files, run faster. dBASE III PLUS is compatible with PC-DOS version 2.0, MS-DOS version 2.1, and all later versions, but if you are running under DOS 3.0 or later, you will need at least 384K of RAM.

Apart from the fact that you cannot upgrade to DOS 3.0, there are several other significant limitations to running dBASE III PLUS on a 256K system. With the minimum amount of memory in your computer, you will be unable to access external programs or execute DOS commands from within dBASE III PLUS. Also, you may not be able to open as many data base files as you need for your application or create enough memory (temporary) variables. For these reasons, it is highly recommended that you plan to upgrade your system to 512K—preferably 640K—although you can get started using the program right away.

CONFIGURING DOS FOR dBASE III PLUS

Before you install or run dBASE III PLUS, you must configure the DOS operating system to optimize the performance of your hard disk and enable you to use dBASE III PLUS to its fullest capacity. To do this, you must understand several important ways that dBASE III PLUS interacts with DOS. You will also need to take several preparatory steps:

- Create or modify the DOS configuration file, CONFIG.SYS
- Make the DOS command processor, COMMAND.COM, available
- If you have a hard disk, create a subdirectory for dBASE III PLUS
- Make sure the date and time are always set
- If you have a serial printer, use the MODE.COM utility to initialize your computer's serial port

If you do not already understand how to do all these things, you should read the following sections in this chapter carefully. If you find the language or concepts in this chapter incomprehensible, consult your DOS manual or an introductory book about MS-DOS.

The CONFIG.SYS File

The DOS configuration file, an ordinary ASCII text file called CONFIG.SYS, contains commands that customize certain aspects of the DOS working environment. The most important commands for dBASE III PLUS users are the FILES command, which specifies the maximum number of disk files that may be in use simultaneously, and the BUFFERS command, which determines how much RAM should be set aside as buffers for disk operations.

The CONFIG.SYS file may contain commands to customize other aspects of the DOS environment, including the number of disk drives in your system, the time and date format, and how often DOS checks the keyboard to see if the operator has pressed CTRL-BREAK to interrupt the current process. It also frequently contains commands that identify device drivers, small programs that are loaded into memory along with DOS when you boot your system. These programs contain special instructions for communicating with non-standard peripheral devices such as some manufacturers' external hard disks, tape backup units, and other mass storage subsystems.

To set up the CONFIG.SYS file for dBASE III PLUS, you have to concern yourself with only the FILES and BUFFERS commands. However, it is important to be aware that this file may also contain commands that are essential for the proper functioning of your hardware or other application software. If you have a hard disk, you should therefore check for the presence of a CONFIG.SYS file and modify its contents if necessary, rather than recreating this file from scratch or copying it onto your hard disk from the dBASE III PLUS distribution disk.

DOS checks for the presence of a CONFIG.SYS file and reads its contents when—and only when—you boot your computer, either by turning on the power or by pressing ALT-CTRL-DEL. Because DOS reads the configuration file only on startup, CONFIG.SYS must be located in the root directory of the disk from which you boot your computer, not in the subdirectory in which dBASE III PLUS is located.

In a system that boots directly from a hard disk, the CONFIG.SYS file must be in the root directory of the hard disk. If you boot from a floppy disk, whether or not you also have a hard disk in your system, CONFIG.SYS must be in the root directory of the boot disk. If you run many applications during the course of a day and reboot your computer each time you switch programs, be sure to reboot from a DOS disk that contains a CONFIG.SYS file properly set up for dBASE III PLUS before you attempt to run the program.

The FILES Command

dBASE III PLUS allows you to work with up to ten data base files at once, and you will also need to work with other types of disk files. Without special instructions in the CONFIG.SYS file, however, DOS cannot keep track of even ten files. Using the method employed by dBASE III PLUS to interact with DOS, the operating system treats the process of transferring data to and from disk files the same as sending and receiving data from physical devices such as the keyboard, monitor, printer, and communications ports. By default, DOS sets aside memory for eight file and peripheral device names, five of which are reserved for physical devices and three of which are for disk files.

You can use the FILES command to increase the number of files and device names permitted by DOS, up to a limit of 255, but no more than 20 may be accessed from a single application program. To maximize the number of files you can open simultaneously from within dBASE III PLUS, you have to configure DOS to allocate memory for 20 file and device names. Make sure that your CONFIG.SYS file contains the following command:

```
FILES = 20
```

If your boot disk already contains a CONFIG.SYS file with a FILES command that specifies 20 or more open files, you need not change this command.

The BUFFERS Command

The term *buffer* describes RAM memory that is used as an intermediary storage, or holding, area for data being transferred between two devices, usually for the purpose of speeding up overall throughput.

One application of this principle that may already be familiar to you is a printer buffer, which is used to store data en route from the computer to a printer. Instead of being sent directly from the computer's memory to the printer, data is first transferred to the buffer, which may be either a memory board in an external box or simply an area of RAM set aside for this purpose. Because data can be sent very fast to the buffer, it may appear to your application program that the entire file has already been printed, and you can proceed to another task while the buffer feeds the remaining data to the printer. This strategy minimizes the time you spend waiting for the printer—an inherently slow, mechanical device—to catch up to the computer, which can transfer data very rapidly.

DOS uses a similar scheme to speed up disk operations by substituting fast memory-to-memory data transfers for the slower process of reading data from the disk. By default, DOS sets aside either two or three (depending on the DOS version) 512-byte memory buffers, and you can increase this number to a maximum of 99. The use of these buffers requires no intervention on your part or special processing by your application software. On each disk access, DOS reads one sector (512 bytes) of data, which is stored in the next available buffer. When all the disk buffers are full, the oldest one is recycled (its current contents are erased) for the next read.

On every read operation, DOS also examines the contents of the memory buffers before reading the disk, so a program that frequently rereads the same sectors will run faster with more buffers. This is because the requested data is likely to be in memory already, and searching the memory buffers is faster than reading the disk.

On the other hand, if you are randomly accessing widely separated parts of a very large file, more buffers may actually slow disk read operations, since DOS must first check all the buffers and then, more often than not, read the disk anyway.

Furthermore, since each buffer occupies 528 bytes of memory (512 for the data plus 16 to keep track of the buffer status), assigning more buffers reduces the amount of RAM available to dBASE III PLUS and leaves less work space for operations such as sorting.

Ashton-Tate recommends using 15 buffers for optimum performance on most hard disks. If you have only 256K of memory, you cannot spare the RAM for more than 4 buffers. As you gain experience—and as your files become larger—you may want to experiment with small variations in these values, but allocating too many buffers may cause seemingly unrelated data entry problems, especially if you have less than 640K of RAM in your system. To configure your system to use 15 buffers, make sure that your CONFIG.SYS file contains the following line:

```
BUFFERS = 15
```

If you have a 256K system and you already have a CONFIG.SYS file, make sure that it does not contain a command that allocates more than 4 buffers. To instruct DOS to use exactly 4 buffers, place the following command in your CONFIG.SYS file:

```
BUFFERS = 4
```

In a 256K system, you might decide, for the sake of simplicity, to omit this line from your CONFIG.SYS file and retain the default setting of 2 or 3 buffers.

Creating or Editing the CONFIG.SYS File

CONFIG.SYS is an ordinary ASCII (American Standard Code for Information Interchange) text file containing one or more commands, each on a separate line. You can create or edit this file with any word processor or text editor that can read and write text files—those containing only characters with ASCII codes between 32 and 127 (the standard keyboard characters, such as letters, numbers, and punctuation marks) and have no embedded word processing or formatting commands. One such editor is the dBASE III PLUS MODIFY COMMAND editor, which is described in Chapter 14. The notepad editors included with desktop accessory packages such as SideKick can also create ASCII files, and many word processors give you the option of saving in ASCII format.

If you do not already have a CONFIG.SYS file on your boot disk, you can copy one of the standard CONFIG.SYS files provided on the dBASE III PLUS System Disk 1 into the root directory of your boot disk. If you have more than 256K of memory, you can use the file named CONFIG.SYS. If you have a 256K system, however, you must use the CONFI256.SYS file and rename it with the standard name recognized by DOS. You can copy this file into the root directory of your hard disk and rename it with a single command.

With a hard disk system in which the hard disk is drive C, you would type

```
COPY A:CONFI256.SYS C:\CONFIG.SYS
```

In a dual-floppy system, place your boot disk in drive A and the dBASE III PLUS System Disk 1 in drive B, and type

```
COPY B:CONFI256.SYS A:\CONFIG.SYS
```

If you do not have a suitable editor or are not sure how to use the one you have, you can use the DOS COPY command to create your CONFIG.SYS file. To do this, make sure you are logged onto the root directory of your boot disk, and type

```
COPY CON: CONFIG.SYS
```

This command instructs DOS to copy characters from the "console" device—your keyboard—to a file called CONFIG.SYS. Keep in mind that you are not using a text editor. When you press ENTER after typing the COPY command, you will see only a blinking cursor on the next screen line, and you have very limited editing capabilities.

Type your CONFIG.SYS entries one at a time, and press ENTER after each one. Within a line, you can correct errors by backspacing and retyping, but once you have pressed ENTER, you cannot back up to a previous line. When you are finished, save the file by pressing F6, which generates the DOS "end-of-file" character, CTRL-Z (represented on the screen as ^Z), and then ENTER.

To create a standard configuration file, you would type the following commands (pressing ENTER after each one):

```
COPY CON: CONFIG.SYS
FILES = 20
BUFFERS = 15
```

Then, press F6 and ENTER to save your new CONFIG.SYS file. If you notice a mistake after you have already entered a line, press F6 to save the file, and repeat the process. The COPY command will replace the old file with the new one.

To add commands to an existing CONFIG.SYS file, you can append your console input to the existing file, rather than writing over it, by substituting the following COPY command for the one in the previous example:

```
COPY CONFIG.SYS+CON: CONFIG.SYS
```

This command tells DOS to copy to the new CONFIG.SYS file all the characters originally in the file, followed by any typed at the console. You can then type new commands and save the resulting file by pressing F6 followed by ENTER.

If you already have a CONFIG.SYS file containing an inappropriate FILES or BUFFERS command, and you do not have an ASCII text editor, the easiest way to solve the problem is to use the COPY command to recreate the CONFIG.SYS file from scratch. First, use the DOS TYPE command to display the current contents of the file, since there may be other commands that you do not want to lose. Type

```
TYPE CONFIG.SYS
```

You may want to use SHIFT-PRTSC to generate a hard copy of this file or make a backup copy on another disk before you overwrite the file with the modified version. Then use the COPY command to create a new CONFIG.SYS file. Type

```
COPY CON: CONFIG.SYS
```

Retype all the commands that you want to keep from the original file as well as the new FILES and BUFFERS commands (the sequence of the commands is immaterial).

MAKING THE DOS COMMAND PROCESSOR AVAILABLE

If you have more than 256K of memory in your computer, you can execute any DOS command, program (.COM or .EXE file), or batch (.BAT) file from within dBASE III PLUS. To do this, you need enough RAM to load COMMAND.COM (the DOS command processor) and the program you wish to run with dBASE III PLUS. In addition, COMMAND.COM must be available on disk.

For the batch files and the intrinsic (built-in) DOS commands, such as DIR, ERASE, RENAME, and COPY, you need only enough additional memory to accommodate COMMAND.COM, which may range in size from about 17K to about 24K (depending on your version of DOS). To run larger applications, such as a word processor or a spreadsheet, you will need 512K or 640K. Don't forget that if you have any RAM-resident utilities, such as a desk accessory, a macro processor, or a print spooler, they further reduce the amount of available memory.

Accessing COMMAND.COM Under DOS 2

All versions of DOS 2 search for COMMAND.COM in the root directory of the disk in the drive from which you boot your computer. Therefore, if you boot your system from a floppy disk, COMMAND.COM must be present on the disk in drive A. Even if you also have a hard disk, you will have to make sure that your boot disk, or another disk containing COMMAND.COM, remains in drive A.

In a dual-floppy drive system, the disk in drive A will be your working copy of the dBASE III PLUS System Disk 2, and for most combinations of DOS and dBASE III PLUS versions, this disk will not have enough free space for COMMAND.COM. If you have this problem, you can forego the ability to run external commands, switch disks whenever you need to run an external command, or after you have gained experience with dBASE III PLUS, eliminate the help files—HELP.DBS and ASSIST.HLP—from your working copy of System Disk 2 to free some space.

If you boot from a hard disk, you will already have a copy of COMMAND.COM in the root directory of your boot disk. Whether you load dBASE III PLUS from a floppy or from the hard disk, DOS can always find COMMAND.COM when it needs to.

Accessing COMMAND.COM Under DOS 3

Under DOS 3, you can use the MS-DOS SET COMSPEC command to instruct DOS to search for COMMAND.COM in any subdirectory on any disk drive in your system. Even if you boot from a floppy disk, you can load COMMAND.COM from your hard disk and avoid having to keep track of which disk is in the floppy drive. The DOS command processor is also loaded into memory much faster from the hard disk than from a floppy.

SET COMSPEC specifies the full path name required to access COMMAND.COM. For example, if you have copied COMMAND.COM into a subdirectory called DBPLUS on drive C, you would use the following command:

```
SET COMSPEC = C:\DBPLUS\COMMAND.COM
```

This command may be typed at the MS-DOS prompt, or for convenience, you can add it to your AUTOEXEC.BAT file. (If you create a batch file named AUTOEXEC.BAT in the root directory of your boot disk, the commands in this file will be executed automatically every time you boot the system. You can create or modify the AUTOEXEC.BAT file using the same techniques outlined for CONFIG.SYS in the previous sections.)

CREATING A SUBDIRECTORY FOR dBASE III PLUS

On a hard disk, it is best to place the dBASE III PLUS program files in a subdirectory rather than in the root directory. Since dBASE III PLUS recognizes DOS path names, you may also wish to create other subdirectories for your data files.

All the examples in this book assume that both the dBASE III PLUS program and the sample data bases are stored on a hard disk called drive C, in a subdirectory named DBPLUS, which is located directly under the root directory (the full path name of this subdirectory is C: \DBPLUS). If your hard disk is not C, or if you wish to use a different subdirectory name, remember to make the appropriate substitutions in the following commands, and in all the examples in the remaining chapters.

To create the subdirectory for dBASE III PLUS, you use the MD (MAKE DIRECTORY) command (you can type MKDIR if you prefer). Type

```
MD \DBPLUS
```

You can log onto this subdirectory (make it the current subdirectory) from any subdirectory on drive C by typing

```
CD \DBPLUS
```

SETTING THE DATE AND TIME

All IBM and compatible computers have a clock that runs as long as the power is on, and many have a battery-powered clock that keeps time even when the computer is turned off. Whenever a file is created or updated, the current date and time are stored, along with the file name, in the disk directory. This information can be very helpful in determining which in a group of related files is the most recent version. And because the DOS date and time are available to dBASE III PLUS for printing on reports and using in calculations, make sure that they are always set correctly.

You can also use the DOS DATE and TIME commands to set the system clock. To determine whether this is necessary, boot your system as you would to run dBASE III PLUS and type

```
DATE
```

DOS will display the current date and prompt you to enter a new date. If the "current" date is "Tue 1-01-1980," you can conclude that it is necessary to reset the clock whenever you reboot your system. It may be that your system contains a multifunction board with a battery-powered clock. You then have to determine the command needed to read the date and the time from this board. If you do not know how to do this, or if you do not have such a clock, you can include the DATE and TIME commands in your AUTOEXEC.BAT file or type them at the DOS prompt before you start up dBASE III PLUS, and enter the current date and time yourself.

USING A SERIAL PRINTER

If your version of dBASE III PLUS can print on a serial printer, you must use the MODE command to initialize the serial port before you attempt to print. Two separate MODE commands are required. The first sets the baud rate (the speed at which data is sent to the printer) and other communications parameters, and the second instructs DOS to redirect printed output from the default output device (the parallel port) to the serial, or communications, port. Assuming that your printer accepts data at 1200 baud, these are the required MODE commands:

```
MODE COM1: 1200,N,8,1,P
MODE LPT1:=COM1:
```

For baud rates other than 1200, you can make the appropriate substitutions in the first MODE command.

These commands can be included in your AUTOEXEC.BAT file if you have only one printer, provided that MODE.COM is available on your boot disk. You can also place the commands in a separate batch file or type them individually at the DOS prompt from any disk or subdirectory that contains a copy of MODE.COM. If you have enough memory in your computer, you can execute the MODE commands from within dBASE III PLUS, but you will probably find it more convenient to take care of this "housekeeping" chore before you load the program.

BACKING UP THE dBASE III PLUS PROGRAM DISKS

dBASE III PLUS is supplied on two floppy disks, labeled System Disk 1 and System Disk 2. In addition, the dBASE III PLUS package includes a disk containing utilities and sample programs, and an on-disk tutorial, neither of which are discussed in this book.

The dBASE III PLUS version 1.0 System Disk 1 is copy-protected using a method called SUPERLoK. Although you can copy the files on this disk, you cannot execute the program from a copy. A backup copy of System Disk 1 is provided in case your original gets damaged. dBASE III PLUS version 1.1 distribution disks are not copy-protected.

Before you begin the installation procedure, be sure to make backup copies of all non-copy-protected dBASE III PLUS disks, and use the backups, except for the copy-protected System Disk 1 version 1.0.

Format enough blank disks to make the required number of copies. If you have a hard disk, be sure to have a copy of FORMAT.COM (the DOS disk-formatting utility program) somewhere on your hard disk (if not, it is a good idea to copy this program from your DOS system disk onto the hard disk to make it readily available for formatting backup data disks). Log onto the subdirectory containing FORMAT. COM and type

```
FORMAT A:
```

If you have two floppy drives, place your DOS system disk (which contains a copy of FORMAT.COM) into drive A and a blank disk in drive B, and type

```
FORMAT B:
```

You will be prompted to confirm that the floppy disk you want formatted is in the specified drive. When the formatting process on that disk is complete, you will be asked to insert another disk or return to DOS.

Next, copy each non-copy-protected disk. If you have floppy disks, or one hard disk and two floppies, place the disk that you want copied in drive A and a blank formatted disk in drive B, and type

```
COPY A:*.* B:/V
```

If you have a hard disk and one floppy drive, it is less convenient to copy directly from one floppy disk to another, since the COPY command will force you to swap disks for each file it copies. You can use DISKCOPY instead, but this does not make as reliable a copy, and if you insert the wrong disk in the drive when you are prompted to switch disks, you can ruin your original.

One safe strategy for copying a floppy disk in a one-floppy-drive hard disk system is to create a new subdirectory on the hard disk, copy the files from the floppy disk to this subdirectory, recopy the contents of the subdirectory to a blank disk, and then erase the files so you can repeat the procedure with another disk.

To copy the dBASE III PLUS disks using this method, use the MD (MAKE DIRECTORY) command to create a temporary subdirectory on your hard disk, and then log onto this subdirectory with the CD (CHANGE DIRECTORY) command. Type

```
MD \TEMP
CD \TEMP
```

Next, place the disk that you want copied into drive A, and copy the files into the new subdirectory, as follows:

```
COPY A:*.*/V
```

Insert a blank formatted disk into drive A, and copy the files from the TEMP directory onto this disk, as follows:

```
COPY *.* A:/V
```

The last step is to erase the files in the TEMP subdirectory. Before you do this, use a DIR command to make sure you are really logged onto the TEMP subdirectory and that there are no other files you need in that directory. When you are sure, type

```
ERASE *.*
```

When you are finished, you may want to remove the temporary directory by logging onto the root directory and using the RD (REMOVE DIRECTORY) command. Type

```
CD \
RD \TEMP
```

It might not be a bad idea, however, to leave this directory intact so you can use it to copy other floppy disks using the same method.

INSTALLING dBASE III PLUS

The exact procedures for installing dBASE III PLUS will vary somewhat, depending on which version you are using and whether you have a hard disk. Before you proceed with the installation, make sure that you have done, or know how to do, the following:

- Create a CONFIG.SYS file or modify your existing CONFIG.SYS file to match your memory and disk configuration
- Make COMMAND.COM available to allow you to run external commands or programs from within dBASE III PLUS

- Create a subdirectory to store the dBASE III PLUS program and data files
- Back up all non-copy-protected dBASE III PLUS distribution disks

If you are unsure how to carry out any of these steps, you might want to reread this chapter, refer to the dBASE III PLUS *Getting Started* pamphlet, or look up unfamiliar DOS commands in your DOS manual or a book on DOS.

RUNNING THE ID PROGRAM FOR dBASE III PLUS VERSION 1.1

Before you can install or run dBASE III PLUS version 1.1, either on a floppy or hard disk system, you must run a program called ID, which identifies you as the owner of the serialized copy you are installing. You should make a backup copy of System Disk 1 before you run the ID program; you may then choose whether to ID the original and then recopy it to serve as a new backup, or to ID the copy.

To prepare to run the ID program, place your copy of System Disk 1 in drive A, and log onto drive A by typing

```
A:
```

Then, type

```
ID
```

You will be asked to enter your name, company name, and dBASE III PLUS serial number, which you can obtain from the label on System Disk 1. If you enter the wrong serial number, the ID program will detect the error and issue a warning. You must enter the correct serial number in order to successfully complete the identification.

Once you have run the ID program, your name, company, and serial number will be prominently displayed on the dBASE III PLUS sign-on screen every time you start up the program. While this does not prevent someone else from copying and using your dBASE III PLUS program, it does enable Ashton-Tate to identify the rightful owner if someone with an illegal copy calls for technical support.

INSTALLING dBASE III PLUS ON FLOPPY DISK SYSTEMS

With all versions of dBASE III PLUS, you can boot your system using any DOS disk that contains an appropriate CONFIG.SYS file, either by turning the system on with this disk in the drive or by pressing ALT-CTRL-DEL to reboot. You can then place System Disk 1 in drive A and use it to start up dBASE III PLUS.

It is generally more convenient to be able to boot directly from System Disk 1. Two steps are required to copy the operating system onto this disk and thus make it bootable. First, you must use the DOS SYS utility program (provided on your DOS disk) to copy two "hidden" files (files that are not displayed in a directory listing) from the DOS disk to System Disk 1. To do this, place your DOS disk in drive A and System Disk 1 in drive B, and type

```
SYS B:
```

Next, copy COMMAND.COM to System Disk 1, by typing

```
COPY COMMAND.COM B:
```

When you type the SYS command, DOS may respond with the error message, "No room for system on destination disk." This may happen if your version of DOS is too large to fit in the space provided on System Disk 1 (which is especially likely if you are running DOS 3) or if you are using an IBM-compatible computer that runs MS-DOS rather than PC-DOS. When you attempt to copy COMMAND.COM to System Disk 1, you may get the error message "Insufficient disk space"; this error condition is also more likely if you are using DOS 3, which has a larger COMMAND.COM file than DOS 2.

If you get the SYS error message with dBASE III PLUS version 1.0, you must continue to boot from a separate DOS disk and then insert System Disk 1 in drive A to start up the program. You cannot erase unneeded files to make room for DOS, because the hidden files must be copied to a certain location (the first tracks) on the disk. If you get the "Insufficient disk space" message, you can erase the help files, but be sure to copy them onto another disk before erasing them from your original System Disk 1.

Because version 1.1 is not copy-protected, users have another alternative: They can use the SYS and COPY commands to transfer a copy of DOS to a blank formatted disk, and then copy only the required files from System Disk 1 to the blank disk. In particular, you can omit the help files—HELP.DBS and ASSIST.HLP—but this method is recommended only after you have used dBASE III PLUS for a while and are sure you can do without on-screen help.

Make sure with any version of dBASE III PLUS that you have a copy of CONFIG.SYS in the root directory of your boot disk that is appropriate for your disk and memory configuration.

INSTALLING dBASE III PLUS ON A HARD DISK

If you are upgrading from dBASE III, which, like dBASE III PLUS version 1.0 is copy-protected with SUPERLoK, you must either install dBASE III PLUS in a different subdirectory or remove the earlier version from your hard disk using the dBASE III UNINSTAL program before you install dBASE III PLUS. You can find instructions for running UNINSTAL in your dBASE III manual or in the following section in this chapter on uninstalling dBASE III PLUS, which uses essentially the same procedure.

To begin the installation procedure, use the CD command to log onto your dBASE III PLUS subdirectory. Type

```
CD \DBPLUS
```

Next, place System Disk 1 into drive A, and log onto drive A by typing

```
A:
```

To begin the installation, type

```
INSTALL C:
```

The installation program will verify that there is enough room on your hard disk for dBASE III PLUS. If you have version 1.0, which is copy-protected, it will check to see that no prior installation has been carried out from System Disk 1. You will be warned that only one installation is permitted and will be asked to confirm that you wish to proceed. With version 1.1, the installation program will determine whether you have run the ID program and will request that you do so if you have not. The installation program will then copy the required files from System Disk 1 onto your hard disk, prompt you to insert System Disk 2 in drive A, and copy the remaining program files from this disk.

A rapidly diminishing number of "IBM-compatible" computers are not sufficiently IBM-compatible to permit installing dBASE III PLUS (or any other SUPERLoK-protected program) on a hard disk. If you have one of these systems, you can still use the DOS COPY command to transfer the dBASE III PLUS program files to your hard disk for faster access. However, you must place your original System Disk 1 in drive A to start up the program.

CAUTIONS FOR USERS OF SUPERLoK-PROTECTED PROGRAMS

When you install any SUPERLoK-protected program on a hard disk — you may have other such programs in addition to dBASE III PLUS — several hidden files are copied into the root directory. If they are moved to any other location on the hard disk, the program will no longer run. Because the files are not displayed in the disk directory, it is easy to forget about them, but you must be sure to avoid using any commands that destroy the files or recopy them onto the hard disk from floppy disks (since they will not end up in exactly the same place).

If you reformat or replace your hard disk, the hidden files will be lost and your copy of dBASE III PLUS will be unusable. Also, you should never use the DOS BACKUP utility to back up the root directory of your hard disk, or the entire hard disk, including all subdirectories, and then restore the files from the backup disks. Although the BACKUP command does not damage the hidden files, RESTORE will copy them to different physical locations on the hard disk, and none of your SUPERLoK-protected programs will work.

One solution to both problems is the UNINSTAL program, supplied with dBASE III PLUS, which disables the copy on the hard disk and resets the installation counter on System Disk 1. Of course, if you are conscientious about performing frequent backups, it is impractical to uninstall and then reinstall dBASE III PLUS every time. A better strategy is to back up the hard disk one subdirectory at a time, working from the root directory, rather than backing up the entire hard disk. You can also back up the entire hard disk, but always remember to restore the files one directory at a time.

You should make every attempt to uninstall all your SUPERLoK-protected programs before you reformat your hard disk. Of course, if you are reformatting in an attempt to resolve read or write errors, or if your hard disk is irreparably damaged and must be replaced, you may not be able to carry out the uninstallation successfully. If this should happen, you can go ahead and reformat or replace the disk and perform a second installation from the backup copy of System Disk 1 provided with the dBASE III PLUS package. You can then contact Ashton-Tate Technical Support to obtain another backup disk.

To run the UNINSTAL program, make sure that you are logged onto the dBASE III PLUS subdirectory on your hard disk, place System Disk 1 in drive A, log onto drive A, and type

```
UNINSTAL C:
```

You will be asked to confirm that you want to continue, you will be notified that the installation count on System Disk 1 has been reset to 1, and finally, you will be informed that dBASE III PLUS has been successfully uninstalled.

STARTING UP dBASE III PLUS

To start up dBASE III PLUS, log onto the appropriate disk drive and subdirectory, and type

```
DBASE
```

dBASE III PLUS will display a sign-on screen summarizing the terms of the software licensing agreement. The version 1.1 sign-on screen includes your name, company, and serial number as you entered them when you ran the ID program. On the bottom line of the screen, dBASE III PLUS will prompt you to "Press ENTER to assent to the License Agreement and begin dBASE III PLUS." If you press ENTER, this message will be cleared immediately, but if you wait long enough, it will disappear on its own. With a floppy disk system, dBASE III PLUS will next ask you to "Insert System Disk 2 and press ENTER, or press CTRL-C to abort."

If you have installed dBASE III PLUS according to one of the standard procedures outlined in this chapter, the program will automatically start up with the ASSIST menu system in control and your screen will look like Figure 2-1. If instead you see a blank screen with a dot and a blinking cursor in the lower left corner, type the following two commands:

```
SET STATUS ON
ASSIST
```

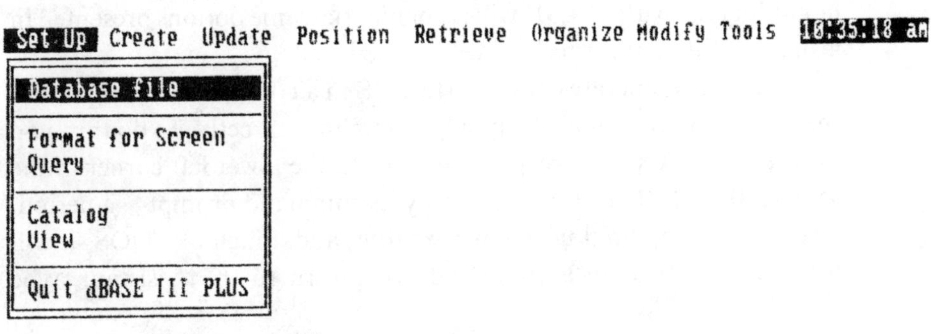

Figure 2-1 *The ASSIST menu*

USING THE ASSIST MENUS

The ASSIST menu system, also referred to as the Assistant, allows you to access many dBASE III PLUS commands through a series of pull-down menus. If you have used Framework II, the appearance and organization of these menus will seem familiar. Those of you who are upgrading from dBASE III will recognize the same options presented in a slightly different format.

You can also operate dBASE III PLUS in a command-driven, rather than menu-driven, mode by typing commands directly. To do this, you must exit the Assistant by pressing ESC. In the lower left corner of the screen, dBASE III PLUS will display its command prompt—a period, or dot—with a blinking cursor next to it, and, much like DOS, it will wait for you to type a command. To return to the Assistant, type ASSIST, or press F2.

When you first begin to work with dBASE III PLUS, the menus can be helpful, since you can use them without having to memorize file names, field names, or the grammar and syntax of the dBASE III PLUS command language. However, not all dBASE III PLUS commands and command options are accessible through the menus, and in some cases using the menus is cumbersome and convoluted, and may even involve more keystrokes than typing commands at the dot prompt.

The worst aspect of working at the dot prompt is that it can be extremely intimidating at first because you must know exactly what you want to do and what commands to type to accomplish your goal. Anyone who does not type or spell well will be at a distinct disadvantage. But although many people find command-driven programs difficult to learn, they can be easy to use once a person gains experience. Typing commands is often faster, more direct, and more flexible than using the menus.

Most of this book concentrates on operating dBASE III PLUS in command-driven mode, with the aim of helping you gain confidence in typing commands at the dot prompt. However, you may want to begin by experimenting with the Assistant. The layout of the ASSIST screen and the keys used to navigate through the menus is common to all dBASE III PLUS menu-driven commands, including the editors used to create screen layouts, report forms, and mailing label formats. You will feel more comfortable using these commands if you already have some experience with ASSIST.

HANDS-ON PRACTICE—SELECTING ASSIST MENU OPTIONS

The Assistant has eight main options, or menus, displayed on the top line of the screen, and the current time is in the upper right corner. One option is always selected; when you first load dBASE III PLUS, it is the **Set Up** option. You can always identify the selected option because its name is highlighted with a bar of inverse video (dark characters displayed on a bright background, instead of the usual light characters on a dark background), and the associated sub-options are displayed in a pull-down menu.

Try moving among the main menu options with the LEFT ARROW and RIGHT ARROW keys. You can jump quickly to the leftmost option (**Set Up**) by pressing the HOME key, and to the rightmost (**Tools**) by pressing END. You can also select a main menu option by typing the first letter of its name.

As you experiment with these commands, you will see that whenever you select a new main menu option, a matching pull-down menu containing the sub-options appears on the screen. Despite the two-dimensional appearance of the screen, the main menu options behave as if they form a loop rather than a linear arrangement—if you move past the last option on the right (**Tools**), the highlight bar will return to the leftmost option (**Set Up**).

Use the arrow keys to select each menu option in turn, and note that some of the sub-options are displayed in brighter characters than others. The bright characters are always used to indicate currently available options, and this changes dynamically as you carry out commands. For example, when you have just entered dBASE III PLUS, all the **Update** options (**Append**, **Edit**, **Display**, **Browse**, **Replace**, and so on) are unavailable, since they all operate on a data base, and no data base is yet open.

Once you have selected a main menu option, you can use the UP ARROW and DOWN ARROW keys to highlight an option in the pull-down sub-option menu. Try these keys, and note that the highlight bar jumps over unavailable options. Pressing PGUP selects the first available option on a menu and PGDN selects the last. Unlike the main menu options, sub-menu selections cannot be made by typing the first letter of the command. To execute your selection, press ENTER.

If executing the selected command requires more input, dBASE III PLUS will continue to pop up additional windows on the screen to display more information and ask you to make further selections from lists of disk drives, files, fields, or options. At any point, you can back up a step by pressing ESC , or you can move to another main menu option with the LEFT ARROW or RIGHT ARROW key.

The main menu options and pull-down menu sub-options of the ASSIST system are illustrated in Figure 2-2.

THE STATUS DISPLAY

The bottom three lines on the screen are occupied by a display that monitors the current status of the working environment, presents additional information about the currently running command, and provides brief instructions for navigating through the menus. The status display is always present when you use the Assistant or the other dBASE III PLUS menu-driven commands. When you work at the dot prompt, you can turn it on or off to suit your preferences by typing

```
SET STATUS ON
```

or

```
SET STATUS OFF
```

The highlighted bar on the third line from the bottom of the screen is called the *Status Bar.* This bar is divided into six regions by double vertical lines, each of which is used for a certain type of information. From left to right, the six regions display the following:

- The currently running command, in this case, ASSIST.

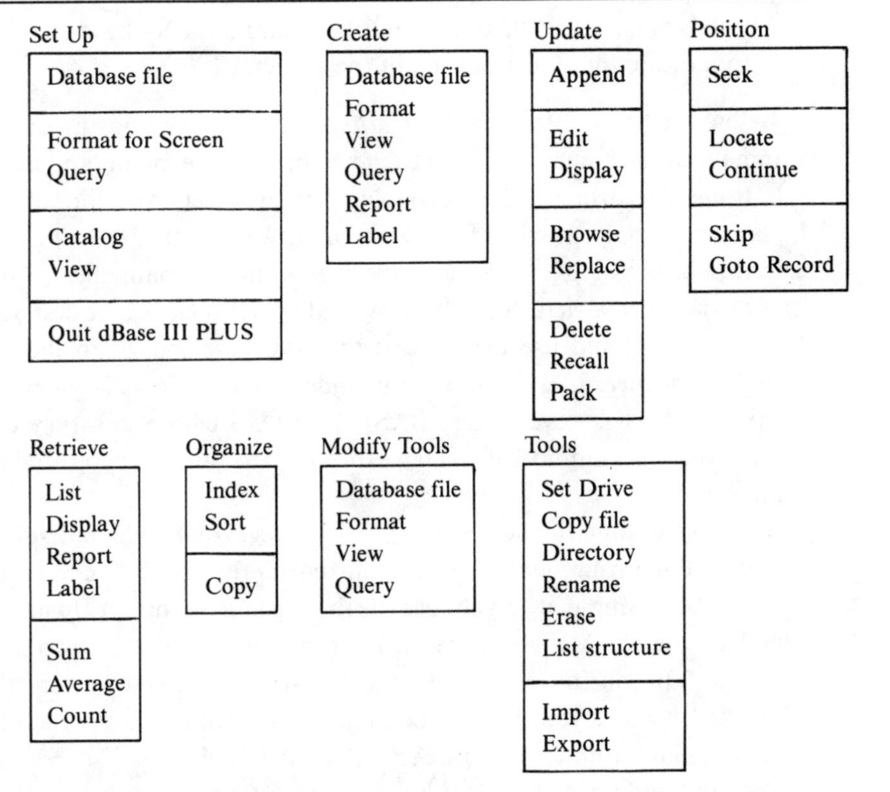

Figure 2-2 *The structure of the ASSIST menu*

- The default disk drive, in this case, drive C.
- The name of the currently selected data base. When no file is open, this space is empty.
- The selected option and total number of options if you are selecting options from a menu, or the current record number and total number of records if a data base is open.
- The status of the INS key (whether you are typing in Insert or Typeover mode) and the deletion status of the current record ("Del" is displayed if the current record has been marked for deletion).

- The status of the NUM LOCK and CAPS LOCK keys. This information is particularly helpful if your keyboard does not have an LED to indicate the status of each of these keys.

Below the Status Bar is a *Navigation Line* that contains a concise summary of the commands used to move through the menus and make selections. This display informs you that you can select an option (within a main menu option) with UP ARROW or DOWN ARROW, execute your selection by pressing ENTER, leave the current menu (main option) and move to another with the LEFT ARROW and RIGHT ARROW, request help by pressing F1, and use ESC to exit the Assistant and go to the dot prompt. The meanings of these commands might not be self-evident to someone who has never used dBASE III PLUS before, but they can serve as a useful reminder if you have forgotten a command you already understand.

The bottom line of the screen is the *Message Line,* which displays additional information describing the currently selected command option. For example, if you choose the first option on the **Set Up** menu, **Database file**, the Message Line explains that this means "Select a data base file." If you move down to the **Format for Screen** option, the Message Line tells you that this command will enable you to "Select a screen design for updating with APPEND and EDIT."

As you build up a command by selecting options from the ASSIST menus, dBASE III PLUS uses the line above the Status Bar, sometimes called the *Action Line* or *Command Line,* to display an equivalent command that you could type at the dot prompt to accomplish the same objective. This is a relatively painless way to begin learning dBASE III PLUS command syntax: Use the menus, which prompt you for the required information in the right sequence, and watch the Action Line for a reminder of what command to type when you begin to work at the dot prompt.

For example, in Chapter 3, you will create a data base file called NWCUST by typing CREATE NWCUST at the dot prompt. Try doing this from the ASSIST menu following these steps:

1. Select **Create** from the main menu.

2. Select **Database file** from the Create menu.

3. Select the disk drive on which to store the file from the displayed list.

4. Enter the name of the file you wish to create.

At this point, your screen should look like Figure 2-3. Note that the Navigation and Message lines always inform you what to do next—in this case, enter a new file name and finish by pressing ENTER. Above the Status Bar, on the Action Line, you can see the command you are

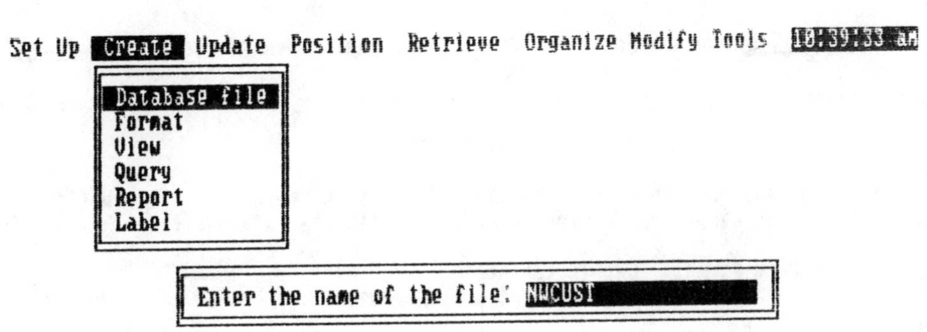

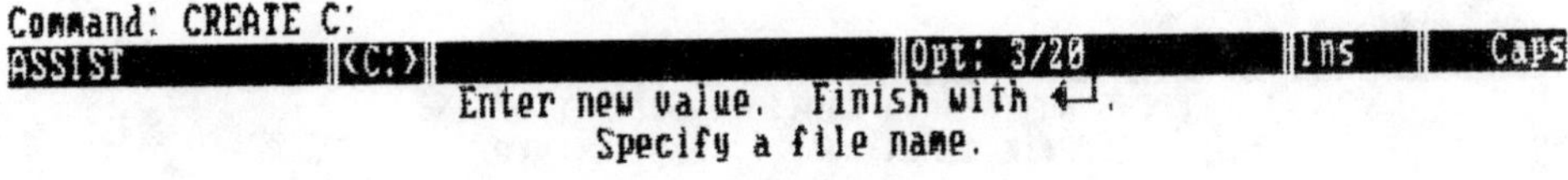

Figure 2-3 *Accessing the CREATE command from the ASSIST menu*

constructing: CREATE C:. When you type in the file name, NWCUST, and press ENTER, the complete command—CREATE C:NWCUST—will be executed immediately.

If you are not ready to proceed to Chapter 3, or if you would prefer to execute the CREATE command from the dot prompt, press ESC instead of ENTER after typing the file name. If you have already pressed ENTER, you can abort the CREATE command by pressing ESC, and then answering Y to the question "Are you sure you want to abandon operation? [Y/N]". You can exit dBASE III PLUS by choosing **Quit dBASE III PLUS** from the Set Up menu.

```
Set Up  Create  Update  Position  Retrieve  Organize Modify Tools  10:43:09 am

                                  CREATE

 CREATE allows the design of a database file structure.  Once the new file
 structure is completed,  enter information into the database file.

      Command Format:  CREATE <database file name>
                       [FROM <structure extended file name>]



ASSIST          ||<C:>||                 ||Opt: 1/6            ||Ins  ||    Caps
                 Press any key to continue work in ASSIST.
                      Create a database file structure.
```

Figure 2-4 *The help screen for the CREATE command*

GETTING MORE HELP

Throughout dBASE III PLUS, both in the Assistant and at the dot prompt, the F1 key serves as a Help key. If you press F1 with an ASSIST command highlighted, you will see a help screen that shows you the syntax of the equivalent command as you would type it at the dot prompt, and the screen further describes the purpose and operation of the selected command. For example, with **Database file** selected from the Create menu, pressing F1 would call up the help screen shown in Figure 2-4.

Whenever a help screen is displayed from the ASSIST menu system, the Navigation Line reminds you to "Press any key to continue working in ASSIST." When you press a key, the help screen disappears, and you are returned to exactly the point from which you summoned help. If you think you will need to refer back to the help screen again before completing your command, you can print a copy of the display by turning on your printer and pressing SHIFT-PRTSC. The graphics characters used to form the lines and boxes in the display may not print correctly on non-IBM-compatible printers, but at least you can preserve the essential information for further reference.

Chapter 3

Planning and Designing a Data Base

Chapter 1 described the process of analyzing your requirements and compiling a list of the items of information to be maintained using dBASE III PLUS. One more preliminary step is required before you can begin entering data: You must translate your list of data items into a dBASE III PLUS *file structure,* which serves as a kind of template, or blank format, for typing in the data.

Try visualizing this step as roughly equivalent to designing a preprinted paper form on which the same information could be recorded. This design process includes deciding how much space to provide for each entry as well as what labels or other informative text to print on the form to guide the person who will be filling in the data.

Once you have settled on the structures for your data bases, you can use the CREATE command to create the empty files into which you will enter data.

DEFINING THE FIELDS

A dBASE III PLUS data base can have up to 128 fields, which may total 4000 bytes (characters). Every item of information that you view as a discrete, self-contained entity should be a separate field. It is also a good idea to place in a separate field any item that you intend to use as a basis for selecting or rearranging records. Even for cases in which this is not strictly necessary, this strategy will greatly simplify the commands and expressions you must use to specify your selection criteria and sorting instructions.

In a mailing list, for example, you could view the city, state, and ZIP code as a single logical unit — the last line of the mailing address — but if you need to send a special mailing to everyone who lives in the state of Texas, or produce mailing labels in ZIP code order, it would be better to use three separate fields.

Names can be even more problematical. To print or view records in alphabetical order, you might create two separate fields for a person's first and last names, and combine them for printing reports and labels. But this structure is not flexible enough to readily accommodate all the variations you may find on your list, such as records having no first name, a company name instead of a person's name, or combined names like "John and Karen Smith" or "John Kelly and Mary Smith." One solution, which will be used in the National Widgets Customer File, is to use a single field for the full name and create another short character field for an account code or ID code, constructed from the last name or company name, which determines alphabetical order.

This ID code field serves another important purpose and illustrates a general principle not limited in its applicability to name and address data bases: It can be used as a unique identifier for each person on the list. Many other types of data bases should also contain a field or combination of fields that uniquely identifies each record. Using techniques that will be described in Chapter 7, you can retrieve any record almost instantly — even in a very large file — based on the contents of this field.

The ability to uniquely identify a record is crucial for many commands that operate on multiple data bases. For example, to display an order record with data from the matching customer record, you must be sure that you can find the right customer. To post transaction data to a customer record (add a transaction amount into a cumulative year-to-date total), dBASE III PLUS must be able to match the transaction with one—and only one—customer record.

Often, it is immediately apparent what the unique field should be. In an inventory data base, it is the part number; in a patient list, it might be a pre-assigned medical record number; in a name and address list, you can easily construct an account code or ID code if one does not already exist. Keep in mind when you assign these codes that since you will use them to search for records, making them easy to remember or reconstruct will greatly facilitate the process of retrieving and editing specified records. An ID code consisting of part of a person's name or company name will be much easier to remember than a numeric account number that bears no relationship to the company it represents.

Not every data base has an obvious candidate for this unique identifier, and sometimes this is because none is required. To continue with the accounts receivable example, the Customer File needs a unique identifier such as an account number, because a company really should have only one record in this file, which dBASE III PLUS must be able to retrieve for a variety of purposes. The related Order File might not have any unique combination of fields; one customer might have many orders, and if each order record represented one line item on an order form (one stocked item), there would be multiple records for the same customer on the same date, and with the same order number or invoice number.

When you define the structure using the dBASE III PLUS CREATE command, you must name the data base and provide four items of information to describe each field:

- *Field name*: The field name is analogous to the text that would be printed on a paper form to identify the information that you want entered into the adjacent space or box.

- *Data type*: dBASE III PLUS recognizes five data types—character, numeric, logical, date, and memo.

- *Field width*: The field width (or length) is the maximum number of characters you need to enter into the field.

- *Decimals*: For numeric fields, you must specify the number of digits to the right of the decimal point.

All these terms are explained more fully in the following sections of this chapter.

FILE AND FIELD NAMES

Before you finalize your data base structures, a few words about file and field names are in order. Developing a consistent scheme for assigning names to files and fields that clearly suggest their contents, and that are easy to type and pronounce, will greatly enhance the "friendliness" and ease of use of your data base, especially for co-workers not privy to the design process.

Under PC-DOS and MS-DOS, a file name can consist of up to eight characters and a three-character extension, separated by a period (which is not displayed in directory listings). Like many other programs, dBASE III PLUS uses the extension to distinguish the different types of files it recognizes: DBF for data base, FRM for report format, LBL for label format, and so on. Extensions are assigned automatically; using most dBASE III PLUS commands, you need not type file extensions unless you wish to deviate from the defaults. When you define file names, you have up to eight characters to work with.

A dBASE III PLUS file name may consist of almost any combination of letters and numbers, except that you cannot use the single letters A through J as file names or begin a file name with a numeric digit. Spaces are not permitted in file names. Although dBASE III PLUS allows you to include any punctuation marks permitted by DOS, it is advisable to avoid using punctuation in all file names, not just those created through dBASE III PLUS. Some communications programs, utilities, and disk format conversion programs cannot access a file with a name containing characters other than the standard letters and numbers.

Using a common prefix for all the files in a system makes it easy to see from a glance at the disk directory which files belong together. With only eight characters at your disposal, you will generally want to use no more than two or three for the prefix. The files in this book will share the prefix NW for National Widgets. Instead of your company name, you might use a prefix like AR for accounts receivable, INV for an inventory data base, or DON for a donor tracking system.

If all your file names have something in common, you can take advantage of the ability of DOS and many DOS utility programs to recognize "wildcard" characters in file names and process files in groups. The two wildcard characters are the question mark (?), which stands for any single character, and the asterisk (*), which stands for any group of any number of characters. The common prefix thus enables you to display, copy, or back up with a single command all the files that make up an application. For example, you could display a directory of all the National Widgets files with the following command:

```
DIR NW*.*
```

With a single command, you could also back up only the National Widgets files from a hard disk to floppies, regardless of which other files are present in the same subdirectory. You would type

```
BACKUP C:\DBPLUS\NW*.* A:
```

When you work with a dBASE III PLUS data base, fields are identified by their names. The field names are used as prompts in the default screens for entering and editing data, and you must choose fields by name when you select from a list presented by the Assistant as well as when you type commands at the dot prompt.

dBASE III PLUS field names may be up to ten characters long. They must begin with a letter, but they can otherwise contain any combination of letters and numbers. Strive to make your field names as descriptive and self-explanatory as possible within the ten-character limit. If you stick with ordinary words and standard abbreviations, your field names will not only be readable but also easy to remember and type—for both you and your co-workers.

No spaces are permitted within field names, and the only allowable embedded punctuation mark is the underscore (_). Some people feel that using underscores to substitute for the prohibited blank space can greatly improve readability, and that a field name like ZIP_CODE is more recognizable than ZIPCODE. Touch typists may find that field names containing underscores are difficult or awkward to type, however. For the most part, the field names in this book do not contain underscores; whether or not you use them is a matter of personal preference.

dBASE III PLUS DATA TYPES

dBASE III PLUS recognizes five *data types*. Different types of calculations and comparisons are permitted on each, and data entered into the various field types is formatted and validated according to different rules. The five data types are defined here:

- *Character fields* may contain any keyboard characters, including letters, numbers, and punctuation marks.
- *Numeric fields* may contain only digits, a decimal point, and a minus sign.
- *Logical fields* may contain only the logical values "true" and "false," which are equivalent to "yes" and "no." Only the characters T, t, Y, y (for "true" or "yes" values), and F, f, N, and n (for "false" or "no" values) may be entered into logical fields.
- *Date fields* contain valid calendar dates, usually displayed in *mm/dd/yy* format (for example, 07/05/88 for July 5, 1988).
- *Memo fields* are variable-length fields that can accommodate up to 5000 characters of free-form text.

ASSIGNING FIELD WIDTHS

Specifying the field widths in a dBASE III PLUS data base is analogous to deciding how long a line or how wide a box to place on a printed form intended to accommodate the same data. The data base structure is more restrictive than a paper form, however. When you fill out a form, you can write smaller or squeeze an extra line of text between two others if the allotted space proves to be too small. dBASE III PLUS gives you no such leeway.

With one important exception (memo fields, which are described in the next section, "Choosing the Appropriate Data Type"), dBASE III PLUS stores data in *fixed-length fields*. This means that for each field, dBASE III PLUS always stores the same number of characters—the number you assigned as the field width when you defined the file structure. If you leave a field partially or completely blank, it is filled out to its maximum length with blank spaces. For example, if you give a name field a length of 30 characters and then enter "Susan Lee" into the field, the full 30 characters are stored on disk—the 9 characters you typed plus 21 blank spaces.

If your fields are too long, you will be wasting disk space, whereas if you make them too short, you will have to abbreviate in ways that may render the information less useful or, more likely, less presentable. Although you should certainly give some thought to assigning field widths judiciously, you will probably guess wrong in at least a few instances. Don't worry too much, however—dBASE III PLUS makes it relatively easy to lengthen or shorten fields later on, even after data has been entered.

You need only specify the widths of character and numeric fields; dates are always 8 characters wide, logical fields take up 1 space, and memo fields require 10. Character fields range in width from 1 to 254 characters, and numeric fields may have up to 19 digits, although dBASE III PLUS uses only 15 digits in its calculations. Up to 15 decimal places are permitted; numbers with zero decimal places are integers (whole numbers). Numeric fields must be wide enough to accommodate the decimal point, if any, and to permit entry of the minus sign in a negative number.

For example, if an account balance ranges from −$10,000.00 to $10,000.00, the field must be 9 digits wide: 2 for the pennies, 1 for the decimal point, 5 for the dollars, and 1 for the minus sign. (Note that you cannot enter commas or dollar signs into a numeric field, although you can add them later for display purposes.)

CHOOSING THE APPROPRIATE DATA TYPE

Almost any kind of data can be stored in a character field, which can contain any combination of keyboard characters. By making all your fields character fields, however, you would sacrifice the ability to manipulate and validate data in special ways that are possible only with other data types. To a certain extent, data of one type can be converted to another, but it is best to avoid such complexity whenever possible.

Only numeric data may be used in mathematical calculations such as addition, multiplication, computing sums and averages, and compiling report totals and subtotals. Fields consisting solely of numeric digits should therefore be made numeric if you need to use them in calculations. For example, in an order record, the selling price and quantity ordered should be numeric so you can multiply them to arrive at the extended price. A customer's year-to-date orders field should also be numeric, because it must accumulate the dollar value of all orders placed during the year, and because you might want to total this field on a customer report.

If you do not foresee using a field in mathematical calculations, it may be preferable to make it a character field. For example, because you would never do arithmetic on an area code, there is no advantage to making it a number, even though it consists entirely of numeric digits. Numeric fields cannot contain embedded punctuation marks (except the decimal point), so a telephone number or social security number (both of which contain dashes) should be a character field. And, as you will see later, it is easier to combine character fields for the purpose of building indexes or displaying data (in an expression like "Area Code: 415") than it is to mix data types.

There are other, subtler distinctions. In true numbers, leading zeroes are meaningless (01001 has exactly the same numeric value as 1001); dBASE III PLUS automatically strips leading zeroes entered into numeric fields and replaces them with blank spaces. Thus, if you made a ZIP code a numeric field (assuming of course, that you had no foreign ZIP codes containing letters or ten-digit ZIP codes with embedded dashes), leading zeroes would be removed from ZIP codes such as 01001, leaving it unclear to the Post Office whether you meant 01001, 10010, or something else entirely.

If you need to arrange records in numerical order based on the contents of a field, the field must either be numeric or you must enter leading zeros so that all your entries in this field occupy the maximum field width. Character data is sorted just as you would alphabetize. While the numeric digits come out in the right order—zero comes before 1, which comes before 2, and so on—character fields are alphabetized one character at a time starting from the leftmost character. Just as any name beginning with A will come before any name beginning with B, regardless of the remaining letters, 10 will come before 2—but not before 02.

Fields that contain the answers to yes-or-no questions should be assigned the logical data type. Since dBASE III PLUS permits only the characters T, F, Y, N, and their lowercase equivalents to be entered into logical fields, using a logical field rather than a character field makes it more difficult to inadvertently enter a meaningless value, for example, by accidentally typing U instead of Y.

Calendar dates should be entered into date fields in order to allow for the validations and specialized operations that are possible with true dates. For example, dBASE III PLUS will not permit the entry of erroneous dates such as 13/42/87 or 02/29/87 (1987 is not a leap year) in a date field. You can choose from several display formats for dates, including the popular American *mm/dd/yy* format and the European *dd/mm/yy* format. Regardless of the display format chosen, dBASE III PLUS can always arrange dates in true chronological order or compare two dates to determine which is earlier or later.

In contrast, if you stored dates in character fields, attempting to sort or compare dates would be subject to some of the same problems outlined earlier for numeric data. Because character fields are alphabetized from left to right, the two digits representing the month in a date stored *yy/mm/dd* format are examined before the two digits that represent the year. Any date in the month of January would therefore be "alphabetized" earlier than any date in February, because 01 comes before 02 in alphabetical order, regardless of the year.

dBASE III PLUS also supports date arithmetic. You may add a number to a date to yield a valid calendar date the specified number of days in the future, subtract a number from a date to yield a past date, and subtract two dates to determine the elapsed time in days. All these calculations are impossible without programming if the dates are stored in character or numeric fields.

Memo fields are often the best way to store variable amounts of free-form text. dBASE III PLUS provides a rudimentary word processor for editing memo fields that offers far better editing capabilities, including word wrap and a search command, than the commands used to edit character fields. Furthermore, if you had more than 254 characters of text (the maximum width of a character field), you would need to divide the entry among two or more fields, and this would make it very awkward to enter and edit the text. Memo fields can also be reformatted to conform to different margins for screen or printer output.

The text entered into memo fields is stored in a separate file on disk. In the main data base file, a memo field occupies only 10 characters, whether or not you have entered any text. Space in the memo text file is allocated dynamically in blocks of 512 characters, so the average length of the text and the number of records that contain entries in this field determine whether using a character or memo field will result in the most efficient use of storage space.

If a relatively small percentage of the records in a file have associated text, using a memo field can result in a considerable savings in disk space, since several long character fields, which would remain blank for most of the records, would be required to store the same information. If more than half the records will contain text, the choice of data type should be based on ease of editing and the anticipated length of the text. For example, if no record is likely to require more than 200 characters, you would be wasting space by using a memo field, since space is allocated 512 characters at a time in the text file.

You should also be aware of several important limitations on using memo fields. You cannot sort or index (two ways to determine the order in which records are displayed or printed) on a memo field, and you cannot do a global search throughout a file based on the contents. Thus, while you could ask dBASE III PLUS to list all the records in which a character field contained the word computer, you could not do the same with a memo field.

A field should be evaluated according to the criteria detailed in this section to see if it requires any of the special treatment that is possible with numeric, date, logical, or memo fields. If not, it should be a character field.

PLANNING THE DATA BASE STRUCTURES

After you have identified all the information that must go into your data bases, you can begin to lay out the file structures. If your application seems simple and straightforward, it will be tempting to turn on the computer, load dBASE III PLUS, and begin creating the files. But even in a small system consisting of only one file, a little advance planning on paper will greatly reduce the amount of time you will spend later making changes. Keep in mind, however, that it is almost impossible to predict all your requirements and that you are not permanently committed to your original file structures, since dBASE III PLUS allows you to modify your file structures without losing any data that is already entered.

The design of the file structures should be guided by the overall goals for any dBASE III PLUS system:

- To carry out all the required operations and produce all the necessary reports
- To use disk space most efficiently
- To optimize the performance of the system
- To maximize the accuracy of the information in the data base

In Chapter 1, a data base was described as a group of records that belong together logically and share the same format. Conversely, data that requires a largely different set of fields should be placed in separate files. For example, storing the required information on National Widgets' customers requires fields for the account number, name, address, phone number, and year-to-date totals, whereas the order data consists of the order date, part number, price, quantity, and extended price.

With 128 fields available, you might consider putting order data into the Customer File, by including multiple sets of identical fields. However, any given customer might have no orders, 1, or 50. If you created five sets of order fields in the Customer File, you would be wasting space if most customers had fewer than five orders, and you would have to create duplicate customer records for those having more. This type of "one-to-many" relationship — one customer might have many orders — generally calls for two separate files.

Since dBASE III PLUS allows you to work with more than one data base at a time and link them based on a field or fields common to both, you can omit from a file any field that can be looked up in another. For example, there is no need to include a field for the item description in the Order File, since this can be looked up in the Inventory File based on a match on the part number. You can thus eliminate a great deal of redundancy, save disk space, and in some cases save time. You might have several hundred inventory items but thousands of order records. If the description field were 25 characters long, 300 copies of this field would occupy 7500 bytes on disk, compared to 75,000 if this field were included in the Order File.

In general, you need not create fields that can be calculated from other fields in the same or another data base, but sometimes including a few such "unnecessary" fields is worthwhile because it gives you instant access to important information. For example, a customer's balance could be calculated by adding all the invoice totals and subtracting all the payments. However, this can be a time-consuming process, one that is best carried out in a batch process for all customer records, not one by one while you are waiting impatiently to see the results. By storing the total in the Customer File, you can make it instantly available for viewing on the screen or printing on a report.

One good way to lay out the data base structures is to start with a blank sheet of paper for each file. Working from your sample documents and lists of required information, and beginning with the file you understand best, write down all the fields you will need. Next, go back and assign field names, types, lengths, and decimal places.

Be sure to give the sequence of the fields some thought, because the placement of fields on the default data entry and editing screens is determined by their positions in the file structure. You need not be overly concerned about writing down all the items in exactly the right order, however; once you have accounted for all the required data, you can go back over your lists and number the fields to remind yourself of the correct sequence when you create the file structures. Figures 3-1, 3-2, and 3-3 illustrate the file design worksheets for the National Widgets system.

CREATING A DATA BASE STRUCTURE

When you work with dBASE III PLUS at the dot prompt, all the commands you type begin with a verb—you are commanding dBASE III PLUS to do something. Commands, file names, and field names may be typed in any combination of uppercase and lowercase letters.

The command for creating a file structure is

```
CREATE
```

If you like, you can also include the name of the file, to create

CREATE *file name*

If you do not include the file name, dBASE III PLUS will prompt you to enter it with "Enter the name of the new file:."

Creating a file involves filling out a table on the screen with the fields listed vertically, and columns for field names, types, widths, and decimal places. The display is arranged in two groups of four columns each, and you can "pan" left or right to view more fields than can fit on the screen at once.

If you are new to dBASE III PLUS, the CREATE screen will be your first introduction to the "full-screen" edit mode used by many dBASE

CUSTOMER FILE

1	Account number or code	ACCOUNT	C	~~5~~ 10	
9	Name	CONTACT	C	25	
2	Company name	COMPANY	C	25	
3	Address	ADDRESS	C	25	
	~~City/State/Zip~~	~~CITY~~	~~C~~	~~35~~	
8	Phone number	TELEPHONE	C	8	
10	Type of computer equipment	EQUIPMENT	C	25	
11	First order date	FIRSTORDER	D		
12	Most recent order date	LASTORDER	D		
13	Year-to-date orders	YTDORDERS	N	10	2
14	Total orders	TOTORDERS	N	10	2
	~~Year-to-date payments~~				
	~~Total payments~~				
4	City	CITY	C	20	
5	State	STATE	C	2	
6	Zip code	ZIP	~~N~~ C	~~5~~ 10	
15	Comments	COMMENTS	M		
7	Include in promotional mailing?	MAIL	L		

Figure 3-1 *The Customer File design worksheet*

ORDER FILE

Customer account number	ACCOUNT	C	10
Product category	CATEGORY	C	6
Part number	PARTNUMBER	C	6
~~Description~~			
Quantity ordered	QUANTITY	N	4
Price	PRICE	N	7 2
Subtotal (Quantity x Price)	SUBTOTAL	N	7 2
Discount	DISCOUNT	N	7 2
Invoice total for this item (Subtotal - Discount)	INVAMOUNT	N	7 2
Invoice number	INVOICE	C	5
Invoice date	INVDATE	D	

Figure 3-2 *The Order File design worksheet*

INVENTORY FILE

1 Product category	CATEGORY	C	6
2 Part number	PARTNUMBER	C	6
3 Description	DESCRIP~~TION~~	C	25
5 Average cost	~~AVGCOST~~ COST	N	7 2
6 Current selling price	PRICE	N	7 2
4 Preferred vendor (code)	VENDOR	C	8

Figure 3-3 *The Inventory File design worksheet*

III PLUS commands for entering and changing information on the screen. All these commands use fundamentally similar cursor movement and editing keys, with a few minor differences that depend on the context.

As you type your field specifications, you can press ENTER to advance from one item to the next and use the arrow keys to move up, down, left, and right to make changes or correct mistakes. A highlighted bar indicates how wide each entry can be. If you fill up the allotted space, the cursor advances automatically to the next item; if not, you must press ENTER or one of the arrow keys. All the cursor movement and editing commands used in CREATE (and the MODIFY STRUCTURE command, which presents an identical screen for changing the structure of an existing file) are listed in Table 3-1.

The Help key, F1, serves as a "toggle"—a switch that turns a function on if it is off, and off if it is on—for a menu that lists some of the cursor movement and editing keys. With the help menu turned on, there is room for 16 fields on the screen (two columns of eight each). If you turn it off, you can see 30 fields at once. When you fill up the screen, the display scrolls to the left, so you can enter another group of 8 or 15 fields, up to a total of 128. The size of a record is also limited to 4000 characters. As you define fields, dBASE III PLUS displays the number of characters remaining in the upper right corner of the screen.

In a file structure with 15 or 20 fields, the arrow keys generally suffice for moving around on the screen and making changes. For larger structures or more extensive editing, you can call up a menu of supplementary command options by pressing CTRL-HOME. There are options that enable you to jump quickly to the top or bottom of the structure (the first or last field) or select any field by number. You can also exit CREATE and return to the dot prompt by choosing the **Save** option, which saves your new or modified structure, or **Abandon**, which exits without saving the new (modified) structure. Just as in the Assistant, you can select an option either by highlighting it and pressing ENTER or by typing the first letter. The various options are summarized in Table 3-2.

When you exit the CREATE command and return to the dot prompt, the data base structure is saved in a disk file with the eight-character file

Table 3-1 Command Keys Used in CREATE and MODIFY STRUCTURE

Control Key	Command Key	Function
CTRL-E	UP ARROW	Move the cursor up to the previous field
CTRL-X	DOWN ARROW	Move the cursor down to the next field
CTRL-D	RIGHT ARROW	Move the cursor right one character
CTRL-S	LEFT ARROW	Move the cursor left one character
CTRL-F	END	Move the cursor right one column
CTRL-A	HOME	Move the cursor left one column
CTRL-B or PGUP	CTRL-RIGHT ARROW	Pan the screen right to display the next group of fields
CTRL-Z or PGDN	CTRL-LEFT ARROW	Pan the screen left to display the previous group of fields
CTRL-G	DEL	Delete the character at the cursor position
	BACKSPACE	Delete the character to the left of the cursor
CTRL-T or CTRL-Y		Delete the characters from the cursor to the end of the word
CTRL-U		Delete the selected field from the structure
CTRL-V	INS	Turn Insert mode on (if it is off) or off (if it is on)
CTRL-N		Insert a new field before (above) the selected field
CTRL-W	CTRL-END	Save the structure and exit
CTRL-Q	ESC	Exit without saving the new or modified structure
	F1	Turn help menu on (if it is off) or off (if it is on)
	CTRL-HOME	Access the menu of special options

name you specified and the extension DBF (for "data base file"). If the structure contains memo fields, dBASE III PLUS also creates a file with the extension DBT (for "data base text") and the same first name as the DBF file to store the text entered into the memo fields.

Table 3-2 *Special Command Options in CREATE and MODIFY STRUCTURE*

Command	**Function**
Top	Move to the first field in the structure
Bottom	Move to the last field in the structure
Field #	Move to any field, specified by number
Save	Save the structure and exit
Abandon	Exit without saving the structure

Note: The menu of special command options is invoked by pressing CTRL-HOME.

HANDS-ON PRACTICE—CREATING THE NATIONAL WIDGETS CUSTOMER FILE

The examples in the next few chapters are drawn from the National Widgets Customer File. For the time being, this is the only structure you need to CREATE.

If you have not yet loaded dBASE III PLUS, do so now. When the ASSIST menu is displayed, press ESC to exit to the dot prompt, and then type the CREATE command as follows:

```
CREATE NWCUST
```

Remember that if you are working on floppy disks you should include the disk drive designator in your file name, entered as B:NWCUST.

For each field, you must type a field name and specify the type. By default, dBASE III PLUS assumes that each new field will be a character field, so you will always see "Character" displayed in the **Type** column. If you do in fact want to create a character field, you can press ENTER to confirm the default and move on to the **Width** column.

There are two ways to change the field type: You can type the first letter of the new data type, or you can press the space bar to cycle through the available types. For example, to create a date field, you can either type **D**, or you can press the space bar twice, until "Date" appears in the **Type** column, and then press ENTER. Note that if you do type a letter, it can be either uppercase or lowercase, and you should not press ENTER afterward, since dBASE III PLUS expects only a single character of input and therefore advances the cursor automatically to the next column. If you do press ENTER, this keystroke will be interpreted as your entry in the next column—as an attempt to move past the **Width** column without entering a valid width.

If you are confused or forget what to do next, watch the Status, Navigation, and Message lines at the bottom of the screen. With the cursor in the **Type** column, the Navigation Line reminds you that you can "Press SPACE to change the field type." As you press the space bar, the message line displays a description of each field type. For example, with "Numeric" selected, this line reads, "Numeric fields contain signed numbers that may be either integer or decimal."

dBASE III PLUS does not require—or allow—you to enter unnecessary information such as the widths of date, logical, and memo fields (which are always 8, 1, and 10 characters, respectively). You can move the cursor into the **Decimals** column only for numeric fields, since this entry does not apply to any other data type. You can move to a previously defined field at any time to make changes, and then return to the bottom of the structure to continue adding fields.

To create the National Widgets Customer File, enter the specifications for the 15 required fields in the Customer File so that your screen matches Figure 3-4.

If you define 128 fields, dBASE III PLUS assumes that you are finished. With a smaller file structure, you can exit CREATE at any time, either by moving to the bottom of the structure and pressing ENTER with the cursor in a blank field name, or by pressing one of the two standard "exit and save" keys used throughout dBASE III

```
                                                    Bytes remaining:   3803

 CURSOR  <-- -->      INSERT        DELETE       Up a field:      ↑
  Char:     ← →     Char:  Ins    Char:   Del    Down a field:    ↓
  Word: Home End    Field: ^N     Word:   ^Y     Exit/Save:     ^End
  Pan:     ^← ^→    Help:  F1     Field:  ^U     Abort:          Esc

    Field Name  Type      Width  Dec          Field Name  Type      Width  Dec

 1  ACCOUNT     Character    10            9  CONTACT     Character    25
 2  COMPANY     Character    25           10  EQUIPMENT   Character    25
 3  ADDRESS     Character    25           11  FIRSTORDER  Date          8
 4  CITY        Character    20           12  LASTORDER   Date          8
 5  STATE       Character     2           13  YTDORDERS   Numeric      10    2
 6  ZIP         Character    10           14  TOTORDERS   Numeric      10    2
 7  MAIL        Logical       1           15  COMMENTS    Memo         10
 8  TELEPHONE   Character     8           16              Character

CREATE          <C:>NWCUST                Field: 16/16          Ins        Caps
                           Enter the field name.
Field names begin with a letter and may contain letters, digits and underscores
```

Figure 3-4 *Creating the National Widgets Customer File*

PLUS: CTRL-END or CTRL-W. You can think of CTRL-END as meaning "End this editing session and save my changes," and CTRL-W as meaning "Write my changes to disk." As was noted earlier, you can also exit by calling up the special Option menu with CTRL-HOME and selecting **Save**.

With the following message, dBASE III PLUS asks you to confirm your intention to exit: "Press ENTER to confirm. Any other key to resume." When you press ENTER, your file structure is saved on disk. If you change your mind and do not want to save the structure as is, you can press any other key on the keyboard and return to the CREATE screen to make further changes or add more fields.

Next, dBASE III PLUS will ask: "Input data records now? (Y/N)." Press N (for No) because you are not ready to begin entering data.

If you use the DOS DIR command to list the disk directory, you will see that your new data base consists of two files: NWCUST.DBF, which contains all the fixed-length fields, and NWCUST.DBT, which contains the text of the memo fields.

DISPLAYING AND PRINTING A FILE STRUCTURE

You can view a file structure on the screen with

```
LIST STRUCTURE
```

or

```
DISPLAY STRUCTURE
```

By including the phrase TO PRINT in the command, you can route the output of this command to the printer as well as to the screen, so you can easily generate a hard copy of the data base structure.

In addition to the field specifications, the display includes a header consisting of the name of the file, the number of records it contains, and the date the file was last updated (modified in any way). At the bottom of the field list is the total record size, obtained by adding up the individual field widths.

The difference between LIST STRUCTURE and DISPLAY STRUCTURE is that the DISPLAY command pauses when the screen is full to allow you to read the display at your leisure and then instructs you to "Press any key to continue...". DISPLAY STRUCTURE is best for viewing data base structures that have many fields. LIST STRUCTURE displays the entire structure without pause, which is fine for a small one that fits on a single screen. It is also more suitable for printing the structure, since the printout will not be disrupted by the "Press any key to continue..." message.

It is a good idea to print a copy of each of your file structures and keep them on hand whenever you are working with the data bases, so you can see at a glance your field names, data types, and data base status information.

HANDS-ON PRACTICE—PRINTING THE CUSTOMER FILE STRUCTURE

You can view the structure of the National Widgets Customer File you just created with the command

```
DISPLAY STRUCTURE
```

Make sure your printer is turned on, and then print the structure by typing

```
LIST STRUCTURE TO PRINT
```

Except for the date of the last update, your printout should match the one shown in Figure 3-5. Note that because you have not yet added any data to the file, the number of records is zero. You might also wonder why the record size is listed as 198, whereas the actual field widths add up to 197 characters. The extra character is required to store a deletion marker added to the record when you request that it be deleted from the file. As Chapter 5 will explain in detail, dBASE III PLUS does not instantly remove a "deleted" record from the disk; it marks the record as deleted, and, if you wish, ignores the record until you later remove it permanently.

To exit dBASE III PLUS at this point, type QUIT at the dot prompt. You can also try CREATEing the National Widgets Order File and the Inventory File for additional practice before you QUIT.

```
Structure for database: C:NWCUST.dbf
Number of data records:        0
Date of last update   : 04/24/87
Field  Field Name  Type       Width     Dec
    1  ACCOUNT     Character     10
    2  COMPANY     Character     25
    3  ADDRESS     Character     25
    4  CITY        Character     20
    5  STATE       Character      2
    6  ZIP         Character     10
    7  MAIL        Logical        1
    8  TELEPHONE   Character      8
    9  CONTACT     Character     25
   10  EQUIPMENT   Character     25
   11  FIRSTORDER  Date           8
   12  LASTORDER   Date           8
   13  YTDORDERS   Numeric       10       2
   14  TOTORDERS   Numeric       10       2
   15  COMMENTS    Memo          10
** Total **                     198
```

Figure 3-5 *The structure of the National Widgets Customer File*

ESTIMATING FILE SIZES

The total record length in the LIST STRUCTURE display is important for another reason: Together with the anticipated number of records in the file, it enables you to estimate how much disk space you will need for your application. Switching data disks with a data base open can severely damage the file, so all the data bases you will ever open simultaneously must fit on one disk. It is also impractical in most cases to split a data base across multiple disks, since this will prevent you from cross-referencing information in different sections of the file.

Suppose, for example, that you have a dual-floppy system with 360K drives and your mailing list data base is greater than 500K. If you split the list alphabetically, it would be relatively easy to retrieve and edit records, since you would always know on which disk a particular name could be found. But dividing the data alphabetically would make it impossible to produce a single set of mailing labels in ZIP code order.

In the National Widgets system, the Customer File has a record length of 198 bytes, and the company anticipates having 700 customers in the near future. The eventual size of this file will therefore be 198 * 700 = 138,600 bytes. Estimating the size of the memo text file is a less precise calculation. If 20 percent of the records contain entries in the COMMENTS field and most have between 500 and 1000 characters, most entries will require two 512-byte blocks, and the .DBT file will have approximately 700 * 0.20 * 1024 = 143,360 bytes.

A similar calculation should be made for each data base file in your application. As you will see in later chapters, data base files are not the only disk files created and used in a dBASE III PLUS application, and they may not be the only large files. Furthermore, you should never allow a data base to take up any more space than about 70 to 80 percent of the total disk capacity. In some situations, you may need even more work space. For example, sorting a file requires that you have free disk space equal to the size of the original file.

The kind of rough estimate outlined here can help you determine the hardware requirements for your system. For example, if you estimate the combined size of your data base files at over 2 million bytes, you can rule out running the system on floppy disks or on a hard disk that is already nearly filled to capacity.

Naturally, it is preferable to do these calculations before you buy a new computer devoted to managing your data bases. If you discover that you are close to exceeding the limitations of your present hardware, you may want to delete or shorten some fields, or reduce the number of records retained in historical files. National Widgets, for example, might choose to maintain only the current month's orders in the Order File instead of an entire year's worth of detail.

Chapter 4

Entering and Editing Data

Once you have defined the structure for a data base, you can begin to enter data and perform the routine daily maintenance procedures required to keep the data accurate and up to date. You will need to call up existing records to view the data on screen, page forward or backward through the file to examine a range of records, edit individual fields, and remove records you no longer need. In most data bases, you will also continue to add records, either at the end of the file or by inserting them in specific positions between existing records.

dBASE III PLUS allows you to carry out these activities by means of a set of *full-screen editing commands,* all of which present a template, or data entry form, derived from your file structure and offer a full complement of commands for moving anywhere on the screen to add, delete, or edit data. Using these full-screen commands, you can view and update files in either of the two styles briefly described in Chapter 1: the "ledger card," or "file card," style, which displays the fields in a record vertically on one or more screens; and the "spreadsheet" style, which displays one record per screen line with the fields lined up in columns.

STRATEGIES FOR TESTING WITH SAMPLE DATA

Before you actually begin to add records to a data base, give some thought to your initial testing strategy. No matter how much advance planning you have done, it is impossible to anticipate every conceivable variation in the data that must be entered, much less all the ways you will want to select and sort data to extract useful information from your files.

Although dBASE III PLUS allows you to change the structure of a data base without losing information that has already been entered, it is best to make these changes while your files are still small. For example, if you add a field to the structure, you will have to call up each existing record to enter data into the new field; shortening a field may force you to search for entries that were truncated and should be edited to fit more gracefully within the new field width.

Your initial testing should be designed to help you verify the following:

- That you have included all necessary fields and have eliminated extraneous fields that are rarely filled in
- That your field widths are neither too long nor too short
- That you have chosen the most appropriate data type for each field
- That you can carry out all necessary calculations
- That you can establish required linkages and carry out transfers of information between files
- That you can specify your selection and sorting criteria
- That you can produce all the requested screen displays and reports

To carry out this testing, you must enter some sample data — usually between 25 and 100 records — into each data base file you have CREATEd. The test data should be drawn from your real application, not from your imagination, to ensure that it is representative of the full range of values that the system will eventually handle. When you invent data for testing purposes, you will likely have a tendency to make the data conform to the file structures, rather than present the challenges that will enable you to verify that your file structures are correct and complete.

During the testing phase, you will also gain valuable insight into some of the non-computer-related problems you may encounter as you convert from manual to computerized procedures. You will uncover any difficulties associated with gleaning the required information from the manual system and interpreting the input documents, and you will be able to estimate how long the initial data entry will take. Any special preparations, such as assigning ID codes or calculating beginning balances, will be brought to your attention, so you can begin to work on these preliminaries early enough to keep the system implementation on schedule.

Entering the test data will help you clarify the data entry sequence. You will be able to outline which fields must be filled in first, so that others may be calculated, and which fields should not be entered at all, because they will be derived from data in other fields or files. Knowing how long data entry will take can also help you more realistically evaluate how much historical data or transaction detail to enter into the data base.

FULL-SCREEN EDITING WITH dBASE III PLUS

The terms *full screen* and *full-screen editing mode* are used to describe all the dBASE III PLUS commands that present data on the screen in a predefined format and offer a variety of cursor movement and editing command keys that you can use to move freely among the fields and enter, change, or delete data.

Table 4-1 lists the cursor movement and editing command keys used in the full-screen APPEND, INSERT, EDIT, and CHANGE commands (which are described in the following sections in this chapter). Notice that many of the commands have both keypad and control key equivalents. For example, to move the cursor right one word, you can press a numeric keypad key—END—or use a control key combination—CTRL-F. In some cases, there is only one choice; and occasionally, there are three.

To use a control key command, you press the CTRL key and continue to hold it down while you press the other key(s) in the combination. If you are unfamiliar with control key commands, it may help to think of CTRL as working much like the SHIFT key—by itself it does nothing, but pressed in combination with other keys, it alters the meanings of those keys and allows you to generate additional characters.

Note also that the NUM LOCK key functions just like the CAPS LOCK key, except that it affects only the numeric keypad. When NUM LOCK is on, the keypad keys produce numbers; when it is off, they generate nonprintable character codes that are used as commands by most programs. If your keyboard does not have an LED (light-emitting diode) that lights when NUM LOCK is on, you can determine the status of this key by looking for the dBASE III PLUS "Num" indicator in the Status Bar or on the top line of the screen.

If you have used other programs with similar command structures, you may already have a strong preference for either the control key or keypad commands. WordStar users will feel right at home with the control key commands, while Lotus spreadsheet users will probably find their hands reaching instinctively for the numeric keypad. When there are alternatives, most of the examples in this book cite keypad commands, but keep in mind that you can always substitute an equivalent command listed in the reference tables.

All the full-screen commands use the field names as prompts, arranged either vertically or horizontally on the screen to identify the data to be entered into each field. Once you have worked with a data base for a while, you will appreciate the value of making your field names clear, readable, and self-explanatory, and arranging them in the most convenient order for data entry and editing.

Table 4-1 *Command Keys Used in APPEND, EDIT, CHANGE, and INSERT*

Control Key	Command Key	Function
CTRL-E	UP ARROW	Move the cursor up to the previous field
CTRL-X	DOWN ARROW	Move the cursor down to the next field
CTRL-D	RIGHT ARROW	Move the cursor right one character
CTRL-S	LEFT ARROW	Move the cursor left one character
CTRL-F	END	Move the cursor right one word
CTRL-A	HOME	Move the cursor left one word
CTRL-G	DEL	Delete the character at the cursor position
	BACKSPACE	Delete the character to the left of the cursor
CTRL-T		Delete characters from the cursor to the end of the word
CTRL-Y		Delete characters from the cursor to the end of the field
CTRL-V	INS	Turn insert mode on (if it is off) or off (if it is on)
CTRL-C	PGDN	Move forward to the next screenful of fields or to the next record
CTRL-R	PGUP	Move backward to the previous screenful of fields or to the previous record
	CTRL-PGDN or CTRL-PGUP	Edit the memo field containing the cursor
CTRL-U		Mark the displayed record for deletion or remove the deletion marker to recover the record
CTRL-W	CTRL-END	Save the record and exit
CTRL-Q	ESC	Exit without saving the record
F1		Turn the help menu on (if it is off) or off (if it is on)

Figure 4-1 shows what the screen would look like while the first record in the National Widgets Customer File is being edited. The Status Bar at the bottom of the screen should already be familiar to you, and the help

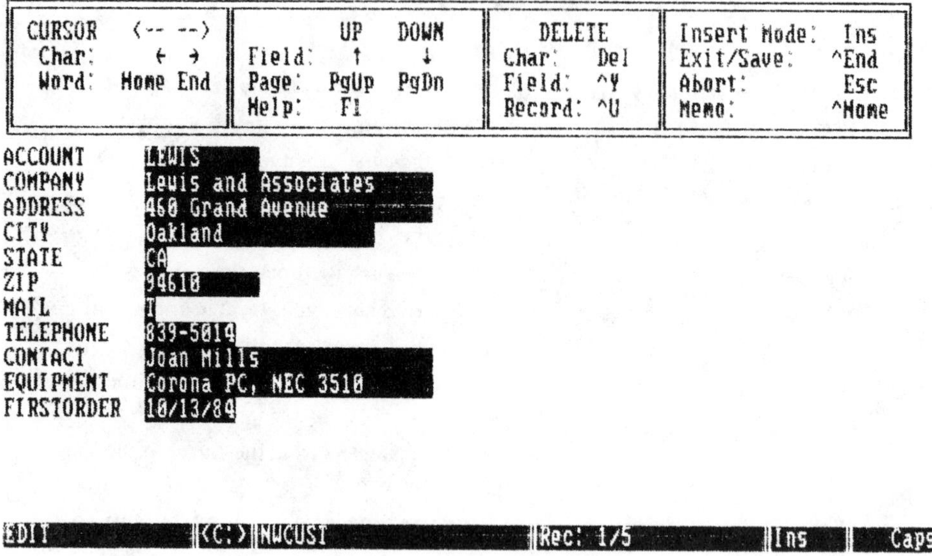

Figure 4-1 *The dBASE III PLUS full-screen editing display*

menu of cursor movement and editing commands resembles the menu displayed by the CREATE command introduced in Chapter 3. As with CREATE, you can turn this menu on or off at any time by pressing F1.

The field names in the data base in use are listed vertically down the left side of the screen. If a character field is too wide to fit on the same line as its prompt, the data will wrap around onto one or more additional lines. Despite this display format, a character field is always treated as one long string of characters, not a formatted paragraph of text. Even if a field occupies multiple lines, you can use only the cursor movement keys that move left and right to edit the data; the UP ARROW and DOWN ARROW keys always move the cursor to the adjacent field.

If there are more fields than will fit on the screen at once, you can use the PGUP and PGDN keys to move up and down in the structure and reveal different sets of fields. Exactly how many fields you can view at once depends on both the field widths and whether the help menu and Status Bar are displayed. With both the menu and Status Bar on the screen, a maximum of 11 fields is visible (fewer if some require more than one line). Turning off the help menu makes room for 17, and if you also turn off the status display with the SET STATUS OFF command, you can view 21 fields.

By default, dBASE III PLUS uses normal text (light characters on a dark background) for the field name prompts and inverse video (dark characters on a light background) for data entered by the user. In the standard full-screen display, the data entry areas are thus delineated by bars of inverse video, and the field widths are evident. When you fill a field completely, dBASE III PLUS sounds a "bell," or electronic beeper, and advances the cursor automatically to the next field. Chapter 12 covers the commands used to change these and other characteristics of the data entry environment to suit your preferences.

In all the full-screen editing modes, dBASE III PLUS formats and validates your entries based on the data type:

- In a *character field,* text is left-justified. Any keyboard characters are permitted, and since there is no way to guess your intentions, dBASE III PLUS performs no special validations on your entries.

- In a *numeric field,* the digits you type appear at the left side of the field until you press DOWN ARROW or ENTER to move to the next field or type a period (.) to indicate that you are ready to enter digits to the right of the decimal point. In either case, dBASE III PLUS right-justifies the number to align with the decimal point (or the right side of the field if no decimal places are defined). Note that if there are decimal places, but all the digits to the right of the decimal point are zeros, you need not type the zeros; they will be filled in automatically when you press ENTER.

- In a *logical field,* the only permissible entries are T, t, Y, and y (for "True" or "Yes") and F, f, N, and n (for "False" or "No"). If you try to type any other character, the cursor will not leave the field until you correct the error; you can, however, leave a logical field blank, in which case it will be treated as if you had entered the logical value .F.

- In a *date field,* you need only enter the six digits representing the month, day, and year. The punctuation marks between the three components of the date—by default, slashes (/)—are supplied automatically, and the cursor jumps over these positions during data entry. Note that you must enter all six digits, and you cannot substitute a space for a leading zero if the month or day is less than 10. dBASE III PLUS tests dates to make sure that the month is between 1 and 12, and that the date is consistent with the number of days in the specified month.

OPENING AND CLOSING DATA BASE FILES

To work with a data base—to add, edit, or display records—it must be open. You open a file with the USE command:

USE *data base file name*

When you open a file, dBASE III PLUS reads the structure from the disk and retains in memory all the essential information recorded there. This includes the field names, lengths, and types; the date the file was last updated; and the total number of records—all the information displayed by the LIST STRUCTURE command. Whenever the status display is on, you can easily determine which, if any, data base is open by glancing at the third segment of the Status Bar, where the file name always appears.

Certain commands, such as CREATE, open a data base automatically. After you CREATE a file structure, the data base remains open, and you can begin adding data immediately. Other commands require that you first open the file in which you want to work. In most cases, if you fail to open a file, you will be prompted for the file name with the message "No database is in USE. Enter file name:". When you type in the name, dBASE III PLUS will open the file and proceed to execute your command.

It is equally important to remember to close a data base — inform dBASE III PLUS that you no longer wish to work with that file — when you are finished with it. Certain crucial information — primarily the number of records in the file — is retained in memory as long as the file is open. It is stored on disk only when you close the data base. If you reboot or turn off the computer without first closing a file, this vital statistic will not be recorded on disk. The next time you try to work with the data base, you will discover that any new records added during the interrupted work session are inaccessible, because even though records are saved one at a time as they are entered, dBASE III PLUS cannot find any record with a number higher than the record count stored with the file structure.

A file is automatically closed when you QUIT from dBASE III PLUS or when you type a USE command to open a different file. If you want to close a file without opening another, you can type

```
USE
```

Think of this command as the verb "USE" followed by no file name, which means, "use no file" or "I don't want to use any file at all." You might want to close and then reopen a file periodically during a long data entry session, just to make sure that a power failure or hardware crash does not leave you with a large number of new records and a mismatched record count. It is also prudent to always close a file before you walk away from the computer if you share your office and your computer equipment with co-workers who are not aware of the danger of rebooting in the middle of a work session with dBASE III PLUS.

USING APPEND TO ADD RECORDS TO A DATA BASE

As its name suggests, the APPEND command is used to add records to the end of a dBASE III PLUS data base (or to an empty data base). To begin adding records, make sure that the right file is open and then type

```
APPEND
```

The APPEND screen looks just like the edit screen illustrated in Figure 4-1. The field names are lined up down the left side of the screen, and a bright bar of inverse video indicates the location and the width of each field. Within a record, you can use the standard dBASE III PLUS full-screen cursor movement and editing commands to move around the screen and make changes or correct mistakes.

dBASE III PLUS assumes that you will want to add more than one record at a time, possibly many records in a single data entry session. When you press ENTER or the DOWN ARROW key to move past the last field in the structure, dBASE III PLUS saves the newly completed record and presents a new blank form for entering the next record. When you have finished adding new records, you can exit APPEND by pressing ENTER with the cursor in the first field of a new blank form.

You can press ENTER to skip over any field you want to leave blank— except the first, since pressing ENTER with the cursor in the first field signals your intention to exit APPEND. To leave the first field blank, you must press the DOWN ARROW key to bypass it.

You may find that after entering several fields, you wish to leave all the remaining fields blank. With the cursor positioned in any field, you can save the current record and advance to the next one by pressing PGDN. If your structure has too many fields to fit on one screen, this command displays the next screenful of fields, so you may have to press PGDN more than once to arrive at a new blank record.

You can minimize the number of times you have to press ENTER to pass over individual fields by designing your data base structures so that fields that are frequently left blank, or that are calculated from other fields, are placed close to the end of the structure. This is not always an easy judgment to make in advance, but you can modify a structure later on if you need to rearrange the fields.

Another way to save the current record and exit APPEND is to press CTRL-END with the cursor positioned in any field. If you want to exit to the dot prompt without saving the current record, whether or not you have entered data in any of the fields, you can press ESC instead. Note also that CTRL-END always saves the current record, so if you press this key with the cursor in the first (or any) field of a blank form, you will (usually unintentionally) enter a blank record into the data base.

HANDS-ON PRACTICE—ENTERING RECORDS IN THE CUSTOMER FILE

You can practice using the APPEND command by adding some sample data to the National Widgets Customer File. If you are not continuing directly from Chapter 3, you must first load dBASE III PLUS, press ESC if necessary to exit the ASSIST menus, and open the Customer File by typing

```
USE NWCUST
```

To invoke the full-screen APPEND command and begin adding records, type

```
APPEND
```

The data for the first sample record is illustrated in Figure 4-2, which shows the appearance of the screen when the help menu is turned off so that all the fields fit on the screen at once. When you are entering the sample data, feel free to turn this menu on or off as often as you like by pressing F1.

As you add records, dBASE III PLUS automatically assigns the next sequential *record number* to each new record. Notice that the Status Bar monitors the total number of records in the file and the current record.

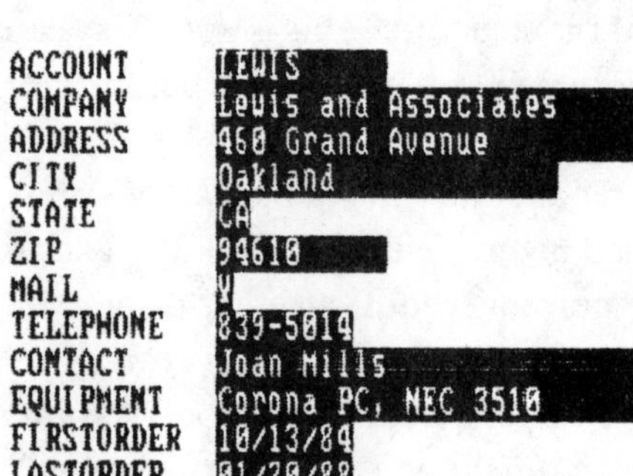

Figure 4-2 *Using APPEND to add the first record to a file*

Before you have completed your first record, the file is considered empty even if you have typed in some data, since you could still abort the entry by pressing ESC. The Status Bar therefore displays the following:

```
Rec: None
```

The ACCOUNT code for the first record is LEWIS, an abbreviation for Lewis and Associates. Enter this field and then the company name and address. Since all these entries are shorter than the field widths, you will have to press ENTER or DOWN ARROW after each field to move on to the next one. When you enter the STATE, MAIL, and TELEPHONE data, the cursor will advance automatically, since these entries fill the fields completely.

If you notice that you have made an error, you can use the cursor movement commands listed in Table 4-1 to move around the screen and make corrections. Remember that you can press INS to alternate between *Insert mode,* in which characters are inserted in the text at the cursor position, and *Typeover mode,* in which the characters you type replace existing ones. You can always tell whether you are typing in insert mode by looking for the "Ins" indicator at the right side of the Status Bar.

This is a good time to make some deliberate errors so you can be sure that you understand how to recover and correct an entry that dBASE III PLUS judges invalid. For example, move to the FIRSTCONT or LASTCONT field, and enter an impossible date such as 13/12/88. dBASE III PLUS will display the following error message on the Message Line at the bottom of the screen: "Invalid date. (press SPACE)".

You must press the space bar to clear the error message and return the cursor to the field; all other keys will be ignored. You will not be able to move the cursor out of the field until you either enter a valid date (of course, dBASE III PLUS cannot determine if you have entered the correct date) or position the cursor at the beginning of the field and press CTRL-Y to erase the data and leave the field blank.

Move the cursor to the MAIL field, and enter a character not permitted in a logical field, such as A or 7. Notice that dBASE III PLUS beeps and refuses to advance the cursor to the next field until you enter a legitimate logical value.

When you reach the last field, COMMENTS, you will see that dBASE III PLUS displays "memo" in the data entry area next to the field name but will not allow you to type anything there. The "memo" serves to remind you that COMMENTS is a memo field, not a short character field. Memo fields are entered and edited using a built-in "word processor," which is described in the next section in this chapter.

In the first record, the COMMENTS field is blank, so you can simply press ENTER to bypass this field and complete your first record. When you do so, dBASE III PLUS will save the record on disk and display a new blank data entry form for entering Record 2. At this point, the

Status Bar displays the following message to indicate that the file contains one record and that you are currently at the end-of-file (EOF)—that is, you are not viewing an existing record:

```
Rec: EOF/1
```

The data for the second record follows. When you reach the COMMENTS field, stop and read the next section to learn how to enter and edit memo fields.

```
Record No.      2

ACCOUNT         ABCPLUMB
COMPANY         ABC Plumbing
ADDRESS         1850 University Avenue
CITY            Berkeley
STATE           CA
ZIP             94703
MAIL            Y
TELEPHONE       861-4543
CONTACT         Ed Williams
EQUIPMENT       Kaypro PC, Epson FX-286
FIRSTORDER      12/01/85
LASTORDER       04/30/88
YTDORDERS          796.41
TOTORDERS         5248.90
COMMENTS
```

USING THE dBASE III PLUS WORD PROCESSOR TO EDIT MEMO FIELDS

A memo field can accommodate up to 5000 characters of free-form text, and dBASE III PLUS provides a rudimentary "word processor" for entering and editing this text. You invoke the memo field editor by positioning the cursor in the data entry area next to the field name and pressing CTRL-PGDN. The editor uses most of the same cursor movement and editing keys as the other full-screen editing modes, plus some commands that are not required for editing shorter character fields. All of the cursor movement and command keys are listed in Table 4-2.

The editor presents you with a relatively blank screen for typing your text. The help menu appears at the top of the screen with the name of the memo field you are editing. To leave more room for text, the editor screen does not include the Status Bar; instead, the "Ins", "Caps", and "Num" indicators are displayed on the top line of the screen.

Like a word processor, the memo editor automatically wraps your text to the next line by inserting a *soft return* whenever you type a line that would otherwise extend beyond the right margin, which is located at column 65. dBASE III PLUS does not allow you to change the right margin in the memo editor, but you can alter the screen display width or print a memo field on a report in either a wider or narrower column.

Whenever a carriage return is required, such as to separate paragraphs, you must press ENTER to create a *hard return*. You can always tell the difference between hard and soft returns, because dBASE III PLUS displays a "<" at the right edge of every line ending in a hard return. Think of a hard return as immutable—it never changes unless you delete it, and it always produces a new line in a printout or screen display.

In contrast, when you add or delete characters so that a line falls short of the right margin or extends beyond it, soft returns are moved in order to adjust the altered text to conform to the standard margins. This process of reformatting edited text takes place one paragraph at a time, and it is not automatic—you must place the cursor within the paragraph you wish to reformat, anywhere *before* the changed section, and press CTRL-KB to realign the text with the margins.

The memo field editor offers a fraction of the advanced editing commands present in relatively simple word processors. You can search forward from the cursor position for a specified string of characters with the CTRL-KF (the *F* means "Find") command, and you can repeat the previous search with CTRL-KL. However, there are no search-and-replace or block manipulation commands.

You can import text from an external file provided that you do not exceed the memo field editor's 5000-character limit. To import a file, you press CTRL-KR (the *R* stands for "read"); dBASE III PLUS will prompt

Table 4-2 *Command Keys Used in the Memo Field Editor*

Control Key	Command Key	Function
CTRL-E	UP ARROW	Move the cursor up to the previous line
CTRL-X	DOWN ARROW	Move the cursor down to the next line
CTRL-D	RIGHT ARROW	Move the cursor right one character
CTRL-S	LEFT ARROW	Move the cursor left one character
CTRL-F	END	Move the cursor right one word
CTRL-A	HOME	Move the cursor left one word
CTRL-B	CTRL-RIGHT ARROW	Move the cursor to the end of the line
CTRL-Z	CTRL-LEFT ARROW	Move the cursor to the beginning of the line
CTRL-G	DEL	Delete the character at the cursor position
	BACKSPACE	Delete the character to the left of the cursor
CTRL-T		Delete characters from the cursor to the end of the word
CTRL-Y		Delete the entire line containing the cursor
CTRL-N		Insert a blank line (a hard return)
CTRL-V	INS	Turn Insert mode on (if it is off) or off (if it is on)
CTRL-C	PGDN	Move forward to the next screenful of text
CTRL-R	PGUP	Move backward to the previous screenful of text
CTRL-KB		Reformat the current paragraph
CTRL-KF		Find a string of characters, searching forward from the cursor position
CTRL-KL		Repeat the previous search
CTRL-KR		Read in the contents of a disk file
CTRL-KW		Write the memo text to a disk file
CTRL-W	CTRL-END or CTRL-PGUP	Save the memo text and return to the data base screen
CTRL-Q	ESC	Exit without saving the new or changed text
F1		Turn the help menu on (if it is off) or off (if it is on)

you to enter the file name. You can also export a memo field to a text file with CTRL-KW (the *W* means "write"). These commands operate on one memo field at a time; there is no easy way to copy the text from a specified memo field in every record in a data base to an external file or to read text into all the records in a file.

To exit the memo field editor and save the text to disk, you can use either of the standard dBASE III PLUS "save and exit" commands—CTRL-END or CTRL-W—or a third alternative used only for memo fields—CTRL-PGUP. If you want to exit without saving your changes or new text, you can press ESC or CTRL-Q.

HANDS-ON PRACTICE—ENTERING MEMO FIELDS

With the cursor in the COMMENTS field in the second customer record, press CTRL-PGDN to invoke the memo editor. If you have already advanced to the third record, you can press PGUP to return to Record 2. Type the following paragraph of text, without pressing ENTER and without backing up to correct mistakes:

```
     This company has several older Kaypro computers in
addition to their newest AT-compatible.  They are still
interested in disks and supplies for the older machines,
and they generally respond to special mailings by calling
and placing an order.
```

Notice that the editor wraps the text into a paragraph. Press ENTER twice to end the paragraph and create an extra blank line, and type another paragraph or more of text—anything you wish—and press ENTER at the end.

Now, go back up to the first paragraph, and change the third line to read, "disks, supplies, and accessories" instead of "disks and supplies". To add words to the existing text, make sure that Insert mode is on by checking for the "Ins" indicator at the top of the screen and pressing INS if necessary.

Delete the words "calling and" from the fourth and fifth lines, and correct any other spelling or typographical errors you may have made. When you have completed the changes, move the cursor to the first line of the first paragraph and press CTRL-KB to reformat the paragraph.

Finally, press CTRL-END to save the text, exit the editor, and return to the APPEND screen, which displays the other fields in Record 2. Notice that the cursor returns to exactly where it was when you invoked the memo editor—the COMMENTS field.

At this point, you have not finished entering Record 2. If you press CTRL-END, dBASE III PLUS will save the record, exit APPEND, and go to the dot prompt. If you press ENTER to move past the COMMENTS field, the record will be saved and dBASE III PLUS will display a blank form for Record 3. However, pressing ESC will abort the entire entry, and dBASE III PLUS will exit to the dot prompt without saving Record 2. If you do this, the text entered in the COMMENTS field will be lost, even though you gave the command to store it on disk, because a memo cannot exist independently of the record it belongs to.

Press ENTER to save Record 2, and enter the following three records into the Customer File:

```
Record No.       3

ACCOUNT      CLEANAIR
COMPANY      Clean Air & Water Society
ADDRESS      2104 Addison Street
CITY         Berkeley
STATE        CA
ZIP          94704
MAIL         N
TELEPHONE    540-7282
CONTACT      Chris Hartley
EQUIPMENT    Compaq Deskpro 286
FIRSTORDER   05/10/85
LASTORDER    05/10/85
YTDORDERS         0.00
TOTORDERS       128.67
COMMENTS


Record No.       4

ACCOUNT      KLEIN
COMPANY      Carol Klein, M.D.
ADDRESS      3107 Telegraph Avenue
CITY         Oakland
STATE        CA
ZIP          94609
```

```
MAIL         N
TELEPHONE    891-2204
CONTACT      Judy Barnes
EQUIPMENT    IBM AT, Quietwriter
FIRSTORDER   10/13/85
LASTORDER    12/28/87
YTDORDERS        0.00
TOTORDERS     1053.89
COMMENTS     Referred by Dr. James Reynolds.


Record No.       5

ACCOUNT      MTK
COMPANY      M.T.K. Industries
ADDRESS      1400 61st Street
CITY         Emeryville
STATE        CA
ZIP          94608
MAIL         Y
TELEPHONE    655-7200
CONTACT      Leslie Cohen
EQUIPMENT    XT clone, Gemini printer
FIRSTORDER   06/23/86
LASTORDER    02/03/87
YTDORDERS      108.59
TOTORDERS      423.92
COMMENTS     Interested in receiving additional information
             on new lines of computer furniture, ergonomic
             workstations, glare screens, and similar items.

             Talk to Leslie about orders, but ask for Joe in
             the Bookkeeping Department for accounts receivable
             questions.
```

Press ENTER with the cursor in the ACCOUNT field of the blank form displayed for Record 6 to exit APPEND and return to the dot prompt.

USING EDIT AND CHANGE TO VIEW AND EDIT RECORDS

You can use the EDIT or CHANGE commands to view and edit data in a full-screen edit mode that is virtually identical to the APPEND screen. These two command verbs serve the same purpose, and you can use them interchangeably. (Most of the examples in this book use EDIT rather than CHANGE, however.) To begin editing records, you type

```
EDIT
```

or

```
CHANGE
```

The resulting screens are identical except for the command verb displayed in the Status Bar. The current record—the one you most recently accessed—is displayed in the standard full-screen format with the cursor positioned in the first field. If you have just finished APPENDing records, the EDIT command will display the last record added to the file. If you are beginning a new work session and have just opened a file with a USE command, the first record in the file will be displayed.

Using any full-screen cursor movement and editing keys listed in Table 4-1, you can move freely among the fields and make any changes you like. Just as in APPEND, you can access a memo field by positioning the cursor in the data entry area next to the field name and pressing CTRL-PGDN.

When you have finished editing a record, you can save your changes and exit to the dot prompt by pressing CTRL-END with the cursor positioned anywhere in the record. If you want to discard the changes and retain the original data, or if you simply want to view the data and have not typed anything, you can exit to the dot prompt by pressing ESC.

The EDIT and CHANGE commands are convenient for flipping through a file, viewing a number of records, and editing some of them. You can page through the file one record at a time by using the PGDN key to move forward and PGUP to move backward. If you are familiar with word processing, you might consider this analogous to reading through a document one page at a time, the "page down" function moving viewing down toward the bottom and the "page up" function moving it back up toward the top. When you use PGDN and PGUP to page through a data base, any changes you make are saved automatically when you leave the current record and move to the next or previous record.

If it seems as if there is little difference between APPEND and EDIT, you are right. In fact, you can access previously entered records directly from the APPEND screen by pressing PGUP. You may page through the file to edit any existing records and then return to adding new records by pressing PGDN with the last record in the file displayed on the screen. If you try this, you will notice that the command displayed in the Status Bar is always APPEND, even when you are editing a record entered earlier, as a reminder that you can still add records, which you cannot do from the EDIT or CHANGE screens.

DELETING AND UNDELETING RECORDS

You can delete a record from a data base by pressing CTRL-U with the record displayed on the screen in any full-screen editing modes. When you press CTRL-U, the record does not disappear from the screen, and it is not removed immediately from the data base—it is only marked, or tagged, as deleted. Of course, there is a way to permanently remove from the disk all records that have been marked as deleted: by using the PACK command, which is described in Chapter 5.

When you are working in any of the full-screen editing modes, you can verify that a record is deleted by the "Del" indicator displayed on the right side of the Status Bar, or, if you have turned off the status display with SET STATUS OFF, on the top line of the screen. You can use EDIT or CHANGE to edit records marked for deletion just as you can any other records in a data base. Also note that the very act of marking a record deleted is no different from making any other editing change, such as changing an address or correcting the spelling of a name. If you press CTRL-U to mark a record deleted, the "Del" indicator appears immediately in the Status Bar. But if you then exit to the dot prompt by pressing ESC, the "Del" indicator will disappear, and the deletion marker will not be saved with the record—just as any other alterations would not be saved.

One reason that deletions are not carried out instantly is that marking them for later removal gives you an opportunity to change your mind.

You can remove the deletion marker, and thereby "undelete" a record, by pressing CTRL-U with the record displayed in any full-screen editing mode. CTRL-U acts as a toggle; it switches the status of a record between deleted and undeleted by setting and removing the deletion marker.

Although the ability to recover a deleted record affords a certain margin of safety, this is not actually the reason dBASE III PLUS carries out deletions the way it does; it is more like a beneficial side effect. Think about what is involved in physically removing a record from a file. Deleting, say, the third record would leave a gap, which could be filled in by copying Record 4 over it. Record 5 could then be moved up into the space formerly occupied by Record 4, and so on.

This amounts to recopying the entire file in place, moving good records up to replace those marked for deletion. This process can take a considerable amount of time, especially if the file is large. Using the method of marking individual records for deletion—and then later removing them permanently all at once—allows you to "delete" a record instantly and choose when you want to spend the time on the slow step of physically erasing them from the file.

HANDS-ON PRACTICE—EDITING, DELETING, AND RECALLING DATA

If you are not continuing directly from the previous examples, load dBASE III PLUS, exit the ASSIST menus, and open the National Widgets Customer File by typing

```
USE NWCUST
```

Enter the full-screen editing mode by typing

```
EDIT
```

Which record you see on the screen depends on what you did last. If you just finished adding records to the file, your last entry, Record 5, will be displayed; if you have reopened the Customer File, you will see Record 1. In any case, use PGUP or PGDN to move to Record 3. If this is your first experience with the editing command keys, you may press one of these keys too many times in rapid succession or hold it down too long. Pressing PGUP to move backward when you are already editing the first record in the file, or using PGDN to move forward when you are already viewing the last record, will cause dBASE III PLUS to exit to the dot prompt. If this happens, just type EDIT again.

Mark Record 3 for deletion by pressing CTRL-U. You should see the "Del" indicator appear in the Status Bar.

Move to the next record by pressing PGDN , correct the street address to read "3204 Telegraph Avenue," and change the value of the MAIL field to "True" by typing Y or T in this field.

Page forward to Record 5 and edit the memo field by placing the cursor in the field and pressing CTRL-PGDN. Move the cursor to the third line and insert the phrase "adjustable chairs" after "screens". Add a new paragraph of text between the first and second paragraphs by moving the cursor to the first line of the second paragraph and pressing CTRL-N twice to insert two new blank lines. Type the following text, and anything else you like:

```
Make sure to send them the new spring catalog as soon as it is
available.
```

Notice that whether or not you are typing in Insert mode, dBASE III PLUS automatically inserts more blank lines to accommodate your text as it wraps the new paragraph.

USING INSERT TO ADD RECORDS IN A SPECIFIED POSITION

When you page through a dBASE III PLUS file using the full-screen EDIT command, records are displayed in the order in which they were entered in the data base. New records entered using the APPEND command are added to the end of the file and are assigned the next sequential number. At times you may prefer to insert a new record between two other records to preserve a particular sequence.

You can add a record in a specific position by using INSERT. INSERT is a full-screen command that uses all the same command and editing keys as APPEND, EDIT, and CHANGE. There is one difference between APPEND and INSERT, however: APPEND continues to add records sequentially until you give an explicit command to exit, while INSERT adds a single record to the file and then returns you to the dot prompt.

You can add a record after the current record by typing

```
INSERT
```

You can add a record before the current record with this variation of the INSERT command:

```
INSERT BEFORE
```

When you add a new record with INSERT or INSERT BEFORE, all records after the point of insertion are moved down to accommodate the new entry. This is comparable to the process (described in the previous section) of physically removing records marked for deletion, and it, too, can be time-consuming in a large file. Chapter 7 describes two more efficient ways to control the actual sequence of records in a data base or the order in which they are displayed, so it is rarely necessary to use the relatively slow and inefficient INSERT command on a large data base. In a small file, however, using INSERT is the easiest way to add a few records in specific places.

HANDS-ON PRACTICE—INSERT

If you are not continuing directly from the previous example, make sure that the National Widgets Customer File is open, enter the full-screen EDIT mode, and use PGUP or PGDN to move to Record 3. You can make changes to this record (make sure the record is still marked deleted when you are finished), and then exit to the dot prompt by pressing CTRL-END. You should be able to confirm, by looking at the "Rec: 3/5" message at the right side of the Status Bar, that Record 3 is in fact the current record.

Add a new record after Record 3 by typing

```
INSERT
```

Notice that the record number indicator in the Status Bar shows you that your new record is number 4 of the total of 6 that are now in the file (or will be, after you complete the new entry). The previous Record 4—Carol Klein—will become Record 5, and the previous Record 5—M.T.K. Industries—will be the new Record 6. Here is the data for the new Record 4:

```
Record No.       4

ACCOUNT      ANDERSON
COMPANY
ADDRESS      3420 19th Street
CITY         San Francisco
STATE        CA
ZIP          94114
MAIL         Y
TELEPHONE    563-8961
CONTACT      John Anderson
EQUIPMENT    Apple IIGS, Imagewriter
FIRSTORDER   08/08/86
LASTORDER    12/01/87
YTDORDERS          0.00
TOTORDERS        832.58
COMMENTS
```

USING BROWSE TO ADD, VIEW, AND EDIT RECORDS

All the full-screen editing commands described thus far—APPEND, EDIT, CHANGE, and INSERT—display the fields from one record in a vertical arrangement on the screen. You can select an alternate way to view your data in which records are laid out horizontally, with one record per line and the fields lined up in columns. This screen format is used by the BROWSE command, which you invoke by typing

```
BROWSE
```

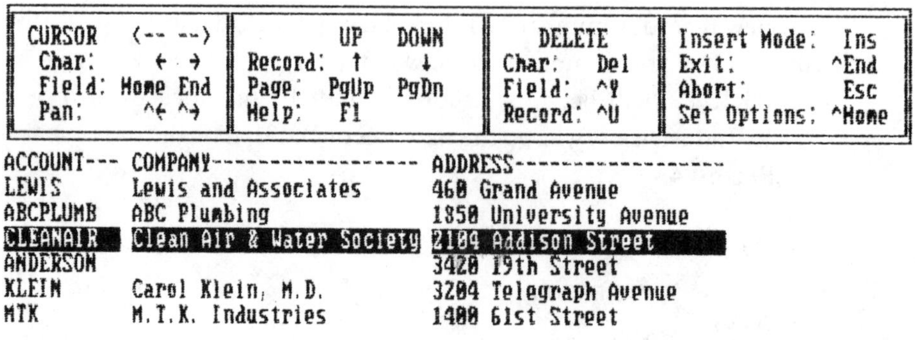

Figure 4-3 *The dBASE III PLUS BROWSE screen*

The appearance of the screen with the first six records in the National Widgets Customer File displayed in BROWSE mode is illustrated in Figure 4-3.

The number of fields that are visible at one time depends on their widths, and the number of records that fit on the screen depends on whether or not the help menu is displayed. With the menu on, you can see 11 records at a time; turning it off increases the number to 17. Whether or not you have SET STATUS OFF, dBASE III PLUS always turns the status display back on in BROWSE mode, so this setting has no effect on how many records may be viewed at once.

As in the other full-screen editing modes, you can use the standard cursor movement and editing command keys to move anywhere on the screen and make changes. You are free to move horizontally—within a record—or vertically—from one record to another. Any changes you make are saved when you leave the record you were editing and move on to the next or previous record. You can exit BROWSE to the dot prompt and save the changes made to the current record with CTRL-END, or exit without saving your changes with ESC.

The Status Bar always displays the current record number—the one containing the editing cursor—and indicates whether or not this record is marked for deletion. You can delete and undelete records using the standard deletion toggle, CTRL-U. Table 4-3 lists all the cursor movement and editing command keys as they are used in BROWSE.

The only limitation on editing through the BROWSE screen is that you cannot access memo fields. The names of memo fields are displayed and you can move the cursor into the fields, but pressing CTRL-PGDN does not invoke the memo field editor; your command is ignored.

Unless your data base has only a few short fields, you will be unable to view all of them at once on the BROWSE screen. You can visualize the data base as a large chart (or worksheet, if you are familiar with spreadsheet programs) with the information in each record spread across one row and the fields lined up in columns. The display screen behaves like a small window that you can position anywhere above this chart to view different portions of the data. You move the window up with PGUP or down with PGDN, and "pan" the display right with CTRL-RIGHT ARROW or left with CTRL-LEFT ARROW.

Table 4-3 *Command Keys used in BROWSE*

Control Key	Command Key	Function
CTRL-E	UP ARROW	Move the cursor up to the previous record
CTRL-X	DOWN ARROW	Move the cursor down to the next record
CTRL-D	RIGHT ARROW	Move the cursor right one character
CTRL-S	LEFT ARROW	Move the cursor left one character
CTRL-F	END	Move the cursor to the next field
CTRL-A	HOME	Move the cursor to the previous field
CTRL-B	CTRL-RIGHT ARROW	Pan to display the next field (on the right)
CTRL-Z	CTRL-LEFT ARROW	Pan to display the previous field (on the left)
CTRL-G	DEL	Delete the character at the cursor position
	BACKSPACE	Delete the character to the left of the cursor
CTRL-T		Delete characters from the cursor to the end of the word
CTRL-Y		Delete characters from the cursor to the end of the field
CTRL-V	INS	Turn insert mode on (if it is off) or off (if it is on)
CTRL-C	PGDN	Move forward to the next screenful of records
CTRL-R	PGUP	Move backward to the previous screenful of records
CTRL-U		Mark the displayed record for deletion or remove the deletion marker to recover the record
CTRL-W	CTRL-END	Save the record and exit
CTRL-Q	ESC	Exit without saving the record
F1		Turn the help menu on (if it is off) or off (if it is on)

If you press the DOWN ARROW key with the cursor in the last record on the screen, the display will scroll to reveal the next record, but dBASE III PLUS does not pan the display left or right unless you press

CTRL-RIGHT ARROW or CTRL-LEFT ARROW. If you begin with the cursor positioned in the leftmost field visible on the screen, pressing ENTER or END moves the cursor to successive fields within the same record until it reaches the last field on the right side of the screen; then it moves down that column. Similarly, you can press HOME to back up to the previous field within a record until you reach the leftmost field on the screen, at which point the cursor begins to move up this column to previous records.

BROWSE offers a menu of options, which you can access by pressing CTRL-HOME. These options are summarized in Table 4-4. There are options that help you move quickly to the top or bottom of the file or to any record, specified by number. There is also a **Lock** option, which allows you to designate one or more fields to remain stationary at the left side of the screen as you pan the display right or left to view other fields. You would generally want to choose for this purpose the field or fields that best enable you to uniquely identify a record.

For example, in the National Widgets Customer File, you might lock the ACCOUNT field so that even when the company name disappears off the left edge of the screen, you can still recognize the customer. The fields you lock need not be the first in the structure; you need only position them at the left edge of the screen before you select the **Lock**

Table 4-4 *Special Command Options in BROWSE*

Command	**Function**
Bottom	Move to the last record in the data base
Top	Move to the first record in the data base
Record No.	Move to any record selected by number
Lock	Specify a field or fields to remain stationary at the left edge of the screen while other fields pan
Freeze	Restrict editing to a specified field
Find	Search the index for a specified value (this option appears only if an index is open)

Note: You can invoke the menu of special command options by pressing CTRL-HOME.

option. You then tell dBASE III PLUS how many fields to lock. To cancel this setting, just choose **Lock** again and enter a zero for the number of fields to lock.

Another option you may find useful is **Freeze**, which restricts editing to a single field. To use this option, you select **Freeze** from the BROWSE options menu and enter the name of the field you wish to edit. You may still pan the display left or right to view any fields in the record, but you cannot move the cursor into any field except the one you have "frozen." To return to accessing the entire record, select **Freeze** again, and leave the field name blank.

You can use the **Freeze** option to partially compensate for the fact that, by default, the cursor moves to the next field within a record before advancing to the next record. This behavior is consistent with APPEND and EDIT, but it detracts from your ability to use BROWSE to view and edit the contents of a single field in a series of records. If your entries fill the field so that the cursor advances automatically, you will have to move left as well as down to return to the desired column. (Another solution to this problem is to pan the display so that the field you want to edit is the last one on the right.)

You can even add records from the BROWSE screen. If you use the DOWN ARROW key to move past the last record in the file, dBASE III PLUS asks if you really intend to add new records with the message "===> Add new records? (Y/N)".

If you pressed DOWN ARROW by mistake, you can press N ("No") to return to editing the last record in the file. If you want to add records, press Y ("Yes"). You can add new records and resume editing at any time by pressing UP ARROW to move back to previously entered records. You will probably find the BROWSE screen less convenient than APPEND if your data base contains more than a few fields, since you must pan the display left or right to enter fields that were not visible initially.

HANDS-ON PRACTICE—BROWSE

Make sure that the National Widgets Customer File is open, and enter the BROWSE mode by typing

```
BROWSE
```

The record you most recently accessed will be displayed at the top of the screen. Unless you have just opened the file, this will not be the first record. Move to the top of the file by pressing CTRL-HOME to call up the options menu and selecting **Top**. You will then see the ACCOUNT, COMPANY, and ADDRESS fields from all six records on the screen.

Experiment with the cursor movement keys to get a feeling for using them to move around on the screen. Notice that all the fields in the record you are editing are highlighted to remind you that this is the current record. Move the cursor into Record 3, which was deleted in an

```
CURSOR   <-- -->  |         UP    DOWN |     DELETE     | Insert Mode:    Ins
 Char:     ←  →   | Record:  ↑     ↓   | Char:    Del   | Exit:          ^End
 Field: Home End  | Page:   PgUp  PgDn | Field:   ^Y    | Abort:          Esc
 Pan:     ^←  ^→  | Help:   F1         | Record:  ^U    | Set Options:  ^Home
```

ACCOUNT---	CITY---------------	STATE	ZIP-------	MAIL	TELEPHONE
LEWIS	Oakland	CA	94610	T	839-5014
ABCPLUMB	Berkeley	CA	94703	T	861-4543
CLEANAIR	Berkeley	CA	94704	F	540-7282
ANDERSON	San Francisco	CA	94114	T	563-8961
KLEIN	Oakland	CA	94609	F	891-2204
MTK	Emeryville	CA	94608	T	655-7200

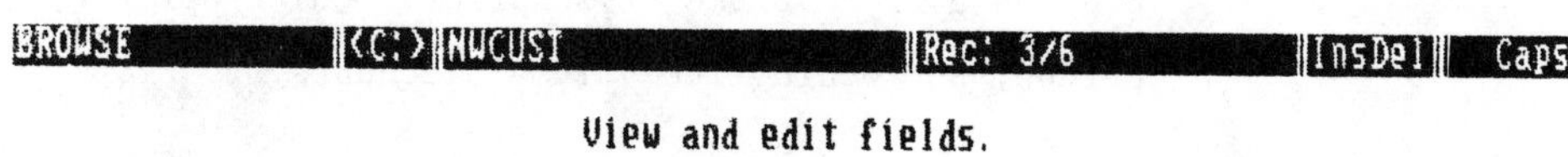

View and edit fields.

Figure 4-4 *Using the Lock and Freeze options in BROWSE*

earlier practice session, and note that the "Del" indicator appears in the Status Bar.

Use the **Lock** option to fix the ACCOUNT field in place on the screen. To do this, make sure that if you have panned the display left or right, the ACCOUNT field is once again displayed in the leftmost column of data on the screen. Then call up the options menu with CTRL-HOME, select **Lock**, and enter 1 as the number of fields to lock.

Pan the display right until the TELEPHONE field is visible on the screen, and choose the **Freeze** option to restrict editing to this field. Notice that only the TELEPHONE field, not the entire record, is highlighted. Your screen should look similar to the one shown in Figure 4-4. Try moving up and down in the data base, and change a phone number if you wish. Return to editing all the fields by selecting the **Freeze** option again and leaving the field name blank.

When you have finished moving through the file and editing data, exit to the dot prompt by pressing CTRL-END to save changes to the current record.

You can stop here, but if you want to add more data to the Customer File, a list of the remaining sample records follow:

```
Record No.       7

ACCOUNT      RAPIDTYPE
COMPANY      RapidType Secretarial Svc
ADDRESS      2457 Union Street
CITY         San Francisco
STATE        CA
ZIP          94123
MAIL         N
TELEPHONE    861-4048
CONTACT      Kathy McDonald
EQUIPMENT    IBM AT, HP LaserJet
FIRSTORDER   03/10/88
LASTORDER    03/10/88
YTDORDERS        348.52
TOTORDERS        348.52
COMMENTS     This company is a word processing and secretarial
             service.  They are looking for one vendor to
             provide a high volume of supplies.  Quick delivery
             and varied product line more important than lowest
             prices, but would like volume discounts.
```

```
Record No.      8

ACCOUNT      PHOENIX
COMPANY      Phoenix Construction
ADDRESS      3214 Pacheco Blvd.
CITY         Martinez
STATE        CA
ZIP          94553
MAIL         T
TELEPHONE    939-8610
CONTACT
EQUIPMENT    Victor 286, TI855
FIRSTORDER   04/28/86
LASTORDER    07/06/86
YTDORDERS          0.00
TOTORDERS        249.57
COMMENTS
```

```
Record No.      9

ACCOUNT      KELLY
COMPANY      Kelly and Sons Furniture
ADDRESS      14800 Bancroft Avenue
CITY         San Leandro
STATE        CA
ZIP          94578
MAIL         N
TELEPHONE    357-7482
CONTACT      Richard Kelly
EQUIPMENT    NEC APC, NEC Pinwriter
FIRSTORDER   01/23/88
LASTORDER    01/23/88
YTDORDERS         87.35
TOTORDERS         87.35
COMMENTS
```

```
Record No.     10

ACCOUNT      GREENTHUMB
COMPANY      Green Thumb Landscaping
ADDRESS      1240 Hearst
CITY         Berkeley
STATE        CA
ZIP          94702
MAIL         Y
```

```
TELEPHONE    549-8901
CONTACT      Celia Lopez
EQUIPMENT    Kaypro PC, Okidata 192
FIRSTORDER   08/16/86
LASTORDER    12/19/86
YTDORDERS          0.00
TOTORDERS        347.73
COMMENTS


Record No.      11

ACCOUNT      HOMEMOVIES
COMPANY      Home Movies Video Rentals
ADDRESS      2982 College Avenue
CITY         Berkeley
STATE        CA
ZIP          94705
MAIL         Y
TELEPHONE    843-1148
CONTACT      Mark Vogel
EQUIPMENT    Columbia, NEC 2010
FIRSTORDER   09/13/87
LASTORDER    09/13/87
YTDORDERS        248.15
TOTORDERS        248.15
COMMENTS     Owner is a friend of Jim's, so they get a 10%
             discount on all orders.  However, they take a
             long time to pay.


Record No.      12

ACCOUNT      SHAPEUP
COMPANY      Shape Up Fitness Center
ADDRESS      2832 Macdonald Avenue
CITY         Richmond
STATE        CA
ZIP          94804
MAIL         Y
TELEPHONE    236-7687
CONTACT      Jeanne Lee
EQUIPMENT    Apple IIc, Okidata 183
FIRSTORDER   02/15/85
LASTORDER    11/12/87
YTDORDERS        435.42
TOTORDERS        867.38
COMMENTS
```

```
Record No.      13

ACCOUNT       FLOORPLAN
COMPANY       Floor Plan Carpet Center
ADDRESS       1482 Lowry Avenue
CITY          South San Francisco
STATE         CA
ZIP           94080
MAIL          Y
TELEPHONE     871-3204
CONTACT       Louise Robbins
EQUIPMENT     NorthStar Advantage
FIRSTORDER    11/20/87
LASTORDER     11/20/87
YTDORDERS          0.00
TOTORDERS        184.18
COMMENTS


Record No.      14

ACCOUNT       JOHNSON
COMPANY       J. Thomas Johnson, CPA
ADDRESS       50 California St., #1032
CITY          San Francisco
STATE         CA
ZIP           94111
MAIL          Y
TELEPHONE     433-6488
CONTACT       Carolyn Sumner
EQUIPMENT     IBM XT, Epson MX-100
FIRSTORDER    06/28/86
LASTORDER     12/06/87
YTDORDERS          0.00
TOTORDERS        168.42
COMMENTS


Record No.      15

ACCOUNT       ELLISMFG
COMPANY       Ellis Manufacturing
ADDRESS       3091 Park Boulevard
CITY          Palo Alto
STATE         CA
ZIP           94306
MAIL          Y
TELEPHONE     494-1421
CONTACT       Barbara Goddard
```

```
EQUIPMENT     Macintosh, Laserwriter
FIRSTORDER    10/18/86
LASTORDER     11/16/87
YTDORDERS         0.00
TOTORDERS       669.00
COMMENTS      Don't accept any orders unless accompanied by
              prepayment.  These people have always been slow
              to pay, and have been avoiding phone calls
              regarding seriously past due balance that is now
              in collections.


Record No.      16

ACCOUNT       IMAGEMAKER
COMPANY       The Image Makers
ADDRESS       1900 Powell St., Ste. 832
CITY          Emeryville
STATE         CA
ZIP           94608
MAIL          Y
TELEPHONE     653-1250
CONTACT       Lisa Burns
EQUIPMENT     IBM AT, NEC 7710
FIRSTORDER    11/12/87
LASTORDER     11/12/87
YTDORDERS         0.00
TOTORDERS       389.50
COMMENTS


Record No.      17

ACCOUNT       WHITNEY
COMPANY       Financial Planning Svcs.
ADDRESS       1800 Peralta, Suite 18
CITY          Fremont
STATE         CA
ZIP           94536
MAIL          Y
TELEPHONE     791-7474
CONTACT       James Whitney
EQUIPMENT     Compaq Deskpro, Brother
FIRSTORDER    10/04/85
LASTORDER     02/13/88
YTDORDERS       201.87
TOTORDERS      1384.45
COMMENTS      This guy likes to talk.  Appreciates good advice,
              but will take up a lot of your time on the phone
              if you go along with it.
```

```
Record No.     18

ACCOUNT      HRINSURANC
COMPANY      H & R Insurance
ADDRESS      1225 Van Ness Avenue
CITY         San Francisco
STATE        CA
ZIP          94109
MAIL         Y
TELEPHONE    398-1441
CONTACT      Jill Henley
EQUIPMENT    Epson Equity III, FX-1000
FIRSTORDER   07/12/86
LASTORDER    10/26/87
YTDORDERS        0.00
TOTORDERS      538.43
COMMENTS


Record No.     19

ACCOUNT      DELTADESGN
COMPANY      Delta Design
ADDRESS      2405 Sycamore Drive
CITY         Antioch
STATE        CA
ZIP          94509
MAIL         Y
TELEPHONE    754-7373
CONTACT      Andrea Bennett
EQUIPMENT    Macintosh, Imagewriter
FIRSTORDER   09/14/87
LASTORDER    09/14/87
YTDORDERS        0.00
TOTORDERS      188.15
COMMENTS     Referred by Chris Johnson.

Record No.     20

ACCOUNT      ARONOFF
COMPANY
ADDRESS      601 First Street
CITY         Benicia
STATE        CA
ZIP          94510
MAIL         Y
TELEPHONE    745-1813
CONTACT      Gina Aronoff
EQUIPMENT    IBM AT, Okidata 132
```

```
FIRSTORDER  10/09/86
LASTORDER   12/14/87
YTDORDERS       0.00
TOTORDERS     232.50
COMMENTS


Record No.     21

ACCOUNT      YORKPUMP
COMPANY      York Pump, Inc.
ADDRESS      632 Charcot Avenue
CITY         San Jose
STATE        CA
ZIP          95131
MAIL         Y
TELEPHONE    946-9975
CONTACT      Sharon Fern
EQUIPMENT    AT clone, Okidata 193
FIRSTORDER   10/18/85
LASTORDER    04/10/88
YTDORDERS        157.38
TOTORDERS        608.42
COMMENTS     Send information on printer stands when flyer is
             ready.
```

The full-screen editing commands described in this chapter enable you to carry out all the routine file maintenance operations listed in the functional definition of data base management presented in Chapter 1. Using APPEND, INSERT, EDIT, CHANGE, and BROWSE, you can add records to a data base, view records on the screen, mark records for later deletion, and make any changes necessary to keep your data accurate and current. The full-screen commands all operate on one record at a time, and with them you can begin to build and maintain your own data bases. Chapter 5 introduces the process of typing dBASE III PLUS commands at the dot prompt to operate on a data base as a whole, to display or print information, and to perform calculations.

Chapter 5

Working at the Dot Prompt: Viewing and Updating Data

Thus far, most of your work with dBASE III PLUS has been in the full-screen editing modes, commands that allow you to view data in a clear, easy-to-read format and move freely from record to record, and from field to field, to enter data and make changes. All these commands are designed to operate on one record at a time; even in BROWSE, which allows you to view more than one record on the screen, you can make changes to only the currently selected record. The full-screen commands are therefore well suited to building new data bases and carrying out the routine maintenance operations required to update your files.

When you work with an existing data base, you will often want to view data, generally from more than one record at a time, without making any changes, and perform calculations without viewing data from the individual records involved. For these purposes, dBASE III PLUS offers commands that operate on a data base as a whole, or on a subset of the records in a file, rather than on a single record. Since these commands may affect far more records than would fit on the screen at once, you execute them by typing them at the dot prompt (or selecting them from the ASSIST menus).

This chapter introduces a group of commands that you can type at the dot prompt to view data from selected fields in one or more records, and thus begin to extract useful information from a data base. Alternatives will also be presented for carrying out some of the same file maintenance operations that you already know how to accomplish using full-screen commands. Depending on the context as well as your personal preferences, you can use any combination of full-screen editing and typing commands at the dot prompt to keep your data bases accurate and current.

THE dBASE III PLUS RECORD POINTER

Whenever a data base is open, dBASE III PLUS keeps track of its position in the file—the record you most recently accessed or the one affected by your last command. This indicator is the *record pointer,* and the record it points to is the *current record.*

Understanding the concept of the dBASE III PLUS record pointer and remembering to be aware of its current position in a file are crucial to working successfully at the dot prompt. Most of the dBASE III PLUS commands you will use to display and print data, and many of the commands that carry out calculations or change data, can operate on a single record, a group of records, or an entire data base. When a command acts on one record, the affected record is the one at the current position of the record pointer, unless you explicitly override this default by including another record number in your command. Some of the many ways you can specify a group of records to be acted on by a dBASE III PLUS command depend on your ability to position the record pointer at the first record in the group before you execute the command.

If you imagine your data base written on a big wall chart laid out like the BROWSE display, you can think of the record pointer as a pointing stick, or a sliding arrow, that moves up and down the chart and enables you to "point out" to dBASE III PLUS which record you want to work with. In all your subsequent work with dBASE III PLUS, it is vital to keep track of the position of the record pointer to ensure that the commands you type operate on the right records.

You already have considerable experience in positioning the dBASE III PLUS record pointer where you want it. In the full-screen editing modes, you position the pointer using cursor movement and command keys. For example, when you press PGDN in EDIT or DOWN ARROW in BROWSE, the record pointer advances to the next record in the file. Because the full-screen commands were designed to facilitate viewing records and making individual editing changes, you are probably accustomed to thinking of these commands as ways to display different records in the file.

However, each of these commands involves two separate steps: First, the record pointer is moved forward or backward, and then the data from the record at the new position of the pointer is displayed on the screen (or, in the case of BROWSE, highlighted) with the cursor in the record to indicate that you may type changes. When you work with dBASE III PLUS at the dot prompt, it is important to distinguish between these two steps, because you may not always need or want to display the data—you may simply want to position the pointer on a particular record and perform some operation on that record or on a group of records beginning with that one.

Whether or not you are aware of the record pointer, and whether or not you have typed any commands to explicitly move the pointer, dBASE III PLUS always keeps track of its position. It is worth reiterating that *the record pointer is always positioned somewhere in the current data base.* When you first open a data base by typing a USE command, the record pointer is positioned at the "top" of the file. In all the examples presented so far, the record at the top of the file is Record 1, the first record entered. (You will see in Chapter 7 that Record 1 is not always at the "top" of a file.) Subsequent editing or display commands may reposition the pointer to any record in the file.

You can always determine the position of the record pointer by looking at the Status Bar, which displays the current record as well as the total number of records in the file. For example, if you entered all of the sample data into the National Widgets Customer File, and you just finished editing the fifth record, you would see the following on the right side of the Status Bar:

```
Rec: 5/21
```

This display informs you that there are 21 records in the file and that the record pointer is currently positioned at Record 5. You might also read this display as "The current record is number 5 out of a total of 21." If the concept of the record pointer still seems confusing or unintuitive, you may find it helpful to keep the status display turned on and keep an eye on the "Rec" indicator as you work in the full-screen editing modes and at the dot prompt.

The record pointer can also be positioned at the end-of-file (EOF), a special location just past the last record in a file. The record pointer will wind up at the end-of-file whenever you attempt to advance it beyond the last record. For example, in the full-screen EDIT command, pressing PGDN with the last record in the file displayed on the screen returns you to the dot prompt and leaves the record pointer positioned at the end-of-file. This fact is reflected in the Status Bar display:

```
Rec: EOF/21
```

As you will see shortly, many commands that process an entire data base leave the record pointer positioned at the end-of-file afterward. The end-of-file is not the same as the "bottom" of the file (you already know how to move to the bottom of a file by selecting the **Bottom** option from the BROWSE options menu). Moving the pointer to the "bottom" of a file places it at a specific record—in all the examples presented so far, the last record entered. If the record pointer is at the end-of-file, it is not positioned at any valid record. This distinction is important, because commands that operate on a single record — the current record — will have no effect if the record pointer is at the end-of-file.

In the previous example, the separation between the act of moving the record pointer and displaying the data is evident. Pressing PGDN is not one of the "official" ways to exit the full-screen EDIT command; its purpose is to advance the record pointer to the next record in the file. If the pointer is already positioned at the last record, PGDN will move it to the end-of-file. Although the pointer moves, there is no "next" record to display, so dBASE III PLUS exits EDIT and returns you to the dot prompt.

Note also that when you use any of the standard exit commands such as CTRL-END or ESC to return to the dot prompt from a full-screen editing mode, the record pointer does not move from its current position. If you are editing Record 3, for example, and you press CTRL-END to save your changes and exit, you will return to the dot prompt with the pointer still positioned at Record 3, a fact that you can confirm by looking at the Status Bar.

USING LIST AND DISPLAY TO VIEW RECORDS

The full-screen editing modes are best suited to viewing and updating records one at a time. Even the BROWSE command, which displays multiple records on the screen, is geared to editing records one by one. If you want to view all or selected fields without making changes, you can use the LIST and DISPLAY commands at the dot prompt.

LIST and DISPLAY are very similar, and as you will see in Chapter 6, you can achieve almost exactly the same results with either command. One difference is that by default LIST operates on all the records in a data base, while DISPLAY acts on only the current record — the one at the position of the record pointer. To display all the records in a data base on the screen, you would type

```
LIST
```

To view only one record, you could type

```
DISPLAY
```

Both commands require that a data base be open; you cannot display data from a file without opening it first or open a file and display its contents with a single command. If you have forgotten to open a file with a USE command, dBASE III PLUS will issue the following warning: "No database is in USE. Enter file name:".

Figure 5-1 illustrates the appearance of the screen after you have opened the National Widgets Customer File when it contained five records and executed a LIST command. By default, LIST displays all the fields from all the records in the file. The record number is included, at the beginning of each record. Records are LISTed in the order in which they were entered into the data base, with each record beginning on a new line, and the fields from each record spread across the screen.

In a small data base with only a few fields, the data will be neatly aligned in columns. If there are too many fields to fit on one line, dBASE III PLUS wraps the data from a record onto as many lines as it requires, which makes the display less readable. In the National Widgets Customer File, a record is 198 bytes long, and thus occupies three lines on the screen.

Recall that when you delete a record, it is not immediately removed from the data base but is marked for later removal. The deletion marker, an asterisk (*), is included in the output produced by the LIST and DISPLAY commands, between the record number and the first data field. In Figure 5-1, you can see that Record 3 is marked for deletion.

By default, dBASE III PLUS displays the field names at the beginning of the output produced by a LIST or DISPLAY command, to serve as "column headings" that identify the data being displayed. The amount of space a field occupies in a LIST or DISPLAY is either the

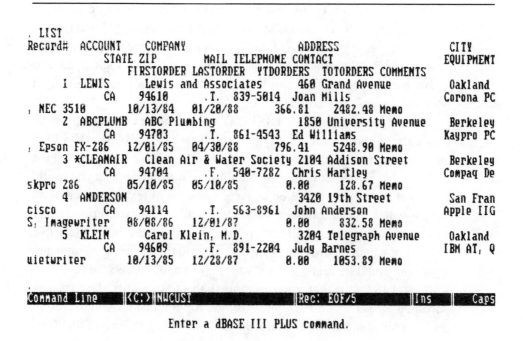

```
. LIST
Record#  ACCOUNT    COMPANY                         ADDRESS                   CITY
             STATE ZIP       MAIL TELEPHONE CONTACT                           EQUIPMENT
                 FIRSTORDER LASTORDER  YTDORDERS  TOTORDERS COMMENTS
      1  LEWIS      Lewis and Associates         460 Grand Avenue             Oakland
             CA     94610       .T.  839-5014  Joan Mills                     Corona PC
, NEC 3510      10/13/84   01/20/88       366.81     2482.48 Memo
      2  ABCPLUMB   ABC Plumbing                 1850 University Avenue       Berkeley
             CA     94703       .T.  861-4543  Ed Williams                    Kaypro PC
, Epson FX-286  12/01/85   04/30/88       796.41     5248.90 Memo
      3 *CLEANAIR   Clean Air & Water Society 2104 Addison Street             Berkeley
             CA     94704       .F.  540-7282  Chris Hartley                  Compaq De
skpro 286       05/10/85   05/10/85         0.00      128.67 Memo
      4  ANDERSON                                3420 19th Street             San Fran
cisco        CA     94114       .T.  563-8961  John Anderson                  Apple IIG
S, Imagewriter  08/08/86   12/01/87         0.00      832.58 Memo
      5  KLEIN      Carol Klein, M.D.            3204 Telegraph Avenue        Oakland
             CA     94609       .F.  891-2204  Judy Barnes                    IBM AT, Q
uietwriter      10/13/85   12/28/87         0.00     1053.89 Memo

.
Command Line  ||<C:>||NWCUST          ||Rec: EOF/5       ||Ins  ||    Caps

                     Enter a dBASE III PLUS command.
```

Figure 5-1 *Using the LIST command to display all the data in a file*

field width or the length of the field name, whichever is greater. You can see from Figure 5-1 that even in a relatively small file having as few as 15 fields (you are permitted a maximum of 128) and a 198-byte record (the maximum is 4000), the data wraps around onto three lines, and the headings are not particularly helpful. You can turn off the field heading display by typing the following command at the dot prompt:

```
SET HEADING OFF
```

As you will see shortly, the headings are much more useful when you LIST only selected fields. If you wish, you can turn the heading display back on with

```
SET HEADING ON
```

You can see from Figure 5-1 that unlike the full-screen commands, LIST and DISPLAY always show logical fields as .T. ("True") or .F. ("False"), even if you entered Y or N. A logical field that was left blank is displayed as .F., which is consistent with the way logical data is evaluated—a logical field can be treated as having a true value only if you have specifically entered .T. or .Y.

The output of a LIST or DISPLAY command does not include the contents of any memo fields in your data base. dBASE III PLUS displays "memo" in place of the actual memo text to remind you that the field is not a character field. Presumably, the rationale is that you would not want the display cluttered by large amounts of text, and there is an easy way to LIST the contents of a memo field, which is described in the next section. Unfortunately, there is also no indication in the LIST display of which records have text entered into the memo field, information that would be useful even if you did not actually see the text.

If you LIST a file that contains more than a few records, the data may scroll up the screen and disappear off the top too fast for you to read it. In Chapter 6, you will see several variations of the LIST and DISPLAY commands that you can use to circumvent this problem, but there are also two control key commands that you can use to temporarily pause any display produced by dBASE III PLUS (and DOS as well). CTRL-S acts as a toggle: it stops the display when it is scrolling and resumes scrolling if it is paused. An alternative command is CTRL-NUM LOCK, which differs from CTRL-S in that it can *only* be used to pause the display. In either case, you can resume scrolling by pressing any key on the keyboard except CTRL-NUM LOCK. To abort a LIST command, and most other dBASE III PLUS commands, and return to the dot prompt to type a new command, you can press ESC.

DISPLAYING SELECTED FIELDS

When your files are small and you are familiar with their contents, using the LIST command is a good way to look for a particular record, see at a glance what data has been entered into a certain field, or quickly scan a data base to spot trends. With a larger structure and more records, this much information can be visually overwhelming, and you will find it difficult to pick out the specific items of interest.

dBASE III PLUS offers an array of options that you can add to the basic LIST and DISPLAY commands to produce a more selective and useful display. If you think of the dBASE III PLUS command language as being similar to English and other natural languages, you can imagine beginning with a simple imperative sentence—a command to do something—and gradually building up a more detailed description of exactly what you want by adding phrases and clauses. In keeping with this analogy, the various parts of a dBASE III PLUS command are often referred to as "phrases," or "clauses."

One way to make the LIST display more informative is to instruct dBASE III PLUS to include only some of the fields in the structure. In most contexts, you will not need to see the entire record, and the extra data only makes it more difficult to find the information you do need on the screen. To LIST or DISPLAY only selected fields, you name them in your command as a *field list.* In dBASE III PLUS, a *list* consists of one or more items of the same kind—such as fields, data base files, or report forms—separated by commas (unless there is only one item in the list). For example, to LIST only the ACCOUNT, COMPANY, and TELEPHONE fields from the National Widgets Customer File, you would type

```
LIST ACCOUNT, COMPANY, TELEPHONE
```

To view the same fields from a single record, you would use

```
DISPLAY ACCOUNT, COMPANY, TELEPHONE
```

The output produced by these commands in a file having only five records is illustrated in Figure 5-2. The fields are displayed in the order in which they were named in the field list, which need not be the same as the order in which they appear in the structure.

You can display the contents of a memo field by naming it explicitly in a LIST command. For example, you could produce the display shown in Figure 5-3 with the following command:

```
LIST ACCOUNT, COMMENTS
```

```
. DISPLAY ACCOUNT, COMPANY, TELEPHONE
Record#  ACCOUNT    COMPANY                    TELEPHONE
      1  LEWIS      Lewis and Associates       839-5014

. LIST ACCOUNT, COMPANY, TELEPHONE
Record#  ACCOUNT    COMPANY                    TELEPHONE
      1  LEWIS      Lewis and Associates       839-5014
      2  ABCPLUMB   ABC Plumbing               861-4543
      3 *CLEANAIR   Clean Air & Water Society  540-7282
      4  ANDERSON                              563-8961
      5  KLEIN      Carol Klein, M.D.          891-2204

.
Command Line   |<C:>|NWCUST          |Rec: EOF/5      |Ins   |   Caps
                    Enter a dBASE III PLUS command.
```

Figure 5-2 *Using DISPLAY and LIST to display selected fields*

```
. LIST ACCOUNT, COMMENTS
Record#  ACCOUNT    COMMENTS
      1  LEWIS
      2  ABCPLUMB       This company has several older Kaypro
                    computers in addition to their newest
                    AT-compatible.  They are still interested in
                    disks, supplies, and accessories for the older
                    machines, and they generally respond to special
                    mailings by placing an order.

      3 *CLEANAIR
      4  ANDERSON
      5  KLEIN      Referred by Dr. James Reynolds.

.
Command Line   |<C:>|NWCUST          |Rec: EOF/5      |Ins   |   Caps
                    Enter a dBASE III PLUS command.
```

Figure 5-3 *LISTing the contents of a memo field*

In all variations of the LIST and DISPLAY commands, dBASE III PLUS by default includes the record numbers and the deletion marker. If you prefer, you can exclude the record numbers by adding the word OFF to your LIST and DISPLAY commands, as in the following:

```
LIST ACCOUNT, COMPANY, TELEPHONE OFF
```

You cannot eliminate the deletion marker, since failing to make some distinction between deleted and nondeleted records would be potentially misleading.

When you type a list of items, such as field names and file names, you need not type a space after each comma, as you would if you were typing a list on paper. You can also type the previous command as follows:

```
LIST ACCOUNT,COMPANY,TELEPHONE OFF
```

Remember that spaces *are* essential between the separate parts of a command. You must always type a space following the verb and between clauses or phrases. If you omit the space after the word "LIST", dBASE III PLUS could not identify the verb in the command, and if you forget the space before "OFF", the last field name in the list would be read as "TELEPHONEOFF"—which is not even a valid field name (it is too long).

USING LIST TO PRINT FOR QUICK REPORTS

When you display fields selectively, with the HEADING option turned ON so that dBASE III PLUS includes field names as column headings, the LIST command produces output in a format that is clear and readable enough to provide useful information to someone who does not understand dBASE III PLUS. You can, in fact, use the LIST command to generate simple printed reports by including TO PRINT in the command. This instructs dBASE III PLUS to route the output of the command to the printer as well as to the screen. To print the same list of account codes, company names, and telephone numbers displayed on the screen in Figure 5-2, you would type

```
LIST ACCOUNT, COMPANY, TELEPHONE OFF TO PRINT
```

In every dBASE III PLUS command, the verb must be the first word. When you build a complex command by adding several discrete clauses or phrases to the basic verb, the order in which you type these optional components is usually unimportant. Thus, you could also type

```
LIST OFF ACCOUNT, COMPANY, TELEPHONE TO PRINT
```

or

```
LIST TO PRINT OFF ACCOUNT, COMPANY, TELEPHONE
```

The order of the command components in the examples in this book was chosen to make the commands read as much as possible like normal English imperative sentences. As you do your own work with dBASE III PLUS, feel free to experiment with different variations to see which ones make the most sense to you.

If your printer is wide enough to accommodate 14-inch paper, or if you can select a "compressed" print mode and thus print more than 80 characters on 8 1/2-by 11-inch paper, you can include more fields in a printout than will fit within a screen line. For example, you could print all the name and address fields in the National Widgets Customer File with:

```
LIST ACCOUNT, CONTACT, COMPANY, ADDRESS, CITY, STATE,
  ZIP OFF TO PRINT
```

Remember that you may type dBASE III PLUS command verbs, file names, and field names in any combination of uppercase and lowercase letters. When dBASE III PLUS displays or prints field headings in a LIST or DISPLAY command, the headings conform to the same combination of uppercase and lowercase letters you used to type the list of field names in the command. To produce a report in which the field name headings are printed using initial capital letters, you could type your LIST command like this:

```
LIST Account, Contact, Company, Address, City,
  State, Zip OFF TO PRINT
```

Note that the case used for the words "LIST", "OFF", and "TO PRINT" does not affect the display in any way.

The printouts produced by LIST TO PRINT commands are relatively crude. The field name headings are printed only once, at the very beginning, and the listings are not paginated—data is printed over the perforations in continuous-form paper, with no provision for top and bottom margins or page numbers. Chapter 9 explains how to print formatted reports, but LIST TO PRINT can still be a valuable tool for producing "quick-and-dirty" reports for situations in which an informal presentation is acceptable.

RETRIEVING AND EDITING PREVIOUS COMMANDS

When you type commands at the dot prompt, dBASE III PLUS retains your last few commands in memory. This command HISTORY, by default, consists of the 20 most recently executed commands. At any point, you can retrieve a command from HISTORY in order to remind yourself about what you just did, repeat a previous command, edit a command and resubmit it in changed form, or add to it.

You can page up and page down through the list of commands in HISTORY with the UP ARROW and DOWN ARROW keys. You might visualize HISTORY as a list, or stack, of commands that is accessed from the bottom up, as if the commands you typed at the dot prompt were progressing up the screen, with the most recent one close by on the line above the command line, and earlier commands gradually pushed off the top of the screen. Pressing UP ARROW at the dot prompt causes dBASE III PLUS to display your previous command, and as you continue to move up, you will see older (earlier) commands closer to the top of the list. When you type your twenty-first command in a work session, the first one is pushed off the top of the HISTORY list and can no longer be retrieved.

To see the entire command HISTORY, you can type

```
LIST HISTORY
```

When you use the arrow keys to retrieve a command from HISTORY, dBASE III PLUS displays the command next to the dot prompt, with the cursor positioned at the first character. To repeat the command in exactly the same form, all you have to do is press ENTER.

You can also use any of the full-screen editing keys to change the command, and when you are ready to resubmit your new command, press ENTER with the cursor positioned anywhere within the line. You can use the RIGHT ARROW and LEFT ARROW keys to move through the command one character at a time, or use HOME and END to move one word at a time. You can delete single characters with DEL or BACKSPACE, you can delete an entire word with CTRL-T, and you can delete all characters to the right of the cursor with CTRL-Y.

Just as in the other full-screen editing modes, dBASE III PLUS defines a "word" as all the characters between the cursor and the next space. If you separate the field names in a list by placing spaces after the commas, you will find it easier to navigate through a list of fields one at a time or delete a single field (a word) from the list.

If you change your mind in the middle of editing a command and decide to type a new command at the dot prompt, you can position the cursor at the beginning of the command line with CTRL-LEFT ARROW and then press CTRL-Y to erase the entire command line and start fresh.

Every command executed from the dot prompt is added to the HISTORY list, regardless of whether you typed the command from scratch or retrieved and reentered a previous command. Thus, if you type LIST, press UP ARROW to retrieve this command, and press ENTER to repeat it unchanged, a LIST HISTORY command will show you that the HISTORY list contains two copies of the LIST command.

RESPONDING TO ERRORS AND REQUESTING HELP

When you type commands at the dot prompt, dBASE III PLUS responds to erroneous commands by displaying a more or less descriptive error message and offering additional help. If the first word in a command is not recognizable as a valid command verb, the error message will be "*** Unrecognized command verb".

If you make a typographical error or forget how to spell one of your field names, the error message is usually "Variable not found". This means that dBASE III PLUS looked for a variable—a field—with the specified name but failed to find one in the data base that is currently open.

In either case, dBASE III PLUS will also display the following offer of help on the Navigation Line below the Status Bar: "Do you want some help? (Y/N)". If you press N (for "No"), dBASE III PLUS will return to the dot prompt, where you can try your command again. If you press Y (for "Yes"), dBASE III PLUS will display a help screen summarizing the syntax and usage of the verb in your command. These help screens are similar but are not identical to the help screens accessed through the ASSIST menus by pressing F1. The help screen for the LIST command is illustrated in Figure 5-4.

Although a message on the Navigation Line invites you to "enter a command," you cannot execute a dBASE III PLUS command from within the help system. This prompt means that you can type another dBASE III PLUS command verb for which you would like help. You can exit from the help system by pressing ESC. When you do so, the help display is cleared from the screen, so you should first use SHIFT-PRTSC to print the screen if you think you may need to refer to it again as you reconstruct your command.

```
                                                              LIST

                              LIST
                              ====

Syntax      :  LIST [<scope>] [<expression list>] [FOR <condition>]
                    [WHILE <condition>] [OFF] [TO PRINT]

Description :  Displays the contents of a database file.
               Used alone, it displays all records.  Use the scope and
               FOR/WHILE clauses to list selectively.  The expression
               list can be included to select fields or a combination
               of fields, such as Cost * Rate.  OFF suppresses the record
               numbers.
```

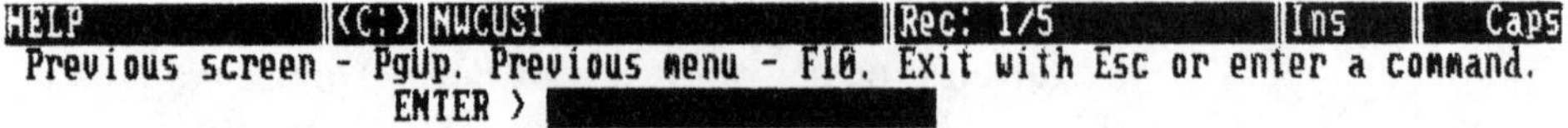

```
HELP            ||<C:>||NWCUST                 ||Rec: 1/5          ||Ins  ||   Caps
 Previous screen - PgUp. Previous menu - F10. Exit with Esc or enter a command.
                      ENTER >
```

Figure 5-4 *The help screen for the LIST command*

The summary screens that describe each command verb form part of a larger menu-driven help system. If the command verb itself is incorrect, dBASE III PLUS cannot determine which specific help screen you need to see, so it displays the initial menu of the help system, shown in Figure 5-5. You can navigate through the help system by making selections from this menu to try to find the information you need.

You will probably find that many of the error messages you receive result not from any true misunderstanding, but from simple typographical errors or because you have forgotten or misspelled field names. Regardless of the cause, you can use the HISTORY feature to avoid having to retype an entire command to correct a minor error. This facility will become increasingly useful as your commands increase in

```
                                                        MAIN MENU

                    Help Main Menu

                    1 - Getting Started
                    2 - What Is a ...
                    3 - How Do I ...
                    4 - Creating a Database File
                    5 - Using an Existing Database File
                    6 - Commands and Functions
```

```
          ENTER >
```

Figure 5-5 *The initial menu in the help system*

both length and complexity.

You can also access the menu-driven help system at any time from the dot prompt. To display the first screen of the help system, you can either press F1 or type

```
HELP
```

In addition to the screens describing each of the command verbs, the help system contains definitions of terms used in dBASE III PLUS, explanations of basic data base concepts, and information about carrying out certain common operations. These screens can be useful when you have no idea why a command failed to produce the intended results or when you cannot remember which command to use for a particular purpose.

If you know the command you need but you cannot recall the exact syntax or all the options, you can request the specific help screen that describes this command by including the verb in the HELP command:

HELP *command verb*

Typing the verb incorrectly calls up the initial menu of the help system, just as if you had asked for help in response to the "Unrecognized command verb" error message.

The help screens may appear to be a bit cryptic at first, but the more you understand the grammar and syntax of the dBASE III PLUS command language, the more useful they will become. You may not be able to learn a new command by reading the help screen, but if you have used a command before and understand the principles behind its operation, you can use the help screens to look up the exact syntax and review the options whose purpose you have forgotten.

HANDS-ON PRACTICE—USING HISTORY AND CORRECTING ERRORS

Make sure that you have loaded dBASE III PLUS and have opened the National Widgets Customer File, if it is not already open, with a USE command as follows:

```
USE NWCUST
```

You can display all the data in the file by typing

```
LIST
```

Try pausing and restarting the display periodically with CTRL-S so you can read the screen. Retrieve the LIST command from HISTORY by pressing UP ARROW, and repeat the command by pressing ENTER. This time interrupt the display by pressing ESC before all the records have scrolled by. Note the record number displayed in the Status Bar, and display just that record by typing

```
DISPLAY
```

If you have turned off the display of field name headings with SET HEADING OFF, turn this display back on with

```
SET HEADING ON
```

If you wish, continue to practice using the UP ARROW and DOWN ARROW keys to page through the list of commands. With any command displayed next to the dot prompt, press CTRL-Y to clear the command line and display the entire command history by typing

```
LIST HISTORY
```

Display the company name, contact person, and telephone number for all National Widgets' customers by typing

```
LIST COMPANY, CONTACT, TELEPHONE
```

Press UP ARROW to retrieve this command from HISTORY, and add the MAIL field between CONTACT and TELEPHONE and the YTDORDERS field after TELEPHONE. To do this, use the RIGHT ARROW or END key to move the cursor to the *T* in TELEPHONE, make sure that you are in Insert mode, and type in the new field name, MAIL, followed by a comma. Then position the cursor after the *E* in TELEPHONE and add a comma and the YTDORDERS field name. The command should now read

```
LIST COMPANY, CONTACT, MAIL, TELEPHONE, YTDORDERS
```

Press ENTER to execute this command, and note that with the two additional fields, the data from each record wraps around onto two screen lines. Retrieve the command again, and add OFF to suppress the record number display in order to fit all the data on one line on the screen as follows:

```
LIST COMPANY, CONTACT, MAIL, TELEPHONE, YTDORDERS OFF
```

Finally, turn on your printer, retrieve the command again, and add TO PRINT to produce a simple report that lists the same data.

```
LIST COMPANY, CONTACT, MAIL, TELEPHONE,
  YTDORDERS OFF TO PRINT
```

Because you can retrieve not only your last command but the most recent 20, you can type any commands you need to determine the cause of an error, and still retrieve the erroneous command to correct and resubmit it. To make a deliberate error, type the following command:

```
LIST ACCOUNT, COMPANY, PHONE
```

This command should result in a "Variable not found" error message. If you want to see the help screen for the LIST command, press Y in response to the offer of help; otherwise, press N to return to the dot prompt. Examining the help screen will enable you to confirm that your command is syntactically correct. The error message should lead you to suspect incorrect spellings of some of your field names, so display the structure by typing

```
LIST STRUCTURE
```

From the resulting display, you can see that the third field in the LIST command should have been TELEPHONE, not PHONE. Press UP ARROW twice to bypass the LIST STRUCTURE command, display the incorrect LIST command on the command line, and change PHONE to TELEPHONE. Press ENTER to execute the corrected command.

USING GOTO TO POSITION THE RECORD POINTER

In the full-screen editing modes, you can move the record pointer forward or backward using command keys such as PGUP and PGDN in EDIT and CHANGE, or UP ARROW and DOWN ARROW in BROWSE. You can also jump to a particular record by using the **Top**, **Bottom**, or **Record No.** options in the BROWSE options menu. At the dot prompt, you can accomplish the same thing with the GOTO command, or GO. To position the record pointer at the top of the file, you would use

```
GOTO TOP
```

or

```
GO TOP
```

You can move to the bottom of the file with

```
GOTO BOTTOM
```

or

```
GO BOTTOM
```

You can also GOTO any record, specified by number, with

GOTO *record number*

or

GO *record number*

Since no dBASE III PLUS command verbs begin with a number, you can even omit the verb entirely, and simply type a number at the dot prompt to move the record pointer to the corresponding record. For example, to move to Record 4, you could type

```
4
```

Unlike the full-screen commands that also position the record pointer, GOTO does nothing else—it does not even display the record, much less present it on the screen in a format suitable for editing. When you first begin to work with dBASE III PLUS, this behavior can be a bit disconcerting, but ultimately, the separation of the positioning and display commands adds flexibility to the dBASE III PLUS command language.

When you use GOTO to position the record pointer to a particular record, dBASE III PLUS makes no assumptions about what you want to do with that record. You might want to edit the data, display it without editing, mark it for deletion, remove a previously entered deletion marker, carry out a computation on the data in the fields, or print it on paper—to name just a few possibilities. The program therefore moves the record pointer and then waits for further instructions.

There are several ways to confirm that a GOTO command has in fact produced the desired result. If the status display is on, you can look at the "Rec" indicator at the right side of the Status Bar to see where the record pointer is positioned. You can also use DISPLAY to view the data on the screen, but it operates on the current record only. Recall that when you invoke the full-screen EDIT and CHANGE commands, the first record displayed is the one at the current position of the record pointer, described in Chapter 4 as "the most recently accessed record." Although you can use PGUP and PGDN to move the record pointer, it is often faster and more efficient to use full-screen commands and GOTO commands typed at the dot prompt.

For example, if you needed to EDIT widely separated records in a large file, you would not want to have to travel from, say, Record 10 to Record 1000, or even Record 100, by pressing PGDN repeatedly! Instead, you could exit the EDIT screen, use GOTO to position the record pointer directly at the next record you need to edit, or, if you do not remember the exact number, to somewhere in the vicinity of the desired record, and then return to the full-screen EDIT mode. Within EDIT, you could still use PGUP and PGDN to move shorter distances.

USING SKIP TO POSITION THE RECORD POINTER

From the dot prompt, you can also move the record pointer forward or backward a specified number of records by using the SKIP command as follows:

SKIP *number of records*

To advance the pointer to the next record, you would type

```
SKIP 1
```

By default, the SKIP command moves forward one record, so you can omit the 1:

```
SKIP
```

You can also move backward by specifying a negative number in the SKIP command. To back up to the previous record, you would type

```
SKIP -1
```

After a SKIP command, dBASE III PLUS displays the new position of the record pointer. For example, if you began with the record pointer positioned at Record 2 and typed SKIP 4, dBASE III PLUS would advance the pointer four records and display the following message:

```
Record No.       6
```

This record number display and the other messages that dBASE III PLUS uses to respond to your commands and confirm the actions taken are called "TALK". This ongoing "conversation" between you and the program is one reason that working at the dot prompt is also referred to as "typing interactively" or working in "interactive mode."

Just like GOTO, the SKIP command does nothing except reposition the dBASE III PLUS record pointer; it does not display or otherwise operate on the record. If you want to see the record to confirm that it really is the one you want, the easiest way to do this is to type

```
DISPLAY
```

USING DELETE AND RECALL TO DELETE AND UNDELETE RECORDS

From any of the full-screen editing modes, you can delete records and recall records previously marked for deletion by pressing CTRL-U. At the dot prompt, you can do the same thing with the DELETE and RECALL commands. By default, both of these commands operate on one record—the one at the current position of the record pointer.

To mark a record for deletion, you can use any command you know (for example, GOTO or SKIP) to move the pointer to the correct record and type

```
DELETE
```

dBASE III PLUS confirms that it has deleted a record with the message "1 record deleted".

You can recover a record that was previously marked for deletion by positioning the record pointer on the correct record and typing

```
RECALL
```

In response, dBASE III PLUS displays the message "1 record recalled".

Normally, deleted records are processed the same way as any other records in a data base. They appear in the output of LIST and DISPLAY commands, they may be edited using any full-screen commands, and, as you will see in later chapters, they are printed on reports and are included in calculations. You can always determine whether a record has been marked for deletion by watching for the "Del" indicator in the Status Bar (or on the top line of the screen if you have turned off the status display) if you are working in one of the full-screen editing modes, or by noting the * displayed next to the record number in a LIST or DISPLAY.

This is acceptable, and even desirable, when you are working with your own data bases. However, you might not want deleted records to be printed on reports intended for use by other people who are less familiar with dBASE III PLUS than you are, and you would almost certainly want to exclude them from calculations and statistics. To cause dBASE III PLUS to ignore deleted records in carrying out all commands that operate on an entire data base, you can type

```
SET DELETED ON
```

To return to displaying deleted records, you would type

```
SET DELETED OFF
```

When DELETED is ON, deleted records are ignored by most dBASE III PLUS commands—they do not appear in the output of LIST and DISPLAY commands, they are not printed on reports or included in calculations, and when you page forward or backward in full-screen editing modes, they are passed over. If, at any time, you want to see deleted records, you can SET DELETED OFF.

To understand this seemingly contradictory terminology, it is helpful to think of DELETED as a kind of *filter*. This term is used by dBASE III PLUS to describe a set of selection criteria applied to a data base, not just for a single command, but for an indefinite period of time. Only records that satisfy the criteria are included in subsequent processing, just as if you had passed the file through a specially designed sieve, which would permit only the correct records to go through. When you SET DELETED ON, you are turning ON this filtering process, which excludes deleted records, or rather, selects records that have not been marked for deletion. SET DELETED OFF turns off the filter and thereby reveals all the records.

By using the DELETED option to selectively ignore deleted records, you can enjoy instantaneous deletion—the "deleted" records seem to disappear from the data base immediately—and the advantage of not having to actually carry out the slower process of physically removing them from the disk.

When DELETED is ON, you can still position the record pointer at a deleted record, but only by using a command that explicitly includes the record number. For example, if Record 3 is deleted, you can access it with

```
GOTO 3
```

You can then DISPLAY, EDIT, or RECALL the record. However, if you execute a SKIP command with the record pointer positioned on Record 2, you will jump directly to Record 4, just as pressing PGDN with Record 2 displayed on the EDIT screen will also pass over the deleted Record 3.

USING PACK TO PERMANENTLY REMOVE DELETED RECORDS

You can permanently remove all deleted records from a data base with the PACK command. To do this, you open the data base and type

```
PACK
```

The PACK command performs the process, described in Chapter 4, of recopying a file in place, minus the deletions. Records are "moved up" in the file into the places formerly occupied by records marked for deletion, and all the records after the first deletion are renumbered. Since it can take some time to PACK a large file, dBASE III PLUS displays a running indicator of its progress, with messages like "6 records copied".

There are no hard and fast rules governing how often to PACK a file. There are two important factors to consider, however. The first is whether you might change your mind and want to RECALL any deleted records. Remember that there is no way to recover deleted records after issuing a PACK command, because the data has been physically over-written on the disk. You might never need to recover certain types of deleted records, such as those deleted because they were entered in error. However, in the course of your normal processing cycle, you may delete records, either one at a time or in groups, based on their contents, such as customers who have not placed an order in over a year. Occasionally, you might want to recover a few such deleted records, although you might work with DELETED ON so as to exclude them from most of your daily processing activities.

The second consideration for deciding when to PACK depends on how many records are marked for deletion, and therefore, how much space they take up. If you have a file of several hundred records and every month you delete two or three, you might PACK only once a year, since the deletions are not occupying much space in your file. When the number of deleted records begins to approach 10 to 25 percent of the total, however, you might want to PACK to reduce the size of the file and thereby recover disk space and speed up the execution of commands that operate on the entire data base.

To understand the effect of deleted records on execution speed, think about how the SET DELETED ON filter works. The status of the DELETED option affects only which records are displayed or processed. To ignore deleted records, dBASE III PLUS must read each record in the file to determine whether it is deleted. If a file contains an unusually large number of deleted records, you may be wasting a great deal of time by reading far more records than you are displaying, and this problem will be more severe on floppy disks than it is on a hard disk. Disk space may also be a factor, especially on a disk that is almost filled to capacity.

Before you PACK, you might want to make sure that you have at least one printed report that includes the deleted records (a technique for selecting only deleted records is introduced in Chapter 8). It is also a good idea to make a backup copy of a data base before you PACK. You can use this backup to recover the deleted records if necessary, but even more importantly, it can help you recover easily from the damage that may occur if a power failure or a hardware crash prevents the PACK command from completing normally. If a PACK command is interrupted, dBASE III PLUS may be unable to determine how many records are in the file, or in extreme cases, to read the data base at all. Your best guarantee of safety is to have a backup copy of the file.

HANDS-ON PRACTICE—PACK

Make sure that the National Widgets Customer File is open, and that DELETED is OFF so you can view deleted records. Position the record pointer at Record 4 by typing

```
GOTO 4
```

Display the record by typing

```
DISPLAY
```

Move the record pointer two records forward in the file by typing

```
SKIP 2
```

dBASE III PLUS should confirm that the record pointer is now positioned at Record 6. If you wish, you can look at this record with a DISPLAY command. Whether or not you do this, mark Record 6 for deletion by typing

```
DELETE
```

Display the account codes and company names with the following LIST command:

```
LIST ACCOUNT, COMPANY
```

You should see that two records are marked for deletion: Record 3, which was deleted from the full-screening EDIT command in Chapter 4, and Record 6, which was just deleted from the dot prompt. Instruct dBASE III PLUS to ignore deleted records by typing

```
SET DELETED ON
```

Retrieve your previous LIST command from HISTORY and repeat it. You should see from the gaps in the record numbers that Records 3 and 6 were not included in the output of the LIST command. However, the Status Bar indicates that 21 records are physically present in the file. (You may see a smaller number if you did not enter all the sample records at the end of Chapter 4.) In fact, you now realize that Record 6 should not have been deleted after all, and the next step will be to RECALL it. Notice, however, from the Status Bar display that the previous LIST command has positioned the record pointer at the end-of-file, so you must first move to Record 6, as follows:

```
GOTO 6
```

DISPLAY the record to confirm that you can in fact view a deleted record, even if you have SET DELETED ON. Then undelete this record by typing

```
RECALL
```

SET DELETED OFF so that you can more easily spot deleted records by the asterisk in a LIST command, and repeat the previous LIST one more time to make sure that only Record 3 is marked for deletion. Finally, remove the deleted records (in this case, it is one record) from the file by typing

```
PACK
```

You can see from the final message displayed that dBASE III PLUS has copied 20 records, or, if your file was smaller, one fewer than the number you started with. The Status Bar also indicates that the record pointer has been repositioned at the top of the file.

This chapter explained the commands that enable you to perform many of the same operations from the dot prompt that you learned to carry out in Chapter 4 in the full-screen editing modes. Sometimes, one approach has a clear advantage over the other. The full-screen commands are better suited for adding and editing data, for example, while the dot prompt commands are more effective for operating on records without looking at all the fields. In other cases, choices may be based on personal preference. For example, if you GOTO a record with the intention of looking at the data and not making any changes, you could use either DISPLAY or EDIT, depending on which display format you prefer.

Some of the command examples in this chapter are already much longer than the simple verbs introduced in Chapter 4. As you learn more options, your commands will soon get even longer. Make sure before you go on that you understand how to use the HISTORY feature to retrieve and edit commands, and that you know how to respond to syntax errors. Keep in mind that you will make many mistakes in your work with dBASE III PLUS, especially if you are not an expert typist. The most important asset you can bring to your work with dBASE III PLUS—far more important than prior computer experience—is an assertive, experimental attitude. A little practice with typing commands, making mistakes, and correcting them will serve you well later on as you construct progressively more complicated commands.

Chapter 6

Working at the Dot Prompt: Stating Simple Selection Criteria

Chapter 5 described how to use the LIST and DISPLAY commands from the dot prompt to display data on the screen and produce simple printed listings. It also introduced several techniques for making these displays more selective—and therefore, more readable and useful. Some of these methods limit the data that appears on each line of the listing; for example, you may include a field list in a LIST or DISPLAY command to cause dBASE III PLUS to display only certain fields or add the OFF keyword to suppress record numbers.

Another aspect of looking at data more selectively is to limit the range of records included in the display. Once a data base grows beyond a few dozen records, you will rarely want to see all of them at once, but picking the ones you need out of a lengthy listing can be difficult and tedious. Chapter 5 presented one of many techniques that you can use to specify which records you want to see. The SET DELETED ON command causes dBASE III PLUS to ignore deleted records or, viewed another way, to select only nondeleted records.

SET DELETED is one method for selecting records based on their contents, since the deletion marker may be considered part of the data in the record. In this chapter, other ways are described for establishing selection criteria based on the contents of a data base, in this case, on the data in one or more fields. You will also learn how to select records based on their position in the file.

By combining these commands and command options in different ways, you can display or print only the fields you need to see from a selected group of records in a data base. With just a few commands in your vocabulary, you can perform sophisticated inquiries and extract meaningful information from the mass of data stored in a dBASE III PLUS file. As you read this chapter, keep in mind that many of the options described in the context of the LIST command are also applicable to most of the commands discussed in later chapters.

THE CONCEPT OF SCOPE

You can limit the range of records acted on by a dBASE III PLUS command based on their position in the file by including a *scope* clause in the command. Every dBASE III PLUS command has a default scope, which determines how many records are processed unless you override it by explicitly typing a different scope. This default is usually either all the records in the file or a single record, the one at the current position of the record pointer. It is always safe to reiterate a default value, so if you forget the default, you can simply type the scope explicitly. The permissible scopes are as follows:

- *ALL:* All the records in the current data base
- *RECORD n:* A single record, specified by number
- *The current record:* A single record, the one at the position of the record pointer (this is available only as a default value)

- *NEXT n:* The group of *n* consecutive records, beginning with and including the current record
- *REST:* All the remaining records in the file, beginning with and including the current record

You have already seen one example of the effects of different default scopes. By default, LIST acts on all the records in a data base, whereas DISPLAY affects only the current record. You can override these standard values by including an explicit scope clause in a LIST or DISPLAY command. Thus, to display all the records in a file, you could use either

```
LIST
```

or

```
DISPLAY ALL
```

To display a single record, the current one, you can use either

```
DISPLAY
```

or

```
LIST NEXT 1
```

When used with any other scope, such as REST or NEXT 10, LIST and DISPLAY display the same records.

There is another, more important difference between these two commands than the default scope. LIST scrolls data continuously, whereas DISPLAY ALL causes dBASE III PLUS to pause the listing when the screen is full and display the message "Press any key to continue . . . " to give you as much time as you need to read the screen. You can then press ESC to abort the listing and return to the dot prompt, or press any other key to display the next screenful of records. Knowing that you can override the default scopes, you can use LIST and DISPLAY interchangeably based on whether or not you prefer the pause.

The selection of the default scope is generally governed by the destructive potential of a command. For most commands that only display or print data, or calculate statistics such as the sum or average of numeric fields, the default scope is ALL (DISPLAY is an exception to this rule), since these commands do not alter or delete data. Commands that do have the potential to change data or delete records have a default scope of one record. For example, the DELETE command acts on the current record only, unless you override this default. Thus, an inadvertent DELETE command that goes unnoticed can remove a maximum of one record from the file.

As you begin to build more complex commands, it will become increasingly important to keep track of the position of the record pointer before and after a command is executed, and this depends on the scope:

- *ALL:* The record pointer is first positioned at the top of the file, the command is executed, and when it completes, the pointer is left at the end-of-file rather than at any valid record.

- *RECORD n:* The record pointer is positioned at the specified record, and it remains there after the command is executed.

- *The current record:* The record pointer remains positioned at the same record after the command is executed.

- *NEXT n:* The record pointer is not moved prior to executing the command, which acts on the current record and enough subsequent records to amount to a total of *n*. After the command completes, the record pointer is positioned at the last record in the group or at the end-of-file if *n* is larger than the number of records remaining.

- *REST:* The record pointer is not moved prior to executing the command, which acts on the current record and all the remaining records in the file. After the command completes, the record pointer is positioned at the end-of-file.

If you visualize the location of the record pointer as the top, or beginning, of the current record, the inclusion of the current record in a NEXT *n* or REST scope will make more sense. The relationship between the scope clause and the record pointer is especially important when you type several commands in a row, some of which depend for proper functioning on the position of the pointer. For example, immediately after executing a LIST command, which leaves the record pointer at the end-of-file, any command with a scope of REST, NEXT *n*, or a single record will have no effect. In this situation, no explicit error or warning message is displayed, although you can often determine from the TALK message or the data (or lack of it) displayed on the screen that no records were processed.

HANDS-ON PRACTICE—USING SCOPE CLAUSES

Make sure that the National Widgets Customer File is open and that the Status Bar is displayed so that you have an easy way to monitor the position of the record pointer. Display all the records in the file in two different ways, using

```
LIST
```

and

```
DISPLAY ALL
```

If your sample file contains more than five records, note that the DISPLAY command pauses after every five records because the screen is full. You can press ESC at any time to interrupt the listing if you do not want to see all the data.

Display the ACCOUNT, COMPANY, and TELEPHONE fields from a single record, Record 4, by typing

```
LIST RECORD 4 ACCOUNT, COMPANY, TELEPHONE
```

Note that since this command explicitly specifies the desired record by number, it displays the right record regardless of the prior position of the record pointer, and that after the command completes, the pointer is positioned at Record 4, as indicated on the Status Bar.

Next, display the same fields from the remaining records in the file by using

```
DISPLAY REST ACCOUNT, COMPANY, TELEPHONE
```

The actual number of records displayed will depend on how many sample records you have entered, but the display should begin with Record 4, and the record pointer should be at the end-of-file when the command completes.

Try to display the "current" record by typing

```
DISPLAY
```

Notice that because the record pointer was positioned at the end-of-file prior to this command, and because DISPLAY does not move the pointer before it is executed, no data is displayed.

STATING SIMPLE CONDITIONS WITH FOR TO VIEW SELECTED RECORDS

You can select which records are displayed or processed based on the data entered into one or more of the fields by including in the command a *condition* that expresses the selection criteria, introduced by the keyword FOR. A condition is any expression that can take on the logical values .T. (True) and .F. (False). In other words, a condition is either true or not for any particular record.

The simplest conditions compare a field to a *constant*. (A constant is an arbitrary value, such as 10 or "San Francisco," that cannot be changed by dBASE III PLUS.) The easiest comparison you can include in a condition tests for equality—it determines whether the data entered into the field is the same as the specified constant value. For example, you could list the ACCOUNT, COMPANY, and TELEPHONE fields from National Widgets' Berkeley customers with

```
LIST ACCOUNT, COMPANY, TELEPHONE FOR CITY = "Berkeley"
```

In the condition in this command, the spaces before and after the equal sign are optional. You can omit them to type the command faster, or include them to improve readability and make it easier to edit the command by moving through the line a word at a time with the HOME and END keys. The previous command could also have been typed this way:

```
LIST ACCOUNT, COMPANY, TELEPHONE FOR CITY="Berkeley"
```

It is not necessary to include the field or fields used as the basis for selecting records in the list of fields processed by the command. In the previous example, the FOR clause instructs dBASE III PLUS to determine which records to display by testing the value of the CITY field, but only the ACCOUNT, COMPANY, and TELEPHONE fields are displayed. When you first begin to experiment with FOR clauses, however, it is a good idea to display all the fields named in each condition to verify that the right records were selected, and thus confirm that you have stated the condition correctly.

When you compare a field to a value, both must be of the same data type—character fields must be compared to character string constants, numeric fields to numbers, and so on. The data type of a field was specified when you defined the data base structure, and the data type of a constant value is determined by the way the value is written. Character strings must be enclosed in double quotation marks ("), single quotation marks ('), or square brackets ([ ]). If a character string contains one of these punctuation marks, you must choose one of the others to surround the entire string. For example, although you may prefer to use double quotes, to compare the contents of the EQUIPMENT field to the text *IBM XT "clone" system,* you must use single quotes or brackets around the character string constant as follows:

```
LIST ACCOUNT, COMPANY, TELEPHONE FOR EQUIPMENT =
  [IBM XT "clone" system]
```

or

```
LIST ACCOUNT, COMPANY, TELEPHONE FOR EQUIPMENT =
  'IBM XT "clone" system'
```

The quotes enable dBASE III PLUS to distinguish a character string constant from an intended field name. In the previous example, if the condition were stated as CITY = Berkeley, dBASE III PLUS would interpret both CITY and Berkeley as field names and assume that you want to display records in which the contents of a field called CITY are the same as the contents of a field called Berkeley. It is perfectly legitimate to compare the contents of two fields, but if dBASE III PLUS fails to find a field named Berkeley in the Customer File, it will display the "Variable not found" error message.

Keep in mind that a constant is an arbitrary value that is taken literally by dBASE III PLUS with no further interpretation, and that every character must be typed exactly as it appears in the data base. Thus, uppercase and lowercase letters are not equivalent, the uppercase letter O is not the same as the digit 0, the lowercase letter l differs from the number 1, and spaces and punctuation marks are as significant as any other characters. Thus, "Berkeley" is not the same as "BERKELEY", "Berkley", or "berkeley".

When dBASE III PLUS compares two character strings, it begins with the first character in the field and examines only as many characters as are present in the string on the right side of the equal sign. You therefore need to type only as many characters as are necessary to precisely identify the group of records you want. For example, the following command would probably suffice to retrieve only customers in Berkeley:

```
LIST ACCOUNT, COMPANY, TELEPHONE, CITY FOR CITY = "Berk"
```

On the other hand, if you typed the following command, intending to view customers in San Francisco, you would also see customers in San Jose, San Rafael, San Leandro, Santa Clara, and any other city having a name that begins with the letters S, a, and n:

```
LIST ACCOUNT, COMPANY, TELEPHONE, CITY FOR CITY = "San"
```

Although this is an easy error to make, you may also want to take advantage of this behavior to retrieve all the records in which one field begins with a specified character string. For example, you could list all people whose account codes begin with the letter B, with the following condition:

```
LIST ACCOUNT, COMPANY, TELEPHONE FOR ACCOUNT = "B"
```

When you compare a numeric field to a constant value, you do not have to surround the numeric constant with any special delimiters. Since dBASE III PLUS field and file names cannot begin with a numeric digit, and there are no commands or keywords that begin with numbers, a constant consisting of digits (and optionally, a decimal point or a minus sign) unambiguously refers to a numeric value. For example, you could list all the customers who did not place any orders during the current year with the following command:

```
LIST ACCOUNT, COMPANY, TELEPHONE, YTDORDERS FOR YTDORDERS = 0
```

Logical constant values are identified by enclosing them between two periods (.). You can regard the period as a special kind of quotation mark that distinguishes the logical values from the single-character constants that they resemble, such as T, N, y, and so on. There is one other fine point to keep in mind when you type conditions involving logical fields. Remember that a condition is defined as any expression that has the value .T. (True) or .F. (False). A logical field by itself fits this definition and therefore constitutes a valid condition, so there is no need to use an equal sign in a logical comparison—in fact, it is wrong to do so.

You can read a LIST command containing a FOR clause something like this: "List these fields for every record in which the following is true . . . ". For example, to display all the records with .T. in the MAIL field, you could use this command:

```
LIST ACCOUNT, COMPANY, TELEPHONE, MAIL FOR MAIL
```

This may be translated as "List the ACCOUNT, COMPANY, TELEPHONE, and MAIL fields for all records in which MAIL is true."

Thus far, all the examples have tested a field and a constant for equality. You can also test a field to see if it is greater than or less than a specified value or not equal to a value. The symbols used to express these relationships are referred to as *comparison operators,* or *relational operators*—they enable you to make comparisons or express relationships between two values. All the comparison operators, the data types they apply to, and their meanings are listed in Table 6-1.

As you can see, most of these comparisons can be carried out on

Table 6-1 *dBASE III PLUS Comparison Operators*

Operator	Data Types	Meaning
=	C, N, D	Equal to
<> or #	C, N, D	Not equal to
>	C, N, D	Greater than
>=	C, N, D	Greater than or equal to
<	C, N, D	Less than
<=	C, N, D	Less than or equal to
$	C	Contained within

character, numeric, or date fields. When applied to character fields, the "greater than" or "less than" comparisons refer to alphabetical order. Thus, the condition CITY >= "S" selects all cities that begin with S or any letter that occurs after S in the alphabet. When applied to date fields, > and < mean later or earlier in chronological order. Comparisons involving constant dates cannot be written as simply as those referring to character, numeric, and logical fields. (See Chapter 8 for a detailed discussion of date comparisons.) Note also that none of the comparison operators may be used to test the contents of a memo field.

One operator reserved for character strings deserves special mention. The *substring operator,* symbolized by a dollar sign ($), tests whether one character string appears anywhere within another. When you read a condition aloud, this operator may be read as "is a substring of" or "is contained in." The $ operator is particularly useful for finding records in which a given sequence of characters occurs at varying positions within a field, since you can test for equality (using the = operator) only if you know the beginning of the string. For example, you might want to list every customer with a contact person whose name is "Smith." Because the names were entered with the first name first, you must use a condition that is true when Smith occurs anywhere within the field:

```
LIST ACCOUNT, COMPANY, TELEPHONE, CONTACT FOR "Smith" $ CONTACT
```

You could read the condition in this command as "Smith is a substring of the CONTACT field" or "Smith is contained in the CONTACT field."

COMBINING A SCOPE AND A CONDITION

You can include both a scope and a condition in a dBASE III PLUS command. Both clauses are evaluated independently, and only records that satisfy both tests will be processed. For example, with the record pointer positioned at any arbitrary record in the Customer File, you could test the next five records and display those in which the CITY field contains the value "San Francisco" with the following command:

```
LIST REST ACCOUNT, COMPANY, TELEPHONE, CITY
  FOR CITY = "San Francisco"
```

The scope and FOR clauses may at first appear contradictory, but in reality they interact to form a combined condition that must be satisfied for a record to be displayed. The scope clause determines how many records should be examined, and of those records only those that pass the test in the condition will actually be processed. Thus, if you typed the previous command with the record pointer positioned at Record 13 out of a total of 20 records in the National Widgets Customer File, five records, Records 13 through 17, would be tested, and of those, only the two in which the CITY field contained "San Francisco", Records 13 and 17, would be LISTed.

COMBINING CONDITIONS

You can combine conditions to form more complex selection criteria by linking them with the *logical operators* .AND., .OR., and .NOT. Like the logical values .T. and .F., these operators must be surrounded by the period delimiters that are used by dBASE III PLUS to identify the logical data type. No spaces are required before or after these operators, and, like any other dBASE III PLUS command words, they may be written in any combination of uppercase and lowercase letters.

When two conditions are combined with .AND., only records that pass both tests are processed. For example, the following command selects customers in San Francisco who have not placed an order during the current year:

```
LIST ACCOUNT, COMPANY, TELEPHONE, CITY, YTDORDERS
  FOR CITY = "San Francisco" .AND. YTDORDERS = 0
```

When conditions are combined with .OR., a record will be processed if it passes either or both tests. Thus, the following command displays all customers in San Francisco (regardless of their year-to-date orders) plus those who have not placed an order during the current year (regardless of where they are located):

```
LIST ACCOUNT, COMPANY, TELEPHONE, CITY, EQUIPMENT
  FOR CITY = "San Francisco" .OR. YTDORDERS = 0
```

The logical operator .NOT. negates a condition; it enables you to select all the records that do not satisfy the specified condition. Thus, you could list all the records in which you have entered .F. or .N. into the MAIL field with

```
LIST ACCOUNT, COMPANY, TELEPHONE, MAIL FOR .NOT. MAIL
```

dBASE III PLUS does not limit you to two conditions; you can combine as many conditions as you need to express complicated selection criteria, as long as you do not exceed the maximum permissible length of a command line—254 characters.

When you translate selection criteria from colloquial English into dBASE III PLUS conditions, there are several common pitfalls. It is easy to choose the wrong logical operator. You might say, for example, "I want to see all the customers in San Francisco and Berkeley." Although you would use the word "and" in this sentence, the two dBASE III PLUS conditions must be linked with .OR. as in the following:

```
LIST FOR CITY = "San Francisco" .OR. CITY = "Berkeley"
```

This command displays all records in which either of the two conditions linked with .OR. is true: *either* the city is San Francisco *or* the city is Berkeley. If you asked for records in which CITY = "San Francisco" .AND. CITY = "Berkeley", no records would be displayed, since the CITY field cannot contain both San Francisco *and* Berkeley.

Also remember that each separate condition linked with .AND. or .OR. must be a complete dBASE III PLUS condition that could stand on its own. You cannot therefore write a condition like CITY = "San Francisco" .OR. "Berkeley" because "Berkeley" by itself is not a valid condition. Although it may seem that there is a closer relationship between conditions that test the value of the same field than between those that do not, dBASE III PLUS does not make this distinction.

Finally, when you combine conditions with .AND., .OR., and .NOT., you must also take into account the order in which the comparisons are evaluated. This subject is covered in greater detail in Chapter 8, but in the meantime, try to avoid mixing different logical operators in a single command.

If a command results in a "Syntax error," "Variable not found," or "Unrecognized phrase/keyword" error message, the most common causes include omitting a required space (say, following the command verb or the word FOR) or comma, misspelling a field name, forgetting to enclose a character field in quotes, omitting a required keyword such as FOR, and combining incomplete conditions with .AND. or .OR. You can either accept or refuse the help offered by dBASE III PLUS. Then you can retrieve the erroneous command from HISTORY and correct it, instead of having to retype it from scratch.

The fact that a command does not generate an error message is no guarantee that it has produced the correct results, however. When you begin to experiment with complex conditions, take the time to double-check your results to ensure that the right records were selected. If you always include in a LIST command the field(s) being tested, you can examine the output to confirm that only records that satisfy the condition in the FOR clause are selected. It is equally important to verify that no records were overlooked. You can do this by reading through a printout of all the relevant fields for the entire data base.

HANDS-ON PRACTICE—USING CONDITIONS

List all the records from the National Widgets Customer File for customers in San Francisco by typing

```
LIST ACCOUNT, COMPANY, TELEPHONE, CITY FOR CITY = "San Francisco"
```

If your data matches the sample file, you should see four records: customers with account codes ANDERSON, RAPIDTYPE, JOHNSON, and HRINSURANC. Retrieve this command from HISTORY and add a second condition so that only customers with more than $500 in total orders are selected. This is the complete command:

```
LIST ACCOUNT, COMPANY, CITY, TOTORDERS FOR CITY = "San Francisco"
  .AND. TOTORDERS > 500
```

Because this command is more than 80 characters long it does not fit on one line in this book or on the screen. When you type a command that is longer than the width of the screen, do not press ENTER in the middle of the command. As you approach the side edge of the screen, the display will scroll to allow you to continue typing on the same line. You can use all the standard full-screen editing commands to move within the line, and the display will pan left or right to allow you to view and edit any portion of the command. Try using HOME and END to move through this command a word at a time, and then press ENTER to execute it. At this point, dBASE III PLUS will wrap the command onto two screen lines so that the entire command is visible as it executes.

The resulting list should include the three Berkeley customers—ABCPLUMB, GREENTHUMB, and HOMEMOVIES—as well as the four customers in San Francisco. Verify by looking at the Status Bar that the record pointer is positioned at the end-of-file.

Try to list the customers in Los Angeles by retrieving your second-to-last command and substituting "Los Angeles" for "San Francisco". This command should produce no output. Try searching for the customers in Oakland who do not own IBM equipment with the command

```
LIST ACCOUNT, COMPANY, CITY, EQUIPMENT FOR CITY = "OAKLAND"
  .AND. .NOT. "IBM" $ EQUIPMENT
```

Again, no records will be listed. To find out why neither command selected any records, display the CITY field from every record in the data base with

```
DISPLAY ALL ACCOUNT, CITY, EQUIPMENT
```

DISPLAY ALL was chosen instead of LIST so that data would not scroll off the screen before you could read it. The listing should enable you to determine that the first LIST command produced no output because there are no Los Angeles customers. This is not an error—the command provided meaningful information about the contents of the file. The second command failed because the contents of the CITY field was typed in uppercase letters, whereas the data was entered using a mixture of uppercase and lowercase letters. You can rectify this by editing the command to read

```
LIST ACCOUNT, COMPANY, CITY, EQUIPMENT FOR CITY = "Oakland"
  .AND. .NOT. "IBM" $ EQUIPMENT
```

USING THE LOCATE COMMAND TO FIND INDIVIDUAL RECORDS

The LIST and DISPLAY commands are used to display or print as a group all the records that satisfy a given condition. These commands are valuable for querying the data base to uncover trends or patterns and for printing quick lists. Sometimes it is more appropriate to search for the matching records one at a time so you can DISPLAY, EDIT, or DELETE them individually. At times, you may also need to retrieve only one record based on some unusual set of criteria. For example, you may have forgotten a customer's account code and company name, but you recall the city and the name of the street.

You can use the LOCATE command to retrieve records one at a time based on the selection criteria applicable to LIST and DISPLAY. You may use any of the scope and FOR clauses described in the preceding sections to express simple or complicated search criteria. The default scope for the LOCATE command is ALL; if you do not override this default, dBASE III PLUS begins at the top of the file and searches for the first record that matches the specified criteria. For example, to find the first customer in San Francisco who has not placed an order this year, you could use

```
LOCATE FOR CITY = "San Francisco" .AND. YTDORDERS = 0
```

When a record is found, the record number is displayed:

```
Record =        3
```

dBASE III PLUS makes no assumptions about what you might want to do with the record; it does not display the data. This is consistent with the behavior of other commands, such as SKIP or GOTO, which position the record pointer and then leave it up to you to decide what to do next. If you do need to see the data, you can use DISPLAY or EDIT to view and change fields.

Having found one match, you can use the CONTINUE command to go on searching for additional records that satisfy the same criteria, starting from the current position of the record pointer (as if you had repeated the LOCATE command with a REST scope). You can type other commands between LOCATE and CONTINUE, but be careful if you use any commands that reposition the record pointer. CONTINUE always causes dBASE III PLUS to resume its search at the current position of the record pointer; it makes no difference how the pointer arrived at that record. You might want to note the record number displayed after each CONTINUE so that you can return to a given record if necessary (with GOTO) before you next issue a CONTINUE command.

When a LOCATE or CONTINUE command fails to find a record that matches your condition within the specified scope, dBASE III PLUS displays the message "End of LOCATE scope." This is not an error message—dBASE III PLUS is simply informing you that in attempting to search further for a record that satisfied your condition, it reached the last of the range of records to be included in the search before finding another match. If the scope encompassed all the remaining records in file, the record pointer will be positioned at the end-of-file; if not, it will point to the last record in the scope.

HANDS-ON PRACTICE—USING LOCATE

Suppose that after looking at the first few records in the Customer File you wanted to find each customer record in which the CONTACT field had been left blank so you could call the company and find out the name of the contact person. Since a blank character field consists entirely of "space" characters, you can carry out this test by comparing the CONTACT field to a single space. Begin by positioning the record pointer at Record 3 and searching forward for the first blank CONTACT field:

```
GOTO 3
LOCATE REST FOR CONTACT = " "
```

This is analogous to searching for the first record in which the CONTACT field begins with any other letter by comparing it to a character string constant consisting of the specified letter. dBASE III PLUS should report that Record 7 is now the current record. Display the record with DISPLAY or EDIT, and confirm that the CONTACT field is indeed blank. Search for the next record that satisfies the same condition by typing CONTINUE, and note that dBASE III PLUS displays the message "End of LOCATE scope" to inform you that there are no other matching records. Look at the Status Bar to verify that the record pointer is positioned at the end-of-file.

USING FILTERS TO VIEW SELECTED RECORDS

Typing LIST or DISPLAY commands individually at the dot prompt, with different scope and FOR clauses in each, is a fast and flexible way to carry out varying inquiries into a data base. At times, however, you will want to work with the same group of records for an extended period of time, perhaps for the duration of a work session. One way to avoid having to type the same FOR clause repeatedly is to retrieve previous commands from HISTORY and edit them to create new commands. If you plan to execute more than a few commands this way, you can use a more efficient method, establishing a FILTER.

A *FILTER* is a condition that, once placed in effect, remains in effect and governs which records are processed by all subsequent dBASE III PLUS commands, until you either exit the program or explicitly cancel the condition. You have already used one specialized type of FILTER, the SET DELETED option, which you can turn ON to limit processing to nondeleted records. You can establish a more generalized FILTER condition by using the SET FILTER command as follows:

SET FILTER TO *condition*

The *condition* can be any valid condition, such as the ones used in the LIST and LOCATE examples in this chapter. In the National Widgets Customer File, for example, you might want to view only San Francisco customers for the remainder of your work session. To do this, you could use the following sequence:

```
SET FILTER TO CITY = "San Francisco"
```

With this FILTER in effect, a LIST command that contains no other clauses will display only San Francisco customers. If you do include a FOR clause, it will be superimposed on the FILTER as if the two conditions had been stated explicitly and combined with .AND.—only records that satisfy both conditions are processed. Thus, you could display only San Francisco customers who had no orders this year with

```
LIST ACCOUNT, COMPANY, TELEPHONE, YTDORDERS FOR YTDORDERS = 0
```

If you include a scope clause as well, the scope is evaluated relative to the FILTER, according to the following rules:

- *ALL:* All the records in the current data base that satisfy the FILTER condition
- *RECORD n:* A single record, specified by number, regardless of whether it satisfies the FILTER condition
- *The current record:* A single record, the one at the current position of the record pointer, regardless of whether it satisfies the FILTER condition
- *NEXT n:* The group of *n* consecutive records, beginning with and including the current record, that satisfy the FILTER condition
- *REST:* All the records beginning with and including the current record, and continuing to the end of the file, that satisfy the FILTER condition

If you have also SET DELETED ON, all scope clauses take both FILTERs into account, so that only nondeleted records that satisfy the condition in the SET FILTER command are selected.

To use FILTERs effectively, keep one crucial fact in mind about the way they operate: dBASE III PLUS tests records against a FILTER condition only when the record pointer is repositioned. For example, GOTO TOP moves the record pointer to the first record that satisfies the FILTER condition, and SKIP positions the pointer at the next record that satisfies the condition.

The SET FILTER and SET DELETED commands do not reposition the record pointer and therefore do not cause dBASE III PLUS to evaluate the current record to determine whether it satisfies the specified condition. If your next command does not move the record pointer either, the current record will be acted on regardless of whether it passes the FILTER test. You can avoid this problem by always remembering to type a command that repositions the record pointer—such as GOTO TOP—immediately after a SET FILTER or SET DELETED command.

Using FILTERs saves you typing time, but it does not speed up processing—dBASE III PLUS must still read every record within the specified scope and test it against the FILTER condition to determine whether or not it should be acted on. Note also that regardless of the FILTERs currently in effect, you can always access any record by number, either with a GOTO command or by including the record number explicitly in a RECORD *n* scope clause.

You can switch to a different FILTER at any time by typing a new SET FILTER command. To cancel a FILTER and return to viewing all records in the data base, use

```
SET FILTER TO
```

This construction is common to many other commands that customize the working environment as well as commands that open and close files. The command that cancels a setting is the same as the one that invoked it, minus the setting itself (in this case, the file name or the condition). Leaving the command line blank beyond the words "SET FILTER TO" implies, "Use no filter" or "I don't want to use any FILTER," just as "USE" means, "I don't want to USE any data base." One exception to this syntax rule is the DELETED option, which in many ways is equivalent to a FILTER but must be canceled with SET DELETED OFF.

USING CREATE/MODIFY QUERY TO CREATE QUERY FILES

You can save a FILTER for later use in a *QUERY file* to avoid having to type the same SET FILTER command repeatedly. dBASE III PLUS provides a full-screen editor for building QUERY files, and it is invoked by typing

```
CREATE QUERY
```

or

```
MODIFY QUERY
```

Although the different command verbs imply that you should use CREATE QUERY to create new QUERY files and MODIFY QUERY to edit existing ones, in practice they can be used interchangeably. You can include the name of the QUERY file in the command:

CREATE QUERY *query file name*

If you do not enter a file name, you will be prompted to enter it with "Enter Query file name".

To define a QUERY file, a data base must be open, so that dBASE III PLUS can display a list of fields available for use in your FILTER condition. If no data base is open when you invoke the QUERY editor, you will be prompted to enter a file name with "No database is in USE. Enter file name:".

The initial screen presented by the QUERY editor is illustrated in Figure 6-1, and the structure of the menus is diagrammed in Figure 6-2. The editor displays a table on the lower half of the screen on which you may enter up to seven conditions, one on each line, by selecting commands from a system of pull-down menus similar to the ASSIST menus. Each condition compares a field to a constant value or expression using one of the comparison operators described earlier in this chapter. If you define more than one condition, you must specify a connector for linking each pair of conditions.

When you first enter the editor, the **Set Filter** option is highlighted, and you may begin filling in line 1 in the table by pressing ENTER. dBASE III PLUS steps you through the definition process by highlighting in sequence the **Field Name**, **Operator**, **Constant/Expression**, and **Connect** options.

Whenever possible, the QUERY editor simplifies the process of defining a complex condition by allowing you to select options from a list.

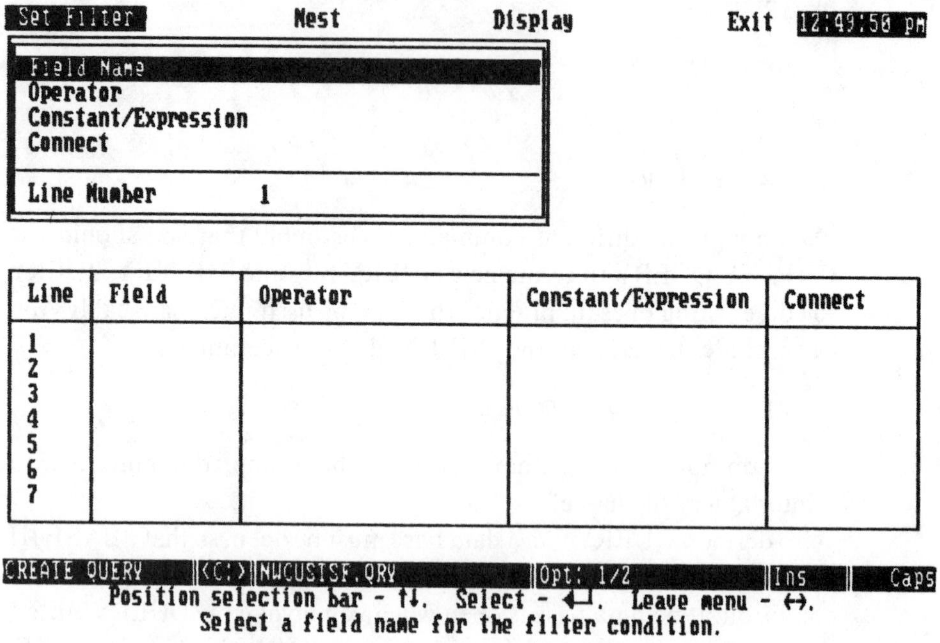

```
Set Filter          Nest          Display          Exit   12:49:50 pm

 Field Name
 Operator
 Constant/Expression
 Connect
 ----------------------
 Line Number        1

| Line | Field | Operator | Constant/Expression | Connect |
| 1    |       |          |                     |         |
| 2    |       |          |                     |         |
| 3    |       |          |                     |         |
| 4    |       |          |                     |         |
| 5    |       |          |                     |         |
| 6    |       |          |                     |         |
| 7    |       |          |                     |         |

CREATE QUERY  ||<C:>||NWCUSTSF.QRY  ||Opt: 1/2  ||Ins  ||  Caps
      Position selection bar - ↑↓.  Select - ↵.  Leave menu - ↔.
           Select a field name for the filter condition.
```

Figure 6-1 *The initial screen presented by the QUERY editor*

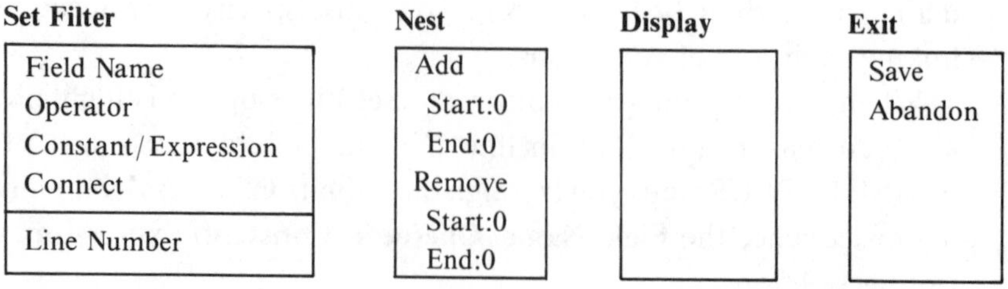

Set Filter	Nest	Display	Exit
Field Name Operator Constant/Expression Connect Line Number	Add Start:0 End:0 Remove Start:0 End:0		Save Abandon

Figure 6-2 *The structure of the QUERY editor menus*

When you choose the **Field Name** option, a box containing the list of fields in the current data base pops up on the screen. As you move through the list with the arrow keys, a second pop-up window displays the data type, field width, and number of decimal places in the highlighted field. Because there are no dBASE III PLUS operators for testing the contents of memo fields, the names of any memo fields in your data base are displayed in dim rather than bright text to indicate that you cannot select them.

Choosing the **Operator** option submenu pops up a box that displays a list of available operators. The choices for character string comparisons are illustrated in the screen shown in Figure 6-3. In addition to the

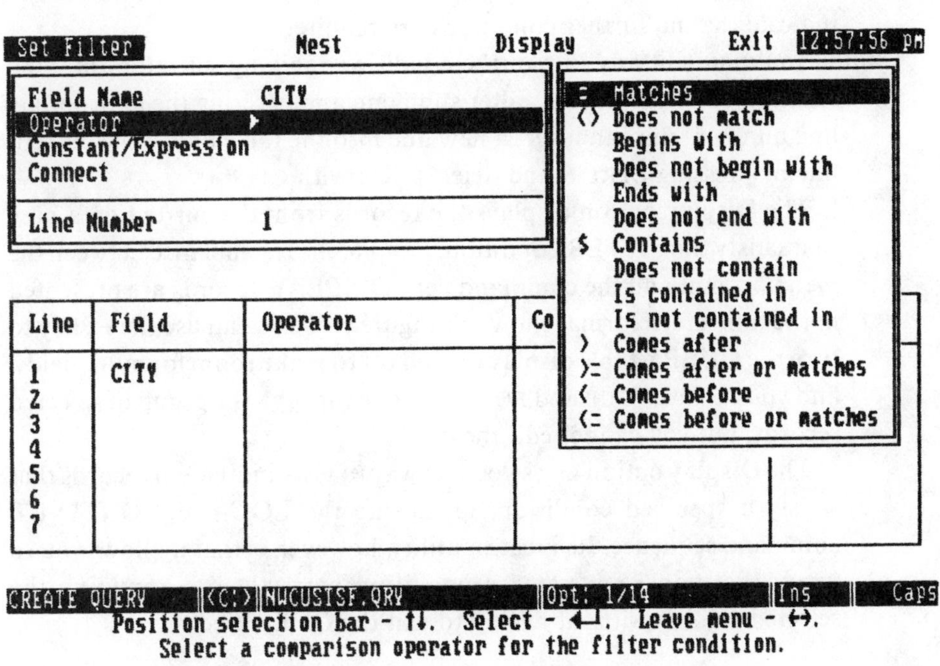

Figure 6-3 Selecting a character string operator in the QUERY editor

straightforward comparisons used in the previous examples in this chapter, you may specify more complex relationships, such as "Ends with" or "Does not contain". (These may also be stated in a SET FILTER command typed at the dot prompt, but doing so requires that you understand more about constructing complex expressions than you have learned so far.)

Next, you enter a constant value or an expression with which to compare the specified field using the specified operator. Just as when you type commands at the dot prompt, character strings must be enclosed in quotes, and logical fields must be surrounded by periods. In Chapter 8, you will learn how to express an arbitrary date and how to build complex expressions.

Finally, if you want to define another condition, you use the **Connect** option to select a logical connector—.AND., .OR., .AND..NOT., or .OR..NOT.—to link the current condition to the next one. You can repeat this procedure up to seven times. After you have entered your last condition, you select "No connector" from the **Connect** option list to indicate that no further conditions are required.

You may edit any line in the condition table by selecting the **Line Number** option in the **Set Filter** submenu and entering the appropriate line number. You can insert a new line into the table above the current line by pressing CTRL-N and delete a line with CTRL-U.

The **Display** option displays the records from the current data base that satisfy the FILTER condition. Despite the resemblance between the menu prompt and the command verb DISPLAY, records are presented in the full-screen format shown in Figure 6-4. You can use the F1 key to turn the QUERY table display on and off to make room for more fields, and you can use PGUP and PGDN to move through the group of selected records, but you cannot edit the data.

The **Display** option gives you one way to view individual records that satisfy a specified condition, much like the LOCATE/CONTINUE command sequence. Its greatest utility, however, is that it allows you to verify that you have stated a condition correctly by examining the selected records without having to exit the QUERY editor.

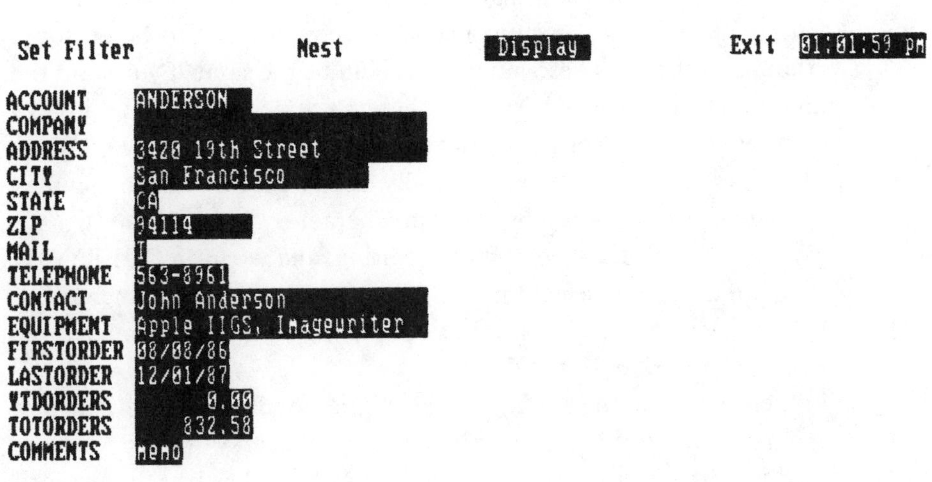

Figure 6-4 *Using the Display option in the QUERY editor*

If the condition is not satisfied by any records in the data base, selecting **Display** generates the message, "No records pass through filter." Obviously, this can occur because you have stated the FILTER condition incorrectly, but it may simply mean that the data base currently contains no matching records—a fact that may provide you with meaningful information.

When you begin to use complex conditions, you may need to group some of the component conditions with parentheses, a process known as *nesting*. You can specify the placement of parentheses in the QUERY table through the **Nest** sub-menu. You use the **Add** option to specify the starting and ending line numbers of the condition(s) to be enclosed within parentheses. These numbers should be the same if you want the parentheses to surround a single line in the table. You remove a set of parentheses by selecting the **Remove** option and specifying the numbers of the lines they currently enclose. The use of parentheses in complex expressions is discussed more fully in Chapter 8.

When you have finished defining, editing, and testing a QUERY, you can save it on disk by selecting the **Save** option in the **Exit** submenu. The QUERY is saved in a file with the name specified when you entered the editor plus the extension .QRY.

When you exit the QUERY editor, the condition just defined is automatically placed in effect. If you used the **Display** option to test the condition, the record pointer will be positioned at the last record displayed. If not, it may not be positioned at a record that satisfies the FILTER condition; just use GOTO TOP to move to the first matching record.

To reuse the same QUERY file in a later work session, you employ a variation of the SET FILTER command:

SET FILTER TO FILE *QUERY file name*

Once a FILTER has been established, it makes no difference whether the condition was read from a QUERY file or was typed directly at the dot prompt. A FILTER condition always controls the selection of records for display or other processing in exactly the same way, and it is always canceled by typing SET FILTER TO.

Using QUERY files enables you to avoid having to type the same FILTER conditions repeatedly. It also eliminates many possibilities for making careless errors that exist when you work at the dot prompt. You might want to use QUERY files to define complex FILTER conditions for other people who are less experienced with dBASE III PLUS. For selection criteria that are used occasionally, it is probably not worth spending the time to define a QUERY file.

HANDS-ON PRACTICE—USING FILTERS AND QUERY FILES

Use the QUERY editor to construct the FILTER condition that selects the customers in San Francisco who have not placed an order this year. Enter the QUERY editor and specify the name of the QUERY file at the same time by typing

```
CREATE QUERY NWCUSTSF
```

If you do not already have the National Widgets Customer File open, enter the file name, NWCUST, when you are prompted to do so.

Select the **Set Filter** option and fill out the screens for the two fields to be tested in the FILTER condition: CITY and YTDORDERS. If you have done everything right, your screen should look like the one shown in Figure 6-5.

The QUERY editor does not allow some of the syntax errors you might make in defining a complex condition at the dot prompt. Field names, operators, and connectors are all selected from lists, so they cannot be entered incorrectly. For errors that it cannot prevent, the QUERY editor issues a warning or error message, but it is not always the same one you would see if you made the same mistake from the dot prompt.

If you try to compare a field to a constant of a different data type, the error message would be more descriptive than the terse "Data type mismatch" displayed at the dot prompt; it informs you of the correct data type for the constant based on the data base field being tested. An example is "This field must contain a valid character expression. Press any key to continue." If dBASE III PLUS cannot precisely determine why an expression is invalid, the error message will be "This field must contain a valid dBASE expression. Press any key to continue."

If you fail to match left and right parentheses, dBASE III PLUS will refuse to display records or exit the editor and will instead display "Cannot display using an invalid filter. Leave Display option." or "Can-

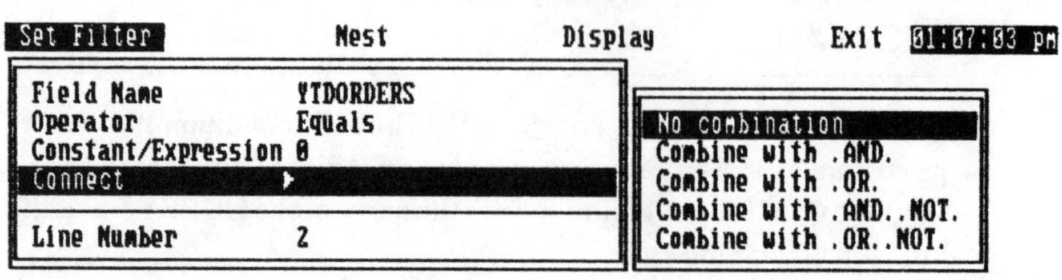

Line	Field	Operator	Constant/Expression	Connect
1	CITY	Matches	"San Francisco"	.AND.
2	YTDORDERS	Equals	0	
3				
4				
5				
6				
7				

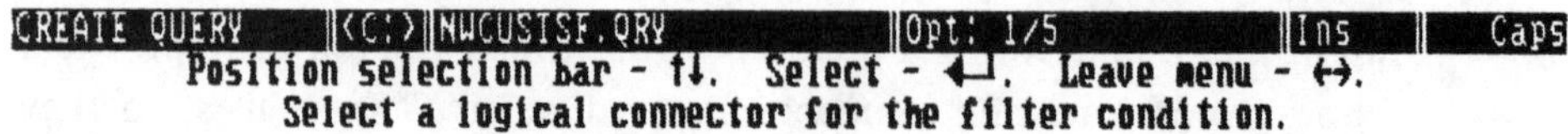

Figure 6-5 *Constructing a QUERY file that selects San Francisco customers with no orders in the current year*

not save an invalid filter. Press any key to continue." In this case, you would get a more explicit error message at the dot prompt: "Unbalanced parenthesis".

Use the **Display** option to page through the selected records, and then exit the QUERY editor by choosing the **Save** option from the **Exit** submenu. From the dot prompt, type a LIST command to verify that the FILTER you just defined is still in effect and that the correct records are selected:

```
LIST ACCOUNT, COMPANY, CITY, YTDORDERS
```

Verify that you can access a record that does not satisfy the FILTER condition by specifying the record by number explicitly in a scope clause:

```
EDIT RECORD 1
```

Note that this customer, LEWIS, is located in Oakland, not San Francisco, and that the YTDORDERS field contains 366.81, not 0. Exit the full-screen editing mode by pressing ESC (since you have not changed any data).

Establish a new FILTER that displays only customers who own IBM equipment by typing a SET FILTER command at the dot prompt:

```
SET FILTER TO "IBM" $ EQUIPMENT
```

Type a DISPLAY command to view the record at the current position of the record pointer. This should still be Record 1, which does not satisfy the FILTER condition. Move the record pointer to the first record in the file that does satisfy the condition by typing

```
GOTO TOP
```

Another DISPLAY or EDIT command will show you that the record pointer is now positioned at Record 4, the record for KLEIN, who owns an IBM AT. Note that you could also have arrived at this record by typing SKIP or pressing PGDN in the full-screen EDIT mode.

Finally, cancel the FILTER by typing SET FILTER TO, and use a LIST command to confirm the fact that no selection criteria are currently in effect.

The new commands in this chapter, although relatively few in number, should substantially increase your ability to extract the information you want from your data base files. Carrying out inquiries based on constantly varying selection criteria by typing commands at the dot prompt is one of the strong points of dBASE III PLUS, since the commands offer a great deal of power, sophistication, flexibility, and convenience. If you have not already done so, this is a good time to experiment further with the sample data in the National Widgets Customer File or to apply some of the same techniques to your own data bases. You need not be concerned about damaging data during these trials, since LIST and DISPLAY only display information—they do not change the contents of records in the current data base.

From now on, it will become increasingly important to recognize the general concepts illustrated by the examples given in this and previous chapters, including the use of field lists, scope clauses, FOR clauses, FILTERs, and QUERY files to narrow the range of data items acted on by dBASE III PLUS commands. These command components, which were illustrated primarily with LIST and DISPLAY, can also be combined in the same ways for use with many other dBASE III PLUS commands.

Chapter 7

Sorting and Indexing

In all the work you have done so far with dBASE III PLUS, both at the dot prompt and in the full-screen editing modes, you have accessed records in the order in which they were entered into a data base. If you impose selection criteria on the file with SET DELETED, SET FILTER, and scope or FOR clauses, not every record will be displayed, but the ones that are will appear in record number order.

In most data base applications, the order of entry is rarely the order in which you want to display or print records, since it usually bears little relationship to the content of the fields. For example, customers might be entered into a data base roughly in chronological order based on their first order dates, whereas you might prefer to view them on the screen in alphabetical order by account code; print reports in order by account code, city, or salesperson; and generate mailing labels in ZIP code order.

Displaying records in the order of entry also gives you no help finding a particular record that you need to view, edit, or delete. When a file is small and you are familiar with the data, this is rarely a problem; you can generally pick out the desired record from the output of a LIST or

DISPLAY ALL command, or use BROWSE to page through the file. You can then specify the record by number in an EDIT, DISPLAY, or GOTO command. If you don't immediately spot the record you need, you can use a LOCATE command to search based on the contents of one or more fields.

All these methods break down rapidly as a data base grows larger, however. Scanning through a file in record number order is as frustrating as flipping through a stack of paper ledger cards, and LOCATE becomes very slow in a data base containing more than a few hundred records. While this is perfectly acceptable for occasional searches based on unusual criteria, it is less than ideal for routinely retrieving records to perform daily file maintenance operations.

This chapter describes two methods for processing records in a dBASE III PLUS data base in a sequence that is different from the order of entry. The first, *sorting,* physically rearranges the records and rewrites them to a new data base in the specified order. The second, *indexing,* retains the original sequence but enables you to display or process the records in a different order. By using one or both of these techniques, you can display or print data in a sequence determined by the contents of one or more fields in the data base, and you can more easily and quickly find individual records.

USING SORT TO REARRANGE THE RECORDS IN A DATA BASE

You can physically rearrange the records in a dBASE III PLUS file, based on the contents of up to ten fields, by using the SORT command. The field or fields used as the basis for sorting a file are referred to as *sort keys* or *key fields.* When you sort, dBASE III PLUS reads records from the data base in use, determines the new order for the records based on the specified keys, and writes the records to a new data base, leaving the original intact. This concept is illustrated schematically in Figure 7-1. To sort based on a single field, you need only specify the name for the sorted

1	LEWIS	Lewis and Associates	...	94610	...
2	ABCPLUMB	ABC Plumbing	...	94703	...
3	ANDERSON		...	94114	...
4	KLEIN	Carol Klein, M.D.	...	94609	...
5	MTK	M.T.K. Industries	...	94608	...
6	RAPIDTYPE	RapidType Secretarial Svc	...	94123	...
7	PHOENIX	Phoenix Construction	...	94553	...
8	KELLY	Kelly and Sons Furniture	...	94578	...
9	GREENTHUMB	Green Thumb Landscaping	...	94702	...
10	HOMEMOVIES	Home Movies Video Rentals	...	94705	...
11	SHAPEUP	Shape Up Fitness Center	...	94804	...
12	FLOORPLAN	Floor Plan Carpet Center	...	94080	...
13	JOHNSON	J. Thomas Johnson, CPA	...	94111	...
14	ELLISMFG	Ellis Manufacturing	...	94306	...
15	IMAGEMAKER	The Image Makers	...	94608	...
16	WHITNEY	Financial Planning Svcs.	...	94536	...
17	HRINSURANC	H & R Insurance	...	94109	...
18	DELTADESGN	Delta Design	...	94509	...
19	ARONOFF		...	94510	...
20	YORKPUMP	York Pump, Inc.	...	95131	...

SORT by ACCOUNT code

1	ABCPLUMB	ABC Plumbing	...	94703	...
2	ANDERSON		...	94114	...
3	ARONOFF		...	94510	...
4	DELTADESGN	Delta Design	...	94509	...
5	ELLISMFG	Ellis Manufacturing	...	94306	...
6	FLOORPLAN	Floor Plan Carpet Center	...	94080	...
7	GREENTHUMB	Green Thumb Landscaping	...	94702	...
8	HOMEMOVIES	Home Movies Video Rentals	...	94705	...
9	HRINSURANC	H & R Insurance	...	94109	...
10	IMAGEMAKER	The Image Makers	...	94608	...
11	JOHNSON	J. Thomas Johnson, CPA	...	94111	...
12	KELLY	Kelly and Sons Furniture	...	94578	...
13	KLEIN	Carol Klein, M.D.	...	94609	...
14	LEWIS	Lewis and Associates	...	94610	...
15	MTK	M.T.K. Industries	...	94608	...
16	PHOENIX	Phoenix Construction	...	94553	...
17	RAPIDTYPE	RapidType Secretarial Svc	...	94123	...
18	SHAPEUP	Shape Up Fitness Center	...	94804	...
19	WHITNEY	Financial Planning Svcs.	...	94536	...
20	YORKPUMP	York Pump, Inc.	...	95131	...

Figure 7-1 *Sorting a data base file*

file and the field on which to base the new sequence:

SORT ON *key field* TO *new file name*

The new file is a data base file with the same structure as the file that provided the data. This new file is created automatically by the SORT command. If a file with the same name already exists on the disk, dBASE III PLUS will issue a warning message and ask your permission to overwrite the existing file, for example, "NWCACCT.dbf already exists, overwrite it? (Y/N)".

If you are intentionally recreating a sorted file, you can press Y ("Yes"). If you have inadvertently used the name of an existing data base that you do not want to overwrite, you can press N and repeat the SORT command with a different file name. If you prefer to be allowed to overwrite existing files without having to answer this question each time, you can disable the "safety" feature by typing

```
SET SAFETY OFF
```

When you sort based on a character field, the new records are arranged in alphabetical order. With a numeric key, you get numerical order, while using a date as the basis for a sort yields chronological order. You cannot sort based on a logical or memo field.

By default, records are sorted in *ascending order,* or low-to-high order. You can also sort in *descending order,* which places the highest key value first, by including the keyword DESCENDING, which may be abbreviated as /D, after the name of the key field. (You can also use ASCENDING, or /A, to indicate ascending order, but this is unnecessary, since ascending order is the default.) To sort the National Widgets Customer File in ascending alphabetical order by account code, you would use the following command:

```
SORT ON ACCOUNT TO NWCACCT
```

To sort the Customer File in descending chronological order by last order date, you could use

```
SORT ON LASTORDER DESCENDING TO NWCDATE
```

or

```
SORT ON LASTORDER /D TO NWCDATE
```

dBASE III PLUS interprets "alphabetical order" in terms of the ASCII codes used internally to represent characters. If you are interested in looking at these codes, you can find an ASCII table in the DOS or BASIC manual that came with your computer. The important point is that the codes for uppercase and lowercase letters are different, and that all uppercase letters come before any lowercase letters. The numeric digits 0 through 9 sort before any letters of the alphabet, as do most punctuation marks.

Fields that contain a consistent mixture of uppercase and lowercase letters, such as an initial capital letter followed by all lowercase letters, present no problems, since character strings are sorted one character at a time starting from the left. However, if data entry was inconsistent, either intentionally or inadvertently, records may not be properly grouped in the sorted file. For example, if you sort the National Widgets Customer File by state and some of the California records contain "CA" in the STATE field while others contain "Ca", the records that contain "CA" will come before "CO" (Colorado) and "CT" (Connecticut), and the "Ca" records will come after (followed by "Co" and "Ct").

You can cause dBASE III PLUS to ignore case and treat uppercase and lowercase letters as equivalent by including the /C option after the key field name in the SORT command. If you specify both the /D and /C options, only one slash is required:

```
SORT ON STATE /CD TO NWCSTATE
```

To sort based on more than one field, you list the sort keys separated by commas (as in any dBASE III PLUS list) in the SORT command. For each field, you can specify any combination of the "/" options. The field listed first determines the main order of the file. If there are multiple records with the same value in this field, they are arranged in the order determined by the second sort key. For example, to sort the National Widgets Customer File in order by state, within each state by city, and within each city by account code, ignoring the case distinction for the STATE and ACCOUNT fields, you would use

```
SORT ON STATE /C, CITY, ACCOUNT /C TO NWCSTATE
```

You can limit the range of records copied to the new file by using a FILTER or by including a scope or FOR clause in the SORT command. Records that have been marked for deletion will be included in the sorted file unless you have SET DELETED ON. As with any other command, if you combine these options, only records that satisfy all the selection conditions will be copied to the sorted file.

Although sorting is easy to understand, it is often not the most efficient way to control the order in which records are displayed or printed, especially if your files are large. Suppose, for example, that you want to view the Customer File on-screen and print reference lists in alphabetical order by account number and print mailing labels in ZIP code order. You also want to print specialized reports by the combination of state, city, and account code described previously and in descending order by first order date. To accommodate all these requirements, you could create four sorted copies of the file:

```
USE NWCUST
SORT ON ACCOUNT /C TO NWCACCT
SORT ON ZIP TO NWCZIP
SORT ON STATE /C, CITY, ACCOUNT /C TO NWCSTATE
SORT ON FIRSTORDER /D TO NWCFIRST
```

You could then use these files interchangeably, selecting for use in any given context the one arranged in the appropriate sorted order. To view customers on-screen, you could USE NWCACCT, for printing labels you could USE NWCZIP, and so on. Although this approach solves the problem, it has several serious drawbacks.

One problem is that although dBASE III PLUS can sort relatively fast, sorting a large file can still take some time, especially if you need to sort in four ways. A more serious problem is that maintaining five copies of the same data — the original data base and the four sorted files — can occupy a considerable amount of disk space, perhaps more than you have or more than you are willing to devote to a single data base. For example, it is reasonable to work with a 2-megabyte data base on a 10-megabyte hard disk, but not if you have to maintain five copies of the file.

Furthermore, keeping all these files up to date can create massive housekeeping problems. Although you may view the five files as equivalent because you know they contain the same data, dBASE III PLUS treats them as separate, unrelated data bases. If you need to add a record or change the value of one of the sort key fields, such as if a customer moves and you change the data in the CITY and ZIP fields, it is up to you to ensure that the changes are reflected in all the relevant files.

When you APPEND a record, it is added to the end of the data base in use. To add new records to all five copies of the Customer File and maintain the correct sequence in each, you would have to APPEND the records to the original file and regenerate the four sorted files or INSERT the new records in their proper positions in each of the sorted files. These alternatives seem even less attractive when you consider the problems involved in editing the sort key fields in existing records, which essentially involves moving each affected record to a new position in one of the sorted files.

There is a solution to all these problems that also affords you the advantage of very fast searches: instead of sorting, you can build indexes. Nevertheless, sorting has its place in your dBASE III PLUS command repertoire. If your data rarely changes or your files are small, and you do not need many different sorted orders, the problems just enumerated are often not very serious.

HANDS-ON PRACTICE—SORTING

Open the National Widgets Customer File and sort the file by account code with the following command:

```
SORT ON ACCOUNT /C TO NWCACCT
```

As dBASE III PLUS sorts, it displays a status message informing you of its progress, but the Customer File is so small that this display will almost immediately reflect the final status of the sort operation: "100% Sorted 20 Records sorted ... Copying text file."

You can see from the Status Bar that the file in use is still NWCUST.DBF and that the record pointer is positioned at the end-of-file after reading all the records. The "Copying text file" message informs you that after writing the sorted data records to the new data base file (NWCACCT.DBF), dBASE III PLUS copies the memo field entries to a matching text file (NWCACCT.DBT). This message does not appear if you sort a data base that is devoid of memo fields.

Open the sorted file by typing a new USE command:

```
USE NWCACCT
```

Use a LIST or DISPLAY command to verify that the records have in fact been rearranged in alphabetical order by account code:

```
DISPLAY ALL ACCOUNT, COMPANY
```

Then reopen the original Customer File by typing

```
USE NWCUST
```

Create the other three sorted copies of the customer data described in the previous section with three more SORT commands:

```
SORT ON ZIP TO NWCZIP
SORT ON STATE /C, CITY, ACCOUNT /C TO NWCSTATE
SORT ON FIRSTORDER /D TO NWCFIRST
```

Open the NWCSTATE file by typing USE NWCSTATE, and verify that the records are grouped correctly by state (although there is only one state, California) and city, and within each city sorted by account code:

```
DISPLAY ALL STATE, CITY, ACCOUNT, COMPANY
```

If you have entered all the sample data, the first screen display should look like the one shown in Figure 7-2.

You can list all the data base files on disk with the DIR (directory) command, which is similar to the DOS DIR command except that by default only data base files are listed. Try this command:

```
DIR
```

Note that the display includes the number of records, the date of the last update, and the size of each file in bytes — the information displayed

```
. DISPLAY ALL STATE, CITY, ACCOUNT, COMPANY
Record#  STATE CITY                ACCOUNT     COMPANY
      1  CA    Antioch             DELTADESGN  Delta Design
      2  CA    Benicia             ARONOFF
      3  CA    Berkeley            ABCPLUMB    ABC Plumbing
      4  CA    Berkeley            GREENTHUMB  Green Thumb Landscaping
      5  CA    Berkeley            HOMEMOVIES  Home Movies Video Rentals
      6  CA    Emeryville          IMAGEMAKER  The Image Makers
      7  CA    Emeryville          MTK         M.T.K. Industries
      8  CA    Fremont             WHITNEY     Financial Planning Svcs.
      9  CA    Martinez            PHOENIX     Phoenix Construction
     10  CA    Oakland             KLEIN       Carol Klein, M.D.
     11  CA    Oakland             LEWIS       Lewis and Associates
     12  CA    Palo Alto           ELLISMFG    Ellis Manufacturing
     13  CA    Richmond            SHAPEUP     Shape Up Fitness Center
     14  CA    San Francisco       ANDERSON
     15  CA    San Francisco       HRINSURANC  H & R Insurance
     16  CA    San Francisco       JOHNSON     J. Thomas Johnson, CPA
     17  CA    San Francisco       RAPIDTYPE   RapidType Secretarial Svc
     18  CA    San Jose            YORKPUMP    York Pump, Inc.
     19  CA    San Leandro         KELLY       Kelly and Sons Furniture
Press any key to continue...
Command Line  ||<C:>||NWCSTATE        ||Rec: 20/20       ||Ins  ||   Caps

                    Enter a dBASE III PLUS command.
```

Figure 7-2 The customer file sorted by state, city, and account code

at the top of the listing produced by the LIST STRUCTURE command. You can list any other disk files by specifying the file name pattern to match. dBASE III PLUS uses the same two wildcard characters as DOS: ?, which stands for any single character, and *, which stands for any group of characters. Display a list of the .DBT files that contain the memo field text from the National Widgets files with

```
DIR NW*.DBT
```

Your screen should look like the one shown in Figure 7-3.

```
. DIR
Database Files    # Records    Last Update     Size
NWCUST.DBF              20     05/25/87        4474
NWCSTATE.DBF            20     05/27/87        4474
NWCACCT.DBF             20     05/27/87        4474
NWCZIP.DBF              20     05/27/87        4474
NWCFIRST.DBF            20     05/27/87        4474

  22370 bytes in     5 files.
2441216 bytes remaining on drive.

. DIR *.DBT
NWCUST.DBT          NWCSTATE.DBT        NWCACCT.DBT         NWCZIP.DBT
NWCFIRST.DBT

  20484 bytes in     5 files.
2441216 bytes remaining on drive.

.
Command Line    ||<C:>||NWCUST           ||Rec: EOF/20       ||Ins  ||     Caps
                      Enter a dBASE III PLUS command.
```

Figure 7-3 *Using the dBASE III PLUS DIR (directory) command*

MAINTAINING A DATA BASE IN SORTED ORDER

If you intend to access a data base in a particular order most of the time, you can periodically sort the file and delete the original. For example, you could eliminate the NWCUST.DBF file after sorting by ACCOUNT to create the NWACCT.DBF file. To retain the name NWCUST.DBF for the file you use most often, you must delete the original file, NWCUST.DBF, and then rename NWCACCT.DBF. You can exit dBASE III PLUS and use the DOS ERASE and RENAME commands for this purpose, or you can use the dBASE III PLUS equivalents. Just remember that a data base that contains memo fields consists of two files with the same first name and different extensions — both must be erased or renamed.

You cannot erase or rename an open file, so if you have just performed the SORT, you must close the original file with a USE command. You can then erase the original file and rename the sorted copy with a sequence of commands such as the following (note that the syntax of the dBASE III PLUS commands differs slightly from the DOS versions):

```
ERASE NWCUST.DBF
ERASE NWCUST.DBT
RENAME NWCACCT.DBF TO NWCUST.DBF
RENAME NWCACCT.DBT TO NWCUST.DBT
```

In a real application, always be sure that you have a backup copy of any file before you erase it.

USING INDEXES TO ACCESS RECORDS IN DIFFERENT ORDERS

An *index* is an auxiliary file that enables you to view a data base in a sequence that is different from the physical order of the records. The syntax of the INDEX command is similar to that of SORT:

INDEX ON *key expression* TO *index file name*

Unlike SORT, however, INDEX does not create another complete data base file. For each record in the associated data base, an index file contains only the value of the *key expression* and a reference to the record number. The file is identified as an index by the extension NDX. (Recall that data base files have the extension DBF.)

If the index key consists of a single field, the index entries are arranged in alphabetical, numerical, or chronological order, depending on the data type of the key field (more complex key expressions will be discussed shortly). You cannot index in descending order simply by adding an option to the INDEX command, but some alternative methods are described in Chapter 8.

To build indexes for the National Widgets Customer File that enable you to access the file in order by account code, ZIP code, and first order date, you could use the following three commands:

```
INDEX ON FIRSTORDER TO NWCFIRST
INDEX ON ZIP TO NWCZIP
INDEX ON ACCOUNT TO NWCACCT
```

A schematic representation of the relationship between the National Widgets Customer File and each of these indexes is illustrated in Figure 7-4. (This is not exactly how a dBASE III PLUS index looks, but it is a good analogy.) Note that each index contains only the field used as the basis for determining the order.

An index is analogous in many ways to the index of a book, which is also an alphabetical list of keywords and references to the location of more complete data. You can consider the index entry in a book equivalent to the contents of a dBASE III PLUS index key and the page number reference equivalent to the record number.

Most dBASE III PLUS indexes are based on one, two, or three short fields, and they are therefore much smaller than the associated data base. By building indexes instead of sorting, you can access a file in several different orders without tying up nearly as much disk space. Indexing is also often faster than sorting, although that may not be true for small files. Even more importantly, dBASE III PLUS can automatically update an index to account for new records or changes to the key field.

After an index is constructed, it remains open with the data base file. You can reopen the index in a subsequent work session by naming it in the USE command that opens the data base:

USE *data base name* INDEX *index file name*

Notice that the keyword INDEX can function as two different "parts of speech." In the INDEX command, it is a verb, instructing dBASE III PLUS to build an index file from scratch. In the USE command, it introduces the clause that identifies the index (or indexes) that should be opened with the data base. Naming an index in a USE command does not construct it; if the specified index cannot be found on the disk, a "File does not exist" error message will be displayed.

If a data base is already open, you can open an index with the SET INDEX command:

```
SET INDEX TO index file name
```

You can also use this command to switch indexes, for example, to print two consecutive reports in different orders.

Whenever an index is open, it governs the sequence in which records are displayed, printed, or otherwise processed by dBASE III PLUS. A LIST command, for example, displays data in indexed rather than record number order. After building the three indexes described previously, a LIST command would display data in account code order (since the NWCACCT index was the last to be constructed), as illustrated in Figure 7-5.

When an index is open, all dBASE III PLUS commands that position the record pointer act relative to the index. GOTO TOP moves the pointer to the record corresponding to the first index entry, and GOTO BOTTOM moves it to the last indexed record. SKIP and SKIP −1 move the pointer to the record referenced by the next or previous index entry, as do the PGUP and PGDN keys in the full-screen editing modes.

To process records in indexed order, dBASE III PLUS constantly reads information from two files: the data base and the index. Whenever a command is executed that requires repositioning the record pointer, the index is read first to determine which record to display next. Based on the record number stored in the index, dBASE III PLUS performs the equivalent of a GOTO command to position the pointer to the right record, where the data is stored.

Although you can SORT based on a list of fields, the INDEX command requires that the key be a single expression. To build an index based on more than one field, you must combine them to form the key. This is easiest with character fields, which can simply be added together,

Record#	Account	Company		ZIP		Firstorder
1	LEWIS	Lewis and Associates	...	94610	...	10/13/84
2	ABCPLUMB	ABC Plumbing	...	94703	...	12/01/85
3	ANDERSON		...	94114	...	08/08/86
4	KLEIN	Carol Klein, M.D.	...	94609	...	10/13/85
5	MTK	M.T.K. Industries	...	94608	...	06/23/86
6	RAPIDTYPE	RapidType Secretarial Svc	...	94123	...	03/10/88
7	PHOENIX	Phoenix Construction	...	94553	...	04/28/86
8	KELLY	Kelly and Sons Furniture	...	94578	...	01/23/88
9	GREENTHUMB	Green Thumb Landscaping	...	94702	...	08/16/86
10	HOMEMOVIES	Home Movies Video Rentals	...	94705	...	09/13/87
11	SHAPEUP	Shape Up Fitness Center	...	94804	...	02/15/85
12	FLOORPLAN	Floor Plan Carpet Center	...	94080	...	11/20/87
13	JOHNSON	J. Thomas Johnson, CPA	...	94111	...	06/28/86
14	ELLISMFG	Ellis Manufacturing	...	94306	...	10/18/86
15	IMAGEMAKER	The Image Makers	...	94608	...	11/12/87
16	WHITNEY	Financial Planning Svcs.	...	94536	...	10/04/85
17	HRINSURANC	H & R Insurance	...	94109	...	07/12/86
18	DELTADESGN	Delta Design	...	94509	...	09/14/87
19	ARONOFF		...	94510	...	10/09/86
20	YORKPUMP	York Pump, Inc.	...	95131	...	10/18/85

Figure 7-4 *The customer file and three indexes that access it in different orders*

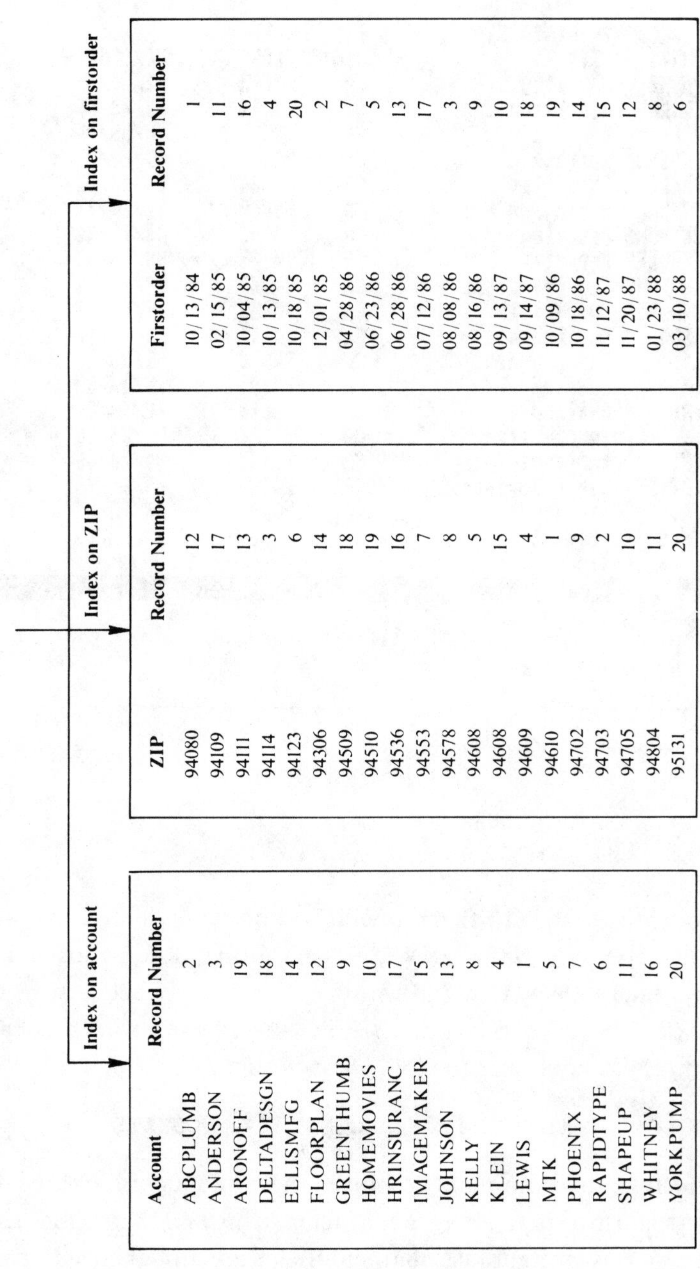

Index on account

Account	Record Number
ABCPLUMB	2
ANDERSON	3
ARONOFF	19
DELTADESGN	18
ELLISMFG	14
FLOORPLAN	12
GREENTHUMB	9
HOMEMOVIES	10
HRINSURANC	17
IMAGEMAKER	15
JOHNSON	13
KELLY	8
KLEIN	4
LEWIS	1
MTK	5
PHOENIX	7
RAPIDTYPE	6
SHAPEUP	11
WHITNEY	16
YORKPUMP	20

Index on ZIP

ZIP	Record Number
94080	12
94109	17
94111	13
94114	3
94123	6
94306	14
94509	18
94510	19
94536	16
94553	7
94578	8
94608	5
94608	15
94609	4
94610	1
94702	9
94703	2
94705	10
94804	11
95131	20

Index on firstorder

Firstorder	Record Number
10/13/84	1
02/15/85	11
10/04/85	16
10/13/85	4
10/18/85	20
12/01/85	2
04/28/86	7
06/23/86	5
06/28/86	13
07/12/86	17
08/08/86	3
08/16/86	9
09/13/87	10
09/14/87	18
10/09/86	19
10/18/86	14
11/12/87	15
11/20/87	12
01/23/88	8
03/10/88	6

```
. DISPLAY ALL ACCOUNT, CITY, STATE, ZIP, FIRSTORDER
Record#  ACCOUNT    CITY                 STATE ZIP        FIRSTORDER
      2  ABCPLUMB   Berkeley             CA    94703      12/01/85
      3  ANDERSON   San Francisco        CA    94114      08/08/86
     19  ARONOFF    Benicia              CA    94510      10/09/86
     18  DELTADESGN Antioch              CA    94509      09/14/87
     14  ELLISMFG   Palo Alto            CA    94306      10/18/86
     12  FLOORPLAN  South San Francisco  CA    94080      11/20/87
      9  GREENTHUMB Berkeley             CA    94702      08/16/86
     10  HOMEMOVIES Berkeley             CA    94705      09/13/87
     17  HRINSURANC San Francisco        CA    94109      07/12/86
     15  IMAGEMAKER Emeryville           CA    94608      11/12/87
     13  JOHNSON    San Francisco        CA    94111      06/28/86
      8  KELLY      San Leandro          CA    94578      01/23/88
      4  KLEIN      Oakland              CA    94609      10/13/85
      1  LEWIS      Oakland              CA    94610      10/13/84
      5  MTK        Emeryville           CA    94608      06/23/86
      7  PHOENIX    Martinez             CA    94553      04/28/86
      6  RAPIDTYPE  San Francisco        CA    94123      03/10/88
     11  SHAPEUP    Richmond             CA    94804      02/15/85
     16  WHITNEY    Fremont              CA    94536      10/04/85
Press any key to continue...
Command Line  ||<C:>||NWCUST          ||Rec: 2/20         ||Ins  ||   Caps

                    Enter a dBASE III PLUS command.
```

Figure 7-5 *Displaying records in indexed order*

or *concatenated*, with the + operator. For example, to build an index that accesses the National Widgets Customer File in order by state, within each state by city, and within each city alphabetically by account code (like the NWCSTATE.DBF file created earlier in this chapter by sorting), you could use the following command:

```
INDEX ON STATE + CITY + ACCOUNT TO NWCSTATE
```

In effect, this command combines the contents of the three separate fields to form a single, longer character string and then builds the index based on this string. Since character fields are alphabetized from left to right, all the index entries with the same first letter in the key will be grouped together. Within this group, they will be arranged according to the second letter, and so on. Thus, when the data base is accessed through this index, all the records with the same value in the first field in the key will appear to be grouped; within this group, the sequence will be determined by the second field in the key, and so on.

To index on a combination of fields of different data types, date and numeric fields must be converted to character fields using a method described in Chapter 8.

HANDS-ON PRACTICE—BUILDING INDEXES

Open the National Widgets Customer File, and with the following sequence of commands, build the four indexes described in the preceding section:

```
USE NWCUST
INDEX ON FIRSTORDER TO NWCFIRST
INDEX ON ZIP TO NWCZIP
INDEX ON STATE + CITY + ACCOUNT TO NWCSTATE
INDEX ON ACCOUNT TO NWCACCT
```

Use a LIST or DISPLAY ALL command to verify that the records are displayed in alphabetical order by account code. Your screen should look similar to the one shown in Figure 7-5. Notice that each record retains its original record number, which reflects the order in which it was entered into the file, although records are displayed on the screen in a sequence determined by the index.

Position the record pointer at the top of the file with GOTO TOP and DISPLAY or EDIT the record. Note that the record at the "top" of the file is not Record 1 but Record 2 (ABC Plumbing), the first record in indexed order—the one corresponding to the entry at the top of the index file.

Move forward in the file by typing SKIP several times, and follow each SKIP command with a DISPLAY to view the records. Try doing the same thing from the full-screen EDIT mode and the full-screen BROWSE mode by paging through the file with the PGUP and PGDN keys. Note that in all cases records are presented in alphabetical order by account code and that all movements of the record pointer take place relative to this sequence.

After returning to the dot prompt, switch to the first order date index by typing

```
SET INDEX TO NWCFIRST
```

Again, use a LIST or DISPLAY ALL command to verify that records are displayed in indexed order, which this time means chronological order by last order date.

USING FIND AND SEEK FOR RAPID RETRIEVAL

In addition to allowing you to view data in a sequence other than the order of entry, index files provide the means to conduct very fast searches based on the contents of the index key. This is done by using the SEEK command:

SEEK *key value*

You have already seen how to use LOCATE to search for records based on the contents of any field or fields. LOCATE works by testing each record until it finds one that matches the specified condition, a process that can take a long time in a large file. SEEK uses an entirely different search strategy to find the *index entry* that matches the specified key value. It then positions the record pointer at the corresponding record in the data base.

To understand how SEEK works, consider again the analogy of a dBASE III PLUS index file and a book index. Suppose you wanted to find the section in this book that describes the SCOPE clause. One strategy, which is analogous to using the LOCATE command, involves starting on page 1 and skimming each page until you find the right one.

By using the index, you can conduct a more efficient search and find any subject you want fast. To look for the topic SCOPE in the index, for example, you would open the index somewhere close to the middle, perhaps at the M section. Knowing that M comes before S, you would move forward in the index, approximately halfway between M and Z, which might leave you in the T section. Realizing that you had gone too far, you would back up and continue the process until you found the "SCOPE" entry. Once you knew the page number, you could quickly "flip" to the correct page. Despite the length of this description, looking up a word in an alphabetical list is actually very fast, as is the operation of the SEEK command. Both the index of a book and a dBASE III PLUS index file are lists of keywords, presorted in alphabetical order, with references to the location of the rest of the information. In both cases, the fast search techniques are based on a knowledge of alphabetical order and an effective scheme for deciding how far to move forward or backward on each pass through the index.

Using a SEEK command, you can retrieve any record in a file, almost regardless of size, in at most a few seconds. By making sure that every data base has an index based on the field or combination of fields that forms the unique (or nearly unique) identifier for each record, you can ensure that you will be able to retrieve any record very quickly in order to view, edit, or delete it.

You need not specify the full key value in a SEEK command, but the portion you enter must start at the beginning of the field. For example, all of the following commands would retrieve the record for ABC Plumbing based on the NWCACCT index:

```
SEEK "ABCPLUMB"
SEEK "ABCPL"
SEEK "ABC"
```

If you specify a partial key that is not unique, a SEEK command will find the record in which the full key value occurs first in the index. Thus, if there were a company called ABC Electrical Services in the National Widgets Customer File with the account code ABCELECT, SEEK "ABC" would retrieve this record rather than ABCPLUMB. Since the index is arranged in alphabetical order, all of the ABCs are adjacent in the index; you could SKIP forward through the file in indexed order until you found the one you wanted. If a data base contains more than one record with the same key value, a SEEK command will retrieve the one with the lowest record number.

Like many other dBASE III PLUS commands, SEEK positions the record pointer without displaying data; it makes no assumptions about what you want to do with the record you have found. Unlike LOCATE, it does not even show you a record number, perhaps because once you begin to use indexes to access records based solely on their contents, you may not care much about the record numbers. If you are interested, you can see from the Status Bar where the pointer is positioned, and you can use DISPLAY or EDIT to view the data.

If dBASE III PLUS fails to find a matching key value in the index, it displays the error message "No find." (This less than grammatical message derives from the verb FIND, a command similar to SEEK that was used in earlier versions of dBASE. For compatibility, dBASE III PLUS still recognizes FIND, but the examples in this book use SEEK.)

USING MULTIPLE INDEXES WITH A DATA BASE

You can open up to seven indexes with a data base by listing them in the USE command that opens the file:

USE *data base name* INDEX *index file list*

There is no limit to the number of indexes that you can construct to access the records in a data base in different orders, provided that you do not try to open more than seven at once. If the data base is already open, you can open the indexes with a SET INDEX command that includes the same list:

SET INDEX TO *index file list*

For example, with the following command, you could open the National Widgets Customer File with the four indexes described thus far:

```
USE NWCUST INDEX NWCACCT, NWCZIP, NWCSTATE, NWCFIRST
```

or

```
USE NWCUST
SET INDEX TO NWCACCT, NWCZIP, NWCSTATE, NWCFIRST
```

Whenever an index is open, it is automatically updated to reflect the addition of new records to the data base and all changes made to the key fields. When you change a field that forms part of the index key in one or more indexes, the index entries are immediately updated and are moved in the index to the positions dictated by the new data. When you APPEND a record, it is added to the end of the data base and is assigned the next sequential record number. A new entry is then added to each open index and is inserted in its proper place so the record can immediately be displayed or processed in correct key order. Marking a record for deletion does not affect any indexes, since the deletion marker is stored in the data base.

When two or more indexes are open, one of them, the *master index,* controls the order in which records are displayed or processed. This is also the only index that can be used for retrieving records with the SEEK command. By default, the master index is the first one named in the USE or SET INDEX command that opened the indexes. The order in which the other indexes are named in these commands is unimportant. In general, therefore, you should first name the index that is used most frequently to SEEK records according to a unique or nearly unique field.

You can designate a new master index at any time with the SET ORDER command:

SET ORDER TO *index file number*

The *index file number* corresponds to the order in which the index file names were listed in the most recent USE or SET INDEX command used to open the indexes. Thus, in the National Widgets example, you could switch to viewing records in ZIP code order with

```
SET ORDER TO 2
```

You could later return to using NWCACCT.NDX as the master index with

```
SET ORDER TO 1
```

Keep in mind that SET ORDER does not renumber the indexes. Regardless of which one is currently the master index, the number associated with each index is determined by its position in the index file list in the last USE or SET INDEX command. To ignore all the indexes and view records in record number order, you can use

```
SET ORDER TO 0
```

After you SET ORDER TO 0, none of the open indexes will be updated to reflect changes to the data base. This command should be used only when you are sure that you will not be adding records or editing the index key fields.

Recall that you can open a new set of indexes with the SET INDEX command, and you can therefore use this command to switch master indexes. But unless you also want to close some of the indexes or open others, SET ORDER is preferable. SET INDEX reopens all the specified indexes from scratch, which involves rereading a portion of each one from the disk, and is therefore slower than SET ORDER, which simply assigns a different index to be used as the master. If you no longer need to have any indexes open, you can close all indexes but still leave the data base open by typing

```
SET INDEX TO
```

This usage is consistent with the USE command, which closes an open data base, and SET FILTER TO, which cancels the current FILTER condition. You can think of it as meaning "I don't want to use any indexes."

You can verify which indexes are open, the key expression for each, and which one is currently the master index by using the DISPLAY STATUS command. DISPLAY STATUS shows you two or more screens of information (depending on how many files are open) about the current status of the working environment, with the pause between screens that all DISPLAY commands produce. Figures 7-6 and 7-7 show what the status display would look like after you open the National Widgets Customer File with the four indexes described in this chapter and then execute a SET ORDER TO 2 command.

```
. USE NWCUST INDEX NWCACCT, NWCZIP, NWCSTATE, NWCFIRST
. SET ORDER TO 2
Master index: C:NWCZIP.ndx
. DISPLAY STATUS

Currently Selected Database:
Select area:  1, Database in Use: C:NWCUST.dbf   Alias: NWCUST
           Index file:  C:NWCACCT.ndx  Key: ACCOUNT
    Master index file:  C:NWCZIP.ndx  Key: ZIP
           Index file:  C:NWCSTATE.ndx  Key: STATE + CITY + ACCOUNT
           Index file:  C:NWCFIRST.ndx  Key: FIRSTORDER
           Memo file:   C:NWCUST.dbt

File search path:
Default disk drive: C:
Print destination:  PRN:
Margin =     0
Current work area =    1

Press any key to continue...
Command Line     ||<C:>||NWCUST                     ||Rec: 2/20          ||Ins  ||    Caps

                        Enter a dBASE III PLUS command.
```

Figure 7-6 *The first screen produced by the DISPLAY STATUS command*

```
ALTERNATE  - OFF  DELETED    - OFF  FIXED      - OFF  SAFETY     - ON
BELL       - ON   DELIMITERS - OFF  HEADING    - ON   SCOREBOARD - ON
CARRY      - OFF  DEVICE     - SCRN HELP       - ON   STATUS     - ON
CATALOG    - OFF  DOHISTORY  - OFF  HISTORY    - ON   STEP       - OFF
CENTURY    - OFF  ECHO       - OFF  INTENSITY  - ON   TALK       - ON
CONFIRM    - OFF  ESCAPE     - ON   MENU       - ON   TITLE      - ON
CONSOLE    - ON   EXACT      - OFF  PRINT      - OFF  UNIQUE     - OFF
DEBUG      - OFF  FIELDS     - OFF

Programmable function keys:
F2  - assist;
F3  - list;
F4  - dir;
F5  - display structure;
F6  - display status;
F7  - display memory;
F8  - display;
F9  - append;
F10 - edit;

.
Command Line   ||<C:>||NWCUST           ||Rec: 2/20        ||Ins ||    Caps
                   Enter a dBASE III PLUS command.
```

Figure 7-7 *The second screen produced by the DISPLAY STATUS command*

Some of the information in the status display may not mean much to you, but you can begin to use this command knowing that it will reveal more information as your understanding of dBASE III PLUS increases. The first screen displays the data bases that are currently open—in this case only one—as well as the list of index files and index key expressions. You are informed which is the master index and that there is a memo text file associated with the data base. If a FILTER were currently in effect, the FILTER condition would also be displayed on this screen.

The second screen of the display includes the current status of many of the dBASE III PLUS SET options and the current meanings assigned to the programmable function keys on the keyboard. If you prefer to eliminate the pause between screens, you can use LIST STATUS instead of DISPLAY STATUS. This variation of the command is better suited to producing a hard copy of the information with LIST STATUS TO PRINT.

HANDS-ON PRACTICE —WORKING WITH MULTIPLE INDEXES AND USING SEEK

If the National Widgets Customer File is not already open, use the following command to open the file as well as the four indexes constructed in the previous practice session:

```
USE NWCUST INDEX NWCACCT, NWCZIP, NWCSTATE, NWCFIRST
```

If the Customer File is already open, open the indexes with

```
SET INDEX TO NWCACCT, NWCZIP, NWCSTATE, NWCFIRST
```

Recall that you can determine whether a file is open by glancing at the Status Bar, and you can use DISPLAY STATUS to view the open index files.

Use a LIST or DISPLAY ALL command to verify that records are displayed in account code order, because the NWCACCT.NDX, which is based on the ACCOUNT field, was named first in the list of index files.

Use a SEEK command to search for the record for Ellis Manufacturing (or another record if you have not entered all the sample data) by its account code, ELLISMFG, and then DISPLAY the record:

```
SEEK "ELLISMFG"
DISPLAY
```

Try searching based on less than the full account code, such as with SEEK "ELLIS", and verify that you can still find the record. Search for a record with the account code XYZ by typing

```
SEEK "XYZ"
```

Note that dBASE III PLUS displays the message "No find" to indicate that this record is not present in the index.

Switch to using the ZIP code index, NWCZIP.NDX, as the master index by typing

```
SET ORDER TO 2
```

Type a DISPLAY STATUS command to verify that you have selected the right index. Your screen should look like the one shown in Figure 7-6. You can press ESC at this point to bypass the rest of the status display, or any other key to examine the status of the SET options and the meanings of the programmable function keys. Turn on your printer, and type LIST STATUS TO PRINT to get a hard copy of the index names and key expressions for later reference.

Use APPEND to add at least one new record to the data base (you can use your own name and address). Exit APPEND and note by looking at the Status Bar that the new record was assigned the next available sequential record number, which will be 21 if you have been following all the examples. Select each of the four indexes in turn with SET ORDER commands, and use a LIST or DISPLAY ALL command that includes the index key fields to confirm that each of the four indexes now contains an entry for the new record; for example,

```
LIST ACCOUNT, CITY, STATE, ZIP, FIRSTORDER
```

This command should display the new record in its proper place in each of the four indexed listings.

REBUILDING AN INDEX

If you ever add records, change the key fields, or PACK a data base without opening one of the indexes associated with the file, the index will no longer match the data base. New records added to a data base without an index open will have no corresponding entries in the index. After a PACK command, the index will contain too many entries, some of which will reference the wrong records or ones that no longer exist in the file. If you edit the key field in a record, the index entry for that record will still contain the obsolete value, and you will not be able to SEEK the record based on its new contents.

Often, a mismatch between a data base and one of its indexes generates an error message the next time you open the index, but sometimes the problem can go unnoticed, and records that should be processed by a command may be passed over while others that should not are included. Certain error messages suggest that there is a potential problem with an index:

- A SEEK command results in a "No find" error message, but you can use a LOCATE command to find the record based on the index key field or see the record in the output of a LIST command.
- Any command results in a "Record is not in index" error message.
- Any command results in a "Record is out of range" error message.

Fortunately, it is easy (if sometimes time-consuming) to rectify these problems, since an index consists of information derived from a data base, and it can be reconstructed whenever necessary. There are two ways to rebuild an index to ensure that it accurately reflects the contents of the key fields in the data base records. The easiest way is to use the REINDEX command, which rebuilds all the currently open indexes based on the original key expressions. To rebuild the four National Widgets Customer File indexes described in this chapter, you could use the following sequence of commands:

```
USE NWCUST INDEX NWCACCT, NWCZIP, NWCSTATE
REINDEX
```

As dBASE III PLUS builds the indexes, status messages are displayed to allow you to monitor the progress of the command.

The REINDEX command is convenient because it does not require that you remember the index key expressions and because it allows you to reconstruct up to seven indexes with a single command. The key expression is stored at the beginning of an index file, where it may be read by dBASE III PLUS in order to REINDEX a file or display the expression in the screen produced by DISPLAY STATUS. For precisely this reason, REINDEX is not always the best way to regenerate the indexes associated with a data base. If an index file is damaged due to a hardware or software failure and dBASE III PLUS cannot read the key expression, you will not be able to use REINDEX.

You can always rebuild an index exactly the same way you constructed it, with an INDEX ON command that specifies the same key expression and the same index file name. You may want to SET SAFETY OFF so that dBASE III PLUS does not ask you to confirm your intention to overwrite the existing indexes. Note that if an index is damaged, you will not be able to open it for any purpose, such as to determine the key expression by typing DISPLAY STATUS. Be sure to generate a printed copy of the index keys before any problems arise, either by marking them on the listing produced by LIST STRUCTURE TO PRINT or by using LIST STATUS TO PRINT with all the indexes open to print the index names and keys.

If you use only one, two, or three indexes with a data base, you might decide to open all the indexes whenever you think you might change data or add records, but this is not always the best strategy. Some applications, particularly those that print many different reports, require more than the seven indexes that may be open at once. Furthermore, opening more indexes slows certain dBASE III PLUS operations. For each new record you add with seven indexes open, eight files must be updated: the data base itself and the seven indexes (plus a ninth, the DBT file, if your data base contains memo fields). Even when you are not actively updating data, dBASE III PLUS must constantly reposition a pointer similar to the record pointer in each index that is open, in case you do make any changes.

The decision about which indexes should be maintained at all times and which can be rebuilt when needed should be based on how much speed degradation you observe during data entry with multiple indexes open and how often you use the indexes. The size of the data base — and therefore, how long reindexing will take — will also affect your decision.

An index that enables you to retrieve records rapidly with SEEK or to control the order in which records are often viewed on-screen should always be kept up to date. An index used to print a report can be rebuilt right before printing the report, especially if the report is printed infrequently. In general, you can carry out slow commands like this one when you are not otherwise using the computer, or even overnight. As a rule of thumb, any index that is used less than once a month need not be maintained all the time, but you must arrive at the right scheduling guidelines for your own situation by experimenting with both approaches and weighing the inconveniences you experience.

STATING CONDITIONS WITH WHILE TO VIEW SELECTED RECORDS

When you impose selection criteria on a data base by adding a FOR clause to a command or by using a FILTER to state the same condition, dBASE III PLUS must read every record to determine whether it satisfies the specified condition. Regardless of how many or how few records are selected, the time required to execute the command is therefore highly dependent on the total number of records in the file.

If the selection criteria are based on fields that make up an index key, you can use an alternative search technique to select the right records without reading through the entire file. Using this strategy, you position the record pointer at the first record in the desired group and then read records in indexed order until the condition is no longer true. To do this, you introduce the condition with the keyword WHILE rather than FOR.

For example, the NWCACCT.NDX index allows you to access the National Widgets Customer File in alphabetical order by account code. To list all customers whose account codes begin with the letters K through M, you could start with the first record having an account code beginning with K and read records in indexed order, knowing that as soon as the record pointer advanced to a record in which the account number started with N, no other records would satisfy the selection criteria.

It makes no difference how you position the record pointer to the first record in the group. If you know the record number, you can use GOTO, or you can exit BROWSE or EDIT with the desired record selected. More commonly, however, you would use a SEEK command to find the first record. For example, to begin a National Widgets customer listing with Kelly and Sons, you could use

```
SEEK "KELLY"
```

Unless you are familiar with the data, you will probably SEEK the first record in the desired group based on a partial key value. For example, if you did not know that KELLY was the first customer whose account code began with K, you could SEEK "K". To find the first record in a ZIP code index in the range 94700 to 94799, you could SEEK "947".

The principle is the same if the index key is made up of multiple fields. Using the NWCSTATE.NDX index, which accesses the Customer File in order by city, state, and account number, you could start a report with the first customer in a California city whose name begins with B with SEEK "CAB". This concept does not extend to indexes based on dates or numeric fields in which you cannot SEEK a partial key value.

Once the record pointer is positioned on the first record in the group, you can include a WHILE clause in your next command to process the remaining records in the group. Unlike FOR, a WHILE clause does not cause the record pointer to be repositioned before the command is executed, and it causes dBASE III PLUS to stop reading records as soon as a record is found that does not satisfy the condition. Thus, to select customers having account codes between K and M, you could use the following sequence of commands, assuming that the Customer File is open and the account code index, NWCACCT.NDX, is the master index:

```
SEEK "K"
LIST WHILE ACCOUNT < "N"
```

Using the ZIP code index, you could select ZIP codes in the range

94700 to 94799 with the following:

```
SEEK "947"
LIST WHILE ZIP < "948"
```

or

```
SEEK "947"
LIST WHILE ZIP <= "94799"
```

Note that the WHILE clause behaves much like a scope, in that it selects records based on their position in the display sequence. The difference is that the condition in the WHILE clause is expressed in terms of the data in the records, which, because of the nature of the index, is tightly linked to the position of the record in the index. If the condition in the WHILE clause is not true for the record at the position of the record pointer when the command is executed, no records will be displayed, just as if you had typed LIST REST or LIST NEXT 5 with the record pointer already positioned at the end-of-file.

You can include both a FOR and a WHILE clause in a command to specify two separate conditions. When you do this, dBASE III PLUS reads records in the group determined by the WHILE clause, and of those records, only those that match the condition in the FOR clause are actually processed. For example, you could list all the customers having ZIP codes between 94700 and 94799 who had no orders this year with the following commands:

```
SEEK "947"
LIST WHILE ZIP <= "94799" FOR YTDORDERS = Ø
```

You can also add a scope, in which case the more restrictive of the scope and WHILE clauses determines which records are processed. Another way to state this is that only records that satisfy all the conditions specified in a command—the scope, FOR, and WHILE clauses—are processed by dBASE III PLUS.

Just as the SEEK command cannot be used for every search, WHILE cannot always substitute for FOR. A WHILE clause selects the right records only when it is used in concert with an index that accesses the file in a specified order — one based on the field or fields in the condition. If you do not already have such an index, you can evaluate some of the same considerations outlined in the previous section to decide whether or not to build one. For reports that are printed frequently, you might speed processing by providing an index that you can use to print only a selected range of records. For a report that is printed only a few times a year, you could use the slower FOR clause.

It is not always possible to use an index and a WHILE clause to speed processing, however. For example, in the National Widgets Customer File, you might want to select customers who own IBM equipment. Because the characters "IBM" might not occur at the beginning of the EQUIPMENT field (a fact that is reflected in the construction of the selection condition "IBM" $ EQUIPMENT), you cannot use an index to access the file in alphabetical order by equipment vendor.

HANDS-ON PRACTICE — USING WHILE CLAUSES

Make sure that the National Widgets Customer File is open as well as the four indexes created earlier in this chapter, and that the ZIP code index is selected as the master index.

The city of San Francisco is defined by the range of ZIP codes between 94100 and 94200. Try to find the first San Francisco ZIP code by specifying the entire key value, for example:

```
SEEK "94101"
```

The National Widgets Customer File does not contain a record with the ZIP code 94101. You can try the next few ZIP codes if you wish. If you keep trying, you will eventually find a record with the ZIP code 94109: Record 17, H & R Insurance. Try the search again using a partial key value:

```
SEEK "941"
```

List all the San Francisco records by specifying the range of ZIP codes in a WHILE clause:

```
LIST ACCOUNT, CITY, ZIP WHILE ZIP < "942"
```

Use a SET ORDER command to select the account code index, NWCACCT.NDX, as the master index, and display the first record, which should be Record 2, ABC Plumbing. Retrieve the previous LIST command from HISTORY and execute it again. This time no records will be displayed, because the condition is not true for the current record in which the ZIP code is 94703. Note that dBASE III PLUS does not consider this an error and therefore does not display an error message. It is up to you to ensure that the condition in a WHILE clause matches the key expression in the active index and that the record pointer is correctly positioned before you execute the command.

Use a SET ORDER TO 3 command to select the NWCSTATE.NDX index, which is based on the STATE, CITY, and ACCOUNT fields. Find the first San Francisco record, based this time on the contents of the STATE and CITY fields, with the following command:

```
SEEK "CASan Francisco"
```

The fact that this index key is composed of more than one field makes no difference to dBASE III PLUS. As in any other SEEK command, you have simply specified the string of characters to search for in the index file.

Use a LIST or DISPLAY ALL command to display the group of San Francisco customers:

```
LIST ACCOUNT, CITY, STATE WHILE STATE = "CA"
  .AND. CITY = "San Francisco"
```

Note that it is not necessary to include the test for the value of the STATE field in this condition, since there is no city named "San Francisco" in any other state. When you use an index in which any combination of key field values could occur, however, it is important to state your conditions carefully so that they test for changes in all the relevant key fields.

This chapter introduced some unfamiliar and difficult concepts. If you do not thoroughly understand indexes at this point, be sure to reread this chapter. Indexes are used throughout this book—and in most of your work with dBASE III PLUS—to display and process records in orders that are more meaningful than the sequence in which they were entered into the file, and to carry out fast searches based on the contents of the index key.

At this point, you have learned most of the major elements of the dBASE III PLUS command syntax. You can begin to think of a dBASE III PLUS command as consisting of discrete, independent components: the verb, and optionally a field list, a scope, a FOR clause, a WHILE clause, and other keywords such as OFF or TO PRINT. In the following chapters, these components are used in many other dBASE III PLUS commands in ways that are analogous to those illustrated thus far primarily with LIST and DISPLAY. Make sure you understand the purpose and usage of common command components before you go on. In the rest of this book, you will combine these clauses into increasingly complex dBASE III PLUS commands just as you would learn to form longer and longer sentences in studying a foreign language.

Chapter 8

Performing Calculations

Chapter 6 introduced the concept of combining data base fields and comparison operators to form dBASE III PLUS expressions, which were used as conditions in FOR and WHILE clauses to express record selection criteria. By definition, a condition is a logical expression, one that evaluates to either true or false. In Chapter 7, you saw an example of a character string expression, when three character fields—STATE, CITY, and ACCOUNT—were concatenated, or added together, to form an index key.

As you continue to work with dBASE III PLUS, you will need to construct more varied and complex expressions that operate on all types of data, not only for establishing more detailed selection criteria, but also for building indexes, specifying data to be printed in reports and mailing labels, and carrying out calculations. This chapter presents the remaining components of the dBASE III PLUS command language and further describes the rules that govern how these components can be combined to form more complex expressions.

This chapter demonstrates ways for using these increasingly sophisticated expressions to perform calculations and display or print the results, and to permanently change the values of fields in a data base.

Keep in mind as you read about constructing expressions that in many of the dBASE III PLUS commands presented in earlier chapters, as well as for most of the other commands in the language, you may substitute any expression of the same data type for the field names used in these examples.

WORKING WITH COMPLEX EXPRESSIONS AND CONDITIONS

An *expression* is a combination of data base fields, memory variables, constants, functions, and operators (these terms are defined shortly). An expression can incorporate elements of more than one data type as long as they are combined according to the rules of dBASE III PLUS syntax, but it always evaluates to a single quantity of a particular data type: character, numeric, date, or logical (you cannot construct memo type expressions).

Bear in mind as you read the examples in the rest of this book that an expression can almost always substitute for a field or a constant of the same data type. The examples in Chapter 5 demonstrated that you can include a *field list* in commands such as LIST or DISPLAY. In fact, these and most other dBASE III PLUS commands accept an *expression list.* For example, you could list, together with some of the fields in the National Widgets Customer File, the time elapsed between each customer's first and last orders with the following:

```
LIST ACCOUNT, COMPANY, TOTORDERS, LASTORDER - FIRSTORDER
```

For a single record, you could do the same with DISPLAY:

```
DISPLAY ACCOUNT, COMPANY, TOTORDERS, LASTORDER - FIRSTORDER
```

In these commands, the expression LASTORDER − FIRSTORDER evaluates to a single quantity, in this case a number, which is equivalent in every way to the other three quantities displayed (ACCOUNT, COMPANY, and TOTORDERS).

USING THE ? COMMAND TO DISPLAY INFORMATION

When you begin to experiment with complex expressions, it is helpful to have a convenient way to display the result of evaluating any given expression quickly. You can use DISPLAY for this purpose; for example, you could have dBASE III PLUS multiply 2 by 4 and show you the result with the command

```
DISPLAY 2 * 4
```

Because the DISPLAY command was intended to operate primarily on data base fields, its output normally includes the current record number from the data base in use and the field name headings, even if they are meaningless or irrelevant. For example, the previous command would produce the following display:

```
Record#  2 * 4
     4       8
```

You can suppress the record number by including the keyword OFF in the DISPLAY command, and you can eliminate the headings with SET HEADING OFF, but two problems still remain. If you attempt to execute a DISPLAY command without having a data base open, dBASE III PLUS will display "No database is in USE. Enter file name:". If a data base is open but is positioned at the end-of-file, the DISPLAY command will produce no output at all.

The ? command provides a general way to display the values of any expressions. For example, to display the result of multiplying 2 by 4, you could use

```
? 2 * 4
```

dBASE III PLUS responds with

```
8
```

To display the values of more than one expression, you list them in the ? command, separated by commas (as in any dBASE III PLUS list). The specified items are displayed with a single space between each pair. For example, the following would display the same data as the DISPLAY command described earlier:

```
? ACCOUNT, COMPANY, TOTORDERS, LASTORDER - FIRSTORDER
```

Because this particular ? command does require that a data base be open, the values of the fields ACCOUNT, COMPANY, TOTORDERS, LASTORDER, and FIRSTORDER are available. However, dBASE III PLUS does not assume that they are field names; they might also refer to memory variables (defined in the next section). If you execute this command without having a data base open, dBASE III PLUS displays "Variable not found" instead of "No data base in use."

The ? command is especially useful for testing a complex expression at the dot prompt before you incorporate it into a report or label form, or include it in a lengthy LIST command. Even if it takes you several tries to get the results you want, these trials will take less time than repeatedly modifying the report or label form, or editing a long LIST command. As you read this chapter, feel free to use this command to experiment on your own and test your understanding of the operators, functions, and expressions illustrated in the examples.

USING MEMORY VARIABLES

The expressions in all these examples were composed of data base fields and constants, combined and related by using the arithmetic, logical, and comparison operators. dBASE III PLUS also allows you to define memory variables to store constant values or the results of performing calculations. A *memory variable,* as the name suggests, is a temporary quantity retained in memory during a work session with dBASE III PLUS. Unless you save memory variables on disk, their values are lost when you turn off the computer or exit dBASE III PLUS.

dBASE III PLUS allows you to define up to 256 memory variables at a time. By default, they can total a maximum of 6000 bytes (although this limit can be increased). Imagine that dBASE III PLUS has provided you with a kind of scratchpad that has 256 separate pages, each of which can contain a single quantity plus a name that identifies what the value represents.

Memory variables can be used to store constant values so that you can employ them throughout a work session in conditions, calculations, reports, or labels without having to retype them. You can also use memory variables to store the results of performing time-consuming calculations, such as the total of a numeric field in a large data base, so that you can use these values later without having to repeat the original calculation. Typically, they are used for separate, unrelated quantities that do not necessarily belong to any one data base file and that do not share a common structure that would merit creating a data base to store them.

Memory variables can take on four of the five data types allowed for data base fields: character, numeric, logical, and date. Like data base field names, memory variable names can be up to ten characters long and can contain an embedded underscore (_). If you name your memory variables strategically, you should be able to remember their names and what the values represent. Beginning all memory variable names with the letter M clearly distinguishes them from data base fields.

When there is a relationship between a memory variable and a field, giving the memory variable a name consisting of the letter M followed by the field name will serve to remind you of the correspondence. For example, if you compute the sum of the YTDORDERS field in the National Widgets Customer File (using the SUM command described later in this chapter), you might assign the name MYTDORDERS to the variable used to store the sum.

Some commands, such as the SUM command just mentioned, can create memory variables automatically; all you need to do is provide the names. You can also create a memory variable by explicitly *initializing* it—naming it and assigning it a value.

You initialize memory variables with the STORE command or the assignment (=) operator. For example, to create a memory variable called MX and assign it an initial value of 1, you could use either

```
STORE 1 TO MX
```

or

```
MX = 1
```

Do not confuse this usage of the equal sign with its meaning in a condition that tests whether the values of two expressions are equal. The command line MX= 1 does not test whether the variable MX currently equals 1; it creates a memory variable called MX and assigns to it the value 1.

Although the = variation is more concise, there is one advantage to using the STORE syntax: You can use it to assign the same value to several variables simultaneously. For example, you could create three variables—MA, MB, and MC—and give them all the value 100.00 with the following command:

```
STORE 100.00 TO MA, MB, MC
```

If you assign a new value to an existing memory variable by specifying a name you have already used in a new STORE command, the variable is essentially recreated from scratch and the old value and data type are lost.

As you might have guessed from the previous examples, dBASE III PLUS determines the data type of a memory variable by the data type of the initial value. Note that the value assigned to a memory variable need not be a constant; you can use any legitimate dBASE III PLUS expression made up of constants, data base fields, functions (which are defined shortly), and other memory variables.

Numeric memory variables are assumed to be integers (whole numbers) that are ten digits long, and by default they have no decimal places. To create a variable with one or more decimal places, you must include them in the initial value, as illustrated in the previous example.

Character memory variables assume the same length as the initial value. Like character fields, they can be up to 254 characters long. Thus, the following command creates a character variable called MCITY, which is eight characters long and has the initial value "Berkeley":

```
STORE "Berkeley" TO MCITY
```

Logical memory variables are initialized by assigning them the logical values .T. (True), .F. (False), or the equivalents, .Y. or .N.:

```
STORE .T. TO MMAIL
```

dBASE III PLUS determines the data types of character, numeric, and logical constants just as it does when it interprets conditions used in FOR and WHILE clauses. Data consisting of only numeric digits is assumed to be a number, text enclosed in any of the standard character string delimiters is assumed to be a character string, and values delimited by two periods are interpreted as logical values.

Initializing date memory variables is complicated by the fact that dBASE III PLUS lacks a standard delimiter, comparable to the quotes used for character fields, that identifies a date as a date. To create a memory variable that has the same value as the FIRSTORDER date field, you could use

```
STORE FIRSTORDER TO MFIRSTORD
```

Assigning a constant value, such as July 5, 1988, to a date variable is more complicated (it is described later in this chapter in the section on "Performing Date Calculations and Comparisons.")

Using memory variables gives you the freedom to type commands that are independent of the precise values on which they operate. For example, suppose that National Widgets wanted to measure the performance of its salespeople by comparing the year-to-date orders for their customers to an arbitrary goal. The company has a different salesperson for each major city in the Bay Area. First, you could store the sales goal and the city in memory variables:

```
STORE 300.00 TO MYTDORDERS
STORE "San Francisco" TO MCITY
```

You could then display each customer's orders as a percent of this total by dividing the data base field YTDORDERS by the memory variable MYTDORDERS (and multiplying by 100 to display the result as a percent rather than a fraction:

```
LIST OFF ACCOUNT, COMPANY, YTDORDERS, YTDORDERS/MYTDORDERS*100
  FOR CITY = MCITY
```

You could easily vary the city or the goal by assigning new values to either or both memory variables and retrieving the command from HISTORY to repeat it unchanged. The resulting display is illustrated in Figure 8-1.

```
. STORE 300.00 TO MYTDORDERS
300.00
. STORE "San Francisco" TO MCITY
San Francisco
. LIST OFF ACCOUNT, COMPANY, YTDORDERS, YTDORDERS/MYTDORDERS*100 FOR CITY=MCITY
 ACCOUNT    COMPANY                       YTDORDERS  YTDORDERS/MYTDORDERS*100
 ANDERSON                                      0.00                      0.00
 HRINSURANC H & R Insurance                    0.00                      0.00
 JOHNSON    J. Thomas Johnson, CPA             0.00                      0.00
 RAPIDTYPE  RapidType Secretarial Svc        348.52                    116.17

. STORE 200.00 TO MYTDORDERS
200.00
. STORE "Berkeley" TO MCITY
Berkeley
. LIST OFF ACCOUNT, COMPANY, YTDORDERS, YTDORDERS/MYTDORDERS*100 FOR CITY=MCITY
 ACCOUNT    COMPANY                       YTDORDERS  YTDORDERS/MYTDORDERS*100
 ABCPLUMB   ABC Plumbing                     796.41                    398.20
 GREENTHUMB Green Thumb Landscaping            0.00                      0.00
 HOMEMOVIES Home Movies Video Rentals        248.15                    124.08

.
Command Line  <C:> NWCUSI              Rec: EOF/20        Ins       Caps

                    Enter a dBASE III PLUS command.
```

Figure 8-1 *Using memory variables for "what-if" analysis*

You can display the names, types, and values of all currently existing memory variables with

```
DISPLAY MEMORY
```

or

```
LIST MEMORY
```

As with any DISPLAY or LIST command, the DISPLAY variant pauses when the screen is full to give you time to read the display, whereas LIST scrolls data continuously. You can also add the phrase TO PRINT to obtain a hard copy of the display.

You can preserve the values of memory variables for use in a later work session by storing them in a disk file with the SAVE command. To save all the variables currently in memory, you would use

SAVE TO *memory file name*

This command creates a file with the extension MEM, which identifies it as a memory variable file. You can also save variables selectively, based on a similarity among their names, by including in the SAVE command a variable name *skeleton,* a pattern made up of text characters and wildcard symbols that describes the variable names you wish to select. You can use the same wildcard characters recognized in DOS and dBASE III PLUS file names: a question mark (?) to symbolize any single character and an asterisk (*) for any group of characters. Thus, you could save all the variables that have names beginning with MX with the following:

```
SAVE ALL LIKE MX* TO MEMFILE1
```

You can also save all variables whose names do not match a certain pattern by using the keyword EXCEPT instead of LIKE. For example, you could save all variables in which the second two letters of the name are not AB with the command

```
SAVE ALL EXCEPT ?AB* TO MEMFILE2
```

The skeleton ?AB* describes file names in which the first position may contain any character, the second must be A, the third must be B, and the rest of the name can be any combination of characters.

You can read the values stored in a memory file back into memory by using the RESTORE command:

RESTORE FROM *memory file name*

When you use this form of the RESTORE command, any variables currently in memory are lost. If you prefer, you can add the set of variables in the file to any that currently exist by including the keyword ADDITIVE in the RESTORE command:

RESTORE FROM *memory file name* ADDITIVE

You can erase the values of variables from memory with the RELEASE command to make room for more variables in the unlikely event that you are nearing the limit of 256, or more likely, so that the output of DISPLAY MEMORY commands is not cluttered by values you no longer need to see. Like the SAVE command, RELEASE allows you to specify a group of variable names in a LIKE or EXCEPT clause, or you can list the variables individually.

HANDS-ON PRACTICE—USING MEMORY VARIABLES

Open the National Widgets Customer File with no indexes so that the record pointer is positioned at Record 1, the record for Lewis and Associates:

```
USE NWCUST
```

Use the ? command to display the fields COMPANY, MAIL, LASTORDER, and YTDORDERS from this record:

```
? COMPANY, MAIL, LASTORDER, YTDORDERS
```

Save the values of these fields in memory variables with STORE commands:

```
STORE COMPANY TO MCOMPANY
STORE MAIL TO MMAIL
STORE LASTORDER TO MLASTORDER
STORE YTDORDERS TO MYTDORDERS
```

Calculate the length of time, in days, that National Widgets has been doing business with this customer by subtracting the FIRSTORDER date from the LASTORDER date, and store the result in a memory variable:

```
STORE LASTORDER - FIRSTORDER TO MDAYS
```

Create five numeric memory variables with the following commands:

```
NUMBER1 = 7
NUMBER2 = 365
STORE 25.128 TO NUMBER3, NUMBER4, NUMBER5
```

Calculate the number of weeks National Widgets has been dealing with Lewis and Associates by dividing MDAYS by NUMBER1, and store the result in another variable:

```
STORE MDAYS / NUMBER1 TO MWEEKS
```

Calculate the number of years by dividing MDAYS by NUMBER2, and store the result in a variable called MYEARS:

```
MYEARS = MDAYS / NUMBER2
```

Display all the active memory variables with

```
LIST MEMORY
```

Your screen should look like Figure 8-2. Note that for a numeric variable dBASE III PLUS shows you the value as displayed and as it is stored internally, which may include more significant digits. You can disregard the "pub" notation, which informs you that a variable is *public;* the distinction between public and *private* variables is meaningful only when you write dBASE III PLUS programs. Save the variables whose names begin with M in one memory file, and the variables that start with NUMBER in another:

```
SAVE ALL LIKE M* TO MEMFILE1
SAVE ALL LIKE NUMBER? TO MEMFILE2
```

Erase the values of all the variables from memory with a RELEASE command:

```
25.128
. STORE MDAYS/NUMBER1 TO MWEEKS
      170.57
. MYEARS=MDAYS/NUMBER2
        3.27
. DISPLAY MEMORY
MCOMPANY    pub   C  "Lewis and Associates
MMAIL       pub   L  .T.
MLASTORDER  pub   D  01/20/88
MYTDORDERS  pub   N          366.81 (        366.81000000)
MDAYS       pub   N         1194  (        1194.00000000)
NUMBER1     pub   N            7  (           7.00000000)
NUMBER2     pub   N          365  (         365.00000000)
NUMBER3     pub   N           25.128 (         25.12800000)
NUMBER4     pub   N           25.128 (         25.12800000)
NUMBER5     pub   N           25.128 (         25.12800000)
MWEEKS      pub   N          170.57 (        170.57142857)
MYEARS      pub   N            3.27 (          3.27123288)
   12 variables defined,        119 bytes used
  244 variables available,     5881 bytes available

.
Command Line   ||<C:>||NWCUST           ||Rec: 1/20        ||Ins   ||   Caps
          Type a command (or ASSIST) and press the ENTER key (←┘).
```

Figure 8-2 *Displaying the values of memory variables*

```
RELEASE ALL
```

If you wish, you can type LIST MEMORY to verify that no memory variables currently exist. Retrieve the variables in the MEMFILE1 file with a RESTORE command:

```
RESTORE FROM MEMFILE1
```

Use a LIST MEMORY command to view these variables, and then restore the remaining variables, adding them to those currently in memory, with

```
RESTORE FROM MEMFILE2 ADDITIVE
```

Again, you may want to type a LIST MEMORY command to confirm that all your variables have been successfully restored from the two memory variable files.

USING dBASE III PLUS OPERATORS

The concept of operators was briefly introduced in Chapter 6, which described the comparison or relational operators used to test the relationship between two values of the same data type. As noted earlier, these operators may be used with character strings, numbers, or dates; depending on the data type, "greater than" and "less than" refer to alphabetical, numerical, or chronological order. An expression that makes use of one of these operators to compare the values of two other expressions always evaluates to the logical value .T. (True) or .F. (False). Chapter 6 also introduced the logical operators .AND., .OR., and .NOT., which are used to link two logical expressions to yield another logical value.

dBASE III PLUS recognizes the four standard arithmetic operators— + (addition), − (subtraction), * (multiplication), and / (division)—as well as exponentiation (raising a number to a power), which is expressed as ^ or **. Note that the symbols used to represent these operators differ from the way the same operations are commonly written on paper. The X cannot be used to represent multiplication, because it could easily be confused with a field or memory variable named X, and the standard division symbol (÷) is missing from the IBM keyboard, although it can be displayed on the screen. The superscript notation generally used for exponentiation is inconvenient for most display screens and printers.

The mathematical operators can be applied to numerical data in the standard ways. The addition and subtraction symbols can also be used, with slightly different meanings, to operate on dates. You can subtract one date from another to yield the number of days elapsed between the two dates, and you can add a number (assumed to represent days) to a date or subtract a number from a date to obtain the calendar date the specified number of days in the future or past.

As described in Chapter 7, where several character fields were combined to form an index key, character strings can be added, or concatenated, with +, which places the beginning of the second string right at the end of the first. If you use the − operator instead, dBASE III PLUS moves all the trailing blanks in both strings to the end of the combined string, a process colorfully described in the original dBASE II manual as "string concatenation with blank squash."

The dBASE III PLUS operators and the types of data on which they operate are summarized in Table 8-1. Note that although many of the operators can be used with more than one type of data, not every combination is possible. For example, the + operator is applicable to character strings, numbers, and dates, but it cannot be used to add a number to a character string or to add two dates together. Attempting to combine data of different types in a way not permitted in the dBASE III PLUS language will result in the "Data type mismatch" error message.

USING dBASE III PLUS FUNCTIONS

A *function* is a specialized operator that adds to the dBASE III PLUS language the ability to perform calculations not possible using only the operators enumerated in the previous section. A function takes a certain kind of input and processes it in a specific way to yield a certain type of output. You can think of a function as a kind of machine that, when given the right raw materials (the input), can predictably crank out a particular product (the output).

For example, the SQRT function takes as its input a number (or numeric expression) and returns as output the square root of the number—a quantity that when multiplied by itself yields the original number. To use this function, you don't have to know how to calculate a square root (although you may once have learned a method for doing so), and you don't need to know how dBASE III PLUS does it. Just remember the name of the function and the type of input it requires.

To include a dBASE III PLUS function in an expression, you write the name of the function followed by a pair of parentheses that enclose the input(s). For example, to display the square root of the number 25, you could use

```
? SQRT(25)
```

Table 8-1 *dBASE III PLUS Operators*

Relational operators

Operator	Data types	Meaning
=	C, N, D	Equal to
<> or #	C, N, D	Not equal to
>	C, N, D	Greater than
>=	C, N, D	Greater than or equal to
<	C, N, D	Less than
<=	C, N, D	Less than or equal to
$	C	Contained within

Logical Operators

Operator	Data types	Value of resulting expression
.AND.	L	.T. if both expressions linked are .T.
.OR.	L	.T. if either expression linked is .T.
.NOT.	L	.T. if following expression is .F.

Mathematical Operators

Operator	Data types	Meaning
+	N	Addition
	C	Concatenation
	D + N	Adds specified number of days to date
−	N	Subtraction
	C	Concatenation, embedded blanks combined at end
	D − N	Subtracts specified number of days from date
	D − D	Elapsed time in days between dates
*	N	Multiplication
/	N	Division
^ or **	N	Exponentiation

If a function requires more than one input, the inputs must be listed (separated with commas, like any other dBASE III PLUS list) in the correct order within the parentheses. For example, the ROUND function, which rounds off a number to a specified number of decimal places, takes two inputs: the numeric value to be rounded off and the number of decimal places. You could use this function in a LIST command that displays the total orders for National Widgets' customers, rounded off to the nearest whole dollar, with the following:

```
LIST ACCOUNT, COMPANY, ROUND(TOTORDERS, 0)
```

Not all functions require that you provide input, but every function reference must include a pair of parentheses. For example, the DATE() function evaluates to the system date, and the DELETED( ) function evaluates to the logical value .T. if the current record in an open data base has been marked for deletion. Strictly speaking, DATE( ), DELETED( ), and other such functions do have input, although it is not supplied by you. DATE( ) takes its input from DOS, which obtains the date from a hardware clock or from the date you entered when you first booted your computer; and DELETED( ) examines the record at the position of the record pointer. The parentheses clearly identify DATE( ) and DELETED( ) as functions, so dBASE III PLUS can distinguish them from data base fields or memory variables of the same names. These functions may be used, like any others, in an expression or a condition. For example, you could display only the deleted records in a data base with the following command:

```
LIST FOR DELETED()
```

Although dBASE III PLUS does offer a number of mathematical functions, performing numerical calculations is not its strong point. Some of the most useful functions are those provided for manipulating character strings. For example, the TRIM function takes as input a character string—a field, a memory variable, or an expression that evaluates to a character string—and returns as output the same character string minus any trailing blank spaces. The expression TRIM(CITY) would thus yield "Berkeley" if the National Widgets Customer File were positioned at a record in which the CITY field contained the character string "Berkeley   ". As you will see in Chapter 9, this function enables you to combine data in separate fields—such as a first name and a last name; or a city, state, and ZIP code—into a more attractive display format.

The LEFT function extracts a portion of a character string, starting at the left side of the field and continuing for a specified number of positions. This function requires two inputs: the original string and the number of characters to be extracted. In Chapter 9 this function is used to print a portion of a long field so as to fit more columns into a crowded report.

The UPPER function converts a character string to all uppercase letters, and the corresponding LOWER function converts to lowercase. You can use these functions in conditions that compare the contents of a field entered in an inconsistent mixture of uppercase and lowercase letters to a constant value, or to convert a field in an index key to uppercase or lowercase and thus avoid the alphabetization problems described in Chapter 7.

As stated earlier, certain operators and functions work only with particular data types. To overcome some of these limitations, dBASE III PLUS provides a number of functions that convert data from one type to another. For example, although you can sort on up to ten fields of any mixture of data types, an index key must be a single expression. You can index on a single character, numeric, or date field to yield an index that accesses a data base in alphabetical, numerical, or chronological order, but to index on multiple fields of different data types, you must convert all the key fields to character strings and then concatenate them to form the key expression.

The DTOC (date-to-character) function converts a date to a character string that looks just like the date. To index the Customer File on the combination of state, city, and last order date, you would index on

```
CITY + DTOC(LASTORDER)
```

The STR function converts a number to a character string. This function has three inputs: the numeric expression to be converted, the length of the resulting string, and the number of decimal places to include. If you omit the length, the output string is ten characters long; if you omit the number of decimals, it is assumed to be zero. Another common application for data type conversion functions such as DTOC and STR is printing a character string prompt followed by the actual data. For example, you could print the following in a report:

```
"Year-to-Date Orders: " + STR(YTDORDERS, 10, 2)
```

In addition to the type conversion functions, dBASE III PLUS offers a full complement of functions for operating on dates. The DOW (day-of-week) function takes a date as input and returns a number corresponding to the day of the week (1 for Sunday, 2 for Monday, and so on). The DAY, MONTH, and YEAR functions extract the individual components of the date as numbers, and a parallel set of functions returns the names of the days and months. The CDOW (character-day-of-week) function yields a character string that spells out the name of the day (for example, "Sunday" or "Monday"), and CMONTH evaluates to the name of the month ("January", "February", and so on). Other important date functions are discussed in the upcoming section "Performing Date Calculations and Comparisons."

Remember that the expression consisting of a function name, the obligatory pair of parentheses, and its inputs (if any) is synonymous with the output of the function and may be used anywhere that an expression of that data type is permitted. For example, the LEFT function takes as input a character string and a number, and yields as output a character string, which can be LISTed, printed on a report, or used in an index key expression.

Among other things, this means that one function may serve as the input to another function. For example, the CDOW function takes a date as input and returns a character string as output. If the DATE() function—which evaluates to a true calendar date, the DOS system date—serves as the input to the CDOW function, the result is the name of the current day of the week. For example, on July 5, 1988, the expression CDOW(DATE()) would yield the character string "Tuesday".

The dBASE III PLUS language offers a wealth of functions for performing mathematical calculations, manipulating character strings and dates, transforming one data type to another, obtaining information about the data base in use in the selected work area, and determining what hardware and operating system software are present. Some of these functions are of interest to programmers, while others can be useful almost immediately. In the remaining chapters in this book, additional functions are presented as they are needed. You will find a complete list of dBASE III PLUS functions in Appendix C.

PRECEDENCE OF OPERATIONS

When dBASE III PLUS evaluates a complex expression, it does not proceed from left to right. Within an expression, dBASE III PLUS performs the indicated operations in the following order:

- Evaluation of functions
- Exponentiation
- Multiplication and division, from left to right
- Numeric addition and subtraction, from left to right
- Character string concatenation
- Evaluation of relational operators, from left to right
- Evaluation of logical operators, in the following order: .NOT., .AND., .OR.

A complex expression is scanned as many times as necessary to adhere to this *precedence* of operations. For example, consider a simple expression intended to calculate a customer's orders from prior years as a percent of the total orders. To perform this computation on a hand-held calculator, you would subtract the YTDORDERS field from TOTORDERS, divide the result by TOTORDERS, and multiply by 100 to convert the result to a percent. If YTDORDERS were 100.00 and TOTORDERS were 400.00, the result would be 75 percent. Your first inclination might be to write the corresponding dBASE III PLUS expression like this:

```
TOTORDERS - YTDORDERS / TOTORDERS * 100
```

Because all multiplication and division operations are carried out before any subtractions, this expression is evaluated by dividing YTDORDERS by TOTORDERS, multiplying this number by 100, and subtracting the result from TOTORDERS. Using the numbers cited in the previous paragraph, you would obtain the value 375.

To override the default order in which expressions are evaluated, you must use parentheses. Any expression containing parentheses is evaluated starting within the innermost set of parentheses and working outward. To force dBASE III PLUS to perform the order calculation correctly, you must add parentheses to the expression listed above as follows:

```
(TOTORDERS - YTDORDERS) / TOTORDERS * 100
```

Equally important is the fact that the logical operators .AND., .OR., and .NOT. are not evaluated strictly from left to right. Consider a condition you might use to select all customers whose invoices total more than $500 and who own either IBM or Compaq equipment:

```
LIST FOR ("IBM" $ UPPER(EQUIPMENT) .OR. "COMPAQ" $ UPPER(EQUIPMENT)
   .AND. TOTORDERS > 500
```

If the parentheses were omitted from this expression, the precedence of .AND. over .OR. would result in selecting all customers who own IBM equipment plus all Compaq owners with more than $500 in invoices.

HANDS-ON PRACTICE—CREATING COMPLEX EXPRESSIONS

Make sure that the National Widgets file is open, and position the record pointer on Record 2. Display the ACCOUNT field, followed by the company name, enclosed in parentheses, with the following expression:

```
? TRIM(ACCOUNT) + " (" + TRIM(COMPANY) + ")"
```

Display the company name and last order date for Lewis and Associates, based on the values stored in memory variables in the previous Hands-On Practice session:

```
? "Last Order Date for " + TRIM(MCOMPANY) + ": " + DTOC(MLASTORDER)
```

Display the year-to-date orders, last order date, and the number of years since the customer's first order with the following commands:

```
? "Year-to-date Orders: " + STR(YTDORDERS,10,2)
? "Last Order Date: " + DTOC(LASTORDER)
? "Years Since First Order: " + STR((DATE() - FIRSTORDER) / 365, 5, 2)
```

Note that in order to combine numeric or date fields with the character string prompts, you must use the STR and DTOC functions to convert these data types to character strings. In the last ? command, the parentheses surrounding the expression (DATE() − FIRSTORDER) are necessary so that dBASE III PLUS performs the subtraction before dividing by 365. In this example, the first input to the STR function is the numeric value that results from evaluating the expression (DATE() − FIRSTORDER) / 365.

Use the date display functions to convert the current date, expressed as the DATE() function, to *dd-Mmm-yyyy* format:

```
? STR(DAY(DATE()),2) + "-" + LEFT(CMONTH(DATE()),3) + "-" +
   STR(YEAR(DATE()),4)
```

In this last example, the DATE() function serves as input to the DAY, CMONTH, and YEAR functions, to yield the day of the month, the name of the month, and the four-digit year, respectively. The two numeric values are converted to character strings with the STR function, and the LEFT function is used to extract the first three characters of the month name. Finally, these components are combined with the dashes used as punctuation to form a single character string.

After typing these commands, your screen should look similar to Figure 8-3. Before you go on, you may want to experiment further with some of the other functions and operators described in this chapter.

PERFORMING DATE CALCULATIONS AND COMPARISONS

Working with dates in dBASE III PLUS is more complicated than manipulating character strings, numbers, and logical fields, partly because dBASE III PLUS does not provide a standard delimiter, or punctuation mark (analogous to the quotes used to identify character strings or the periods used to surround logical values) to identify a date as a date. This makes it more difficult to express an arbitrary date, such as January 1, 1988, for use in conditions and calculations.

```
. ? TRIM(ACCOUNT) + " (" + TRIM(COMPANY) + ")"
ABCPLUMB (ABC Plumbing)
. ? "Last Order Date for " + TRIM(MCOMPANY) + ": " + DTOC(MLASTORDER)
Last Order Date for Lewis and Associates: 01/20/88
. ? "Year-to-date Orders: " + STR(YTDORDERS,10,2)
Year-to-date Orders:      796.41
. ? "Last Order Date: " + DTOC(LASTORDER)
Last Order Date: 04/30/88
. ? "Years Since First Order: " + STR((DATE() - FIRSTORDER) / 365, 5, 2)
Years Since First Order:  1.52
. ? STR(DAY(DATE()),2) + "-" + LEFT(CMONTH(DATE()),3) + "-" + STR(YEAR(DATE()),4
)
10-Jun-1987
.
Command Line    ||<C:>||NWCUST           ||Rec: 2/20          ||Ins   ||   Caps

                     Enter a dBASE III PLUS command.
```

Figure 8-3 *Using functions and memory variables in complex expressions*

The only way to express a specific date is to use the CTOD (character-to-date) function, which converts a character string that looks like a date, such as 01/01/88, to a true date. For example, to list the customers whose most recent order was before January 1, 1988, you could use the following command:

```
LIST ACCOUNT, COMPANY, LASTORDER FOR LASTORDER < CTOD("01/01/88")
```

As mentioned earlier, you can index on a combination of character and date fields by converting date to a character string using the DTOC function. However, once you have converted a date to a character string, dBASE III PLUS no longer views it as a date, but simply as a sequence of digits and punctuation marks. If you index on a date in *mm/dd/yy* format that is converted to a character string with DTOC, this string is processed one character at a time, starting from the left. All the records with the same month are indexed in a group, within which they are grouped by day, and finally by year. Thus, any record in which the month is January will index before any record in February, regardless of the year.

To achieve true chronological order, you must choose an alternate display format for dates, one in which the year comes first, followed by the month, and then the day. dBASE III PLUS allows you to select six display formats for dates by using the SET DATE command:

SET DATE *date format*

The standard date format is called AMERICAN, and the *yy.mm.dd* format (which uses periods instead of slashes), is called ANSI. In ANSI format, the date January 10, 1988, would be displayed as

```
88.01.10
```

You can select the ANSI date format with

```
SET DATE ANSI
```

and return to the standard format with

```
SET DATE AMERICAN
```

If you do not object to entering and editing data using the ANSI date format, you can simply SET DATE ANSI for most of your work with dBASE III PLUS. If you prefer, you can continue to enter and edit dates in AMERICAN format and switch to ANSI format just to build an index for a particular purpose, such as printing a report. Because the SET DATE command controls only the display format for dates, not the way they are stored internally, it makes no difference which format is in effect when you enter data.

Whenever you update an index based on a date converted to a character string with the DTOC function, you must be careful not to mix ANSI and AMERICAN dates. If you object to the ANSI display format, it is safest to rebuild such an index immediately prior to printing the report that requires it, rather than always opening the index with the data base. Note that because the index controls the sequence in which records are processed, regardless of display format, you can SET DATE AMERICAN to print the report.

HANDS-ON PRACTICE—WORKING WITH DATES

Make sure that the Customer File is open, and LIST the customers who have placed orders since January 1, 1988, with the following command:

```
LIST ACCOUNT, COMPANY, LASTORDER, YTDORDERS FOR LASTORDER >= CTOD("01/01/88")
```

Look for customers for which either the first or last order date field is blank:

```
LIST ACCOUNT, COMPANY FOR DTOC(FIRSTORDER) = " " .OR. DTOC(LASTORDER) = " "
```

If you have entered all the sample data exactly as presented in this book, none of the records should pass this test.

Switch to the ANSI display format for dates and list the contents of the two date fields in the data base:

```
SET DATE ANSI
LIST ACCOUNT, CITY, FIRSTORDER, LASTORDER
```

Build an index that accesses the Customer File by city, and within each city by last order date:

```
INDEX ON CITY + DTOC(LASTORDER) TO NWCDATE
```

Retrieve the previous LIST command from HISTORY and repeat it to verify that the records are in fact grouped by CITY and arranged chronologically within each city. Then switch back to AMERICAN date format and repeat the LIST one more time to verify that the records are still displayed in the correct order, regardless of the date display format:

```
LIST ACCOUNT, CITY, FIRSTORDER, LASTORDER
SET DATE AMERICAN
LIST ACCOUNT, CITY, FIRSTORDER, LASTORDER
```

USING REPLACE TO CHANGE THE CONTENTS OF A DATA BASE FIELD

You already know how to individually change the contents of any field in any record in a data base by using the EDIT, CHANGE, and BROWSE commands. You can change data in more than one record at a time, without viewing the affected records, with the REPLACE command. The basic form of this command is

REPLACE *field* WITH *expression*

You can use any combination of scope, FOR, and WHILE clauses to specify the range of records to be processed. The *field* may be a character, numeric, logical, or date field (you cannot alter the contents of a memo field except by using the dBASE III PLUS memo editor), and the *expression* may be any legitimate dBASE III PLUS expression of the same data type. For example, in the National Widgets Customer File, you could zero out the YTDORDERS field at the end of each year to prepare to accumulate the new year-to-date total with

```
REPLACE ALL YTDORDERS WITH 0
```

If you had any doubt about whether the state abbreviations had all been entered consistently in uppercase letters, you could convert them to uppercase with

```
REPLACE ALL STATE WITH UPPER(STATE)
```

Notice that in this command the expression that specifies the new value for the STATE field includes a reference to the field itself. If this seems "circular" to you, consider the way that dBASE III PLUS executes the command: First it evaluates the expression following the keyword WITH—which can be made up of any combination of fields, constants, and memory variables—and then it substitutes the result into the named field, overwriting the previous value.

Recall that when dBASE III PLUS executes any command that can process an entire data base, it reads all the records defined by the scope and WHILE clauses, even if a FILTER or FOR clause narrows the range of records that are actually affected by the command. Thus, three consecutive REPLACE ALL commands will cause dBASE III PLUS to make three passes through the data base, and in a large file this can be very time-consuming.

One way to speed up this process is to REPLACE more than one field on each pass through the data base. The only restriction on the number of fields that you can change with a single REPLACE command is the limit on the length of any dBASE III PLUS command: 254 characters. The fields need not be of the same data type, and the new values can be the same or different, but you must name each field and its replacement value explicitly, even if some are the same. For example, you could convert the ACCOUNT and STATE fields to uppercase letters and zero the year-to-date and total orders fields with the following:

```
REPLACE ALL ACCOUNT WITH UPPER(ACCOUNT), STATE WITH UPPER(STATE),
  YTDORDERS WITH 0, TOTORDERS WITH 0
```

Note that the scope, FOR, and WHILE clauses always determine which records are acted on by an entire command. You cannot apply different selection criteria to separate field replacements executed with a single REPLACE command.

Another way to facilitate the operation of the REPLACE command is by the strategic use of indexes. As was pointed out in Chapter 7, the most efficient way to limit processing to a set of records grouped together in indexed order is to use a SEEK command to position the record pointer on the first record in the group, and then use a WHILE clause to express the selection criteria so that dBASE III PLUS stops reading records as soon as the pointer advances beyond the last record in the group.

If your selection criteria do not depend on an index key and the scope of a command is ALL, processing is faster with no indexes open. When dBASE III PLUS reads through a file in indexed order, it must alternately read data from two files: the data base and the index. Because consecutive index entries may refer to records that are widely separated on the disk, finding the "next" record can involve moving the disk drive head further.

You can also gain speed by processing a file in sequential order when the selection criteria are based on the position of the records in the data base. For example, the fastest way to replace the first order date with the current date in "new" customer records is to position the record pointer on the first new record and include the REST scope in the REPLACE command:

```
REPLACE REST FIRSTORDER WITH DATE()
```

This command will work correctly only if all new entries are grouped at the end of the file. If you are not sure where the new records begin, you can position the record pointer anywhere prior to the first new entry and combine the REST scope with a FOR clause that selects the desired records. In this example, you could test for a blank first order date by using the DTOC function to convert the date to a character string and checking the first character of the resulting string (any nonblank date will have either a zero or a 1 in the first position):

```
REPLACE REST FIRSTORDER WITH DATE() FOR DTOC(FIRSTORDER) = " "
```

This strategy may select too many records if there are longstanding customers whose first order date was never recorded. This detailed example illustrates an important point about working with potentially destructive commands. Whenever possible, verify that your expressions are correct and that your scope, FOR, and WHILE clauses select the right group of records by using a LIST command before you carry out a more dangerous REPLACE or DELETE that affects many records. For example, you could use the following command to display the present values of the fields that would be affected by the REPLACE command in the previous example:

```
LIST REST ACCOUNT, COMPANY, FIRSTORDER, LASTORDER FOR DTOC(FIRSTORDER) = " "
```

From the resulting list, you might see that some of the records in which the FIRSTORDER field is blank have very low record numbers (indicating that they were not entered recently) or have a later date in the LASTORDER field.

You must also process a file in sequential order if you want to REPLACE an index key field. Suppose, for example, that you wanted to change all state abbreviations for California customers to uppercase letters. You might try to do this by opening the Customer File with the state/city/account index, positioning the record pointer on the first California record with a SEEK command, and then, knowing that "CA" comes before "Ca" in indexed order, using the following:

```
REPLACE STATE WITH "CA" WHILE STATE = "Ca"
```

This strategy will fail because whenever an index key field is changed (by REPLACE, EDIT, or any other command), the entry for that record is moved immediately to its new position in the index. With an index open, dBASE III PLUS interprets the "next" record as the one corresponding to the next index entry. When the STATE field is changed from "Ca" to "CA", the index entry moves to join the other "CA" records. Thus, the "next" record will not have "Ca" in the STATE field, and processing will stop. To REPLACE the contents of an index key field, you must therefore close the index, process the file in record number order, and then rebuild the index.

USING SUM, COUNT, AND AVERAGE TO COMPILE STATISTICS

Earlier in this chapter, methods were described for displaying calculated values with the LIST, DISPLAY, and ? commands, which do not save the results, and for storing a computed value in a data base with REPLACE. You can also compile statistics based on all or selected records in a data base without altering the field contents, by using the SUM, AVERAGE, and COUNT commands.

The SUM and AVERAGE commands can compute statistics for any numeric fields or expressions for the range of records selected by any combination of a FILTER, a scope, a FOR clause, and a WHILE clause. If you need to accumulate more than one SUM or AVERAGE, you can speed processing by including up to 32 separate expressions in a single command rather than making multiple passes through the data base. As with REPLACE, the same record selection criteria must apply to all calculations. For example, you could add up the total year-to-date and overall orders for National Widgets' San Francisco customers with

```
SUM YTDORDERS, TOTORDERS FOR CITY = "San Francisco"
```

You could obtain the average values of the same fields with

```
AVERAGE YTDORDERS, TOTORDERS FOR CITY = "San Francisco"
```

If you do not include an explicit list of expressions in a SUM or AVERAGE command, all numeric fields will be processed. Keep in mind that you are not limited to computing the sums and averages of single data base fields. A SUM or AVERAGE command can operate on any expression that evaluates to a number. Thus, although you cannot calculate an "average date," you can determine the average elapsed time between two dates, which is a true numeric value (a number of days). For example, National Widgets could calculate the average length of time it has done business with its San Francisco customers together with the average year-to-date and total orders with:

```
AVERAGE YTDORDERS, TOTORDERS, DATE() - FIRSTORDER FOR CITY = "San Francisco"
```

The COUNT command returns the number of records that satisfy selection criteria that you establish, as with any other command, by using any combination of a FILTER, a scope, a FOR clause, and a WHILE clause. For example, you could determine how many customers in San Francisco have placed an order during the current year with:

```
COUNT FOR CITY = "San Francisco" .AND. YTDORDERS > 0
```

The COUNT, SUM, and AVERAGE commands read through the selected records, compile the specified statistics, and display the results without storing them in any form. The appearance of the screen after executing the four previous commands is illustrated in Figure 8-4. Unless you have SET HEADING OFF, the statistics are identified by the usual field name labels. If you need access to the values after subsequent commands have scrolled the statistics off the top of the screen, you can use the PRTSC key to produce a hard copy.

You can also save the calculated results in memory variables so you can redisplay them at will and make them available for use in further calculations. To do this, you name the memory variables that will contain the sums, counts, or averages; for example:

```
AVERAGE YTDORDERS, TOTORDERS, DATE() - FIRSTORDER TO MYTDORD, MTOTORD, MDAYS
  FOR CITY = "San Francisco"
```

HANDS-ON PRACTICE—REPLACING FIELDS AND PERFORMING CALCULATIONS

Make sure that the Customer File is open with no indexes, and convert all the entries in the ACCOUNT and STATE fields to uppercase letters with a REPLACE command:

```
REPLACE ALL ACCOUNT WITH UPPER(ACCOUNT), STATE WITH UPPER(STATE)
```

Note that the message "21 record(s) replaced," shows you that the replacement was conducted for all records in the file, regardless of whether the fields already contained uppercase characters.

Open the NWCDATE index created in the previous Hands-On Practice session to access the Customer File in order by city and last order date, and find the first San Francisco record with a SEEK command:

```
SEEK "San Francisco"
```

Change the value of the MAIL field to .F. (False) for all San Francisco customers who have placed an order on or after December 1, 1987, so that they are not included in the next promotional mailing:

```
REPLACE MAIL WITH .F. FOR LASTORDER >= CTOD("12/01/87")
  WHILE CITY = "San Francisco"
```

```
. SUM YTDORDERS, TOTORDERS FOR CITY = "San Francisco"
     4 records summed
   YTDORDERS      TOTORDERS
      348.52        1887.95
. AVERAGE YTDORDERS, TOTORDERS FOR CITY = "San Francisco"
     4 records averaged
 YTDORDERS  TOTORDERS
     87.13     471.99
. AVERAGE YTDORDERS, TOTORDERS, DATE() - FIRSTORDER FOR CITY = "San Francisco"
     4 records averaged
 YTDORDERS  TOTORDERS  DATE() - FIRSTORDER
     87.13     471.99                  178
. COUNT FOR CITY = "San Francisco" .AND. YTDORDERS > 0
     1 record
.
Command Line    ||<C:>||NWCUST         ||Rec: EOF/20       ||Ins    ||    Caps
                      Enter a dBASE III PLUS command.
```

Figure 8-4 *Using the SUM, AVERAGE, and COUNT commands*

In this command, the WHILE clause makes dBASE III PLUS stop reading records as soon as it encounters the last San Francisco customer. Within this group of records, only those in which the date field LASTORDER is later than the arbitrary date expressed using the DTOC function will be affected. Note that the index NWCDATE.NDX was built using the ANSI date format, but currently the date display format is AMERICAN. This command does not depend on processing records in chronological order. Regardless of the display format, dBASE III PLUS can always determine which of two dates is greater (later). If your file matches the sample data, the MAIL field should be replaced in three records.

Close the index to return to processing records in the order of entry, and use a SUM command to compute the year-to-date and total orders for all of National Widgets' customers, and save the results in two memory variables:

```
SET INDEX TO
SUM YTDORDERS, TOTORDERS TO MYTD, MTOTAL
```

Note that SUM TO MYTD, MTOTAL would have produced exactly the same results, since these are the only two numeric fields in the structure.

Open the account code index, and display the percentage of the total represented by each customer who has placed an order this year by comparing the data base field values to the memory variables:

```
SET INDEX TO NWCACCT
LIST OFF ACCOUNT, COMPANY, YTDORDERS, YTDORDERS/MYTD*100, TOTORDERS,
  TOTORDERS/MTOTAL*100 FOR YTDORDERS > 0
```

Your screen should look like the one shown in Figure 8-5.

The commands in this chapter illustrate one of the strong points of dBASE III PLUS: the power and flexibility it offers for carrying out ad hoc queries into a data base when you type commands at the dot prompt. The query process is fast and immediate because it requires little prior preparation. For repeated inquiries, you can add convenience and improve your efficiency by using indexes, FILTERs, and QUERY files.

```
. SUM YTDORDERS, TOTORDERS TO MYTD, MTOTAL
     20 records summed
   YTDORDERS     TOTORDERS
     2760.50      16553.52

.
. LIST OFF ACCOUNT, YTDORDERS, YTDORDERS/MYTD*100, TOTORDERS, TOTORDERS/MTOTAL*1
00 FOR YTDORDERS > 0
 ACCOUNT      YTDORDERS  YTDORDERS/MYTD*100  TOTORDERS  TOTORDERS/MTOTAL*100
 ABCPLUMB        796.41               28.85    5248.90                 31.71
 HOMEMOVIES      248.15                8.99     248.15                  1.50
 KELLY            87.35                3.16      87.35                  0.53
 LEWIS           366.81               13.29    2482.48                 15.00
 MTK             108.59                3.93     423.92                  2.56
 RAPIDTYPE       348.52               12.63     348.52                  2.11
 SHAPEUP         435.42               15.77     867.38                  5.24
 WHITNEY         201.87                7.31    1384.45                  8.36
 YORKPUMP        167.38                6.06     608.42                  3.68

.
Command Line   |<C:>|NWCUST              |Rec: EOF/20      |Ins |   Caps

                     Enter a dBASE III PLUS command.
```

Figure 8-5 Displaying the Customer File percentages

This chapter also introduces the elements of dBASE III PLUS syntax, such as operators and functions, and describes the rules by which they can be combined into complex expressions and conditions. Some of the most useful applications are illustrated in the examples, yet the commands presented here barely scratch the surface. As you work with dBASE III PLUS, try to review these command components periodically, particularly the list of available functions in Appendix C, to make sure that you do not overlook features that might be useful to you.

Chapter 9

Printing Reports and Labels

You have already seen that dBASE III PLUS allows you to echo to the printer the screen output of a LIST or DISPLAY command by including the phrase TO PRINT in the command. Commands such as LIST STRUCTURE TO PRINT and LIST STATUS TO PRINT are especially useful for documenting file structures, index keys, and the status of the working environment for future reference. Using LIST TO PRINT and DISPLAY TO PRINT are also the fastest, most immediate ways to produce a quick printout of the contents of selected fields from selected records in a data base in a clear and readable format.

dBASE III PLUS also provides menu-driven editors, similar to the QUERY editor described in Chapter 6, which enable you to define standard formats for printing mailing labels and columnar reports. These predefined formats, which include a description of the page layout and the data to be printed, are stored on disk for repeated use. By using report and label forms, you can reprint the same report or set of labels without having to repeat the definition steps. You can reuse the same basic page layout to print data from different sets of records, based on different FILTERS and FOR clauses, and to reflect changes made in the course of daily updates and file maintenance operations. By sorting or indexing the data base, you can print records in different orders and define additional selection criteria based on WHILE clauses.

Using report and label forms differs in two important ways from using LIST TO PRINT to produce "quick and dirty" printed listings. Separating the definition and printing steps enables you to create detailed report instructions, including page numbers, page and column headings, and the accumulation of up to two levels of subtotals. Report forms are useful for producing attractively formatted reports in standard layouts that are easily interpreted by people who are unfamiliar with dBASE III PLUS or even unfamiliar with computers. The LIST command, which requires no prior preparation and yields output instantly, is more appropriate for constantly changing, ad hoc inquiries and calculations in which the content of the display is more important than its appearance.

USING CREATE/MODIFY LABEL TO DEFINE AND EDIT LABEL FORMS

To define a mailing label format, you use the full-screen label form editor, which is invoked by typing

```
CREATE LABEL
```

or

```
MODIFY LABEL
```

As with the other full-screen editors that create stored formats, you can use the CREATE and MODIFY variations interchangeably, regardless of whether you are defining a new format or editing an existing one. If you wish, you can include the name of the label form in the command:

CREATE LABEL *label form name*

If you do not enter a file name, dBASE III PLUS will prompt you to enter it with the message "Enter label file name:".

Since a label form draws heavily (although not exclusively) on information stored in a data base, dBASE III PLUS requires that a data base be open when you create or edit a label form. If there isn't a data base open when you invoke the label form editor, you will be prompted to enter a file name with the message "No database is in USE. Enter file name:".

Although you can name a data base at this point, you cannot also specify an index file. Although you may wish to open an index before you actually print labels, the index does not have to be open while you define the label form, since the label form itself contains no instructions about the sequence in which records should be printed. At various times, you might use the same label form to print records in different orders by opening different indexes, or in record number order by opening the data base with no index.

The label form editor has two pull-down menus. The **Options** submenu enables you to define the page layout and label dimensions, and the **Contents** submenu is used to specify the data to print on each line of the label. The initial screen presented by the label form editor, which displays the contents of the **Options** submenu, is illustrated in Figure 9-1. The cursor movement and editing commands are displayed in a help menu above the Status Bar. You can turn off this menu by pressing F1, but since this does not make room for displaying any additional information on the screen, there is little advantage to doing so.

When you select the **Options** submenu, the **Predefined size** option is highlighted, and the Message Line at the bottom of the screen reminds you that you can "Select a standard label size". There are five predefined label layouts, each of which is described in terms of the width and height of a label in inches and the number of labels across the page. Associated with each predefined size is a set of dimensions that define the page layout: the width and height of each label, the left page margin, the number of lines printed (vertically) between consecutive rows of labels and spaces printed (horizontally) between adjacent labels, and the number of labels across the page.

The predefined sizes and the corresponding label specifications are listed in Table 9-1, along with the range of permissible values that each parameter may take on. The relationship between these parameters and the resulting printed labels is illustrated in Figure 9-2.

Except in the brief descriptions that identify the predefined formats,

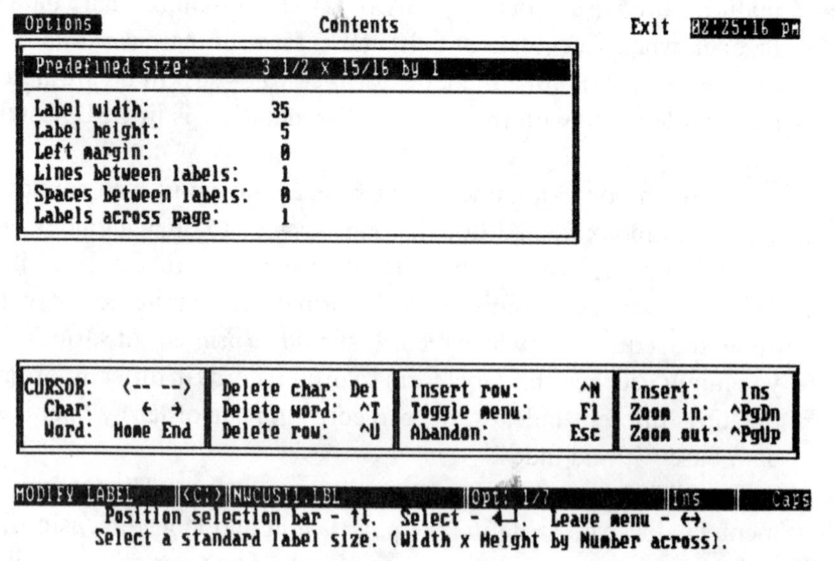

Figure 9-1 *The initial screen presented by the label form editor*

all label dimensions are defined in units of *printer movement,* not inches. The left margin, the label width, and the number of spaces between labels (if you are printing more than one across) are specified in *characters,* and the number of lines per label and lines between labels are in *lines.* The predefined sizes assume that you are printing at 10 characters per inch (cpi) horizontally and 6 lines per inch (lpi) vertically, which are the default settings on most printers.

It is entirely up to you to match the values you enter for these settings to the character pitch and line spacing you plan to use for printing labels. For example, if your labels are 4 inches wide and 1 inch deep, you must define the width of a label as 40 (characters) and the height as 6 (lines) to print at 10 cpi, 6 lpi. To print in a "compressed" mode at 16 cpi, with a vertical line spacing of 8 lpi, you would define the same label as 64 characters wide and 8 lines high.

In the **Options** submenu of the label form editor, you may step through the standard label layouts by pressing ENTER with the

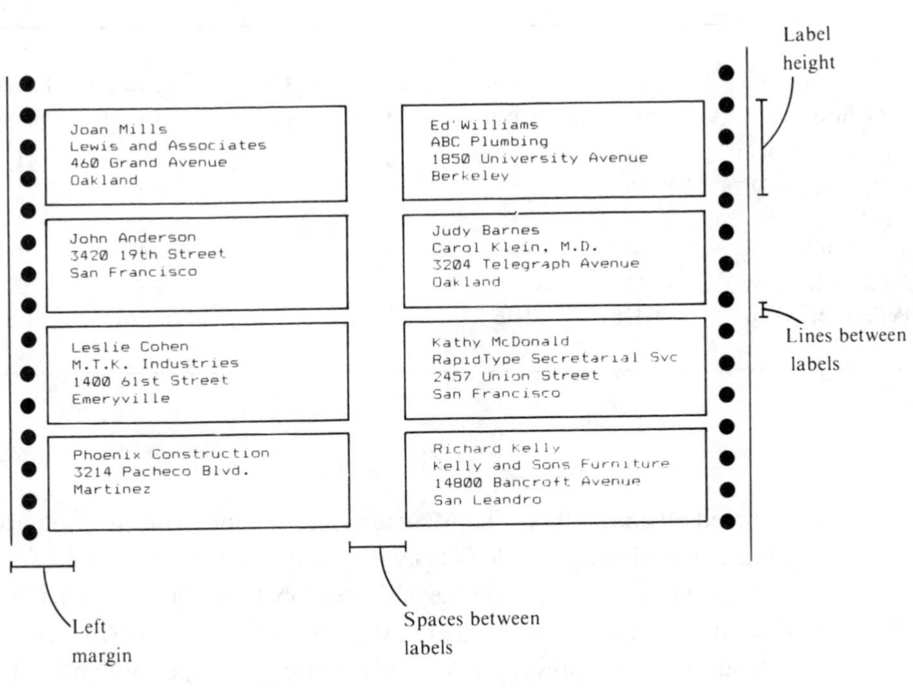

Figure 9-2 *The label page layout settings*

Predefined size option selected. If none of these formats suits your purpose, you can choose the closest match and change any or all individual parameters to conform to the spacing of your labels. To change a setting, you highlight the appropriate option, press ENTER, and then either type in the new value or use the UP ARROW or DOWN ARROW key to increase or decrease the numeric value displayed one unit at a time.

After you have defined the basic page layout, you specify the contents of each line on the label through the **Contents** submenu. This menu displays a pull-down menu box containing a series of numbered lines. The total number of lines corresponds to the value of the **Label height** setting established through the **Options** submenu.

The contents of a label line may consist of a *list* of legitimate dBASE III PLUS *expressions* of any data types. Although in most contexts dBASE III PLUS permits expressions up to 254 characters long, the length of the expression list that specifies the contents of a label line may

Table 9-1 *Predefined Label Sizes*

Predefined size	Label width	Label height	Left margin	Lines between	Spaces between	Labels across
3 1/2 x 15/16 by 1	35	5	0	1	0	1
3 1/2 x 15/16 by 2	35	5	0	1	2	2
3 1/2 x 15/16 by 2	35	5	0	1	2	3
4 x 1 7/16 by 1	40	8	0	1	0	1
3 2/10 x 11/12 by 3	32	5	0	1	2	3
Permissible range	1-120	1-16	1-120	0-16	0-120	1-5

not exceed 60 characters. The Message Line reminds you that you are not limited to printing single fields with the message "Enter a field/expression list to be displayed on the indicated label line". The lines may be entered in any order; just use the UP ARROW and DOWN ARROW keys to highlight a line, and press ENTER to select it. As you type your entry, the screen will scroll to permit an expression or list longer than the width of the menu box.

While you are entering or editing a label line, you can press F10 at any time to pop up a box containing a list of field names from the data base in use. As you use the arrow keys to move through this list, another pop-up window displays the data type, field width, and number of decimals, as illustrated in Figure 9-3. When you press ENTER, the highlighted field is entered into your expression list at the cursor position. You can construct an expression list using any combination of typing and selecting fields from the menu, and when the list is complete, you press ENTER to finish defining the label line.

If you specify more than one expression to be printed on a line, the items in the list are printed with trailing blanks removed, and with one blank space separating each pair. This often gives you exactly the output you want. For example, you could combine a first name and a last name stored in separate fields to print the full name on a mailing label. Listing the fields separately also permits you to print several fields of different data types on one line without having to convert all fields to character strings and combine them into a single string. In other cases, a list will work but is less than ideal. For example, to print the CITY, STATE, and ZIP fields from the National Widgets Customer File on one line on a mailing label, you could enter the contents of the line as

```
CITY, STATE, ZIP
```

This command would produce the following output on the label for John Anderson:

```
San Francisco CA 94114
```

Although this is perfectly legible, you might prefer to print these fields in a standard format:

```
San Francisco, CA  94114
```

To achieve this result, you can combine the three fields into a single expression by removing the trailing blanks from the CITY field with the TRIM function and adding two character string constants to separate

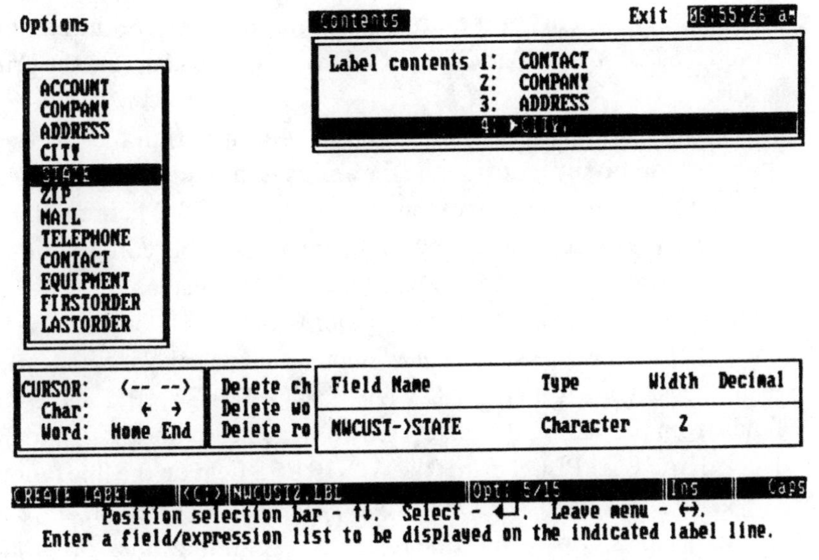

Figure 9-3 Selecting a field name from a list

the fields: one containing the comma and the blank space that follow the CITY field and another consisting of two blank spaces printed between the state and ZIP fields:

```
TRIM(CITY) + ", " + STATE + "  " + ZIP
```

You save a label form by selecting the **Save** option from the **Exit** submenu. The form is saved on disk in a file with the extension LBL, which identifies it as a label form.

DISPLAYING AND PRINTING LABELS

You can display and print labels with the LABEL FORM command:

LABEL FORM *label form name*

Labels are always displayed on the screen as dBASE III PLUS processes the file. If the total line width is more than 80 characters, each line of output will wrap around to two or more screen lines, making the display somewhat less readable. You can add the phrase TO PRINT to direct the output to the printer as well as to the screen. You might want to view at least part of the label run on the screen to verify that you have correctly specified the contents of the label lines, and then retrieve the command from HISTORY to add the TO PRINT phrase and generate the printed labels.

You can control the order in which records are printed by sorting or, more commonly, by indexing the file and making sure that the appropriate index is open when you execute the LABEL FORM command. You can specify selection criteria by using any reasonable combination of a FILTER, a scope, a FOR clause, and a WHILE clause.

dBASE III PLUS automatically suppresses blank lines resulting from empty fields (or expressions that evaluate to strings of blank spaces). For example, if you print the CONTACT, COMPANY, and ADDRESS fields from the National Widgets Customer File on lines 1, 2, and 3 of a label, dBASE III PLUS prints the ADDRESS field on the line following the CONTACT field if COMPANY is blank. As a result, if you are printing labels two or more across, corresponding lines on adjacent labels may contain different data, but this is generally not a problem.

Because of the range of label sizes permitted by dBASE III PLUS, you can use "label forms" to produce many printed formats besides mailing labels. For example, you could print the contents of a data base (not necessarily a name and address list) on continuous-form index cards or Rolodex cards, or print two- or three-across "labels" on plain paper to serve as a reference list. These applications are limited by three factors: the maximum height of a label (16 lines, plus 16 lines between labels), the fact that you cannot deliberately include blank lines to improve the appearance and readability of the printout, and the lack of a command for pausing between records to print on single cards, envelopes, or sheets of paper.

HANDS-ON PRACTICE—PRINTING MAILING LABELS

Make sure that the National Widgets Customer File is open, and invoke the label form editor by typing

```
CREATE LABEL NWCUST1
```

Starting with the default predefined label size, 3 1/2 by 15/16 by 1, define the page layout for printing on mailing labels that are four inches wide and one inch high. Note that "15/16" refers to the actual measurement of the label; with 1/16 inch between labels, the distance from the top of one label to the top of the next is one inch, or six lines. Change all the necessary parameters so that your screen matches Figure 9-4.

Next, select the **Contents** submenu to define the contents of the four lines of data on the label. Note that you can also produce the correct vertical spacing by entering the **Label height** as six lines and the **Lines between labels** as zero (or five and one, respectively).

Select each label line from the **Contents** submenu, and define the four lines of data as follows, either by choosing fields from the list invoked by pressing F10 or by typing the expressions yourself:

```
1:  IIF(CONTACT <> " ", "ATTN: " + CONTACT, " ")
2:  COMPANY
3:  ADDRESS
4:  TRIM(CITY) + ", " + STATE + ZIP
```

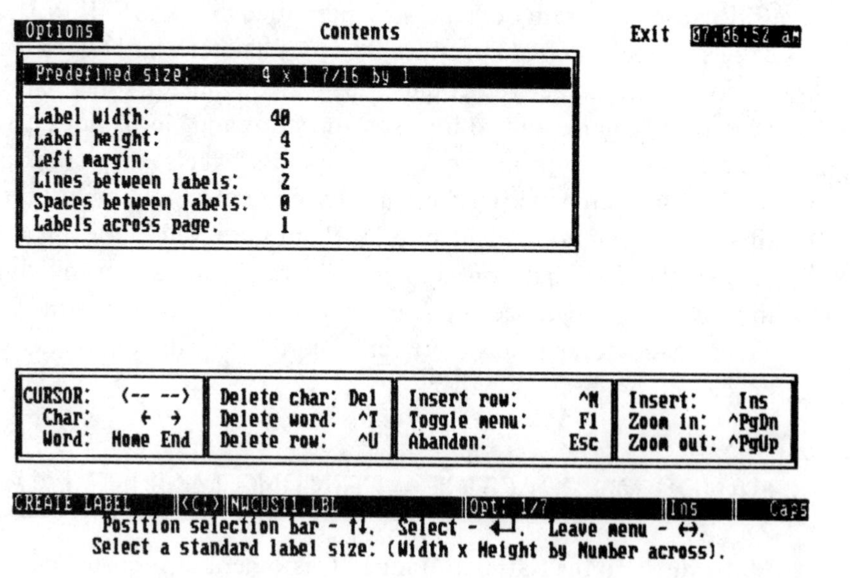

Figure 9-4 *The specifications for printing one-up labels from the Customer File*

The expression on the first line of the label uses the IIF function to test the value of the CONTACT field. If the condition is true—that is, the CONTACT field is not blank, the text "ATTN: ", followed by the CONTACT name, is printed. If the condition is false, the IIF function evaluates to a blank space, and dBASE III PLUS suppresses the blank line. If you had specified the contents of line 1 as "ATTN: " + CONTACT, this expression could never be blank, and the text "ATTN: " would be printed by itself on the label if the CONTACT field were blank.

The expression on line 4 combines five separate character strings into one expression:

- The result of operating on the CITY field with the TRIM function to remove trailing blanks
- A character string consisting of a comma and a blank space
- The STATE field
- A character string consisting of two blank spaces
- The ZIP field

Save the label form by selecting the **Save** option from the **Exit** submenu.

Open the ZIP code index for the Customer File and display the labels on the screen by typing

```
SET INDEX TO NWCZIP
LABEL FORM NWCUST1
```

You want to print labels for those customers in Berkeley, Oakland, and Emeryville whose total orders amount to $400 or greater and who have .T. in the MAIL field. The desired geographical area is bounded by the ZIP code range 94600 to 94799. First, position the record pointer on the first record in this region:

```
SEEK "946"
```

Then, print labels using a WHILE clause that makes dBASE III PLUS stop reading records at the end of the ZIP code range, and a FOR clause that selects only those customers that match the other two criteria:

```
LABEL FORM NWCUST1 WHILE ZIP <= "94799" FOR TOTORDERS >= 500 .AND. MAIL
```

If you have a printer, you can add the phrase TO PRINT to send the output to the printer as well as to the screen. If you have entered all the sample data, the resulting printout should look like Figure 9-5.

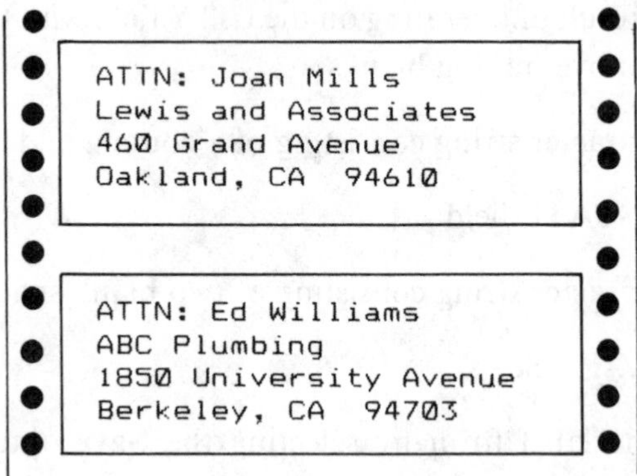

Figure 9-5 *Printing labels for customers in Oakland and Berkeley who have more than $400 in orders*

USING CREATE/MODIFY REPORT TO DEFINE AND EDIT REPORT FORMS

The dBASE III PLUS report generator provides for printing columnar reports with optional column totals and up to two levels of subtotals on numeric fields. You define report forms much the same way as label forms, using a similar full-screen editor invoked with

```
CREATE REPORT
```

or

```
MODIFY REPORT
```

As with any of the full-screen editors, you can use the CREATE and MODIFY variations interchangeably, and you may include the name of the report form in the command that invokes the editor:

CREATE REPORT *report form name*

If you do not enter the report file name, you will be prompted for it with the message, "Enter label file name:". If you have not already opened a data base, you will be prompted to enter the file name with "No database is in USE. Enter file name:".

The report form editor functions much like the label form editor, but because reports may vary more than mailing labels, there are more submenus and options. The initial screen displayed by the report editor is illustrated in Figure 9-6, and the structure of the menus is diagrammed in Figure 9-7. When you enter the report editor, the region above the Status Bar is occupied by a menu of cursor movement and editing commands that alternates with a diagram of the report layout; you can switch between the two at any time by pressing F1.

As with the label form editor, you define the basic page layout of a report by using the **Options** submenu, and specify the contents of the individual columns on a report (which are analogous to the lines on a mailing label) through the **Columns** submenu. You can also use the **Groups** submenu to request one or two levels of subtotals and enter a heading that introduces each group of records.

DEFINING THE PAGE LAYOUT

Figure 9-8 illustrates a simple report based on the National Widgets Customer File, with the page layout parameters indicated on the printout. When you first enter the editor to create a new report form, you will see the default page layout options displayed in the **Options** submenu box; you can select, in any order, the options whose values you want to change. The options, their purposes, and the default settings are as follows:

- **Page title:** Up to four lines of 60 characters each, which will be

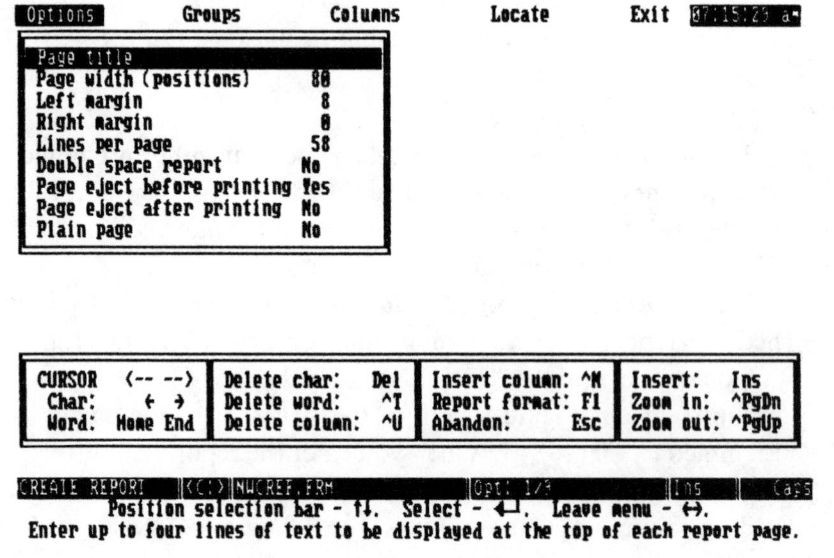

Figure 9-6 *The initial screen displayed by the report editor*

printed centered in the space between the left and right margins at the top of each page of the report

- **Page width (positions):** The total width of the page, expressed in characters, including the left and right margins. Permissible values range from 1 to 500 characters.

- **Left margin:** The width in characters of the blank space at the left side of the page.

- **Right margin:** The width in characters of the blank space at the right side of the page. The left and right margins should be set to approximately the same value, because they are used to center the page title lines.

Options

Page title
Page width (positions)
Left margin
Right margin
Lines per page
Double space report
Page eject before printing
Page eject after printing
Plain page

Groups

Group on expression
Group heading
Summary report only
Page eject after group
Sub-group on expression
Sub-group heading

Columns

Contents
Heading
Width
Decimal places
Total this column

Locate

Exit

Save
Abandon

Figure 9-7 *The structure of the report editor menus*

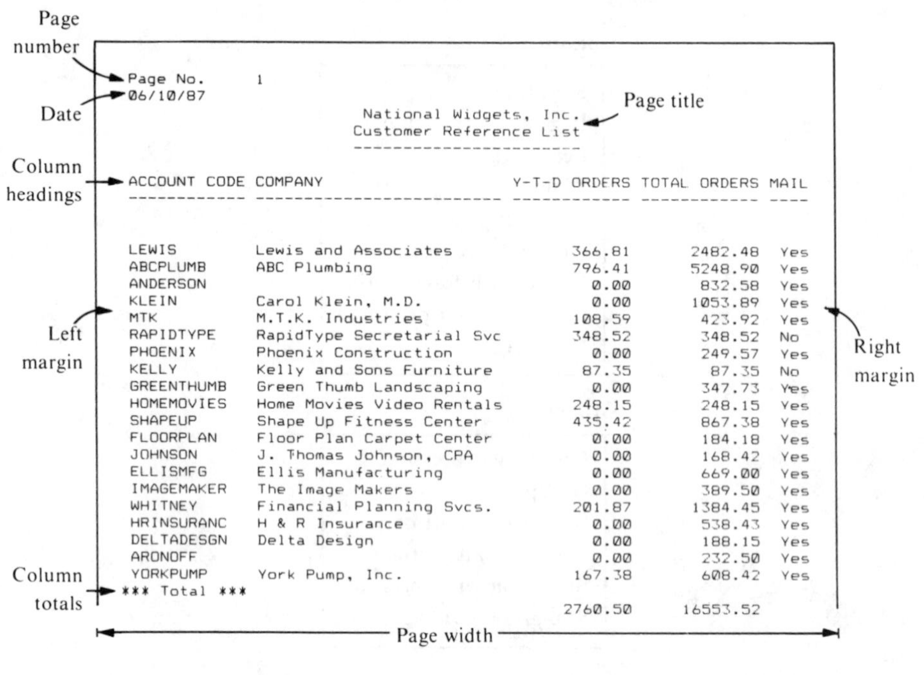

Page No. 1
06/10/87

National Widgets, Inc.
Customer Reference List

ACCOUNT CODE	COMPANY	Y-T-D ORDERS	TOTAL ORDERS	MAIL
LEWIS	Lewis and Associates	366.81	2482.48	Yes
ABCPLUMB	ABC Plumbing	796.41	5248.90	Yes
ANDERSON		0.00	832.58	Yes
KLEIN	Carol Klein, M.D.	0.00	1053.89	Yes
MTK	M.T.K. Industries	108.59	423.92	Yes
RAPIDTYPE	RapidType Secretarial Svc	348.52	348.52	No
PHOENIX	Phoenix Construction	0.00	249.57	Yes
KELLY	Kelly and Sons Furniture	87.35	87.35	No
GREENTHUMB	Green Thumb Landscaping	0.00	347.73	Yes
HOMEMOVIES	Home Movies Video Rentals	248.15	248.15	Yes
SHAPEUP	Shape Up Fitness Center	435.42	867.38	Yes
FLOORPLAN	Floor Plan Carpet Center	0.00	184.18	Yes
JOHNSON	J. Thomas Johnson, CPA	0.00	168.42	Yes
ELLISMFG	Ellis Manufacturing	0.00	669.00	Yes
IMAGEMAKER	The Image Makers	0.00	389.50	Yes
WHITNEY	Financial Planning Svcs.	201.87	1384.45	Yes
HRINSURANC	H & R Insurance	0.00	538.43	Yes
DELTADESGN	Delta Design	0.00	188.15	Yes
ARONOFF		0.00	232.50	Yes
YORKPUMP	York Pump, Inc.	167.38	608.42	Yes
*** Total ***				
		2760.50	16553.52	

Figure 9-8 *The report page layout*

- **Lines per page:** The total number of lines to be printed on a page, including lines used for page titles and column headings. Permissible values range from 1 to 500 lines.

- **Double space report:** Whether or not a blank line should be printed between records.

- **Page eject before printing:** Whether or not a page eject command should be sent to the printer before beginning to print a report.

- **Page eject after printing:** Whether or not a page eject command should be sent to the printer after printing a report.

- **Plain Page:** Whether or not the page number, date, page title, and column headings should be printed on each page of a report. Choosing "Yes" suppresses the page number and date and causes dBASE III PLUS to print the headings on the first page of the report only.

When you select an option that permits a long, variable entry, such as **Page title**, a box pops up on the screen into which you type your text. For numeric entries, you can either type a new value next to the prompt or use the UP ARROW or DOWN ARROW key to increase or decrease the displayed value one unit at a time. For the options that permit only "Yes" or "No" settings, you can toggle between the two alternatives by pressing ENTER.

As with labels, dBASE III PLUS largely leaves it up to you to ensure that your page layout is appropriate to the physical dimensions of the paper (or display screen, if you intend to view the report on the screen) and the horizontal and vertical spacing used by your printer. The page width depends on the actual width of the paper in inches as well as horizontal spacing (the number of characters per inch). The number of lines per page depends on the length of the page in inches and the number of lines per inch printed.

The report editor verifies that the total space allocated to the left and right margins does not exceed the page width, and it does not permit the sum of the individual column widths to exceed the total report width. But if the report is too wide for the physical page, the data will wrap around onto multiple lines with no warning. Similarly, dBASE III PLUS prints the number of lines specified in the **Lines per page** option and then sends a page eject command to the printer. It is up to you to ensure that the number of lines is appropriate to the combination of physical page length and vertical spacing, and to position the paper in the printer a few lines down from the top of the page to create a "top margin."

dBASE III PLUS does not formally provide for accessing any of your printer's special fonts or attributes, although a method for doing so is described later in this chapter. If you want to underline the page title or column headings, you must include the underline characters (such as dashes) as one of the title or heading lines.

The best choices for the two **Page eject** options and the **Plain page** setting may vary with the context in which a particular report is printed or to suit your personal preferences. You might want to eject the paper before printing a report if you often use other print commands (for example, LIST TO PRINT or LIST STRUCTURE TO PRINT) that cannot paginate a listing and you do not want to have to remember to advance the paper manually by pressing the printer's form feed button before printing a formatted report. Issuing the Page eject after printing is more appropriate if you often print several consecutive reports or use other print commands after printing a formatted report. You might choose "No" for both of these options in order to print several related short reports on the same page. Finally, the **Plain page** option is useful for printing a report to a disk file to edit with a word processor or to transfer the data to another program such as a spreadsheet.

DEFINING THE COLUMN CONTENTS

A report can contain up to 24 columns, in which you can print the result of evaluating any valid dBASE III PLUS expression. You use the **Columns** submenu to define the report columns by entering the following items for each:

- **Contents:** A single expression up to 60 characters long to print in the column.
- **Heading:** Up to four lines of heading text to print at the top of the column.
- **Width:** The width of the column expressed in characters. The default value is the width of the column contents or the heading, whichever is greater, but you can increase or decrease this value.
- **Decimal places:** For numeric expressions, the number of decimal places to print. For a data base field, this defaults to the number of decimal places defined in the file structure, but you can increase or decrease the value.

- **Total this column:** For numeric expressions, whether or not grand totals and, optionally, subtotals should be printed for the column. The default is "Yes". If no subtotal breaks have been defined through the **Group** submenu, only grand totals are printed.

Be careful not to confuse the *contents* of a column — the expression that specifies the data to be printed in the column — with the *column heading*. The contents expression is validated to make sure that it is syntactically correct and does not reference nonexistent fields or memory variables. The column headings can contain any text and need not resemble the field or variable names in the expressions that form the column contents.

Headings are printed left-justified over character, memo, date, and logical fields, and right-justified over numeric fields. Character, memo, date, and logical data are also left-justified within the specified column width, and numeric values are right-justified. If the column is narrower than the data, character and memo fields are wrapped to fit in the specified column width.

The **Decimal places** and **Total this column** options apply only to numeric data; if the expression that specifies the contents of a column does not evaluate to a number, these options are displayed in dim text and may not be selected.

With the **Contents** option selected, you can move forward to the next column by pressing PGDN or backward with PGUP. You can delete a column with CTRL-U and add a new column at the end of the list by pressing PGDN with the last defined column visible on the screen. To insert a new column between two existing columns, use PGUP or PGDN to select the column that will follow the new one, and press CTRL-N to insert a new column before (to the left of) that column.

When you move the main menu selection cursor to the **Columns** option, the help menu above the Status Bar is automatically replaced by a diagram of the report layout. The report layout display, which is shown in Figure 9-9, provides a rough guide to the final appearance of the report. The column headings are displayed exactly as they will print, and each space in a report line is represented by one of the symbols shown in Table 9-2.

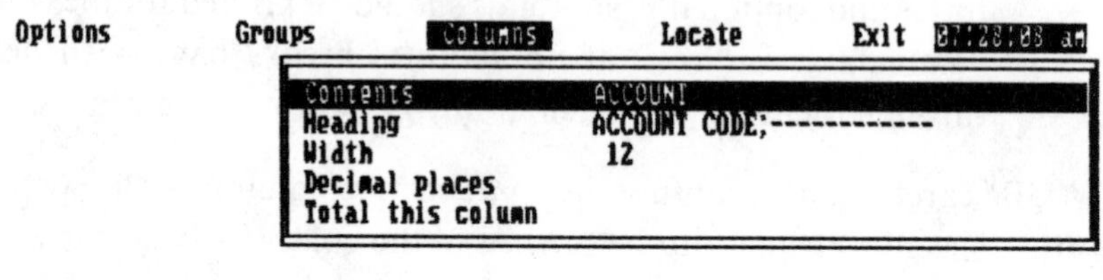

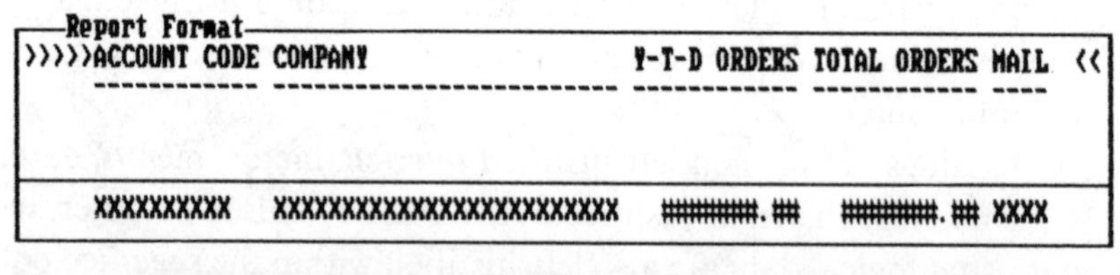

CREATE REPORT <C:> NWCREF1.FRM Column: 1 Ins Caps
Position selection bar - ↑↓. Select - ↵. Prev/Next column - PgUp/PgDn.
Enter a field or expression to display in the indicated report column.

Figure 9-9 *The report editor Columns submenu and layout display*

Table 9-2 *The Symbols Used in the Report Layout Diagram*

Symbol	Meaning
>	Left margin
<	Right margin
—	Undefined space between margins
X	Character data
9	Numeric data, no totals requested
#	Numeric data, totals requested
L	Logical data
M	Memo field
mm/dd/yy, yy.mm.dd, and so on	Date (representation depends on current date display format)

In a report that has more than a few columns, selecting a column by repeatedly pressing PGUP or PGDN can be tedious. You can use the **Locate** submenu to jump quickly to any column in a report. The **Locate** pull-down menu displays the expression that defines the contents of each report column; you move through the list with the UP ARROW and DOWN ARROW keys and select one by pressing ENTER with the desired column highlighted. The report editor then automatically selects the **Columns** submenu and displays the chosen column specifications.

You save a report form by selecting the **Save** option from the **Exit** submenu. The form is saved on disk in a file with the extension FRM, which identifies it as a report form.

You can display or print a report with the REPORT FORM command as follows:

REPORT FORM *report form name*

The report is always displayed on the screen, but you can also add the phrase TO PRINT to direct the output to the printer. As with labels, you can view the report on the screen to verify that the page layout is clear and attractive, and that you have correctly specified the column contents expressions, and then retrieve the command from HISTORY to add the TO PRINT phrase and generate the hard copy.

Just as you can with labels, you can control the order in which records are printed by sorting or indexing the data base, and specify selection criteria by using any reasonable combination of a FILTER, a scope, a FOR clause, and a WHILE clause.

HANDS-ON PRACTICE—PRINTING REPORTS

Make sure that the National Widgets Customer File is open, and invoke the report form editor by typing

```
CREATE REPORT NWCREF1
```

Define the page layout options for a Customer Reference List that could be displayed on the screen or printed on 8 1/2- by 11-inch paper as follows:

```
Page title                  National Widgets, Inc.
                            Customer Reference List
                            -----------------------
Page width (positions)       80
Left margin                   5
Right margin                  5
Lines per page               58
Double space report         No
Page eject before printing  No
Page eject after printing   Yes
Plain page                  No
```

If you enter the page title last, the appearance of the screen as you type the title will match Figure 9-10. The page width and margins were chosen so that the report would fit on the screen.

Next, define the contents of the first report column. Move to the **Columns** submenu, and press ENTER to select the **Contents** option. Press F10 to display the field list, press ENTER to select ACCOUNT from the list, and press ENTER again to complete the **Contents** entry. Select the **Heading** option, and enter the following two lines of heading text:

```
ACCOUNT CODE
------------
```

dBASE III PLUS permits four lines of column heading text, but in this report you need only two. After typing the 12 dashes that underline the words ACCOUNT CODE, you can either press ENTER three times to bypass the last two lines, or you can press CTRL-END to complete the entry. Notice that the heading is displayed on one line in the **Columns** menu box, with semicolons indicating the line breaks, rather than on four separate lines. Because the heading is wider than the ACCOUNT field, the column width defaults to 12, the width of the heading text. Press PGDN to display a blank column definition screen in preparation for entering the specifications for the next column.

Define the remaining four columns as follows:

```
Contents            COMPANY
Heading             COMPANY
                    -------------------------
Width                25

Contents            YTDORDERS
Heading             Y-T-D ORDERS
                    ------------
Width                12
Decimal places        0
Total this column   Yes
```

```
Contents               TOTORDERS
Heading                TOTAL ORDERS
                       ------------
Width                    12
Decimal places            0
Total this column      Yes

Contents               IIF(MAIL, " Yes", " No")
Heading                MAIL
                       ----
Width                    5
```

You can either select fields from the list produced by pressing F10 or type the expressions yourself. Note that for numeric fields, you must change the number of decimal places to zero, since the report editor sets the default to match the two decimal places defined in the data base structure.

Figure 9-10 *Entering the report title*

The expression in the last column is designed to display the text " Yes" or " No" in place of the logical values .T. and .F., which might not be readily understandable to people who are unfamiliar with dBASE III PLUS. The IIF function in this expression tests the value of the MAIL field. If it is true, the text " Yes" is printed; otherwise, " No" is printed. The extra spaces within the quotation marks that delimit these character strings are intended to indent the text one space from the beginning of the column heading.

Use the PGUP and PGDN keys as necessary to review the five column entries. With the first column selected, your screen should look similar to Figure 9-9. Save the label form by selecting the **Save** option from the **Exit** submenu.

Open the ACCOUNT code index for the Customer File and display the report by typing

```
SET INDEX TO NWCACCT
REPORT FORM NWCREF1
```

Reprint the report, selecting only those customers who have placed an order this year, by retrieving the last command from HISTORY and adding the FOR clause as follows:

```
REPORT FORM NWCREF1 FOR YTDORDERS > 0
```

If you have a printer, you can also add the phrase TO PRINT to produce a hard copy of this report. Your printout should match Figure 9-11 if you have entered all of the sample data.

PRINTING REPORTS WITH SUBTOTALS

In addition to the grand totals printed at the end of a report, dBASE III PLUS permits two levels of subtotals, referred to in the report editor as *groups* and *subgroups,* but identified on the report itself as *subtotals* and *subsubtotals.* You specify the fields that determine the location of the subtotal breaks through the **Groups** submenu in the report form editor.

The groups, or subtotals, form the outer, or larger grouping of records, within which records are arranged according to the subgroup, or subsubtotal fields. For example, to print subtotals by state, and within each state subsubtotals by city, you would define the grouping

```
Page No.        1
06/10/87
                        National Widgets, Inc.
                        Customer Reference List
                        -----------------------

ACCOUNT CODE COMPANY                      Y-T-D ORDERS TOTAL ORDERS MAIL
------------ ------------------------- ------------ ------------ ----

ABCPLUMB     ABC Plumbing                    796.41      5248.90  Yes
HOMEMOVIES   Home Movies Video Rentals       248.15       248.15  Yes
KELLY        Kelly and Sons Furniture         87.35        87.35  No
LEWIS        Lewis and Associates            366.81      2482.48  Yes
MTK          M.T.K. Industries               108.59       423.92  Yes
RAPIDTYPE    RapidType Secretarial Svc       348.52       348.52  No
SHAPEUP      Shape Up Fitness Center         435.42       867.38  Yes
WHITNEY      Financial Planning Svcs.        201.87      1384.45  Yes
YORKPUMP     York Pump, Inc.                 167.38       608.42  Yes
*** Total ***
                                            2760.50     11699.57
```

Figure 9-11 *Printing the Customer Reference List*

expression as the STATE field and the subgroup expression as the CITY field. The **Groups** submenu includes the following options:

- **Group on expression:** The field or expression that defines the larger, or outer level of subtotals.
- **Group heading:** Up to 50 characters of text to print before the set of records in each group. This text is followed by the current contents of the field that defines the group.
- **Summary report only:** Whether or not to print every record in the report. If you choose "Yes", the individual records are suppressed and only the subtotals, subsubtotals, and grand totals are printed.
- **Page eject after group:** Whether or not to send a page eject command to the printer after each subtotal is printed. If you choose "Yes" for this option, each group will begin on a new page. You might want to do this to distribute the report sections to different people or departments.
- **Subgroup on expression:** The field or expression that defines the smaller, or inner level of subtotals (the subsubtotals).

- **Subgroup heading:** Up to 50 characters of text to print before the set of records in each subgroup. This text is followed by the current contents of the field that defines the subgroup.

It is up to you to ensure that your file is either sorted or indexed by the same fields that define the subtotal groups. As dBASE III PLUS prints the report, it adds the data from each record into the subtotals and subsubtotals. Whenever the record pointer advances to the next record, dBASE III PLUS checks to see whether either of the expressions that specify the subtotal breaks has changed. If the value of the subgroup expression has changed, the subsubtotals are printed and zeroed out to prepare to accumulate statistics for the next subgroup. If the value of the group expression has changed, the subtotals are printed and zeroed out as well. Unless records are read in a sequence that matches the specified subtotal breaks, there will be more than one group of records with the same value for the group or subgroup expression, and the totals will be meaningless.

OVERRIDING DEFAULTS WITH COMMAND LINE OPTIONS

Some of the options defined through the **Options** sub menu in the report editor can also be specified by adding keywords to the REPORT FORM command. Any options included in the REPORT FORM command take precedence over the settings saved with the report. The following are the keywords and the options they override:

- *NOEJECT:* This keyword prevents dBASE from sending a page eject to the printer before printing the report. This is equivalent to selecting "No" for the **Page eject before printing** option.

- *PLAIN:* This keyword causes dBASE III PLUS to omit the page number and date, and print the page titles and column headings on only the first page of the report. This is equivalent to choosing "Yes" for the **Plain page** option.

- *SUMMARY:* This key word causes dBASE III PLUS to print only the subtotals, subsubtotals, and totals, not the individual detail records. This is equivalent to choosing "Yes" for the **Summary report only** option.

You may also include in the REPORT FORM command an additional line of heading text preceded by the HEADING keyword. This text is printed on the first line of the page along with the page number. Unlike the three special keywords listed above, the HEADING option has no equivalent report editor menu option. This is consistent with the intended purpose of the heading: to allow you to include in a report an "extra" line of text describing a particular report run without having to edit the report form again. For example, you might use this heading to reiterate the selection criteria so it is clear to anyone reading the report which records have been selected:

```
REPORT FORM NWCREF1 TO PRINT FOR YTDORDERS >= 500
  HEADING "Customers With Over $500 in Orders This Year"
```

If you specify a HEADING and also include the PLAIN keyword, the extra heading line will not be printed, since the PLAIN option prevents dBASE III PLUS from printing the page number and date lines.

ACCESSING SPECIAL PRINTER FEATURES

If your printer can change type style, character pitch, line spacing, or other print attributes under software control, you can make use of many of these special features in dBASE III PLUS reports. Some applications include fitting a wide report onto 8 1/2-inch-wide paper by printing in compressed print (16 to 20 characters per inch, depending on the printer) on a dot matrix printer, switching between 10- and 12-pitch on a letter quality printer, using the "near letter quality" or "correspondence quality" print mode of a dot matrix printer for the final copy of a report, and printing a field on a mailing label in boldface type.

Most microcomputer printers (dot matrix, daisy wheel, laser, and other types) are controlled by two types of commands: single *control characters* and *escape sequences* (command sequences that begin with ESC, the character whose ASCII code is 27). For example, on Epson FX-series printers, CTRL-O turns on compressed print, and double-strike printing is initiated with ESC-G and canceled with ESC-H.

Your printer manual should have a complete list of the commands used to access these special features. Because there is no one standard notation for describing printer control codes, you may find any mixture of decimal (base 10) ASCII codes, hexadecimal (base 16) ASCII codes, and key names (such as "ESC-G"). A good ASCII table, such as the one in your BASIC or DOS manual, can be helpful in translating the ASCII codes to the decimal numbers required by dBASE III PLUS.

You cannot send a command sequence like ESC-G to a printer simply by pressing the ESC key followed by the G key. ESC has its own meaning within dBASE III PLUS, namely, to cancel the command or operation in progress, and pressing G would just produce a G on the screen. Instead, you must express the control and escape characters with their ASCII codes using the CHR function. CHR, which may be read as "the character whose ASCII code is . . . ", takes one input, the decimal (base 10) ASCII code of the character you want to access.

To send the ESC-G sequence to the printer from the dot prompt, you must first turn on the printer so that it echoes characters displayed on the screen, and then display the characters that make up the command using the CHR function for nonprinting characters. You can toggle the printer echo on with either of two commands recognized by DOS for this purpose: CTRL-P or CTRL-PRTSC. You then display the printer control command with

```
? CHR(27) + "G"
```

You can turn the printer echo off with the same command used to turn it on. Note that the ? command will be printed on the page, so be sure to issue this command before you line up the paper in the printer where you want to begin printing the report. When the report or label run is complete, you can return the printer to its default state either by sending it a command to cancel the attributes you have set or by turning it off and then on again to reinitialize it.

To a limited extent, you can make use of special print attributes within a printed format. Remember that the contents of a report column or label line may consist of any dBASE III PLUS expression, including functions. You could therefore print the company name field on a mailing label in double-strike mode by specifying the contents of the appropriate line in the label form as (for an Epson printer):

```
CHR(27) + "G" + COMPANY + CHR(27) + "H"
```

This technique is readily applicable to one-up labels, but if you try it with- two or three-across labels, or in a report form, you will see that the printer control characters disrupt the vertical alignment of the columns. dBASE III PLUS counts the four printer control characters (ESC, G, ESC, and H in the previous example) among those that form the COMPANY line, although they are not actually printed on the page. In the second and subsequent columns of labels, the COMPANY line will therefore be offset to the right.

Although you can specify the contents of a report column as an expression, the page titles and column headings are assumed to be literal character strings. If you type an expression like the one in the previous example for a page title, it will be printed on the page exactly as you type it instead of causing dBASE III PLUS to boldface the text.

HANDS-ON PRACTICE—PRINTING REPORTS WITH SUBTOTALS

Make a copy of the report form designed in the previous Hands-On Practice session with the following COPY command:

```
COPY FILE NWCREF1.FRM TO NWCREF2.FRM
```

In a moment you will edit the new report form to add subtotals and three new columns of data. One of these will contain the number of days elapsed since the customer's last order, but National Widgets needs to be able to calculate this quantity based on any arbitrary date, not necessarily the system date, which could easily be expressed using the DATE() function. To allow this date to vary in different report runs, you can store it in a memory variable called MDATE, which will be entered into the column contents expression. This variable must exist when you edit the report form, although its value is significant only when the report is printed. Initialize the variable as the last day of the current month, as you would if you were printing this month's report. For example, for April 1988, you would use

```
STORE CTOD("04/30/88") TO MDATE
```

Invoke the report form editor by typing

```
MODIFY REPORT NWCREF2
```

To fit the additional data on the report, increase the page width to 132 columns. No other changes to the page layout options are necessary.

Select the **Groups** submenu, and define two levels of subtotals based on the contents of the STATE and CITY fields. Here are the subtotal specifications:

```
Group on expression       STATE
Group heading             CUSTOMERS IN THE STATE OF
Summary report only       No
Page eject after group    No
Sub-group on expression   CITY
Sub-group heading         CUSTOMERS IN THE CITY OF
```

Next add the three new columns of data. The first new column contains the LASTORDER field and is located between the COMPANY and YTDORDERS columns. Move to the **Locate** submenu, and select the YTDORDERS column by highlighting the contents of this column and pressing ENTER. You will be returned to the **Columns** submenu with the YTDORDERS column displayed in the pull-down menu box.

Press CTRL-N to insert a new column to the left of the selected column. The menu box will clear to accommodate the new column specifications, and you will see a question mark (?) displayed in the column's position in the report diagram, indicating that dBASE III PLUS knows nothing as yet about the contents of this column. Enter the following to define the column:

```
Contents            LASTORDER
Heading             LAST ORDER
                    ----------
Width                10
```

Press PGDN to select the YTDORDERS column again, and press CTRL-N again to add another new column to the left of YTDORDERS (and to the right of the new LASTORDER column). This column will contain the number of days elapsed since the customer's last order, using the memory variable MDATE as a reference point. No subtotals are required. Here are the specifications:

```
Contents            MDATE - LASTORDER
Heading             DAYS AGO
                    --------
Width                 8
Decimal places        2
Total this column   No
```

Return to the **Locate** submenu, and select the last column, MAIL. Press PGDN to add a new column at the right edge of the report. This column will display the memo field COMMENTS in a column 30 characters wide:

```
Contents            COMMENTS
Heading             COMMENTS
                    ------------------------------
Width                30
```

Use PGUP and PGDN to browse through the report columns, and then select the **Locate** submenu to view all the column contents together. Your screen should look something like Figure 9-12. Note the symbols used in the report diagram to represent different types of data and to distinguish numeric columns that are subtotaled from those that are not.

Save your changes by selecting the **Save** option from the **Exit** submenu. Switch to the city/state/ZIP code index with the command:

```
SET INDEX TO NWCSTATE
```

If you have added or changed data since this index was constructed, rebuild it before printing the report with

```
REINDEX
```

If your printer cannot accommodate wide paper but can print in compressed print, find the control code that initiates this mode in your printer manual. For example, if you have an IBM Graphics Printer, an Epson, or a compatible model, the command is CTRL-O , the character with the decimal ASCII code 15. To send this code to the printer, press CTRL-P or CTRL-PRTSC , and then type

```
? CHR(15)
```

Press CTRL-P or CTRL-PRTSC again, line up the paper at the top of a fresh page, and print the report by typing

```
REPORT FORM NWCREF2 TO PRINT
```

Since this report is more than 80 columns wide, the screen is less readable than that produced by NWCREF1.FRM. Your printout should look similar to Figure 9-13.

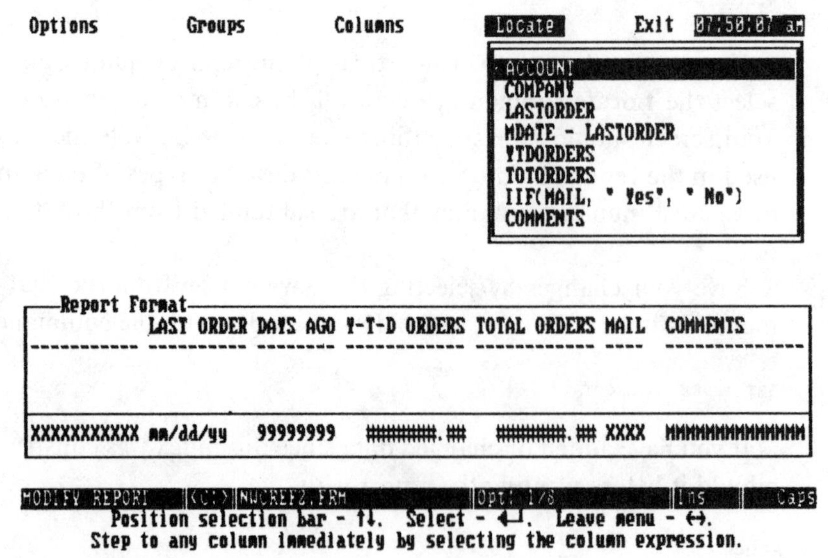

Figure 9-12 *Defining the Customer Reference List with subtotals*

```
Page No.
06/15/87
                                    National Widgets, Inc.
                                   Customer Reference List
                                   -----------------------

ACCOUNT CODE COMPANY                  LAST ORDER DAYS AGO Y-T-D ORDERS TOTAL ORDERS MAIL  COMMENTS
------------ ------------------------ ---------- -------- ------------ ------------ ----  ------------------------------


** CUSTOMERS IN THE STATE OF CA

* CUSTOMERS IN THE CITY OF Antioch
DELTADESGN   Delta Design             09/14/87        229         0.00       188.15 Yes  Referred by Chris Johnson.

* Subsubtotal *
                                                                  0.00       188.15

* CUSTOMERS IN THE CITY OF Benicia
ARONOFF                               12/14/87        138         0.00       232.50 Yes
* Subsubtotal *
                                                                  0.00       232.50

* CUSTOMERS IN THE CITY OF Berkeley
ABCPLUMB     ABC Plumbing             04/30/88          0       796.41      5240.90 Yes
GREENTHUMB   Green Thumb Landscaping  12/19/86        498         0.00       347.73 Yes
HOMEMOVIES   Home Movies Video Rentals 09/13/87       230       248.15       248.15 Yes  Owner is a friend of Jim's, so
                                                                                         they get a 10% discount on all
                                                                                         orders.  However, they take a
                                                                                         long time to pay.

* Subsubtotal *
.                                                              1044.56      5844.78
.
.
* CUSTOMERS IN THE CITY OF Emeryville
IMAGEMAKER   The Image Makers         11/12/87        170         0.00       389.50 Yes
MTK          M.T.K. Industries        02/03/87        452       108.59       423.92 Yes  Interested in receiving
                                                                                         additional information on
                                                                                         computer furniture, ergonomic
                                                                                         workstations, glare screens,
                                                                                         etc.

* Subsubtotal *
.                                                                108.59       813.42
.
.
* CUSTOMERS IN THE CITY OF Fremont
WHITNEY      Financial Planning Svcs. 02/13/88         77       201.87      1384.45 Yes
* Subsubtotal *
                                                                201.87      1384.45

* CUSTOMERS IN THE CITY OF Martinez
PHOENIX      Phoenix Construction     07/06/86        664         0.00       249.57 Yes
* Subsubtotal *
                                                                  0.00       249.57

* CUSTOMERS IN THE CITY OF Oakland
KLEIN        Carol Klein, M.D.        12/28/87        124         0.00      1053.89 Yes  Referred by Dr. James
                                                                                         Reynolds.

* CUSTOMERS IN THE CITY OF South San Francisco
FLOORPLAN    Floor Plan Carpet Center 11/20/87        162         0.00       184.10 Yes
* Subsubtotal *
                                                                  0.00       184.10

** Subtotal **
                                                               2760.50     16553.52

*** Total ***
                                                               2760.50     16553.52
```

Figure 9-13 Printing the Customer Reference List with subtotals

PRINTING REPORTS AND LABELS TO DISK

In general, dBASE III PLUS offers little control over the position and format of the page number, date, titles, and subtotal identifiers. One way to overcome these and other formatting problems is to save an image of the printed report in a disk file, and edit this file with a word processing program to add the print enhancements.

You can print a report or a set of mailing labels to a text file on disk by specifying the file name in a TO FILE clause in the REPORT or LABEL command:

LABEL FORM *label form name* TO FILE *text file name*

or

REPORT FORM *report form name* TO FILE *text file name*

The TO FILE and TO PRINT options are not mutually exclusive. There are three possible destinations for a dBASE III PLUS report: the screen, which is always selected by default; the printer; and a text file on disk. One or all of these can be active at the same time.

You can edit the text file created by the TO FILE clause with any word processor or editor that can read standard ASCII text files. Using the word processor, you can add print enhancements such as boldfacing and true underlining, and change the format of the labels "* Subsubtotal *", "** Subtotal **", and "*** Total ***" that identify the subtotal and total lines.

This alternative is most appropriate for relatively short reports, up to a maximum of 50 pages. With large data files, you can easily generate a text file that does not fit on your disk, or more likely, that is too large to edit easily with your word processor.

The dBASE III PLUS report and label editors allow you to easily define a variety of printed formats that can include the result of evaluating any legitimate dBASE III PLUS expression. The best features of the built-in report and label generators are this flexibility in defining calculations within a record and the ease of use of the full-screen editors. In a broader sense, however, the report generator is quite limited. It offers little control over the detailed format of the page title, column headers, and subtotal header and footer lines; it supports only two levels of subtotals; and the only statistics it can accumulate are subtotals. There are several categories of reports that it cannot print at all; for example, full-page formats such as insurance forms or invoices. As you will see in Chapter 11, you are also limited in the ways that you can print data drawn from more than one data base.

Chapter 10

Creating Custom Data Entry Screens

All dBASE III PLUS full-screen editing commands that display no more than one record at a time — APPEND, EDIT, INSERT, and CHANGE — use the same standard screen layout. The field names are aligned vertically on the left side of the screen as prompts, and the data entry areas are to the right. By default, dBASE III PLUS displays the field names in light characters on a dark background and displays the data in inverse video (dark characters on a light background).

As long as you are careful to choose meaningful and descriptive field names, the standard data entry screen is more than adequate for many applications. The existence of a standard format also enables you to begin working with a new file immediately, without having to spend time designing a screen layout. Even if you intend to define a custom screen, it is often best to wait until you have entered some sample data and completed your initial testing. If the testing phase reveals, as it usually does, that modifications to the file structure are necessary, you will not have to redesign the data entry screen.

Although many users find the default screen perfectly acceptable, there are good reasons to design custom screens. In a data base that has many short fields, for example, you can fit more data on the screen at once. You can use longer, more descriptive field prompts and display informative messages to explain the purpose of a field or list the permissible entries.

dBASE III PLUS does not limit you to one custom screen per data base, so you can create multiple screens for different tasks or users. You can design a screen to resemble an existing printed form, which can be reassuring for a less knowledgeable user and speed up data entry when you are working from the printed form. If some operations do not require access to all of the fields, or some users should not see certain data, you can create screens that include only some of the fields in a file. To prevent anyone from inadvertently or intentionally altering sensitive data or fields whose values should be calculated, you can choose which fields can be updated and which are only displayed.

Custom screens also enable you to carry out more extensive data formatting and validation. You can do such things as convert a state abbreviation to uppercase letters or insert the punctuation in a telephone number or social security number to reduce the possibility that inconsistent data entry will cause problems in later sorting, indexing, or search operations. You can prevent the entry of inappropriate characters, such as letters in a telephone number or digits in a state abbreviation, and you can test numeric and date fields to ensure that an entry falls within a specified range of values.

USING CREATE/MODIFY SCREEN TO CREATE FORMAT FILES

dBASE III PLUS saves the instructions for drawing a custom screen image in a *format file,* an ASCII text file that contains commands to display prompts as well as display, collect, format, and validate data. You can create a format file with a text editor much as you would write a dBASE III PLUS program, but unless you are familiar with the dBASE III PLUS programming language, it is easier to use the full-screen editor provided for this purpose. You invoke the editor with

CREATE SCREEN *screen file name*

or

MODIFY SCREEN *screen file name*

As with any of the full-screen editors, you can use the CREATE and MODIFY variants interchangeably. If you do not include the *screen file name* in the command, dBASE III PLUS will prompt you to enter it. Unlike the QUERY, report, and label form editors, CREATE/MODIFY SCREEN does not require that a data base be open initially. Because you can create a new data base and define a screen layout at the same time, as well as design a screen for an existing file, the editor provides menu options for naming the data base later.

The screen editor has three main submenus: **Set Up**, **Modify**, and **Options**. If you enter the editor without having a data base open, you must either choose a data base from the list presented by the **Select Database File** option to design a screen for an existing file or name a new data base to create by selecting the **Create New Database File** option.

The screen editor also differs from the other full-screen editors in that it is not entirely menu-driven. As you design a screen, you alternate between executing commands through the menu system and editing the screen image directly on a *blackboard;* you toggle between these two modes by pressing the F10 key. As you type on the blackboard, you can use the INS key to toggle between Insert and Typeover modes, and delete characters by pressing DEL. You can insert a blank line between two existing lines by pressing CTRL-N; delete a line, including all fields and text, with CTRL-Y; or delete a single field with CTRL-U. Both delete options remove the reference to the field from the screen without removing the field from the data base structure.

If you are working with an existing data base, you can use the **Load Fields** option on the **Set Up** submenu to transfer one or more fields to the blackboard with the field names as default prompts. When you select **Load Fields**, the screen editor displays the names of the fields in the current data base in a pop-up window. You select a field by using the UP

ARROW or DOWN ARROW key to highlight the field and then pressing ENTER; you can "unselect" a field the same way. Selected fields are indicated by a small triangle displayed to the left of the field name. The appearance of the screen with several fields from the Customer File selected is illustrated in Figure 10-1.

After selecting one or more fields, you can press F10 or use the LEFT ARROW or RIGHT ARROW key to exit the **Set Up** submenu. When you return to the blackboard, the selected fields are aligned vertically, together with the field name prompts, with the first field positioned where you left the cursor when you pressed F10 to enter the menu system. Thus, if you select all the fields in the structure, your screen will look like the standard dBASE III PLUS data entry screen. You can also add fields to a screen one at a time, without the field name prompts, through the **Modify** submenu, which is described in the next section.

You can draw continuous single or double lines and boxes, like the ones that form the pull-down menus in the screen editor itself, with the **Draw a window or line** option in the **Options** submenu. You choose the type of border by pressing ENTER with either **Single** or **Double** highlighted, and you define the size and location of the box by moving the cursor to one of the corners, pressing ENTER, and repeating the process for the diagonally opposite corner.

Producing a horizontal or vertical line is no different from drawing a box, but if the diagonally opposite corners are on the same row or column, a line rather than a box will result. To expand or contract a box, you place the cursor within one of the borders, press ENTER, and then move left, right, up, or down to indicate the new position of the side of the box that contains the cursor. There is no way to erase a line or a box (although you can use the method just described to contract it to a single character), so you may want to leave this step for last.

You can move a single field or a box and its contents by positioning the blackboard cursor within the field or box and pressing ENTER. You can then use the arrow keys to drag the selected item around the screen, and press ENTER again to release it in its new position. You cannot move text or prompts this way, presumably because it is easy enough to delete and retype them.

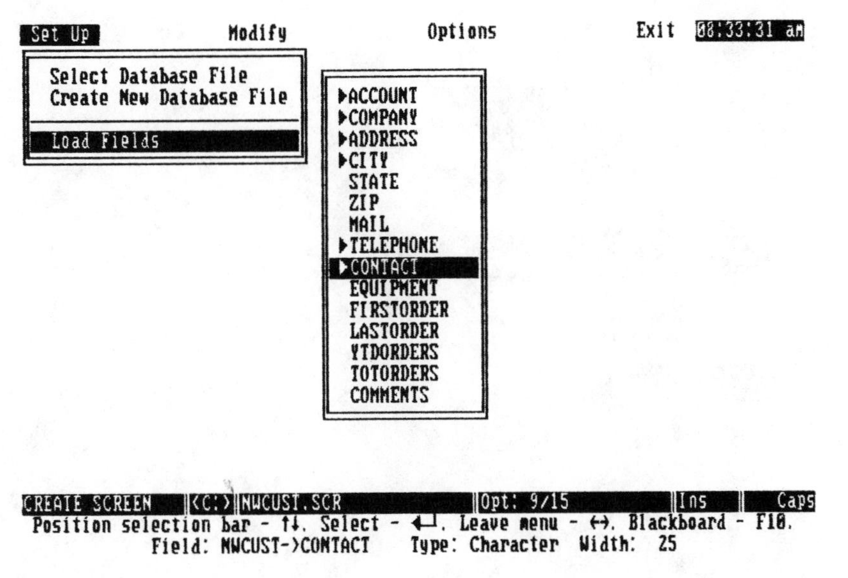

Figure 10-1 *Loading fields onto the blackboard from the Customer File*

Whenever the cursor is positioned within a field on the blackboard, dBASE III PLUS displays the name, data type, and width of the field on the Message Line at the bottom of the screen. For example, for the STATE field from the National Widgets Customer File, this line would read, "Field: NWCUST—>STATE Type: Character Width: 2."

The data entry area is indicated by an inverse video bar as wide as the field that is filled with characters symbolizing the data type. dBASE III PLUS uses X for character fields, 9 for the digits of numeric and date fields, and L for logical fields; memo fields are displayed as "MEMO." Figure 10-2 illustrates the appearance of the screen after you have loaded all the fields from the Customer File onto the blackboard, inserted several blank lines, and moved the STATE and ZIP fields onto the same line as CITY.

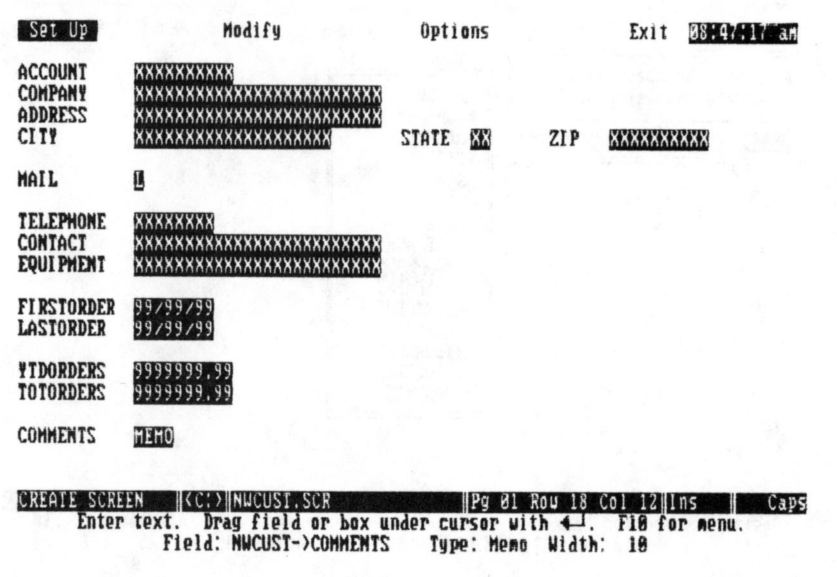

Figure 10-2 *The Customer File fields displayed on the blackboard*

dBASE III PLUS translates the image formed by the text and fields you place on the blackboard into the instructions that make up the format file. Although you can move freely around the blackboard and position text or fields anywhere you like based on the appearance of the screen, it is helpful to understand the coordinate system used by dBASE III PLUS to describe the screen layout. A screen can contain multiple "pages," each of which consists of 25 rows and 80 columns. The rows are numbered from zero to 24, with row zero at the top of the screen, and the columns are numbered from zero to 79 from left to right. When you are typing on the blackboard, the fourth section of the Status Bar displays the page, row, and column numbers that identify the cursor position.

It is best not to place fields or text on line zero, although the screen editor will allow you to do so. If you SET STATUS OFF, dBASE III PLUS uses the top row on the screen for the Caps, Ins, and Del indicators, as well as for certain error messages, and these messages will overwrite your screen display. If you prefer to work with the Status Bar displayed, you must also leave lines 21, 22, and 23 free.

A dBASE III PLUS data base can contain up to 128 fields—more than you can generally fit on one screen. The screen editor can generate a format file with multiple "pages" by automatically inserting a *soft page break* every 25 lines. When you use a multipage format file to enter or edit records, pressing PGDN clears the screen and displays the next page, and PGUP returns you to the previous page. Because the screen editor creates 25-line pages, you must SET STATUS OFF while working with a multipage format file.

You save a custom screen by choosing the **Save** option in the **Exit** submenu. The screen is saved in two disk files; they have the same file name (the one you specified when you entered the editor) but different extensions. The *format file,* which has the extension FMT, draws the screen and collects the data. The *screen file,* which has the extension SCR, stores the screen image in a form used internally by the editor; this file is essential for using the editor to modify an existing format file with the screen editor. Remember that if you later rename the FMT file, you should also rename the SCR file.

USING A FORMAT FILE TO UPDATE A DATA BASE

The format file created by the screen editor draws a custom screen layout that substitutes for the standard data entry screen used by the full-screen APPEND, EDIT, INSERT, and CHANGE commands. When you work with a custom screen, you can use all the usual cursor movement and editing command keys to move around the screen and enter and edit data. If new records are APPENDed using a format file that does not allow access to all the fields in a data base structure, the fields that are not displayed, and therefore not collected, remain blank.

When you exit the screen editor, the format file is automatically put in effect. You can open the format file in a later work session by using the SET FORMAT command:

SET FORMAT TO *format file name*

To cancel the format file and return to using the standard dBASE III PLUS data entry screens, you can use either

SET FORMAT TO

or

CLOSE FORMAT

A format file, like an index, is used only in conjunction with a data base; the format file is therefore closed automatically when you close the data base with a USE command.

HANDS-ON PRACTICE—CREATING A FORMAT FILE

Enter the screen editor by typing

```
CREATE SCREEN NWCUST
```

If the National Widgets Customer File is not already open, choose the **Select Database File** option from the **Set Up** submenu to open it. Next, select the **Load Fields** option and mark all the fields by highlighting each one in turn and pressing ENTER. Press F10 to return to the blackboard. You will see all the fields aligned on the screen in a format that resembles the standard full-screen APPEND or EDIT display.

Move the cursor to the line containing the CITY field, and retype the STATE and ZIP prompts, but leave room to add the data base fields on the same line. Move the STATE field to the right of its prompt by positioning the cursor within the field, pressing ENTER, moving the cursor to the new location of the field, and pressing ENTER again. Notice that the field itself does not move with the cursor; it assumes its new position only when you complete the "drag" operation by pressing ENTER at the new field location. Move the ZIP field the same way.

Delete the old STATE and ZIP prompts by positioning the cursor within the appropriate lines and pressing CTRL-Y. Add blank lines to the screen by pressing CTRL-N so that the screen looks like the one shown in Figure 10-2. Using the cursor movement and editing keys, change the data entry prompts and add additional text to the screen so that your screen matches that of Figure 10-3.

You must move all the prompts and fields in a few spaces from the left edge of the screen and add one blank line at the top to make room to draw a double-lined box around the entire screen image. To draw the box, press F10 to exit the blackboard and return to the menu system. Select the **Double bar** option from the **Options** submenu. The screen editor will redisplay the blackboard. Move the cursor to the upper left corner of the screen, press ENTER, move to the lower right corner, and press ENTER again to complete the box.

Press F10 again to return to the menu system, and select the **Save** option from the **Exit** submenu to save your screen.

Position the data base at any record, such as Record 4, with a GOTO command, and type EDIT to view the record using the screen layout defined by the format file:

```
GOTO 4
EDIT
```

Use the PGUP and PGDN keys to navigate through the file and view several records, and then press CTRL-END to return to the dot prompt. Close the format file by typing

```
SET FORMAT TO
```

Verify that dBASE III PLUS is again using the standard data entry screens by typing the EDIT command again to view the current record.

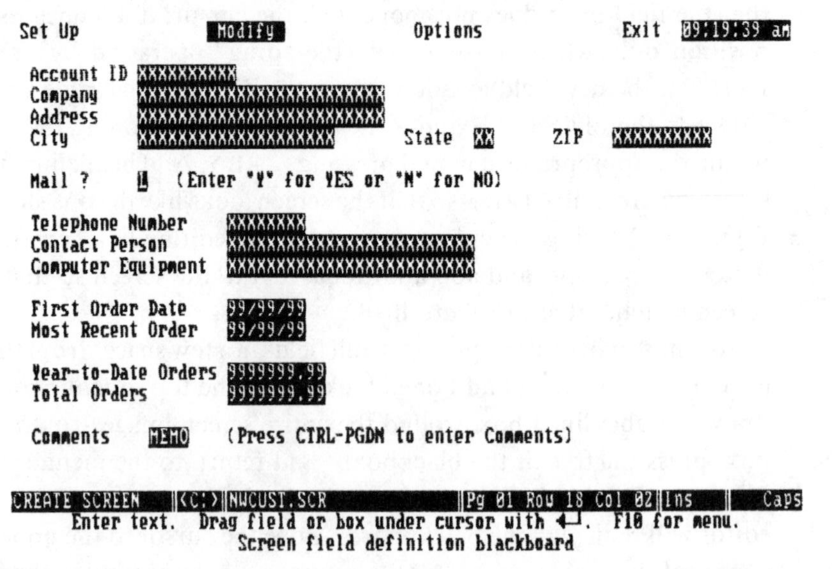

Figure 10-3 *Revising the data entry screen for the Customer File*

FORMATTING AND VALIDATING DATA

You can alter the default format of a field through the **Modify** submenu. You select the field to be modified by positioning the blackboard cursor within the field before pressing F10 to return to the menu system. The **Action** option toggles between two display modes: Edit/GET, which allows the user to enter or edit data, and Display/SAY, which displays the field but does not permit the user to make changes.

In all full-screen editing modes, dBASE III PLUS validates and formats your entries to a certain extent: only numbers, a decimal point, and a minus sign can be entered into numeric fields; only valid calendar dates are accepted in date fields; and only .T. (T, t, Y, or y) and .F. (F, f, N, or n) are permitted in logical fields. You can add a wider variety of validation and formatting rules to a custom screen by using *functions*, *templates*, and *ranges*, which are specified when you select the three options in the **Modify** submenu that have similar names: **Picture Function**, **Picture Template**, and **Range**.

A *range* is used to impose an upper and lower limit on the values that may be entered into a particular date or numeric field. For example, to limit entries into a sales tax rate field to numbers between zero and 10, you could define the lower limit as zero and the upper limit as 10. To restrict entries in the LASTORDER date field in the Customer File to dates in the current year, you would enter 01/01/88 as the lower limit and 12/31/88 as the upper limit (that is, in 1988).

When a format file containing range specifications is used to update a data base, entering a value outside the permissible range causes dBASE III PLUS to display an error message such as "Range is 0.00 to 10.00 (press SPACE)" on the Message Line below the Status Bar or on line zero if you have SET STATUS OFF. Pressing the space bar clears the error message, but the cursor will not advance to the next field until you have entered an acceptable value.

The range affects only newly entered or changed data. If you edit a customer record using a format file that restricts entries in the LASTORDER field to dates in 1988, an existing entry of 07/11/86 will not generate an error message, whereas an attempt to type this date into the field would result in the error message "Range is 01/01/88 to 12/31/88".

A *function* consists of one or more characters that symbolize the overall display format or data entry rules for a field. Some functions affect only the format used to display existing data. For example, the C function causes CR (credit) to be displayed after a positive number, and X displays DB (debit) after a negative number.

Other functions transform or validate the data that is entered into a field. For example, the A function permits only letters of the alphabet (not numbers or punctuation marks) to be entered into a character field, and S allows you to scroll a long character field through a narrower space on the screen. Many functions operate on both displayed and entered data. For example, the exclamation symbol (!) causes character fields to be displayed in uppercase letters and entered data to be converted to uppercase letters.

You can combine the individual function symbols in any reasonable way. For example, using both C and X (entered either as CX or XC) for a numeric field causes dBASE III PLUS to display CR after the field if it is greater than zero and DB if it is less than zero. The combined function A! permits only letters of the alphabet in a character field and automatically converts these characters to uppercase.

When you choose the **Picture Function** option, a box like the one illustrated in Figure 10-4 pops up to display the function symbols that are appropriate to the data type of the selected field and the action defined for the field (Display/SAY or Edit/GET). All the function symbols and their meanings for displayed and entered data are listed in Table 10-1.

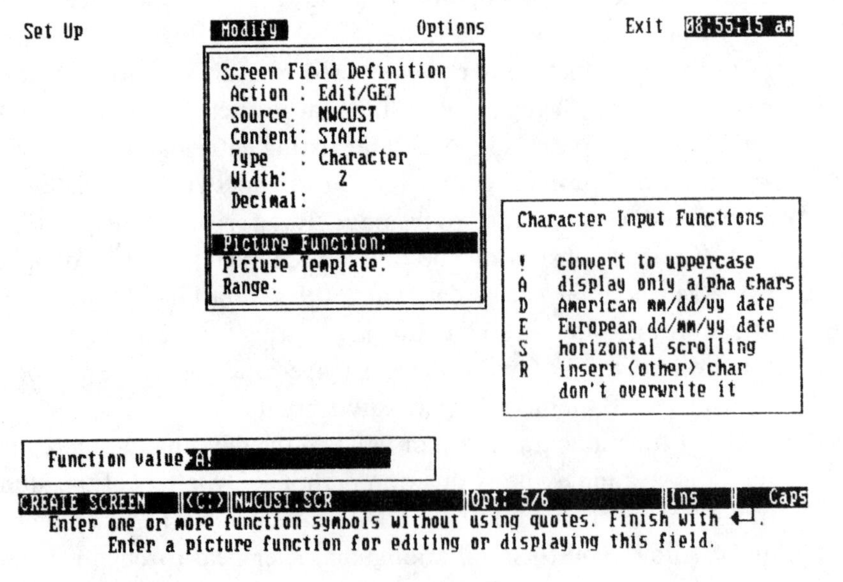

Figure 10-4 *Choosing a function to format the STATE field*

Table 10-1 *dBASE III PLUS Function Symbols*

Symbol	Data Types	Meaning with Display/SAY	Meaning with Edit/GET
C	N	Display CR (credit) after a positive number	None
D	N	Display DB (debit) after a positive number	None
(	N	Display a negative number in parentheses	None
B	N	Display a number left-justified	Display numbers left-justified (data is stored right-justified)
Z	N	Display a zero value as blank spaces (but including any decimal point)	Display a zero value as blank spaces (data is stored as zero)
D	C, N, D	Display in American date format (mm/dd/yy)	Display in American date format (dates are stored in the format determined by Set Date command)
E	C, N, D	Display in European date format (*dd/mm/yy*)	Display in European date format (dates are stored in the format determined by Set Date command)
A	C	None	Permit only alphabetic characters
!	C	Display data in uppercase	Convert entered data to uppercase letters
R	C	None	Extra characters in a template are used for display only and do not become part of the data
Sn	C	Display the first *n* characters of the data	Scroll the data through a space *n* characters wide

You can exercise more precise control over the format of a field by using a template. A *template* consists of a set of symbols, one for each position in the data field, which specify, character by character, the display format or the characters that can be entered. For example, each exclamation point (!) in a template converts the character displayed or entered in the corresponding position to uppercase, and an A allows only an alphabetic character to be entered. A 9 permits only a digit or minus sign, and a comma can be inserted between two digits by using a template such as 9,999,999.99 (a comma is displayed only if there are digits on both sides).

If a template contains any symbols other than the standard template characters, they are inserted into the field in the specified positions. During data entry, the cursor passes over these fixed characters. For example, the picture 999-9999 may be used to format the TELEPHONE field in the Customer File as three digits, a dash (supplied automatically by dBASE III PLUS), and four more digits.

For numeric fields, the symbols affect only the display format. Normally, "extra" symbols inserted into character fields are stored in the data base, but you can use the R (Raw) function to cause these characters to be used for display purposes only. Thus, a TELEPHONE field collected with the picture 999-9999 must be eight characters wide (to accommodate seven digits and the dash), unless you also specify the R function, in which case the dash is not stored and the field can be seven characters wide.

Table 10-2 lists all the dBASE III PLUS template symbols, the data types they apply to, and their meanings for displayed and entered data.

You can define any combination of a range, a function, and a template for a given field. For example, you might specify the range 10,000 to 20,000 for a numeric field, together with the (function to display negative values enclosed in parentheses, and the template 99,999.99 to add a comma when the field is displayed.

Many of the templates described in the foregoing examples require more space than the actual field width. In other cases, however, you may want to collect a wide field in a smaller space with the S function. After you specify the S function, you must also change the display width on the screen to match by positioning the cursor within the field on the

Table 10-2 *dBASE III PLUS Template Symbols*

Symbol	Data Types	Meaning with Display/SAY	Meaning with Edit/GET
A	C	Display character unchanged	Permit only alphabetic character
X	C	Display character unchanged	Permit entry of any character
!	C	Display character in uppercase	Convert alphabetic character to uppercase
L	C	Display character unchanged	Permit only T, t, Y, y, F, f, N, n
	L	Display character unchanged	Permit only logical value
Y	L, C	Display character unchanged	Permit only Y, y, N, n
9	C	Display character unchanged	Permit only a numeric digit
	N	Display character unchanged	Permit numeric digit or minus sign
#	C	Display character unchanged	Permit numeric digit, space, minus sign, or decimal point
	N	Display character unchanged	Permit numeric digit, space, or minus sign
$	N	Display character if present, or a "$" in place of a space	None
*	N	Display character if present, or an "*" in place of a space	None
,	C	Display a "," if a digit is present on both sides	Insert a "," into data
	N	Display a "," if a digit is present on both sides	None
OTHER	C	Display symbol in place of data character With R function, symbol is inserted into data field	Insert symbol into data With R function, symbol is displayed only
	N	Symbol is inserted into data field	None

blackboard and pressing either INS or DEL to adjust the size of the data entry area. Note that this combination does not have the same effect as selecting the **Width** option in the **Modify** menu, which changes the field width in the data base structure.

HANDS-ON PRACTICE—USING RANGES, FUNCTIONS, AND TEMPLATES

Make sure that the Customer File is open, and edit the format file created in the previous Hands-On Practice session by typing

```
MODIFY SCREEN NWCUST
```

Press F10 to access the blackboard, move the cursor within the ACCOUNT field, and press F10 again to return to the menu. Note that whenever you switch back to the menu system from the blackboard, the **Modify** option is automatically selected. Choose the **Picture Function** option in the **Modify** submenu, and enter the exclamation function symbol (!) in the menu box that pops up in the lower left corner of the screen. This function will cause dBASE III PLUS to display the ACCOUNT field in uppercase letters, and to convert all characters entered into this field to uppercase.

Using the same sequence of commands, define the combined function !A for the STATE field to permit only letters of the alphabet to be entered into this field, and convert the entries to uppercase letters.

Specify a template for the TELEPHONE field that automatically inserts the dash and permits only numeric digits to be entered into the other character positions in the field. To do this, position the blackboard cursor within the TELEPHONE field, press F10 to return to the menu, and select the **Picture Template** option in the **Modify** submenu. Type the following template in the menu box that pops up in the lower left corner of the screen:

```
999-9999
```

Using the same command sequence, specify the template Y for the logical field MAIL to display the logical values .T. and .F. as Y and N and permit only these characters to be entered into the field.

The next step is to insert commas in the display format for the numeric fields YTDORDERS and TOTORDERS, and at the same time prevent entries into these fields. To make room for the two extra characters, move the blackboard cursor into each of these fields, and press INS twice to add two spaces to each data entry area. Press F10 to return to the menu system, and press ENTER with the **Action** option in the **Modify** submenu highlighted to switch the status of the field to Display/SAY. Then use the **Picture Template** option to define the following template for both fields:

```
9,999,999.99
```

Notice when you return to the blackboard that these fields are no longer displayed in inverse video, which identifies data entry areas.

Finally, define a range for the LASTORDER field that restricts entries in this field to dates in the current calendar year. To do this, position the blackboard cursor within the field, press F10 to return to the menu system, and select the **Range** option in the **Modify** submenu. Enter January 1 of the current year as the **Lower Limit** of the range, and December 31 as the **Upper Limit**, as shown in Figure 10-5 (if the year is not 1988, you can make the appropriate adjustment). When you return to the blackboard, your screen should look like the one shown in Figure 10-6.

Save the modified screen, and try entering a new record to observe the effects of the various formatting options. Notice that the cursor passes over YTDORDERS and TOTORDERS since you are no longer allowing entry in these fields. Deliberately try to enter incorrect data; for example, type a number in the STATE field, and enter a date outside the range defined for the LASTORDER field.

```
Set Up        Modify           Options           Exit  09:54:08 am
            Screen Field Definition
             Action : Edit/GET
             Source:  NWCUST
             Content: LASTORDER
             Type    : Date
             Width:      8
             Decimal:

            Picture Function:
            Picture Template:
            Range:                   Input Range
                                      Lower Limit:01/01/88
                                      Upper Limit:12/31/88

MODIFY SCREEN  <C:> NWCUST.SCR        Pg 01 Row 13 Col 22 Ins      Caps
                     Enter new value.  Finish with ←┘.
           Enter the maximum and minimum values allowed for this field.
```

Figure 10-5 *Entering a range for the LASTORDER date field*

USING THE SCREEN EDITOR TO CHANGE OR CREATE A FILE STRUCTURE

You can use the screen editor to make permanent changes to the structure of an existing file or create a new file structure as you design the screen layout. All these changes are effected through the **Modify** submenu, which provides an alternative to the **Load Fields** option in the **Set Up** submenu for adding fields to a screen. To use this method, you position the blackboard cursor where you want to collect the field, and press F10 to return to the menu.

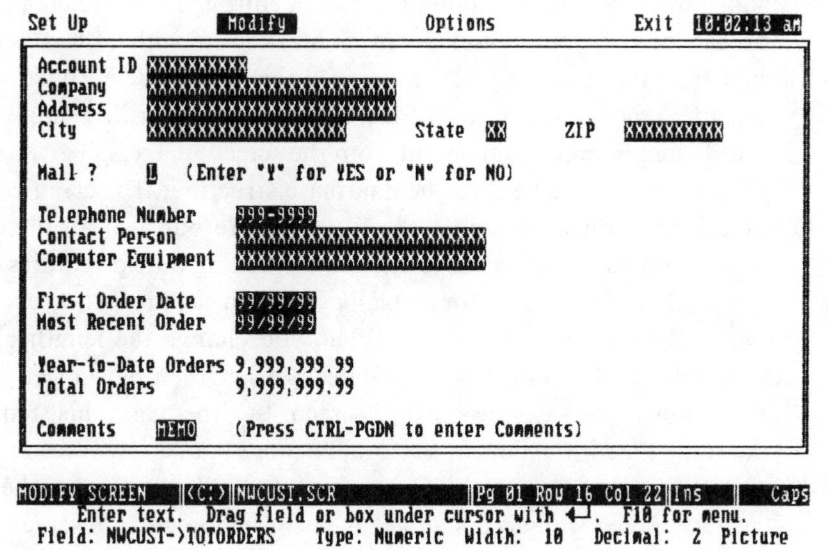

Figure 10-6 *The revised Customer File input screen*

When you select **Content**, a box pops up to display the list of fields in the current data base. You can select an existing field to add to the screen by using the UP ARROW and DOWN ARROW keys to highlight the desired field and pressing ENTER, or you can add a new field to the structure by selecting **<NewField>**, the first item on the list. If you choose an existing field, its name, width, and data type will be displayed in the **Modify** menu box; if you are defining a new field, you must fill in these settings yourself. Note that unlike **Load Fields**, this method for adding fields to a screen limits you to adding only one field at a time and does not place the field names on the screen as prompts.

To edit an existing field, you position the blackboard cursor within the field before returning to the menu, and then use the **Screen Field Definition** options in the **Modify** submenu to alter the field width, data type, or, for numeric fields, the number of decimal places. You cannot change the field name through the screen editor. If you are creating a new data base, deleting a field from the blackboard with CTRL-U causes dBASE III PLUS to ask you whether you also want to delete it from the structure; when you edit a screen that accesses an existing data base, CTRL-U simply removes the field from the screen image.

If you add a new field to the data base structure, the screen editor immediately adjusts not only the file structure but also all the data records to match your new specifications. Adding a field requires that dBASE III PLUS insert enough blank spaces in each record to accommodate the data you will enter. When you change the length of an existing field, the data base is updated (to lengthen or shorten each record) when you save the finished screen. In either case, this step can take some time if the data base contains more than a few records.

Note also that the new field is added at the beginning of the file structure. When you access a data base through a custom screen, the order of the fields in the structure is immaterial, but if you still use the standard full-screen editing displays, you may find it inconvenient to be unable to select the order of the fields. Chapter 11 describes a more efficient way to change the structure of a large file.

Unless you are sure about your file structure, it is inadvisable to use the CREATE SCREEN editor to create a new data base. In most applications, the initial data entry and testing phase reveals that some fields are too long or too short, that you have omitted an essential field, or that you have included fields that are rarely filled in and that you later consider unnecessary. After you make the necessary adjustments to the structure, you will have to redesign the screen to match. You can avoid this extra step by postponing the creation of your custom screens until you have entered enough data and completed enough of the preliminary testing to ensure that your file structure is reasonably close to its final form.

HANDS-ON PRACTICE—MODIFYING THE CUSTOMER FILE STRUCTURE

Make sure that the Customer File is open, and use the screen editor to modify the NWCUST format file. At the same time, add a field for the telephone area code to the file structure. This field does not need a separate screen prompt. It will be displayed and entered immediately to the left of the telephone field in a format like the following:

```
(415) 624-9035
```

Make room for the new field by inserting six blank spaces to the left of the data entry area for the TELEPHONE field. Type the parentheses that will surround the area code, position the cursor inside the parentheses, and press F10 to return to the menu system. Notice that because the cursor is not located in a field, **Content** is the only available option in the **Modify** submenu. Select the **Content** option, and from the field list that pops up choose **<NewField>**. Define the characteristics of the new field as follows:

```
Content:          AREACODE
Type    :         Character
Width:            3
Picture Template: 999
```

Notice that when you add the field, dBASE III PLUS modifies the structure of the file immediately and translates the data to conform to the new structure. As the file is converted, dBASE III PLUS displays a message above the Status Bar to allow you to monitor how far it has progressed in adding records to the new structure. Save your modified screen and file by choosing the **Save** option from the **Exit** submenu, and examine the new structure with

```
LIST STRUCTURE
```

Notice that the new field is now the first in the structure.

Since the area code for most of National Widgets' customers is 415, you could save some time by entering this value in all the records with a REPLACE command:

```
REPLACE ALL AREACODE WITH "415"
```

In a real application, you would still have to edit individually the records that required different entries in the AREACODE field.

Using format files to customize the data entry screens used with the dBASE III PLUS full-screen APPEND, EDIT, INSERT, and CHANGE commands represents a giant step toward customizing the dBASE III PLUS working environment for an application and its users. You can draw attractively formatted screens with borders, descriptive prompts, and data entry instructions, and you can validate and format data as it is displayed or collected. These features will enable you to make the data entry and update process fast and natural, and will render your data base less susceptible to careless errors and inconsistent data entry.

Chapter 11

Working with Multiple Data Bases

Thus far, all the dBASE III PLUS commands and procedures described in this book have acted on a single data base file (in some cases, they were opened together with auxiliary files such as index and format files). Chapters 11 and 12 illustrate ways to use some of these commands to manipulate data drawn from two or more data bases and introduce other commands intended specifically for working with multiple files.

dBASE III PLUS allows you to create a new data base containing some or all of the data in an existing file, add records from one file to another of similar structure, and create a new file consisting of summarized data from an existing data base. In addition to carrying out these "batch-type" operations, dBASE III PLUS permits you to open two or more files simultaneously and establish linkages between pairs of files based on common fields. To illustrate these concepts, this chapter introduces the two remaining data bases that make up the National Widgets system: the Order File and the Inventory File. Using the three National Widgets files, a variety of practical techniques are presented for displaying or printing data from related records and for updating one file based on information contained in another.

Although dBASE III PLUS provides several powerful tools for establishing the logical relationships between files, most of the responsibility for ensuring that records are matched properly and updated correctly lies with you. You must design your file structures so that they support the required relationships, remember to enter identical values into the key fields so that dBASE III PLUS can find the matching records, and make sure that the integrity of the data is preserved as you add, edit, and delete records. It is also essential to develop strategies for verifying that related files are linked correctly and that data is transferred as intended, since in most cases, dBASE III PLUS does not warn you about potential problems.

USING COPY TO EXTRACT A PORTION OF A DATA BASE

You can create a new data base that contains some or all of the data in the file that is currently open by using the COPY command. In its simplest form, COPY makes an exact copy of the original data base:

COPY TO *new data base file*

For example, you could use the following sequence of commands to copy the data in the National Widgets Customer File to a new file called CUSTOMER:

```
USE NWCUST
COPY TO CUSTOMER
```

The COPY command first duplicates the structure of the open data base to create a new, empty file with the specified name. dBASE III PLUS then reads records from the open file one at a time, just as it does when executing a LIST or REPORT command, and APPENDs matching records to the new file.

If you want to create an exact duplicate of an existing data base, the DOS COPY command or the dBASE III PLUS equivalent will do the job faster. Both commands can copy any disk file, not just data bases. You must therefore specify the full file name, including the extension, and when you copy a data base that contains memo fields, you must remember to copy both the DBF and DBT files. For example, outside dBASE III PLUS, you could copy the Customer File with the following DOS command:

```
COPY NWCUST.DB? CUSTOMER.DB?
```

The question mark (?) in the file name specification is the DOS wildcard character that stands for any single character. The foregoing COPY command thus operates on all files with the first name NWCUST and an extension consisting of the characters DB followed by any single character, such as DBF and DBT.

You can use the RUN command to execute COPY—or any other DOS command, program, or batch file—from within dBASE III PLUS if you have more than 256K of RAM and COMMAND.COM is available (as described in Chapter 2). There are two ways to type a RUN command:

RUN *DOS command*

or

! *DOS command*

To copy the Customer File from within dBASE III PLUS, you would use:

```
RUN COPY NWCUST.DB? CUSTOMER.DB?
```

The dBASE III PLUS equivalent, COPY FILE, uses a slightly different syntax and can act on only one file at a time. You would therefore need two commands to copy a data base that has memo fields:

```
COPY FILE NWCUST.DBF TO CUSTOMER.DBF
COPY FILE NWCUST.DBT TO CUSTOMER.DBT
```

dBASE III PLUS does not allow you to use COPY FILE to duplicate a data base that is currently open, since this command reads the source file from the disk. You can be sure that the version on disk reflects all the latest additions and changes only after the file is closed. For the same reason, you should never use a DOS command to copy or rename an open file, although DOS does not issue a warning.

The advantages of the slower dBASE COPY command are its flexibility and the control it offers over the structure and contents of the new file. You can specify the fields in the new file structure with a FIELDS clause, determine the record sequence by indexing or sorting the source file, and select the records to be transferred with any combination of FILTER, scope, FOR, and WHILE clauses. Records marked for deletion are copied with the deletion marker to the new file, unless you have SET DELETED ON.

For example, the following command sequence lets you copy, in alphabetical order by account code, the company name, contact information, and dollar totals for customers in San Francisco who have placed an order during the current year:

```
USE NWCUST INDEX NWCACCT
COPY TO NWCUSTSF FIELDS ACCOUNT, COMPANY, TELEPHONE, YTDORDERS, TOTORDERS
  FOR CITY = "San Francisco" .and. YTDORDERS > 0
```

You can copy a file structure alone, to create a new empty data base, by adding the keyword STRUCTURE to the COPY command:

COPY STRUCTURE TO *new file name* FIELDS *field list*

One application of the COPY command is to extract a specific set of records for a co-worker who has no need for the rest of the data. You might also want to move selected records to a separate file to speed processing if you need to carry out extensive inquiries or calculations on a relatively small portion of a large file. Although you could use a FILTER to restrict processing to the desired set of records, dBASE III PLUS would still have to read the entire file each time you used a command such as LIST or COUNT.

USING APPEND FROM TO COMBINE DATA BASES

You can combine two files by using the APPEND FROM command. Recall that APPEND by itself invokes a full-screen mode in which you add records to a data base one at a time. APPEND FROM reads records into the currently open data base from another file:

APPEND FROM *data base name*

dBASE III PLUS matches fields in the two files by name. The fields need not be in the same order in the two structures, they do not have to be the same length, and there can be other, nonmatching fields in either file. The fields can even be of different data types, provided that the contents are plausible for the new data type. For example, data can be moved from a numeric or date field into a character field, and character data that "looks like" a number or a date can be transferred to a true date or numeric field.

Data that came from a shorter field is padded with blank spaces to its new width, and character fields that are too long are truncated to fit. If a numeric value is too long, the field is filled with asterisks to indicate *numeric overflow,* since truncating a number would render the data meaningless. Extra fields in the open file remain blank, and fields in the file that provide the new data but have no counterparts in the open file are simply not appended.

These relationships are shown in Figure 11-1, which illustrates schematically the way that data would be added from a hypothetical mailing list file called MAILLIST.DBF to the National Widgets Customer File.

Records that are marked for deletion in the file that provides the data are transferred, unless you have SET DELETED ON, but they are not

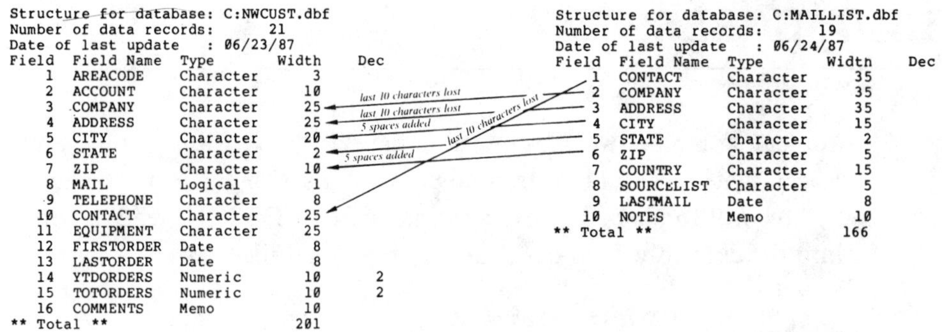

```
Structure for database: C:NWCUST.dbf
Number of data records:      21
Date of last update   : 06/23/87
Field  Field Name  Type       Width    Dec
    1  AREACODE    Character      3
    2  ACCOUNT     Character     10
    3  COMPANY     Character     25
    4  ADDRESS     Character     25
    5  CITY        Character     20
    6  STATE       Character      2
    7  ZIP         Character     10
    8  MAIL        Logical        1
    9  TELEPHONE   Character      8
   10  CONTACT     Character     25
   11  EQUIPMENT   Character     25
   12  FIRSTORDER  Date           8
   13  LASTORDER   Date           8
   14  YTDORDERS   Numeric       10      2
   15  TOTORDERS   Numeric       10      2
   16  COMMENTS    Memo          10
** Total **                     201
```

```
Structure for database: C:MAILLIST.dbf
Number of data records:      19
Date of last update   : 06/24/87
Field  Field Name  Type       Width    Dec
    1  CONTACT     Character     35
    2  COMPANY     Character     35
    3  ADDRESS     Character     35
    4  CITY        Character     15
    5  STATE       Character      2
    6  ZIP         Character      5
    7  COUNTRY     Character     15
    8  SOURCELIST  Character      5
    9  LASTMAIL    Date           8
   10  NOTES       Memo          10
** Total **                     166
```


Fields 1, 2, 8, 9, 11, 12, 13, 14, 15, and 16 remain blank.

Fields 7, 8, 9, and 10 are not transferred.

Figure 11-1 *Appending records from MAILLIST.DBF to NWCUST.DBF*

marked as deleted in the file in use. You cannot use a FILTER to APPEND records selectively, but you can use a FOR clause, provided that the expression used to state the condition includes only fields that are common to both files; any reference to a field not present in the file in use will result in a "Variable not found" error message. You can work around this limitation by using a COPY command to extract the desired records from the file that provides the data and then APPENDing the resulting file into the original.

By strategic use of the COPY and APPEND commands, you can maintain files with similar structures but different data and either combine them or split off selected records for specific purposes. For example, you might have several mailing list files with the same name and address fields but other structural differences. If you rarely mail to everyone on all the lists, maintaining separate files maximizes processing speed in each. For the occasional combined mailing, you can APPEND several files into one. If you frequently mail to the entire list, however, it is more convenient to store all the names in one file. To access specific subsets of the list, you can either COPY records to a separate file or use a combination of FILTER, scope, FOR, and WHILE clauses to select the desired records.

When you design new files, you may not be able to predict how you will want to split or combine them later, but it is always prudent to use the same names for fields that have similar purposes. This may mean that a field name is not always entirely descriptive of its contents. For example, you might end up calling a mailing list field CONTACT instead of NAME to match a customer file, or using generic field names such as FIRSTDATE rather than FIRSTMAIL or FIRSTORDER.

USING TOTAL TO CONDENSE AND SUMMARIZE DATA

Chapter 9 described one way to summarize data in a dBASE III PLUS data base file: by printing a report with subtotals, or printing only the subtotals by including the SUMMARY keyword in the REPORT FORM command. You can accumulate the same totals, but write them to another data base instead of printing them, by using the TOTAL command:

TOTAL ON *key expression* TO *new file name*

This command reads records from the currently open file and creates a new data base with the same structure to contain the totals. This file is always recreated from scratch; you cannot add records to it with consecutive TOTAL commands. The operation of the TOTAL command is represented schematically in Figure 11-2.

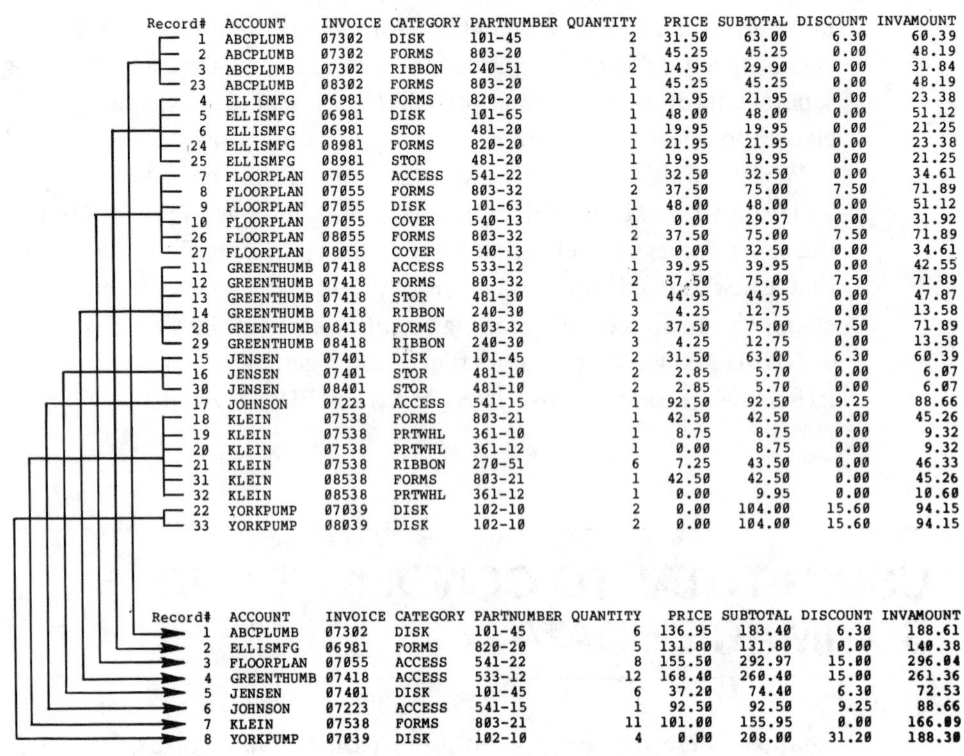

Record#	ACCOUNT	INVOICE	CATEGORY	PARTNUMBER	QUANTITY	PRICE	SUBTOTAL	DISCOUNT	INVAMOUNT
1	ABCPLUMB	07302	DISK	101-45	2	31.50	63.00	6.30	60.39
2	ABCPLUMB	07302	FORMS	803-20	1	45.25	45.25	0.00	48.19
3	ABCPLUMB	07302	RIBBON	240-51	2	14.95	29.90	0.00	31.84
23	ABCPLUMB	08302	FORMS	803-20	1	45.25	45.25	0.00	48.19
4	ELLISMFG	06981	FORMS	820-20	1	21.95	21.95	0.00	23.38
5	ELLISMFG	06981	DISK	101-65	1	48.00	48.00	0.00	51.12
6	ELLISMFG	06981	STOR	481-20	1	19.95	19.95	0.00	21.25
24	ELLISMFG	08981	FORMS	820-20	1	21.95	21.95	0.00	23.38
25	ELLISMFG	08981	STOR	481-20	1	19.95	19.95	0.00	21.25
7	FLOORPLAN	07055	ACCESS	541-22	1	32.50	32.50	0.00	34.61
8	FLOORPLAN	07055	FORMS	803-32	2	37.50	75.00	7.50	71.89
9	FLOORPLAN	07055	DISK	101-63	1	48.00	48.00	0.00	51.12
10	FLOORPLAN	07055	COVER	540-13	1	0.00	29.97	0.00	31.92
26	FLOORPLAN	08055	FORMS	803-32	2	37.50	75.00	7.50	71.89
27	FLOORPLAN	08055	COVER	540-13	1	0.00	32.50	0.00	34.61
11	GREENTHUMB	07418	ACCESS	533-12	1	39.95	39.95	0.00	42.55
12	GREENTHUMB	07418	FORMS	803-32	2	37.50	75.00	7.50	71.89
13	GREENTHUMB	07418	STOR	481-30	1	44.95	44.95	0.00	47.87
14	GREENTHUMB	07418	RIBBON	240-30	3	4.25	12.75	0.00	13.58
28	GREENTHUMB	08418	FORMS	803-32	2	37.50	75.00	7.50	71.89
29	GREENTHUMB	08418	RIBBON	240-30	3	4.25	12.75	0.00	13.58
15	JENSEN	07401	DISK	101-45	2	31.50	63.00	6.30	60.39
16	JENSEN	07401	STOR	481-10	2	2.85	5.70	0.00	6.07
30	JENSEN	08401	STOR	481-10	2	2.85	5.70	0.00	6.07
17	JOHNSON	07223	ACCESS	541-15	1	92.50	92.50	9.25	88.66
18	KLEIN	07538	FORMS	803-21	1	42.50	42.50	0.00	45.26
19	KLEIN	07538	PRTWHL	361-10	1	8.75	8.75	0.00	9.32
20	KLEIN	07538	PRTWHL	361-12	1	0.00	8.75	0.00	9.32
21	KLEIN	07538	RIBBON	270-51	6	7.25	43.50	0.00	46.33
31	KLEIN	08538	FORMS	803-21	1	42.50	42.50	0.00	45.26
32	KLEIN	08538	PRTWHL	361-12	1	0.00	9.95	0.00	10.60
22	YORKPUMP	07039	DISK	102-10	2	0.00	104.00	15.60	94.15
33	YORKPUMP	08039	DISK	102-10	2	0.00	104.00	15.60	94.15

Record#	ACCOUNT	INVOICE	CATEGORY	PARTNUMBER	QUANTITY	PRICE	SUBTOTAL	DISCOUNT	INVAMOUNT
1	ABCPLUMB	07302	DISK	101-45	6	136.95	183.40	6.30	188.61
2	ELLISMFG	06981	FORMS	820-20	5	131.80	131.80	0.00	140.38
3	FLOORPLAN	07055	ACCESS	541-22	8	155.50	292.97	15.00	296.04
4	GREENTHUMB	07418	ACCESS	533-12	12	168.40	260.40	15.00	261.36
5	JENSEN	07401	DISK	101-45	6	37.20	74.40	6.30	72.53
6	JOHNSON	07223	ACCESS	541-15	1	92.50	92.50	9.25	88.66
7	KLEIN	07538	FORMS	803-21	11	101.00	155.95	0.00	166.09
8	YORKPUMP	07039	DISK	102-10	4	0.00	208.00	31.20	188.30

Figure 11-2 *The mechanism of operation of the TOTAL command*

As in printing a report, the data base that generates the totals must be sorted or indexed on the key expression, the field or fields that define the subtotal groups, so that all the records that contribute to a subtotal are processed in sequence. When the TOTAL command completes, the new file will contain one record for each subtotal group in the original data base.

By default, TOTAL acts on all numeric fields, but you may include a FIELDS clause to specify that only certain fields be totaled. If a total is too large to fit in its field, the field will be filled with asterisks to identify numeric overflow. You can control the range of records that contribute to the totals by using any combination of FILTER, scope, FOR, and WHILE clauses.

One reason for generating a summary file rather than printing a report is to maintain an ongoing record of the summarized data. To illustrate this application, consider the National Widgets Order File, NWORDER.DBF, which contains one record for each item ordered by each customer. The structure of the Order File is illustrated in Figure 11-3, and the sample data is listed in Figure 11-4. Since the Hands-On Practice sessions in this chapter draw extensively on the order data, you may want to take a few minutes now to CREATE the file, add some or all the sample records, and build the NWOACCT.NDX index, which is based on the ACCOUNT field.

```
Structure for database: C:NWORDER.dbf
Number of data records:       33
Date of last update   : Ø6/21/87
Field  Field Name  Type        Width    Dec
    1  ACCOUNT     Character      1Ø
    2  INVOICE     Character       5
    3  CATEGORY    Character       6
    4  PARTNUMBER  Character       6
    5  QUANTITY    Numeric         4
    6  PRICE       Numeric         7      2
    7  SUBTOTAL    Numeric         7      2
    8  DISCOUNT    Numeric         7      2
    9  INVAMOUNT   Numeric         7      2
** Total **                       6Ø
```

Figure 11-3 *The structure of the National Widgets Order File*

Record#	ACCOUNT	INVOICE	CATEGORY	PARTNUMBER	QUANTITY	PRICE	SUBTOTAL	DISCOUNT	INVAMOUNT
1	ABCPLUMB	07302	DISK	101-45	2	31.50	63.00	6.30	60.39
2	ABCPLUMB	07302	FORMS	803-20	1	45.25	45.25	0.00	48.19
3	ABCPLUMB	07302	RIBBON	240-51	2	14.95	29.90	0.00	31.84
4	ELLISMFG	06981	FORMS	820-20	1	21.95	21.95	0.00	23.38
5	ELLISMFG	06981	DISK	101-65	1	48.00	48.00	0.00	51.12
6	ELLISMFG	06981	STOR	481-20	1	19.95	19.95	0.00	21.25
7	FLOORPLAN	07055	ACCESS	541-22	1	32.50	32.50	0.00	34.61
8	FLOORPLAN	07055	FORMS	803-32	2	37.50	75.00	7.50	71.89
9	FLOORPLAN	07055	DISK	101-63	1	48.00	48.00	0.00	51.12
10	FLOORPLAN	07055	COVER	540-13	1	0.00	29.97	0.00	31.92
11	GREENTHUMB	07418	ACCESS	533-12	1	39.95	39.95	0.00	42.55
12	GREENTHUMB	07418	FORMS	803-32	2	37.50	75.00	7.50	71.89
13	GREENTHUMB	07418	STOR	481-30	1	44.95	44.95	0.00	47.87
14	GREENTHUMB	07418	RIBBON	240-30	3	4.25	12.75	0.00	13.58
15	JENSEN	07401	DISK	101-45	2	31.50	63.00	6.30	60.39
16	JENSEN	07401	STOR	481-10	2	2.85	5.70	0.00	6.07
17	JOHNSON	07223	ACCESS	541-15	1	92.50	92.50	9.25	88.66
18	KLEIN	07538	FORMS	803-21	1	42.50	42.50	0.00	45.26
19	KLEIN	07538	PRTWHL	361-10	1	8.75	8.75	0.00	9.32
20	KLEIN	07538	PRTWHL	361-12	1	0.00	8.75	0.00	9.32
21	KLEIN	07538	RIBBON	270-51	6	7.25	43.50	0.00	46.33
22	YORKPUMP	07039	DISK	102-10	2	0.00	104.00	15.60	94.15
23	ABCPLUMB	08302	FORMS	803-20	1	45.25	45.25	0.00	48.19
24	ELLISMFG	08981	FORMS	820-20	1	21.95	21.95	0.00	23.38
25	ELLISMFG	08981	STOR	481-20	1	19.95	19.95	0.00	21.25
26	FLOORPLAN	08055	FORMS	803-32	2	37.50	75.00	7.50	71.89
27	FLOORPLAN	08055	COVER	540-13	1	0.00	32.50	0.00	34.61
28	GREENTHUMB	08418	FORMS	803-32	2	37.50	75.00	7.50	71.89
29	GREENTHUMB	08418	RIBBON	240-30	3	4.25	12.75	0.00	13.58
30	JENSEN	08401	STOR	481-10	2	2.85	5.70	0.00	6.07
31	KLEIN	08538	FORMS	803-21	1	42.50	42.50	0.00	45.26
32	KLEIN	08538	PRTWHL	361-12	1	0.00	9.95	0.00	10.60
33	YORKPUMP	08039	DISK	102-10	2	0.00	104.00	15.60	94.15

Figure 11-4 *Order File sample data*

At the end of each year, National Widgets might summarize the order data by customer and save the totals in a historical file that contains one record per customer per year. The Order File might then be emptied in preparation for entering the following year's orders. To create the customer totals, you would open the Order File with the account code index and use a TOTAL command to generate the summary records:

```
USE NWORDER INDEX NWOACCT
TOTAL ON ACCOUNT TO NWORDTOT
```

The contents of the summary file, NWORDTOT.DBF, are shown in Figure 11-5. This file contains one record for each customer represented in NWORDER.DBF. Since no field list was included in the TOTAL command, all numeric fields were totaled, but not all the totals represent meaningful quantities. It makes little sense to total a field such as QUANTITY, because this field may be expressed in varying units for different items.

Note that non-numeric fields take their values from the first record in each subtotal group. The contents of the ACCOUNT field are important, because they identify the subtotal group, but the other non-numeric "totals" are essentially meaningless—you cannot add character or date fields, and the records that contribute to each subtotal may contain widely varying values in these fields. For example, a customer may order many different products from several categories.

Since the TOTAL command offers no direct control over the structure of the summary file, you must either ignore the unwanted fields in subsequent commands or eliminate them from the structure. One way to do this is to use the MODIFY STRUCTURE command, which is described

Record#	ACCOUNT	INVOICE	CATEGORY	PARTNUMBER	QUANTITY	PRICE	SUBTOTAL	DISCOUNT	INVAMOUNT
1	ABCPLUMB	07302	DISK	101-45	6	136.95	183.40	6.30	188.61
2	ELLISMFG	06981	FORMS	820-20	5	131.80	131.80	0.00	140.38
3	FLOORPLAN	07055	ACCESS	541-22	8	155.50	292.97	15.00	296.04
4	GREENTHUMB	07418	ACCESS	533-12	12	168.40	260.40	15.00	261.36
5	JENSEN	07401	DISK	101-45	6	37.20	74.40	6.30	72.53
6	JOHNSON	07223	ACCESS	541-15	1	92.50	92.50	9.25	88.66
7	KLEIN	07538	FORMS	803-21	11	101.00	155.95	0.00	166.09
8	YORKPUMP	07039	DISK	102-10	4	0.00	208.00	31.20	188.30

Figure 11-5 *Order data summarized by customer*

in the next section. Another method involves defining a new file structure that contains only the required fields and using APPEND FROM to read in the contents of the file created by the TOTAL command.

This alternative allows you to accumulate the results of successive TOTAL commands into a single historical file. The structure of NWORDACC.DBF, a hypothetical customer order history file for the National Widgets system, is illustrated in Figure 11-6. Since this file stores annual customer totals, it also contains a field for the year, which can be filled in with a REPLACE command after the total records are created and appended. Here is the full command sequence:

```
USE NWORDER INDEX NWOACCT
TOTAL ON ACCOUNT TO NWORDTOT
USE NWORDACC
APPEND FROM NWORDTOT
REPLACE YEAR WITH YEAR(DATE()) FOR YEAR = 0
```

USING MODIFY STRUCTURE TO CHANGE THE STRUCTURE OF A FILE

The MODIFY STRUCTURE command enables you to change the structure of an existing file using a full-screen editor that uses the same cursor movement and editing commands as CREATE. You can add or delete fields, move fields to new positions in the structure, lengthen or shorten fields, and change data types (provided that the new data type is consistent with the contents of the field)—all without losing data.

MODIFY STRUCTURE works much like APPEND FROM; it creates a temporary copy of the file structure to which all your changes are applied. When you press CTRL-W or CTRL-END to save the new structure, the data is appended from the old file into the new structure. Fields are matched by name, and the data is lengthened or shortened to fit in the new structure. When you save the new structure, dBASE III PLUS reminds you of the importance of field names by displaying the message "Database records will be APPENDED from backup fields of the same name only!!!"

```
Structure for database: C:NWORDACC.dbf
Number of data records:      0
Date of last update    : 06/16/87
Field  Field Name  Type       Width    Dec
    1  ACCOUNT     Character     10
    2  YEAR        Numeric        4
    3  SUBTOTAL    Numeric        7      2
    4  DISCOUNT    Numeric        7      2
    5  INVAMOUNT   Numeric        7      2
** Total **                      36
```

Figure 11-6 *The structure of the customer order history file*

MODIFY STRUCTURE does allow you to change field names without losing data, but you cannot make any other alterations to the file structure at that time. You can make all your other changes in one session with MODIFY STRUCTURE and then edit the field names in a second pass. When you press CTRL-END to save the modified structure, dBASE III PLUS asks you to confirm that fields should be matched on the basis of position rather than name by asking, "Should data be COPIED from backup for all fields? (Y/N)".

HANDS-ON PRACTICE—COPY, APPEND FROM, AND TOTAL

In this Hands-On Practice session, you will create a data base that maintains an ongoing summary of National Widgets' orders by part number and add to this file the order data for the current year. The strategy employed is similar to the one outlined in the previous section for summarizing data by customer.

If you have not already done so, CREATE the National Widgets Order File, NWORDER.DBF, based on the structure listed in Figure

11-3, and enter some of the sample data that is shown in Figure 11-4.

The ongoing summary file, NWORDPRT.DBF, should have fields for product category, part number, quantity ordered, dollar value of the order, discount, actual invoice amount, and year in which the order was placed. To create this file, copy the structure of the Order File:

```
USE NWORDER
COPY STRUCTURE TO NWORDPRT
```

Next, open the (still empty) summary file, use MODIFY STRUCTURE to delete the unneeded fields—ACCOUNT, INVOICE, and PRICE—and add a field for the year. The CATEGORY field will be retained so that the data can be further summarized by product category if necessary. Here is the command sequence:

```
USE NWORDPRT
MODIFY STRUCTURE
```

You can use all of the cursor movement and editing commands displayed in the help menu to move around the screen and make changes. First, make sure that the ACCOUNT field is highlighted, and press CTRL-U to delete this field. Notice that the following fields are moved up and renumbered to fill in the gap. Press CTRL-U again to delete the INVOICE field, use the DOWN ARROW key to move down to the PRICE field, and press CTRL-U to delete this field as well.

Insert the YEAR field between the PARTNUMBER and QUANTITY fields by using the UP ARROW key to highlight the QUANTITY field and pressing CTRL-N to insert a new field before the highlighted field. dBASE III PLUS opens a new blank line on which you can enter the specifications for YEAR, a numeric field with a width of four digits and no decimal places.

After defining the YEAR field, your screen should look like Figure 11-7. Press CTRL-END to exit MODIFY STRUCTURE. dBASE III

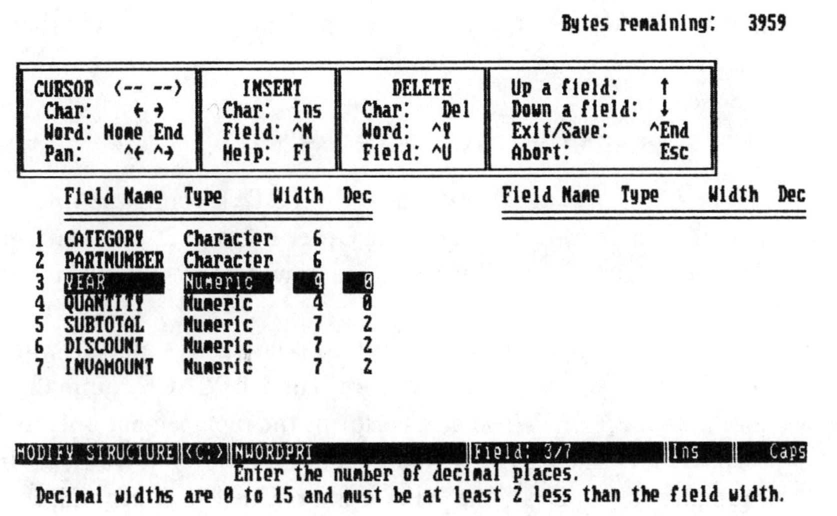

Figure 11-7 *Using MODIFY STRUCTURE to edit a data base structure*

PLUS requests confirmation with the message "Press ENTER to confirm. Any other key to resume." Check the structure, and if it is correct press ENTER to save the file structure on disk.

Before you can summarize the orders by part number, you must index the Order File by the PARTNUMBER field so that all the orders for each item will be read in a group:

```
USE NWORDER
INDEX ON PARTNUMBER TO NWOPART
```

Next use a TOTAL command to generate the summary records. The order data will be totaled in a temporary file called NWTEMP, which has the same structure as the Order File. You can then read the contents of this file into NWORDPRT.DBF and fill in the YEAR field with a

REPLACE command. Here is the command sequence (which assumes that the NWOPART.NDX index is open) for generating the totals:

```
TOTAL ON PARTNUMBER TO NWTEMP
USE NWORDPRT
APPEND FROM NWTEMP
REPLACE YEAR WITH YEAR(DATE()) FOR YEAR = 0
```

The status message displayed by the TOTAL command informs you that 33 records were read from the Order File and 20 summary records were generated. This means that 20 items were represented among the 33 order records.

Note that although the summary file is currently empty, it will not be the next time you run this procedure. The REPLACE command therefore tests the YEAR field and performs the replacement only in "new" records, identified by a blank—that is, zero—YEAR field. In this example, the value of the YEAR is obtained in a general way—by applying the YEAR function to the system date, expressed by the DATE( ) function, to extract the year. If you run this procedure after the end of the year, such as when summarizing 1988 in January 1989, you could state the replacement value explicitly:

```
REPLACE YEAR WITH 1989 FOR YEAR = 0
```

For analyzing sales trends, National Widgets might want to view the records in NWORDPRT in various orders, such as by CATEGORY, PARTNUMBER, and YEAR, or in descending order by SUBTOTAL. To build an index based on a combination of character and numeric fields, the numeric field YEAR must be converted to a character string with the STR function. To index in descending numerical or chronological order, you can subtract the numeric or date field from a larger constant value. When subtracted from the same number, a larger value will yield a smaller result and will thus index first (for example, 100 − 98 is a smaller quantity than 100 − 2).

Build an index that accesses the NWORDPRT.DBF file by CATEGORY, PARTNUMBER, and YEAR, and then list the contents of the file with the following commands:

```
INDEX ON CATEGORY + PARTNUMBER + STR(YEAR,4) TO NWORDPRT
LIST
```

Build an index based on CATEGORY and, in descending order, SUBTOTAL, and list the result with the following:

```
INDEX ON CATEGORY + STR(9999.99 - SUBTOTAL,4) TO NWORDSUB
LIST
```

If you entered all of the sample data into the Order File, your screen should look similar to Figure 11-8.

Record#	CATEGORY	PARTNUMBER	YEAR	QUANTITY	SUBTOTAL	DISCOUNT	INVAMOUNT
15	ACCESS	541-15	1988	1	92.50	9.25	88.66
13	ACCESS	533-12	1988	1	39.95	0.00	42.55
16	ACCESS	541-22	1988	1	32.50	0.00	34.61
14	COVER	540-13	1988	2	62.47	0.00	66.53
4	DISK	102-10	1988	4	208.00	31.20	188.30
1	DISK	101-45	1988	4	126.00	12.60	120.78
2	DISK	101-63	1988	1	48.00	0.00	51.12
3	DISK	101-65	1988	1	48.00	0.00	51.12
19	FORMS	803-32	1988	8	300.00	30.00	287.56
17	FORMS	803-20	1988	2	90.50	0.00	96.38
18	FORMS	803-21	1988	2	85.00	0.00	90.52
20	FORMS	820-20	1988	2	43.90	0.00	46.76
9	PRTWHL	361-12	1988	2	18.70	0.00	19.92
8	PRTWHL	361-10	1988	1	8.75	0.00	9.32
7	RIBBON	270-51	1988	6	43.50	0.00	46.33
6	RIBBON	240-51	1988	2	29.90	0.00	31.84
5	RIBBON	240-30	1988	6	25.50	0.00	27.16
12	STOR	481-30	1988	1	44.95	0.00	47.87
11	STOR	481-20	1988	2	39.90	0.00	42.50
10	STOR	481-10	1988	4	11.40	0.00	12.14

Figure 11-8 *The order category summary file indexed by CATEGORY and SUBTOTAL*

WORKING WITH MULTIPLE DATA BASES

The commands described in the first part of this chapter enable you to transfer data between files, but they all operate on one data base at a time. dBASE III PLUS also allows you to work with up to ten data bases simultaneously, each in a separate *work area.* You may switch freely among work areas to view data from several data bases without having to close and then reopen any files. At times you might want to open two or three files at once just to take advantage of this convenience, but the ability to open several files simultaneously is most useful for working with multiple related files and viewing or updating matching records based on the contents of a common field or fields.

When you first load dBASE III PLUS, work area 1 is active. You use the SELECT command to switch from one work area to another, using any of the following three methods to identify the desired area. You can refer to work areas by number (1 through 10) or by the equivalent letter (A through J). For example, you could select work area 2 with

```
SELECT 2
```

or

```
SELECT B
```

Once a work area contains an open data base, you can also select it by the file's *alias.* An alias is an alternate name for a data base, up to 10 characters long, which you designate in the USE command that opens the file. For example, you could open the National Widgets Customer File in work area 2 with two indexes and assign to it the alias CUSTOMER with the following commands:

```
SELECT 2
USE NWCUST INDEX NWCACCT, NWCZIP ALIAS CUSTOMER
```

For the remainder of your work session, you could then move to work area 2 with

```
SELECT CUSTOMER
```

If you do not specify an alias, dBASE III PLUS assigns the file name (in this example, NWCUST) as the alias. dBASE III PLUS retains no record of the alias after a file is closed, so you may open the same file with a different alias in a subsequent work session.

You do not have to use the ten work areas in sequence, opening your first file in work area 1 (A), the second in area 2 (B), and so on. When you work frequently with the same set of related files, you may prefer to associate each data base with a particular work area, so in a given situation you might end up opening files in areas 2, 4, and 7. In general, however, it is easier to remember the file alias than the number of the work area containing the file; and if you use aliases, it makes no difference which area is used for any of your files.

dBASE III PLUS maintains a separate record pointer in each work area, which does not move when you switch to another area. Thus, you always have access to data from the current record in any open file. Fields in all files except the one in the current work area are referred to by a combination of the file alias and field name, for example, CUSTOMER—>CONTACT for the CONTACT field in the NWCUST.DBF file opened with the alias CUSTOMER. This expression might be read aloud as "customer contact" or "customer file contact field."

Although dBASE III PLUS permits you to open ten data bases at once, a tighter restriction is imposed by MS-DOS. MS-DOS allows an application program to open at most 15 disk files at once. This limit includes data base files, indexes, format files, report and label form files, memory variable files, and if a data base contains memo fields, the DBT file used to store the memo text. Thus, if you opened the Customer File as described in the previous example, and you invoked the NWCUST format file to draw a custom screen, a total of five files would be open in work area 2: NWCUST.DBF, NWCUST.DBT, NWCACCT.NDX, NWCZIP.NDX, and NWCUST.FMT. In practice, since you will almost always use at least one index with each data base, you can open 3 to 5 data bases, but this is sufficient for most purposes.

You can close a single data base by SELECTing the appropriate work area and typing

```
USE
```

You can close all open data bases and return to work area 1 with a CLOSE command:

```
CLOSE DATABASES
```

ACCESSING RELATED RECORDS FROM TWO FILES

The primary motivation for opening multiple data bases simultaneously is to access related records from two or more files. Once you have opened the files, you can find the matching records by using a variety of methods, many of which do not depend on establishing any formal relationships between files. For example, you might open the National Widgets Customer File and Order File in work areas 1 and 2 with the following sequence:

```
SELECT 1
USE NWCUST INDEX NWCACCT ALIAS CUSTOMER
SELECT 2
USE NWORDER INDEX NWOACCT ALIAS ORDER
```

You could then search for a particular customer and display the customer record, as well as all the matching order records, with the following command sequence:

```
SELECT CUSTOMER
SEEK "ABCPLUMB"
DISPLAY
```

```
SELECT ORDER
LIST FOR ACCOUNT = "ABCPLUMB"
```

One way to improve this search strategy is to state the condition in the FOR clause more generally so that it applies to any customer:

```
LIST FOR ACCOUNT = CUSTOMER->ACCOUNT
```

The condition ACCOUNT = CUSTOMER—>ACCOUNT selects records in which the contents of the ACCOUNT field in the currently selected file (the Order File) match the ACCOUNT field in the file whose alias is CUSTOMER. Since dBASE III PLUS does not move the record pointer in the Customer File when you move to the Order File work area, this condition always selects Order File records that match the "current" Customer File record (the one named in the most recent SEEK command).

After searching for another customer record, you could return to the Order File, retrieve this command from HISTORY, and repeat it unchanged to view the new customer's orders. If you plan to use this command sequence more than a few times in a row, you can use a FILTER to state the same condition:

```
SELECT ORDER
SET FILTER TO ACCOUNT = CUSTOMER->ACCOUNT
```

The FILTER, which behaves exactly like LIST FOR, is convenient, but if the Order File is large, finding matching records will be slow. There is a more efficient way to display a given customer's orders, however, based on the fact that the Order File is indexed by ACCOUNT. You can use a SEEK command to find the first matching order record and then state the condition in the LIST command in a WHILE clause:

```
SELECT ORDER
SEEK "ABCPLUMB"
LIST WHILE ACCOUNT = "ABCPLUMB"
```

In this command sequence, SEEK positions the record pointer at the first order record in which the specified condition is true, and the WHILE clause causes dBASE III PLUS to cease reading records at the end of the group defined by the contents of the ACCOUNT field. The account code can be expressed in general terms, in both the SEEK and LIST commands, so that the same commands work with any customer:

```
SELECT ORDER
SEEK CUSTOMER->ACCOUNT
LIST WHILE ACCOUNT = CUSTOMER->ACCOUNT
```

USING SET RELATION TO LINK TWO DATA BASES

The method described in the preceding section for accessing related Customer and Order File records depended solely on your ability to state selection criteria that define the matching sets of records. If the relationship between two files is based on a common field or fields, and if an index exists based on this common key, you can establish a more formal linkage based on the key expression by using the SET RELATION command. The syntax is as follows:

SET RELATION TO *key expression* INTO *file alias*

The two files must be open, in any two work areas, and the file you intend to process must be selected. The field(s) that make up the key expression must be present in both files, although they need not have the same names. The file accessed through the RELATION—the file whose alias is named in the SET RELATION command, also referred to as the *related file*—must be indexed on the key expression. The selected file may be indexed on any expression or not at all.

Once the RELATION is SET, any commands that move the record pointer in the selected file cause dBASE III PLUS to automatically position the related file to the matching record based on the common key expression. If there is more than one such record, the RELATION finds the first, just as SEEK would. If there is no match, the record pointer in the related file is positioned at the end-of-file, and all fields in the "current record" in this file will appear to be blank.

You can SET up to ten RELATIONs at a time, but you can SET only one RELATION from any given work area. You cancel the linkage between two files with

```
SET RELATION TO
```

SET RELATION is most useful when each record in the selected file has only one matching record in the related file. For example, you could open the Customer and Order files and link them by the common field ACCOUNT with the following sequence:

```
SELECT 1
USE NWCUST INDEX NWCACCT ALIAS CUSTOMER
SELECT 2
USE NWORDER ALIAS ORDER
SET RELATION TO ACCOUNT INTO CUSTOMER
```

For each order there should be exactly one matching customer (although it is conceivable that there could be more than one, or none, due to data entry errors). With the files linked in this way, dBASE III PLUS always positions the Customer File on the record that matches the current Order File record; you can display any fields from both files. For example, you could use a GOTO command to access a particular order record (chosen at random in this example) and display the customer company name along with (or instead of) the account code and other selected fields from the order record:

```
SELECT ORDER
GOTO 5
DISPLAY ACCOUNT, CUSTOMER->COMPANY, CATEGORY, PARTNUMBER, QUANTITY
```

If the operation of the SET RELATION command still seems mysterious, it may help to recall that you can obtain exactly the same results—for a single order record—by using a SEEK command to find the matching customer. The following command sequence produces the same results as the previous example:

```
SELECT ORDER
GOTO 5
SELECT CUSTOMER
SEEK ORDER->ACCOUNT
SELECT ORDER
DISPLAY ACCOUNT, CUSTOMER->COMPANY, CATEGORY, PARTNUMBER, QUANTITY
```

When SET RELATION is used to access one record at a time, the only advantage of using it is convenience—it requires fewer commands to display several consecutive sets of matching customer and order records than would using an individual SEEK for each record. The real benefit of SET RELATION is that it offers access to the matching record in the related file *for every record in the selected file* that is processed by commands such as LIST, DISPLAY, REPORT, LABEL, and REPLACE. As dBASE III PLUS moves the record pointer in the selected file to execute any of these commands, it also does the equivalent of a SEEK command "behind the scenes" in the related file. For example, with the Customer and Order files linked with SET RELATION (as described earlier in this section), you could display the matching customer name with every order record:

```
SELECT ORDER
LIST ACCOUNT, CUSTOMER->COMPANY, CATEGORY, PARTNUMBER, QUANTITY
```

Keep in mind that the ability to access data from the current record in the Customer File depends only on this file being open. Using this facility to produce a *meaningful* list of fields from matching records in two files depends on the RELATION. Thus, if you neglected to link the files with SET RELATION, the previous LIST command would not produce an error message. However, the record pointer in the Customer File would not move as the pointer advanced through the Order File, and the same COMPANY field would be displayed for every order record—the one from the customer record that was "current" the last time the customer work area was selected.

Even if the files are properly linked, you may not get the results you want if there is not a perfect one-to-one correspondence between records in the selected and related files. In the previous example, if the Order File was positioned at a record for which there was no matching customer record, the Customer File would be positioned at the end-of-file, and COMPANY, along with all other fields in this file, would appear blank. If there is more than one matching customer record, only the first can be accessed through the relation.

The strategy for "looking up" data in one file based on fields in another is equally applicable to printing reports and labels. Thus, you could include the customer company name field on an order summary report by specifying the contents of the appropriate report column as CUSTOMER—>COMPANY. The expression CUSTOMER—>COMPANY makes sense to the report editor only if the NWCUST.DBF file is open in any work area when you create (or edit) the report. When you print the report, the files must also be linked with SET RELATION to ensure that for each order record printed the right customer record is retrieved.

USING REPLACE TO TRANSFER DATA BETWEEN FILES

Based on the examples presented thus far, you might conclude that SET RELATION may be used only to display data from matching records in two files, but there is no such limitation. You may also use data from the related record in calculations, including those that change the values of fields in the selected file.

Figure 11-9 illustrates the structure of the third data base in the National Widgets system, the Inventory File, and Figure 11-10 lists the sample data. To try the examples in the remaining Hands-On Practice sessions in this chapter, you will need to CREATE this file, enter the sample data, and build the NWICATPT.NDX index, which is based on the combination of the CATEGORY and PARTNUMBER fields.

For each record in the Order File, there should be only one matching inventory record, based on the common CATEGORY and PARTNUMBER fields. To fill in the standard prices from the Inventory File, you could open the two files and link them with SET RELATION based on the common key expression CATEGORY + PARTNUMBER:

```
SELECT 1
USE NWINVENT INDEX NWICATPT ALIAS INVENTORY
SELECT 2
USE NWORDER ALIAS ORDER
SET RELATION TO CATEGORY + PARTNUMBER INTO INVENTORY
REPLACE ALL PRICE WITH INVENTORY->PRICE
```

```
Structure for database: C:NWINVENT.dbf
Number of data records:       50
Date of last update    : 06/09/87
Field  Field Name  Type        Width    Dec
    1  CATEGORY    Character       6
    2  PARTNUMBER  Character       6
    3  DESCRIP     Character      25
    4  COST        Numeric         7      2
    5  PRICE       Numeric         7      2
** Total **                       52
```

Figure 11-9 *The structure of the National Widgets Inventory File*

This command is not a special form of the REPLACE command. You can REPLACE a field with the result of evaluating any legitimate dBASE III PLUS expression of the same data type, and INVENTORY—> PRICE, which represents the contents of a single data base field, is a perfectly legitimate expression. As with any other REPLACE command, you can use any combination of FILTER, scope, FOR, and WHILE clauses to process order records selectively. For example, to fill in the standard price in new records in which the PRICE field remains blank (zero), you could use:

```
REPLACE ALL PRICE WITH INVENTORY->PRICE FOR PRICE = 0
```

For these REPLACE commands, which must read every record in the Order File, the file was opened with no indexes to speed processing. The sequence in which order records are read has no bearing on the use of SET RELATION to link the two files. Regardless of how the record pointer in the Order File arrives at a particular record, the sole effect of the RELATION is to position the Inventory File record pointer to the matching record. Since this is done with the equivalent of a SEEK

Record#	CATEGORY	PARTNUMBER	DESCRIP	COST	PRICE
1	DISK	101-42	5-1/4" SSDD Soft Sector	19.00	28.00
2	RIBBON	270-10	NEC 7700 Cloth Ribbon	4.20	6.95
3	PRTWHL	321-11	NEC Courier 10	8.45	12.50
4	PRTWHL	321-18	NEC Emperor P.S.	9.60	15.00
5	DISK	101-40	5-1/4" SSDD 10 Sector	19.00	28.00
6	DISK	101-41	5-1/4" SSDD 16 Sector	19.00	28.00
7	DISK	101-44	5-1/4" DSDD 16 Sector	21.00	31.50
8	DISK	101-43	5-1/4" DSDD 10 Sector	21.00	31.50
9	DISK	101-45	5-1/4" DSDD Soft Sector	21.00	31.50
10	DISK	101-60	5-1/4" SSDD 10 Sector	23.50	38.00
11	DISK	101-61	5-1/4" SSDD 16 Sector	23.50	38.00
12	DISK	101-62	5-1/4" SSDD Soft Sector	22.80	38.00
13	DISK	101-63	5-1/4" DSDD 10 Sector	29.40	48.00
14	DISK	101-64	5-1/4" DSDD 16 Sector	29.40	48.00
15	DISK	101-65	5-1/4" DSDD Soft Sector	28.75	48.00
16	PRTWHL	321-15	NEC Prestige Elite 12	8.45	12.50
17	PRTWHL	341-51	Qume Courier 10	4.80	7.95
18	PRTWHL	341-54	Qume Prestige Elite 12	4.80	7.95
19	PRTWHL	341-52	Qume Courier 12	4.80	7.95
20	PRTWHL	361-10	Diablo Courier 10	5.20	8.75
21	PRTWHL	361-15	Diablo Manifold 10	5.20	8.75
22	PRTWHL	361-18	Diablo Courier Legal 10A	5.20	8.75
23	RIBBON	270-11	NEC 7700 Multistrike	4.20	6.95
24	RIBBON	270-13	NEC 3500 Multistrike	7.80	13.50
25	RIBBON	270-12	NEC 3500 Cloth	7.20	12.95
26	RIBBON	270-50	Diablo Hytype II Cloth	4.50	6.95
27	RIBBON	270-51	Diablo Hytype II Multi	4.75	7.25
28	RIBBON	270-53	Diablo 620 Multistrike	6.50	9.50
29	RIBBON	270-72	Qume Multistrike	3.50	5.95
30	RIBBON	240-50	Epson MX/FX80	5.20	9.45
31	RIBBON	240-51	Epson MX/FX100	9.75	14.95
32	RIBBON	240-30	Okidata 80, 81, 82, 83	2.75	4.25
33	RIBBON	240-31	Okidata 84	3.00	4.95
34	FORMS	803-20	14-1/2 x 11" Green bar	28.50	45.25
35	FORMS	803-21	14-1/2 x 11" White	24.00	42.50
36	FORMS	803-32	9-1/2 x 11" White	24.50	37.50
37	FORMS	803-31	9-1/2 x 11" Green bar	25.00	37.50
38	FORMS	820-20	3-1/2 x 1" Labels, 1-up	14.50	21.95
39	FORMS	820-23	3-1/2 x 1" Labels, 4-up	39.50	64.95
40	COVER	540-10	Dust cover, Apple II	16.50	24.95
41	COVER	540-12	Dust cover, IBM PC, XT	18.50	29.95
42	COVER	540-11	Dust cover, Macintosh	17.00	26.50
43	STOR	481-10	5-1/4" Disk Case, Blue	1.15	2.85
44	STOR	481-20	Locking Disk Storage Tray	12.50	19.95
45	STOR	481-30	Oak Disk Storage Case	29.75	44.95
46	ACCESS	533-12	Plexiglas Printer Stand	24.50	39.95
47	ACCESS	541-15	Terminal Swivel Mount	68.00	92.50
48	ACCESS	508-13	Polaroid Glare Screen	16.30	24.95
49	ACCESS	508-14	Polaroid Glare Screen	14.40	21.95
50	ACCESS	541-22	Non-magnetic Copy Stand	21.00	32.50

Figure 11-10 *Inventory File sample data*

command, the Inventory File must be indexed on the common key expression to support the RELATION.

This command will produce the results you expect only if there is a one-to-one relationship between the Order File and the Customer File. If dBASE III PLUS fails to find a matching inventory record for a particular order record, the Inventory File will be positioned at the end-of-file, where the PRICE field (and every other field) takes on a blank, or zero, value. dBASE III PLUS does not regard this as an error condition; it simply transfers the 0 value to the PRICE field in the Order File without issuing any warning.

You can detect such problems before you perform the REPLACE command by using a LIST command to display the matching fields from both files:

```
LIST CATEGORY, PARTNUMBER, INVENTORY->CATEGORY, INVENTORY->PARTNUMBER
```

If the output of this LIST command included any records in which the inventory fields were blank or in which the corresponding fields did not contain identical values, you could correct these problems before executing the REPLACE command. A blank value might result from a missing inventory record or an incorrectly entered part number (in either file), while mismatched values would occur if you failed to link the files with SET RELATION or if the Inventory File index has been damaged.

You could make it even easier to spot mismatches by displaying only those records in which some Inventory File field differs from its counterpart in the Order File, for example:

```
LIST ACCOUNT, CATEGORY, PARTNUMBER FOR PARTNUMBER <> INVENTORY->PARTNUMBER
```

The important point is that dBASE III PLUS leaves it largely up to you to test for these kinds of problems before you carry out potentially destructive commands such as REPLACE.

ESTABLISHING ONE-TO-MANY RELATIONSHIPS

SET RELATION is less automatic but is still useful when there is more than one record in the related file that matches each record in the selected file. For example, considered from the point of view of the Order File, its relationship with the Customer File is one-to-one: for each order there is one customer. From the point of view of the Customer File, the relationship is one-to-many: for each customer there may be many orders.

SET RELATION provides only limited help in working with files that have a one-to-many relationship to carry out operations such as displaying a customer record with all matching orders. You can link the files based on the match between ACCOUNT fields, this time from the Customer File into the Order File:

```
SELECT 1
USE NWORDER INDEX NWOACCT ALIAS ORDER
SELECT 2
USE NWCUST INDEX NWCACCT ALIAS CUSTOMER
SET RELATION TO ACCOUNT INTO ORDER
```

When you move the record pointer to any record in the Customer File, dBASE III PLUS does an internal SEEK to position the record pointer in the Order File to a matching record. If there is more than one match, RELATION finds the same record as an explicit SEEK would—the first one—and it is entirely your responsibility to devise a way to access the entire set of related records. You can do this with a WHILE clause, as described earlier in this chapter:

```
SELECT CUSTOMER
SEEK "ABCPLUMB"
SELECT ORDER
LIST WHILE ACCOUNT = CUSTOMER->ACCOUNT
```

In this example, SET RELATION is a convenience; it relieves you of the necessity to use a separate SEEK command in the Order File.

HANDS-ON PRACTICE—WORKING WITH MULTIPLE RELATED FILES

Open the three files in the National Widgets system, and link them with SET RELATION, as follows:

```
SELECT 1
USE NWINVENT INDEX NWICATPT ALIAS INVENTORY
SELECT 2
USE NWORDER INDEX NWOACCT ALIAS ORDER
SET RELATION TO CATEGORY + PARTNUMBER INTO INVENTORY
SELECT 3
USE NWCUST INDEX NWCACCT, NWCZIP ALIAS CUSTOMER
SET RELATION TO ACCOUNT INTO ORDER
```

The first SET RELATION command in this sequence links the Order and Inventory Files based on the common CATEGORY and PARTNUMBER fields so that for each order record, matching inventory data is available. The second SET RELATION command links the Customer and Order Files. Since there may be more than one order record matching any given customer record, this RELATION will be used only to find the first order record.

If you lose track of which files are open, and in which work areas, you can always type

```
DISPLAY STATUS
```

The resulting status display is shown in Figure 11-11. The display includes all open files and indexes, and indicates the selected work area. You can also determine the currently selected work area (identified by the file open in this area) by looking for the alias in the Status Bar, or if you have SET STATUS OFF, by typing DISPLAY to view the current record or DISPLAY STRUCTURE to definitively identify the file.

Find the customer record for ABC Plumbing with a SEEK command:

```
SEEK "ABCPLUMB"
```

```
. SET RELATION TO CATEGORY + PARTNUMBER INTO INVENTORY
. SELECT 3
. USE NWCUST INDEX NWCACCT, NWCZIP ALIAS CUSTOMER
. SET RELATION TO ACCOUNT INTO ORDER
. DISPLAY STATUS

Select area:  1, Database in Use: C:NWINVENT.dbf   Alias: INVENTORY
    Master index file:  C:NWICATPT.ndx  Key: CATEGORY + PARTNUMBER

Select area:  2, Database in Use: C:NWORDER.dbf   Alias: ORDER
    Master index file:  C:NWOACCT.ndx  Key: ACCOUNT
    Related into: INVENTORY
    Relation: CATEGORY + PARTNUMBER

Currently Selected Database:
Select area:  3, Database in Use: C:NWCUST.dbf   Alias: CUSTOMER
    Master index file:  C:NWCACCT.ndx  Key: ACCOUNT
           Index file:  C:NWCZIP.ndx  Key: ZIP
            Memo file:  C:NWCUST.dbt
    Related into: ORDER
    Relation: ACCOUNT
Press any key to continue...
Command Line    ||<C:>||CUSTOMER            ||Rec: 2/21         ||Ins ||   Caps

                        Enter a dBASE III PLUS command.
```

Figure 11-11 *Working with three files at once*

Select the Order File, and verify that with a DISPLAY command it is positioned at the first record for ABCPLUMB. Select the Inventory File, and verify that it is positioned at the record matching the current order record with another DISPLAY. Return to the Order File, and list all the orders for ABCPLUMB as well as the full item description and cost from the Inventory File, with the following:

```
SELECT ORDER
LIST ACCOUNT, CATEGORY, PARTNUMBER, INVENTORY->DESCRIP, INVENTORY->COST,
  PRICE WHILE ACCOUNT = CUSTOMER->ACCOUNT
```

Your screen should look similar to Figure 11-12. Select the Customer File and repeat the inquiry process for another customer. You will probably find it easier to type short commands, such as SELECT ORDER, and more expedient to retrieve longer commands, such as LIST, from HISTORY. This time the customer is selected by record number:

```
SELECT CUSTOMER
GOTO 4
DISPLAY
SELECT ORDER
LIST ACCOUNT, CATEGORY, PARTNUMBER, INVENTORY->DESCRIP, INVENTORY->COST,
  PRICE WHILE ACCOUNT = CUSTOMER->ACCOUNT
```

Select the Order File, and display all items showing a profit margin greater than 40 percent. The margin is calculated by subtracting the COST from the PRICE, dividing the result by the PRICE, and multiplying by 100 to convert the decimal value to a percentage. This computation will use the actual price charged (the PRICE field from the Order

```
. DISPLAY
     2      ABCPLUMB   ABC Plumbing                 1850 University Avenue    Berk
eley              CA 94703      .T. 861-4543 Ed Williams                  Kaypro PC,
 Epson FX-286   12/01/85 04/30/88      796.41     5248.90 Memo

. SELECT ORDER
. DISPLAY
     1  ABCPLUMB   07302 DISK   101-45     2   31.50    63.00     6.30   60.39

. SELECT INVENTORY
. DISPLAY
     9  DISK   101-45 5-1/4" DSDD Soft Sector     21.00    31.50

. SELECT ORDER
. LIST ACCOUNT, CATEGORY, PARTNUMBER, INVENTORY->DESCRIP, INVENTORY->COST, PRICE
 WHILE ACCOUNT = CUSTOMER->ACCOUNT
     1  ABCPLUMB    DISK    101-45 5-1/4" DSDD Soft Sector      21.00    31.50
     2  ABCPLUMB    FORMS   803-20 14-1/2 x 11" Green bar       28.50    45.25
     3  ABCPLUMB    RIBBON 240-51 Epson MX/FX100                 9.75    14.95
    23  ABCPLUMB    FORMS   803-20 14-1/2 x 11" Green bar       28.50    45.25

Command Line   <C:>  ORDER              Rec: 4/33          Ins        Caps
                         Enter a dBASE III PLUS command.
```

Figure 11-12 *Displaying data from two related files*

File) and the standard cost stored in the Inventory File:

```
SELECT ORDER
LIST FOR (PRICE - INVENTORY->COST) / PRICE * 100 >= 40
```

USING UPDATE TO TRANSFER DATA BETWEEN DATA BASES

The UPDATE command allows you to change the values of fields in one file based on data in another. The file to be updated and the file that provides the data must be open, in any two work areas, and the work area containing the file to be updated must be selected. For each record in the file being updated, there can be any number of records in the file that provides the data. In fact, UPDATE is best suited for operating on files that have a one-to-many relationship. The National Widgets Customer and Order files are good examples of such files. For one-to-one relationships, you can use the more straightforward REPLACE command.

The UPDATE command requires that the two files share a common field. The most efficient of several ways to use UPDATE is to build an index for the file being updated based on the common field that identifies matching records in the two files, and read the file that provides the data in record number order. Because this is not the only way to use UPDATE, you must include the keyword RANDOM in the command to indicate that the file that provides the data is in random order with respect to the common field. The general format for the UPDATE command is

> UPDATE ON *common field* FROM *file alias* RANDOM REPLACE *field WITH expression*

You can REPLACE more than one field with a single UPDATE command, subject only to the limitation that the command line may not exceed the 254-character maximum length.

When dBASE III PLUS executes the UPDATE, it updates the

selected file based on records read from the file named in the UPDATE command; these records are in random order with respect to the key expression. For each record in this file, dBASE III PLUS uses the equivalent of a SEEK to find the matching record in the selected file, which is indexed on the common key expression. When a match is found, each field listed after the REPLACE keyword is replaced with the result of evaluating the specified expression.

For example, you could use UPDATE to "post" order data to the Customer File with the following sequence:

```
SELECT 1
USE NWORDER ALIAS ORDER
SELECT 2
USE NWCUST INDEX NWCACCT ALIAS CUSTOMER
UPDATE ON ACCOUNT FROM ORDER RANDOM REPLACE YTDORDERS WITH
  YTDORDERS + ORDER->INVAMOUNT, TOTORDERS WITH TOTORDERS + ORDER->INVAMOUN
```

In this example, the Customer File is opened with an index based on the ACCOUNT code, the field that is used to determine which record to update for a given order record, and the Customer File is selected. The UPDATE command instructs dBASE III PLUS to update the Customer File based on data contained in the Order File, which is in random order with respect to the ACCOUNT field, the common key field used to identify the matching records. The UPDATE command does exactly the same thing, but for each record in the Order File, as if you had typed the following commands at the dot prompt:

```
SELECT CUSTOMER
SEEK ORDER->ACCOUNT
REPLACE NEXT 1 YTDORDERS WITH YTDORDERS + ORDER->INVAMOUNT,
  TOTORDERS WITH TOTORDERS + ORDER->INVAMOUNT
SELECT ORDER
SKIP
```

The UPDATE command always reads every record in the file that provides the data. If you do not want to process the entire file, you must copy the selected records to a temporary file and use this file to perform the UPDATE. For example, you might want to transfer data to the Customer File from the "new" (previously unposted) Order File records. In this case, the most likely way to identify the "new" records is by keeping track of the last invoice number posted in the previous batch.

If it were invoice "08299", you could post the new invoices with the following sequence of commands:

```
USE NWORDER
COPY TO NWTEMP FOR INVOICE >= "08300"
USE NWTEMP ALIAS ORDER
SELECT 2
USE NWCUST INDEX NWCACCT ALIAS CUSTOMER
UPDATE ON ACCOUNT FROM ORDER RANDOM REPLACE YTDORDERS WITH
  YTDORDERS + ORDER->INVAMOUNT, TOTORDERS WITH TOTORDERS + ORDER->INVAMOUNT
```

The methods described in this chapter for working with multiple related data bases depend partially on the initial data base design, because the files must share common fields if dBASE III PLUS is to identify the matching records. If this fundamental requirement is met, you can use a few basic tools to establish the relationships. You can build indexes based on the common fields, use SEEK or SET RELATION to find the matching records, and WHILE clauses to process groups of related records efficiently.

More important, these techniques depend on your ability to maintain the integrity of the data entered in the files. You must ensure that identical values are entered into corresponding fields in related files, that a field intended as a unique record identifier never takes on the same value in two different records, and that matching records are added to related pairs of files where necessary. If you change the contents of the index key field in one of several related files, you must make sure to change the contents of the same field in all records in the other related files.

For the most part, dBASE III PLUS does nothing to maintain data integrity automatically. You can use the basic tools outlined in this chapter—in particular, SET RELATION—to detect problems such as an order record that has no matching customer or inventory record, but dBASE III PLUS cannot prevent erroneous data from being entered into the files in the first place. Working with multiple files requires attention to detail and error detection strategies to find potential problems before you carry out file update procedures that depend on the accuracy of the data in the files.

Chapter 12

Customizing the Working Environment

One of the best features of dBASE III PLUS is that you can get started right away by using built-in defaults for many aspects of the data entry environment. You can later customize data entry to suit your preferences and the demands of your application. As you gain experience, you will undoubtedly form strong opinions about which defaults you want to change. dBASE III PLUS offers a full complement of SET commands, many of which have already been introduced in earlier chapters, that you may combine as you wish to create a personalized working environment. This chapter elaborates on the use of SET commands and introduces the CONFIG.DB file, a configuration file used to save your settings so that they become the defaults for future work sessions.

In addition to the SET commands that control general aspects of the working environment at the dot prompt and in the full-screen editing modes, dBASE III PLUS provides for constructing customized views of the data in one file or a set of related files. You have already learned about some of these tools—format files, FILTERs, and QUERY files—as they apply to working with a single data base. This chapter introduces additional commands and strategies that can be used to view and update data in multiple related files, and perform the necessary housekeeping operations to manage the many disk files that make up a large application.

USING SET COMMANDS

Many of the SET commands used by dBASE III PLUS to customize the working environment and the appearance of the screen in the full-screen editing modes were introduced as necessity arose in earlier chapters. For example, you already know how to quiet the beeper with SET BELL OFF, use SET HEADING OFF to eliminate the field name headings from the output of commands such as LIST or SUM, and make room for more data on the screen by turning off the status display with SET STATUS OFF. You can change the values of these and many other settings in three ways:

- By typing SET commands at the dot prompt
- By using the menu-driven SET command, which allows you to make selections from pull-down menus
- By saving the settings in a configuration file called CONFIG.DB

Thus far, all the examples in this book used the first of these methods: typing SET commands individually at the dot prompt. If you want to change many settings at once, say at the beginning of a work session, or if you need a reminder about what options are available, the menu-driven SET command is more convenient. To enter the menu system, you type

```
SET
```

Figure 12-1 illustrates the initial screen displayed by the SET command, and the structure of the menus is diagrammed in Figure 12-2. Most of the options described in earlier chapters can be found on the **Options** submenu, which lists the settings in alphabetical order as well as their current values. You can see from the Status Bar that there are 25 options on this submenu, too many to fit on the screen at once. To view the remaining options, you select **Options** and then use the PGDN or DOWN ARROW key to move down through the list.

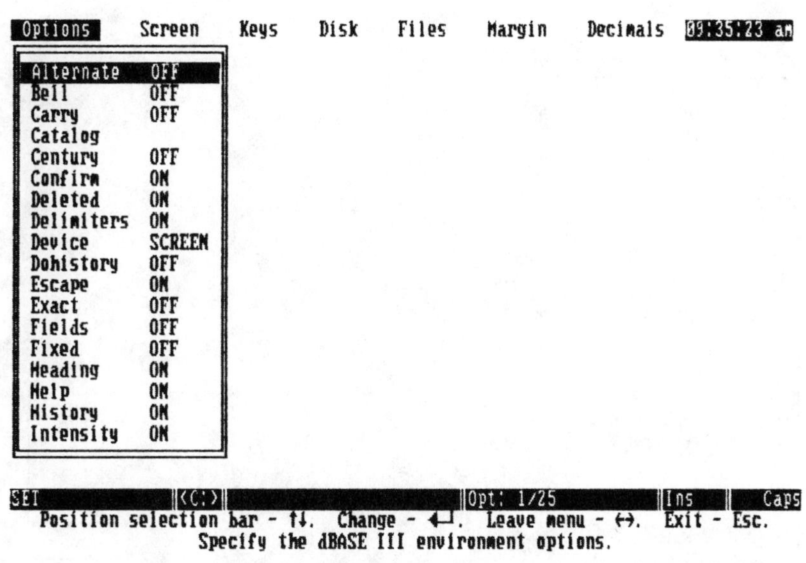

Figure 12-1 *The initial screen displayed by the SET command*

Many of the settings on the **Options** submenu are *toggles* that may take on two values: ON or OFF. Just as you operate a push-button toggle switch, you use the same command to turn an option ON if it is OFF or OFF if it is ON. To change the toggle, you use the arrow keys to highlight the desired option, and then press ENTER to switch to the alternate value.

When you first look at the SET menu, it may seem as if you are being confronted with a bewildering array of options. Keep in mind that many of the available options are of interest only to programmers and that the utility of others will become apparent only as you gain more experience with dBASE III PLUS. If you prefer, you can continue to work with the default settings in effect.

Options

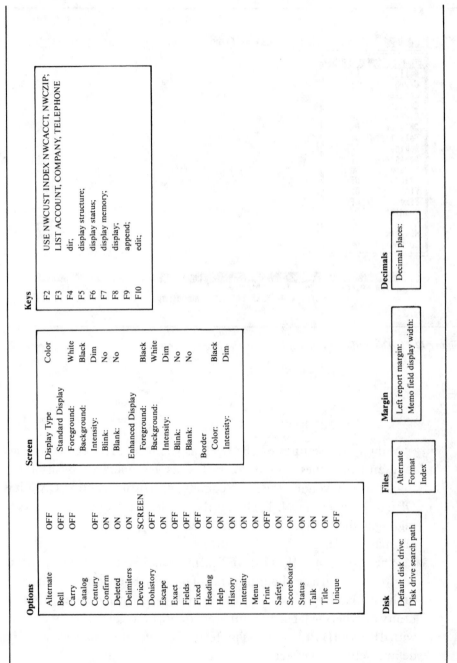

Alternate	OFF
Bell	OFF
Carry	OFF
Catalog	
Century	OFF
Confirm	ON
Deleted	ON
Delimiters	ON
Device	SCREEN
Dohistory	OFF
Escape	ON
Exact	OFF
Fields	OFF
Fixed	OFF
Heading	ON
Help	ON
History	ON
Intensity	ON
Menu	ON
Print	OFF
Safety	ON
Scoreboard	ON
Status	ON
Talk	ON
Title	ON
Unique	OFF

Screen

Display Type	Color
Standard Display	
Foreground:	White
Background:	Black
Intensity:	Dim
Blink:	No
Blank:	No
Enhanced Display	
Foreground:	Black
Background:	White
Intensity:	Dim
Blink:	No
Blank:	No
Border	
Color:	Black
Intensity:	Dim

Keys

F2	USE NWCUST INDEX NWCACCT, NWCZIP;
F3	LIST ACCOUNT, COMPANY, TELEPHONE
F4	dir;
F5	display structure;
F6	display status;
F7	display memory;
F8	display;
F9	append;
F10	edit;

Disk

Default disk drive:
Disk drive search path

Files

Alternate
Format
Index

Margin

Left report margin:
Memo field display width:

Decimals

Decimal places:

Figure 12-2 *The structure of the SET menus*

The following is a summary of the options, some of which you already know, that you may want to change (the default values are shown in parentheses):

- ***Bell*** *(ON):* Whether the bell (beeper) sounds when you fill a field completely or make an error
- ***Carry*** *(OFF):* Whether the values entered into each new record are used as defaults for the next record appended
- ***Confirm*** *(OFF):* Whether you must always press ENTER to advance the cursor to the next field, even if the data completely fills a field
- ***Deleted*** *(OFF):* Whether deleted records are ignored by most commands
- ***Delimiters*** *(OFF):* Whether data entry areas are delineated by punctuation marks (by default, colons are used as delimiters)
- ***Heading*** *(ON):* Whether the expressions displayed by commands such as LIST, DISPLAY, and SUM are included in the output as "column headings"
- ***Help*** *(ON):* Whether dBASE III PLUS responds to error messages by offering help: "Do you want some help? (Y/N)"
- ***Intensity*** *(ON):* Whether data entry areas (fields) are distinguished from background text (field name prompts) by the use of different colors or visual attributes
- ***Menu*** *(ON):* Whether dBASE III PLUS displays a help menu of cursor movement and editing command keys when you first enter any full-screen editing mode
- ***Print*** *(OFF):* Whether data and text displayed on the screen are also echoed to the printer
- ***Safety*** *(ON):* Whether dBASE III PLUS asks for confirmation before overwriting an existing disk file

- ***Scoreboard** (ON):* Whether status indicators and error messages are displayed on the top line of the screen if you also SET STATUS OFF
- ***Status** (OFF):* Whether or not the bottom three lines of the screen are used for the Status Bar, Navigation Line, and Message Line

Several options on the other submenus may also be of immediate interest. If you are working on floppy disks, you can use the **Default drive** option on the **Disk** menu to set the default drive to B (or whatever letter identifies your floppy disk), so that you do not have to include the disk drive designator in all your file names.

If you have a color monitor, you may want to experiment with the screen colors using the **Screen** submenu. dBASE III PLUS divides the screen into three areas, defined not by their location but by their use: The *Standard* display area refers to text displayed by dBASE III PLUS (normally white characters on a black background), the *Enhanced* area is used for entered data (normally inverse video, or black characters on a light background), and the *border* is the perimeter of the screen that lies outside the 25-line by 80-column display area. You can set the border color and individually change the foreground and background colors used for the Standard and Enhanced areas.

Most, but not all of the environment settings may be changed from the SET menu. One useful option that cannot is the choice of the actual delimiter character used to mark the beginning and the end of data entry areas when you have SET DELIMITERS ON. You can choose the characters with

SET DELIMITERS TO *delimiter character(s)*

If you specify one character, it is used at both the beginning and the end of the field; if you specify two, the first is displayed at the beginning and the second at the end. For example, you could substitute square brackets for the default delimiter (the colon) with the command

```
SET DELIMITERS TO "[]"
```

The SET menu also offers options to reprogram the function keys (a topic that is covered later in this chapter), change the default left margin for reports, adjust the display width used for memo fields in LIST or DISPLAY commands, and specify the number of decimal places used when calculated results are displayed.

Some option selections are governed solely by personal style. For example, when a field is filled, some people find hearing a bell annoying, while others are reassured by this audible reminder, like the bell on a typewriter that signals the end of a line. The nature of your data base may also play an important role. When you update a file with short fields that are always completely filled in, you might SET CONFIRM OFF to eliminate an extra keystroke (pressing ENTER after each field). In a name and address data base, however, fields that are rarely filled (such as a street address) often alternate with fields that invariably are filled (a state abbreviation or ZIP code); you may prefer to SET CONFIRM ON if you find this inconsistency disconcerting.

HANDS-ON PRACTICE—SET

To invoke the menu-driven SET command, type

```
SET
```

Press ENTER to select the **Options** submenu, and use the UP ARROW and DOWN ARROW keys to browse through the available options. For any option you want to change, press ENTER to switch to the alternate value. If you don't have any preferences, select the following settings:

```
BELL:          OFF
CONFIRM:       ON
DELETED:       ON
DELIMITER:     ON
HELP           OFF
STATUS:        ON
```

Use the RIGHT ARROW key to select the **Screen** menu, and experiment with different color combinations or monochrome display attributes. To do this, press ENTER with any of the color areas highlighted to step through the available choices. You can see the effects of your changes immediately in a small box that pops up to display exactly how the Standard and Enhanced areas would look using the selected display attributes. Figure 12-3 illustrates this screen.

In addition to changing the colors themselves, you can vary the intensity of any color by highlighting the **Intensity** option and pressing ENTER to toggle between Bright and Dim. You can also make a color blink or blank out an area entirely, but these options are generally used by programmers for small, specific areas on a screen—you would not normally want an entire data entry screen to blink.

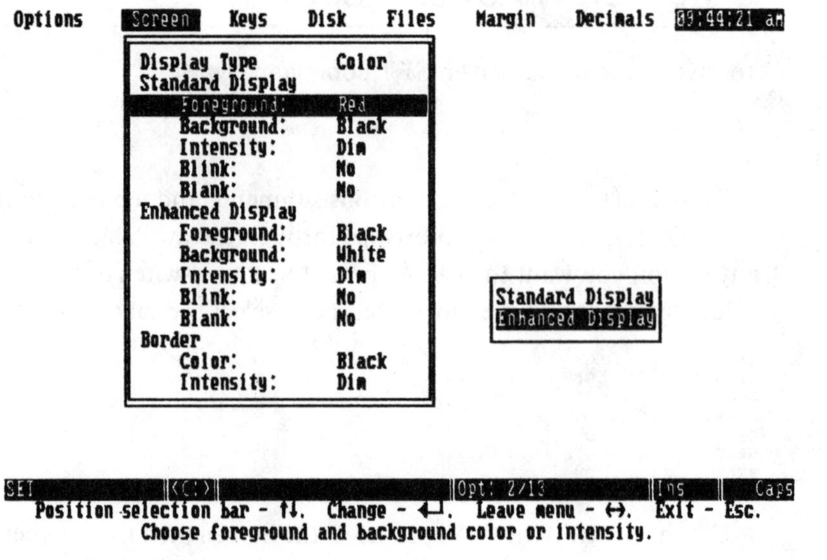

Figure 12-3 *Selecting screen colors from the SET menu*

When you are satisfied with your color selections, use the RIGHT ARROW key to move to the **Disk** menu. Select the default disk drive by pressing ENTER until the correct drive designator appears next to the prompt. Note that you can also specify a default search path for files not found in the current directory.

Press the RIGHT ARROW key again (twice) to move to the **Margin** submenu, and set the left report margin to 5 to add five characters to the left edge of printed reports (in addition to the left margin specified in the report or label form). Use the **Memo field display width** option to change the display width for memo fields to 30 characters so that you can fit more fields on the screen in a LIST or DISPLAY command that includes memo fields.

When you are satisfied with your selections, press ESC to exit the SET menu. Note that unlike most of the other full-screen editors, SET saves each option as you change its value, and exiting with ESC does not result in losing your settings. To view the effects of your changes, type

```
DISPLAY STATUS
```

You might also want to APPEND a new record or EDIT existing records to observe the differences in the data entry environment.

REPROGRAMMING THE FUNCTION KEYS

You can further customize the working environment by assigning your own meaning to any programmable function key (most keyboards have either 10 or 12) except F1, which is reserved for use as a HELP key. You can alter function key assignments either through the **Keys** submenu in the full-screen SET command, or by typing a SET FUNCTION command at the dot prompt. Reprogramming the function keys enables you to issue frequently used commands with a single keystroke. You might, for example, redefine the F2 key to open a file:

```
SET FUNCTION 2 TO "USE NWCUST INDEX NWCACCT, NWCZIP;"
```

The semicolon in the command string symbolizes a carriage return. This SET command causes the F2 key to have the same effect as typing

USE NWCUST INDEX NWCACCT, NWCZIP and then pressing ENTER. You can store more than one command in a single function key by including more than one semicolon within the command string:

```
SET FUNCTION 3 TO "SEEK CUSTOMER->ACCOUNT; DISPLAY;"
```

Note that a function key assignment can represent any sequence of keystrokes; they are typed for you by dBASE III PLUS when you press the designated key. A key might represent one command, more than one command, or part of a command. For example, you might want to use the LIST command to display the same set of fields from a data base but vary the record selection criteria. You could use a function key to store the constant portion of your command:

```
SET FUNCTION 4 TO "LIST ACCOUNT, COMPANY, TELEPHONE FOR "
```

When you press F4, dBASE III PLUS types LIST ACCOUNT, BALANCE FOR (including the space after "FOR"), and you can complete the command by typing your condition and pressing ENTER.

USING A CONFIG.DB FILE TO ESTABLISH THE DEFAULT ENVIRONMENT

The options you select, either through the menu-driven SET command or by typing individual SET commands at the dot prompt, remain in effect only for the duration of your work session. dBASE III PLUS retains no permanent record of the settings, so if you exit to DOS and reload dBASE III PLUS, the program's default settings will again be in effect.

You can save your own personalized default settings in a configuration file called CONFIG.DB. This file, which is analogous to the DOS configuration file CONFIG.SYS, is an ordinary ASCII text file with each command on a separate line. You can create or edit the file CONFIG.DB with any word processor or text editor that can read and write ASCII files, including the dBASE III PLUS program editor (which is covered in Chapter 14), or you can use the COPY command, as described in Chapter 2 in the section on CONFIG.SYS.

Just as DOS reads CONFIG.SYS only when you boot your computer, dBASE III PLUS checks for the CONFIG.DB file only when you start up the program. If you edit the configuration file from within dBASE III PLUS, you must exit and reload the program to see the effects of your changes. The CONFIG.DB file must be located in the directory from which you load dBASE III PLUS. If the CONFIG.DB file is missing, the default settings are automatically placed in effect, and you can always override the settings specified in the CONFIG.DB file by typing new SET commands at the dot prompt.

The syntax used in CONFIG.DB differs in several respects from the equivalent SET commands. Most SET commands take the form

SET *option value*

or

SET *option* TO *value*

The equivalent CONFIG.DB commands take the form

option = *value*

In some cases, there are other minor differences. For example, the following is a typical sequence of SET commands:

```
SET BELL OFF
SET CONFIRM ON
SET DEFAULT TO C
SET DELETED ON
SET DELIMITER ON
SET DELIMITER TO "[]"
SET INTENSITY OFF
SET STATUS ON
SET FUNCTION 2 TO "USE NWCUST INDEX NWCACCT, NWCZIP;"
SET FUNCTION 3 TO "SEEK CUSTOMER->ACCOUNT; DISPLAY;"
SET FUNCTION 4 TO "LIST ACCOUNT, COMPANY, TELEPHONE FOR "
```

The options listed in the previous example would appear as follows in CONFIG.DB:

```
BELL = OFF
CONFIRM = ON
DEFAULT = C
DELETED = ON
DELIMITER = ON
DELIMITER = []
INTENSITY = OFF
STATUS = ON
F2 = "USE NWCUST INDEX NWCACCT, NWCZIP;"
F3 = "SEEK CUSTOMER->ACCOUNT; DISPLAY;"
F4 = "LIST ACCOUNT, COMPANY, TELEPHONE FOR "
```

For several CONFIG.DB options, there are no equivalent SET commands. Most of these options govern advanced aspects of memory allocation that do not concern beginning dBASE III PLUS users, but there is one that you should know about. The COMMAND option allows you to specify a dBASE III PLUS command to be executed immediately when you load dBASE III PLUS. For example, you could display a list of available data bases with the following entry:

```
COMMAND = DIR
```

The COMMAND command is responsible for the fact that dBASE III PLUS displays the ASSIST menu when the program is first loaded. The default CONFIG.DB file provided with dBASE III PLUS consists of the following two lines:

```
COMMAND = ASSIST
STATUS = ON
```

If you prefer to bypass the Assistant, you can remove the COMMAND= ASSIST entry from the CONFIG.DB file, create a new configuration file that has no COMMAND command, or substitute your own to execute a command of your choice.

Appendix E contains a summary of the correct syntax for all the CONFIG.DB entries recognized by dBASE III PLUS.

VIEWING AND EDITING SELECTED FIELDS

In addition to the commands that allow you to customize general aspects of the working environment, both at the dot prompt and in the full-screen editing modes, dBASE III PLUS offers a variety of tools for creating customized views of the data in one or more files. You have already seen some of these methods. For example, you can add a field list to commands such as DISPLAY, LIST, and COPY to restrict processing to certain fields. For full-screen editing, you can design format files that include only certain fields in a data base.

You can also add a field list to an EDIT, CHANGE, or BROWSE command to view and edit selected fields using the standard dBASE III PLUS editing screen. The field list determines which fields are displayed and the order in which they are presented. For example, you could update the COMMENTS field in the National Widgets Customer File while displaying the ACCOUNT, COMPANY, and YTDORDERS fields for reference with:

```
EDIT FIELDS COMMENTS, ACCOUNT, COMPANY, YTDORDERS
```

or

```
CHANGE FIELDS COMMENTS, ACCOUNT, COMPANY, YTDORDERS
```

This technique is ideal for updating a few fields in many records in a data base, especially if the fields are located toward the end of the structure, and using the standard EDIT screen would force you to skip all intervening fields by pressing PGDN, ENTER, or DOWN ARROW repeatedly. Often, the fields whose values uniquely identify a record—they are entered initially and rarely change afterward—are placed near the top of the structure, while the fields you need to access more often later on are further down.

For editing certain standard groups of fields or inquiries that are repeated frequently, you might prefer to design format files, which draw "prettier" screens and permit more extensive data formatting and validation. Using a field list with EDIT or CHANGE is more appropriate for occasional or varying queries that do not merit spending the time to create format files.

The BROWSE command also accepts a field list and displays the named fields only, in the specified order. BROWSE has one significant limitation compared with EDIT and CHANGE: It does not allow you to access memo fields.

BROWSE offers its own set of options, some of which were described in Chapter 4, for further refining your view of a data base. The WIDTH option, which is not accessible from the menu of special options invoked by pressing CTRL-HOME, allows you to specify the maximum display width for character fields and thus fit more fields on the screen at once. The WIDTH setting applies equally to all character fields.

When you display fields, such as ACCOUNT and COMPANY in the previous example, not for editing but simply to help you identify records, the first 10 or 15 characters of the field may serve the purpose. Regardless of the display width, you can edit all the data in the field; as you move the cursor left or right, the data scrolls to reveal more characters, just as when you use the S function in a format file to collect a long character field in a narrower space. For example, the following would set the display width for character fields to 20 characters so that all listed fields fit on the screen at once:

```
BROWSE WIDTH 20 FIELDS AREACODE, TELEPHONE, CONTACT, ACCOUNT, COMPANY
```

Once a file grows larger than a few hundred records, it is inconvenient to locate a particular record in BROWSE by paging up and down 20 records at a time. If an index is open, you can execute a SEEK command without exiting the BROWSE screen. This option, labeled **Find** (to match the alternate indexed retrieval command retained for compatibility with dBASE II), is accessed through the special options menu; it is displayed on the menu only if an index is open.

When you press CTRL-HOME to display the menu and select **Find**, dBASE III PLUS prompts you to "Enter search string" and then executes the SEEK. If dBASE III PLUS fails to find a matching record, the error message "** Not Found **" is displayed below the Status Bar; if a record is found, the screen is redrawn with the specified record at the top.

ACCESSING FIELDS FROM MULTIPLE DATA BASES

All the commands described in the preceding sections allow you to access fields from more than one data base. In EDIT, CHANGE, and BROWSE, you can access fields from any data base open in any of the ten work areas, just as you can with a LIST command. But if the resulting display is to be meaningful, the files must share a common field or fields and must be linked with SET RELATION based on this common key expression. For example, you could edit Order File records while viewing the matching customers' company name and equipment with the following sequence of commands:

```
SELECT 1
USE NWCUST INDEX NWCACCT ALIAS CUSTOMER
SELECT 2
USE NWORDER INDEX NWOACCT ALIAS ORDER
SET RELATION TO ACCOUNT INTO CUSTOMER
EDIT FIELDS ACCOUNT, INVOICE, CATEGORY, PARTNUMBER, QUANTITY, PRICE,
  SUBTOTAL, DISCOUNT, INVAMOUNT, CUSTOMER->COMPANY, CUSTOMER->EQUIPMENT
```

Since you can access data from only one matching record in the related file, this technique is most useful for performing "lookups" when there is a one-to-one relationship between files. When you work with files that have a one-to-many relationship, SEEK retrieves only the first of a group of matching records. Nevertheless, you might occasionally want to SET RELATION from the file with "one" record into the file with "many." For example, you could display Order File fields while editing records in the Customer File. Although you could view only one order record per customer, it would be sufficient to determine whether a customer had any orders at all; if not, the RELATION would position the Order File at the end-of-file, and all the fields would appear blank.

Note also that although this command was presented as a tool for viewing data, you can make changes to any fields displayed on the screen, and the changes will be stored in the respective data bases.

USING SET FIELDS TO ACCESS SELECTED FIELDS

If you frequently need to display or edit certain groups of fields, you can avoid having to retype the field list repeatedly by using the SET FIELDS command to restrict the fields that are accessible through the EDIT, BROWSE, LIST, and many other commands. The syntax of the SET FIELDS command is:

SET FIELDS TO *field list*

Because you might want to select more fields than you can specify in a single 254-character command, successive SET FIELDS commands add fields to the list rather than creating a new field list. You can select all the fields in a file with

```
SET FIELDS TO ALL
```

The following command sequence makes available the same set of fields that were specified in the last example in the previous section:

```
SELECT 1
USE NWCUST INDEX NWCACCT ALIAS CUSTOMER
SELECT 2
USE NWORDER INDEX NWOACCT ALIAS ORDER
SET RELATION TO ACCOUNT INTO CUSTOMER
SET FIELDS TO ALL
SET FIELDS TO CUSTOMER->COMPANY, CUSTOMER->EQUIPMENT
EDIT
```

You can disable the field list temporarily to view all fields in all open files with

```
SET FIELDS OFF
```

and then place the list back in effect with

```
SET FIELDS ON
```

By default, dBASE III PLUS assumes that the field list is OFF and that all fields are available. When you use a SET FIELDS command to specify the field list, this command also activates the field list, as if you had typed SET FIELDS ON. Using SET FIELDS differs in one way from adding a field list to an EDIT, CHANGE, or BROWSE command: SET FIELDS cannot be used to change the order in which fields are presented on the screen. Fields from the selected work area are always displayed first, followed by fields from unselected work areas, in all cases, in the order they occur in the file structure.

With a field list in effect, any attempt to process a field not included in the list results in a "Variable not found" error message, and if you SELECT a work area containing a file with no available fields and execute a command such as EDIT, dBASE III PLUS responds with "No fields to process".

When a field list is used to access fields from two data bases linked with SET RELATION, all the specified fields from both files are visible when you select the file that initiates the RELATION. With the related file selected, only fields from this file are accessible, because from the related file there is no path back to the matching record(s) in the data base that initiates the RELATION.

When you APPEND records to either file, the field list is ignored. All the fields from the selected file—none from other work areas—are displayed. This may seem confusing at first, but it would not make sense to prohibit you from entering data into all the fields in a new record; whereas when you are simply viewing data, no harmful consequences result from limiting access to certain fields.

When two files are linked with SET RELATION, you might want to be able to view fields from the related file while adding records to the file that initiates the relation. For example, making the EQUIPMENT field from the Customer File visible as orders are entered enables you to verify that the ordered items are at least reasonable purchases for a given customer. In addition, you might hope to detect missing customer records or misspelled account codes by observing the failure of dBASE III PLUS to find the matching customer for a new order.

All these potentially desirable operations are impossible, largely because of the way SET RELATION works. Remember that dBASE III PLUS performs the internal SEEK that retrieves the related record at the instant the record pointer moves in the selected file. When you APPEND a record to the selected file, dBASE III PLUS immediately positions the record pointer on the new record. At this point, all fields are blank, including the one(s) on which the RELATION is based, so the related file is positioned at the end-of-file. Entering data into the new record does not move the record pointer, so the related file is not repositioned either.

dBASE III PLUS offers little help in ensuring that related files always contain matching data. You can neither verify that the customer exists when you enter an order record nor automatically add a matching customer record if one is missing. Because much of the burden for maintaining the integrity of your data bases rests with you, it is worth thinking about how you can verify that your files do contain matching data. For example, after adding a batch of orders, you could use the technique described in Chapter 11 to detect mismatches between the Customer and Order files:

```
SELECT 1
USE NWCUST INDEX NWCACCT ALIAS CUSTOMER
SELECT 2
USE NWORDER INDEX NWOACCT ALIAS ORDER
SET RELATION TO ACCOUNT INTO CUSTOMER
LIST ACCOUNT, CATEGORY, PARTNUMBER, QUANTITY FOR ACCOUNT <> CUSTOMER->ACCOUNT
```

USING VIEW FILES TO CREATE A CUSTOMIZED DATA ENTRY ENVIRONMENT

By using the commands described in this and the last chapter, you can create highly customized data entry environments for particular purposes. dBASE III PLUS allows you to store a description of the working environment in a VIEW file so you can easily recreate a complex environment in a subsequent work session. The VIEW file, which has the extension VUE, may include specifications for some or all of the following:

- One or more data base files and the work area in which to open each
- The indexes, if any, to open with each data base
- How to link the files with SET RELATION
- A field list made up of fields from all work areas
- One format file for accessing fields from one or more files
- A FILTER to establish record selection criteria
- The work area to select when the VIEW is placed in effect

These specifications describe exactly what the term VIEW implies: a highly customized view of the data contained in one or more files. You can create or edit a VIEW using a full-screen editor invoked with

```
CREATE VIEW
```

or

```
MODIFY VIEW
```

The VIEW editor offers four main menu options. The **Set Up** option displays a list of available data base files from which you may select up to ten; the work areas are assigned in sequence, starting with work area 1. There is no way to assign an alias to a file by using the VIEW editor.

You choose a file by using the UP ARROW and DOWN ARROW keys to highlight the file name and then pressing ENTER. Selected files are indicated by a triangle that appears to the left of the file name; you can "unselect" a file (remove it from the VIEW) by highlighting the name and pressing ENTER again. Since you can choose up to ten data bases, the list of file names remains on the screen until you exit the **Set Up** submenu by pressing the LEFT ARROW or RIGHT ARROW key to move to another main menu option.

After you choose each file, another pop-up box displays a list of index files. You can choose one or more for each data base; the first one you select is designated the master index — the one that controls the order in which records are processed, and the one that you may use to SEEK records — just as if you had named this index first in a USE or SET INDEX command.

You use the **Relate** option to establish a chain of relations between pairs of data bases. You can establish a straight chain of relations of any length. For example, you could SET RELATION from the Customer File into the Order File, and from the Order File into the Inventory File (although this particular setup might not be very useful). First you select the file that initiates the RELATION (the Customer File in this example) and then select the related file from another pop-up box. Finally, you specify the key expression used to link the data bases.

Just as at command level, you can SET only one RELATION from a given work area. From the dot prompt, however, you can SET RELA-

TION into the same file from two other files, whereas you cannot do this from the VIEW editor. This limit is consistent with the purpose of a VIEW, which is used to provide a particular view of your data; dBASE III PLUS does not intend that when you use a VIEW you would switch work areas (although once you gain some experience, you may want to).

The **Set Fields** option allows you to construct a field list, which may include fields from each of the data bases that make up the VIEW. By default, all the fields in all the files are selected. You select and "unselect" fields from a list displayed in a pop-up box by pressing ENTER with the desired field highlighted. For reference, another pop-up box displays the data type and the length of the highlighted field.

The **Options** submenu allows you to specify a format file (which must already exist) to draw a custom screen for updating the files in the VIEW, and a FILTER condition to define record selection criteria. The VIEW editor does not allow you to name a previously defined QUERY file as a substitute for typing a FILTER condition.

To save the VIEW on disk, you choose the **Save** option from the **Exit** submenu. When you exit the editor, the VIEW file is automatically placed in effect.

You can also create a VIEW file "on the fly" from the dot prompt by opening all the required files, issuing the appropriate SET commands, and then typing

CREATE VIEW *view file name* FROM ENVIRONMENT

A view created in this way will include file aliases specified in the USE commands that opened the file. Regardless of how it was created, you invoke a VIEW with

SET VIEW TO *view file name*

You cancel a VIEW file indirectly when you close the data bases it accesses (usually with CLOSE DATABASES).

Using a VIEW file simplifies the process of opening two or more data base files, linking them with SET RELATION, and creating a highly customized environment for viewing and editing records. Creating a

VIEW enables you to later accomplish with a single command—SET VIEW—a task that would otherwise require five or more commands. A less knowledgeable user can then easily open a set of files that you have created without having to remember the file names or understand the complexities of SET RELATION and SET FIELDS. In theory, such a user might not even realize that the data on the screen was drawn from not one but several related data base files.

VIEW files, like the individual commands that they incorporate—SET RELATION and SET FIELDS—are most useful for viewing and updating data in one file while displaying and possibly editing fields from a related file at the same time. When you work with several unrelated data bases open simultaneously in multiple work areas to avoid having to repeatedly type different USE commands, a VIEW would actually limit your activities, since it permits only one format file, one FILTER, and one field list. The VIEW is intended to do what its name implies—to give you a customized view into the data stored in one or more data base files, working from the point of view of one of the files, and presenting fields from the other related file(s) as if they were included in the record in the selected file.

HANDS-ON PRACTICE—CREATING A VIEW FILE

Earlier in this chapter, in "Using SET FIELDS to access Selected Fields," the Customer and Order files were opened and linked with SET RELATION to edit order records while you view certain fields from the Customer File. Make sure that any open data bases are closed, and then open the Customer and Order files as described previously, with the following command sequence:

```
CLOSE DATABASES
SELECT 1
USE NWCUST INDEX NWCACCT ALIAS CUSTOMER
SELECT 2
USE NWORDER INDEX NWOACCT ALIAS ORDER
SET RELATION TO ACCOUNT INTO CUSTOMER
SET FIELDS TO ALL
SET FIELDS TO CUSTOMER->COMPANY, CUSTOMER->EQUIPMENT
```

Save this environment in a VIEW file by typing

```
CREATE VIEW NWORDCST FROM ENVIRONMENT
```

Use a DISPLAY STATUS command to verify that the right files are open and that the Order File work area is selected. EDIT an order record to confirm that the customer fields are visible, and then move through the Order File with PGUP and PGDN. The customer data should change to match the ACCOUNT field in the Order File.

Press ESC to return to the dot prompt, and try the EDIT, APPEND, and BROWSE commands in both work areas. In all cases, you should see that when the Order File is selected, fields from both files are visible, whereas in the Customer File work area, only COMPANY and EQUIPMENT are displayed. Type DISPLAY STRUCTURE from both work areas. You will see that the selected fields are marked with a ">" next to the field name. Finally, close all open files, including the VIEW, with

```
CLOSE DATABASES
```

Use the VIEW editor to modify the VIEW file by typing

```
MODIFY VIEW NOWRDCST
```

Note the triangular markers that identify NWCUST and NWORDER as data bases included in the VIEW file you are editing. Select the SET FIELDS option to add the customer CONTACT, YTDORDERS, and TOTORDERS fields to the VIEW. dBASE III PLUS will display the names of the two active data bases in a pop-up box. Select NWCUST by pressing ENTER with the file name highlighted. The VIEW editor will display a list of fields, with COMPANY and EQUIPMENT marked as selected. Select each of the three new fields by highlighting each field in turn and then pressing ENTER. Your screen should look like Figure 12-4.

Press the RIGHT ARROW key twice, once to exit the **Set Fields** option and once to move to the **Options** submenu. Define a FILTER condition that selects only orders in the DISK category by entering the condition

```
CATEGORY = "DISK"
```

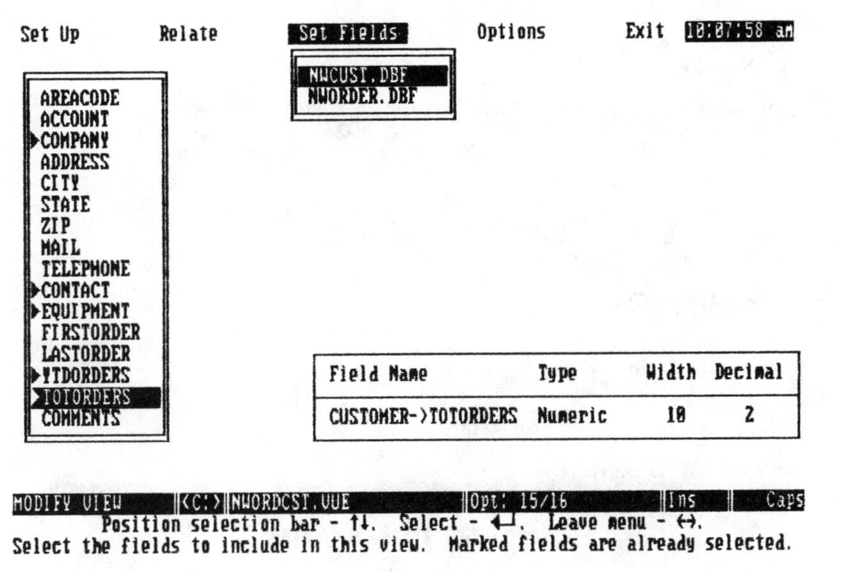

Figure 12-4 *Selecting the fields to be included in a VIEW*

Finally, save the modified VIEW by choosing the **Save** option on the **Exit** menu. From the dot prompt, invoke the new VIEW with

```
SET VIEW TO NWORDCST
```

Again, type DISPLAY STATUS to verify the status of the working environment. Your screen should match Figure 12-5. Page through the Order File again using EDIT or CHANGE, and note the new set of fields and the effect of the FILTER. Find a record for ABC Plumbing, and change the COMPANY field contents to A.B.C. Plumbing. Press ESC to return to the dot prompt, select the Customer File, and DISPLAY the record to confirm that the change was saved:

```
SELECT CUSTOMER
DISPLAY
```

```
. SET VIEW TO NWORDCST
. DISPLAY STATUS

Select area:  1, Database in Use: C:NWCUST.DBF   Alias: CUSTOMER
    Master index file:  C:NWCACCT.NDX  Key: ACCOUNT
           Memo file:   C:NWCUST.dbt

Currently Selected Database:
Select area:  2, Database in Use: C:NWORDER.DBF   Alias: ORDER
    Master index file:  C:NWOACCT.NDX  Key: ACCOUNT
Filter: CATEGORY = "DISK"
    Related into: CUSTOMER
    Relation: ACCOUNT

File search path:
Default disk drive: C:
Print destination:  PRN:
Margin =    0
Current work area =    2  Delimiters are '[' and ']'

Press any key to continue...
Command Line    <C:> ORDER             Rec: 1/33          Ins      Caps
                      Enter a dBASE III PLUS command.
```

Figure 12-5 *The environment defined by the NWORDCST.VUEVIEW*

USING CATALOG FILES TO GROUP THE FILES IN AN APPLICATION

As a data base application grows and matures, it invariably generates many disk files. A system with two or three main data bases might well encompass dozens of files, including indexes, format files, QUERY files, VIEW files, and data bases created by extracting, totaling, or archiving records derived from the main files. As a system grows, it becomes increasingly important to develop a system for keeping track of the purpose and use of all files that belong to the application.

One way to make it easier to identify files is to assign names that are descriptive of the contents but are within the eight-character file name limit. dBASE III PLUS provides a more formal way to group the files that make up an application, by recording the essential facts about each file in a data CATALOG. You create a new CATALOG or open an existing CATALOG with

```
SET CATALOG TO catalog file name
```

You can close a catalog with

```
SET CATALOG TO
```

When a CATALOG is open, every command that opens or creates files causes dBASE III PLUS to check the CATALOG, and if the specified files are not already present, add them to the CATALOG. By default, dBASE III PLUS also prompts you to enter an 80-character *title* that serves as a longer description of the purpose of the file. If you prefer not to have to pause to enter this description, you can disable the query with

```
SET TITLE OFF
```

The purpose of a CATALOG is to group the files that make up an application. You can maintain as many separate CATALOGs as you need. Since there is no objective way to determine which files belong together, you must be careful to open the right CATALOG file when you work with any given set of files. If you need to open an occasional unrelated file, you can temporarily turn off the CATALOG update process with

```
SET CATALOG OFF
```

and reactivate it with

```
SET CATALOG ON
```

dBASE III PLUS updates the CATALOG to reflect all changes in the set of files it defines. If you delete a file from the disk using the dBASE III PLUS ERASE command, its CATALOG entries are deleted, and if you RENAME a data base, the CATALOG entries are updated to reflect the new name. Because you might erase or rename files from outside dBASE III PLUS or without activating the CATALOG, dBASE III PLUS checks when you open a CATALOG that all the file names it references actually exist and deletes any "orphan" CATALOG entries for which there are no matching disk files.

Whenever a CATALOG is open, even if you have SET CATALOG OFF, you can use a *CATALOG query clause* in any command that opens files in order to display a list of the available files of the appropriate type that belong to the application. To do this, you substitute a question mark for the file name. For example, you could display a list of data bases in the current CATALOG by typing

```
USE ?
```

In response to a CATALOG query clause, dBASE III PLUS displays a list of file names in a pop-up box on the screen. You can scroll through this list with the UP ARROW and DOWN ARROW keys and make a selection by pressing ENTER. As you scroll through the file names, another pop-up box displays the title you entered as a description for the highlighted file, as illustrated in Figure 12-6.

Although the file title is helpful for identifying the file you want, this example does not illustrate the best use of the CATALOG, since you could easily determine which data bases belonged to the National Widgets system with a DIR command:

```
DIR NW*
```

The real value of the CATALOG is that it keeps track of which auxiliary files—indexes, format files, and QUERY files—are associated with the data bases, information that is difficult or impossible to determine with certainty any other way. For example, with the Customer File open, you could display a list of associated index files by typing

```
SET INDEX TO ?
```

The resulting screen, which displays the names of the indexes and in the "title" box the index key expressions, is shown in Figure 12-7.

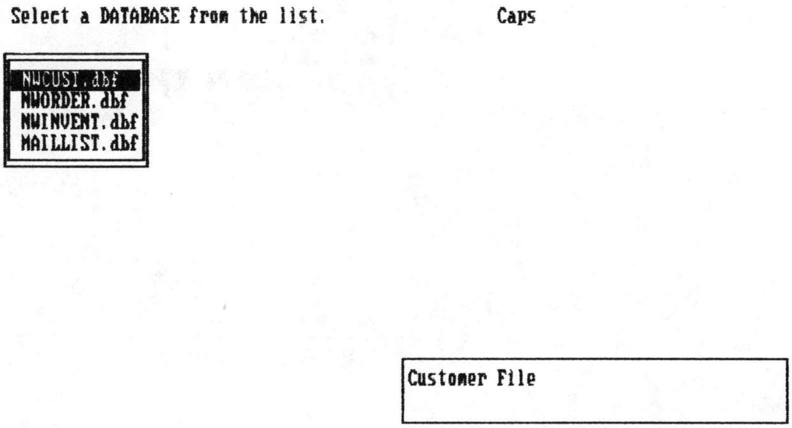

```
Select a DATABASE from the list.                Caps

NWCUST.dbf
NWORDER.dbf
NWINVENT.dbf
MAILLIST.dbf

                                         Customer File
```

Figure 12-6 *Using a CATALOG query clause to select a data base file*

A CATALOG is an ordinary dBASE III PLUS data base file that is opened in work area 10 when you type the SET CATALOG command. CATALOG files are not included in the list of data bases displayed by the DIR command, because they have the extension CAT rather than the standard DBF. If you type DISPLAY STATUS with a CATALOG open, you will see the file name in work area 10. Note also that a CATALOG counts as an open file, so if your application is nearing the 15-file limit, you may have to forego the use of a data CATALOG.

dBASE III PLUS also maintains a CATALOG of available CATALOG files in a *master CATALOG* called CATALOG.CAT; this enables you to use a CATALOG query clause to choose which CATALOG you want to activate:

```
SET CATALOG TO ?
```

```
STATE + CITY + ACCOUNT

. SET INDEX TO ?
Command Line    ||<C:>||NWCUST          ||Rec: 1/21        ||Ins    ||   Caps
    Position selection bar - ↑↓.  Select - ↵.  Leave menu - ↔.
        Select index file(s) to be used with the chosen file.
```

Figure 12-7 *Using a CATALOG query clause to select index files*

The structure of the CATALOG is illustrated in Figure 12-8. The fields are used for the following purposes:

- *PATH:* The full path name needed to find the file, from the current subdirectory.
- *FILE_NAME:* The file name, including its extension.
- *ALIAS:* The file name, excluding its extension.
- *TYPE:* The standard extension that identifies the file type, regardless of the actual extension you have given the file.
- *TITLE:* For most files, the 80-character description you entered when the file was first added to the CATALOG. For index files, this field contains the index key expression.

```
Structure for database: C:NW.CAT
Number of data records:       5
Date of last update   : 05/04/87
Field  Field Name  Type       Width    Dec
    1  PATH        Character     70
    2  FILE_NAME   Character     12
    3  ALIAS       Character      8
    4  TYPE        Character      3
    5  TITLE       Character     80
    6  CODE        Numeric        3
    7  TAG         Character      4
** Total **                     181
```

Figure 12-8 *The structure of a CATALOG data base*

- *CODE:* A numerical code used to identify files that are used together (for example, a data base and its associated indexes and format file). The CODE values are assigned sequentially and have no relationship to the work area in which a file was opened.
- *TAG:* A four-character field provided for your use (it is not used by dBASE III PLUS).

You can update a CATALOG as you would any other data base file, with commands such as APPEND, EDIT, BROWSE, and DELETE, but you should never change its structure (if you do, dBASE III PLUS can no longer recognize the file as a CATALOG). To access an active CATALOG, you can SELECT 10. You can also open a CATALOG with a USE command, but because the file extension is CAT rather than the default DBF, you must specify the extension in the USE command, for example:

```
USE NW.CAT
```

Sometimes the automatic CATALOG update can yield unexpected results. If you move an application to a new disk drive or directory and then reuse a previously created CATALOG, dBASE III PLUS will delete all the CATALOG entries, because the files with the path names stored in the CATALOG no longer exist.

In addition to its utility in helping to open files, the CATALOG also provides a convenient way to document on paper the files that make up an application. Because the CATALOG is stored as an ordinary dBASE III PLUS data base file, you can build an index to access the entries in a particular order, LIST the contents, or even define a report form to print the file in a more readable format.

HANDS-ON PRACTICE—USING A DATA CATALOG

Close any open data bases by typing

```
CLOSE DATABASES
```

Create and open a new CATALOG by typing

```
SET CATALOG TO ?
```

Because no catalog named NW.CAT yet exists, dBASE III PLUS asks you to confirm your intention to create a new catalog with the message "Create new file catalog? (Y/N)". Press Y to create the catalog. dBASE III PLUS next prompts you to enter a title for this catalog with "Enter title for file NW.cat:". Enter "National Widgets Accounts Receivable System" or a title of your choice. dBASE III PLUS displays the message "File catalog is empty". This is not an error message; it simply informs you that there are no files in the CATALOG—not surprising, since it was just created.

Open each of the files in the National Widgets system to add the names to the CATALOG, and then close all files in preparation for testing the CATALOG query clause. You can make up your own titles or use the ones suggested in the command sequence that follows:

```
USE NWCUST INDEX NWCACCT, NWCZIP, NWCSTATE ALIAS CUSTOMER
     Title: Customer File
SET FORMAT TO NWCUST
     Title: Format file for updating Customer File
USE NWORDER INDEX NWOACCT ALIAS ORDER
     Title: Order File
USE NWINVENT INDEX NWICATPT ALIAS INVENTORY
     Title: Inventory File
SET VIEW TO NWORDCST
     Title: View for editing order records
CLOSE DATABASES
```

Type DISPLAY STATUS, and note that the CATALOG is still open in work area 10. SELECT work area 10, and use the BROWSE command to view the data:

```
BROWSE WIDTH 20
```

If you are not satisfied with any of the descriptions you entered in the TITLE field, you can edit these entries now. Exit BROWSE by pressing CTRL-END, and return to work area 1 with SELECT 1. Use a CATALOG query clause to display the available data bases:

```
USE ?
```

Scroll through the files and watch the pop-up box in the lower right corner of the screen; it displays the title for the highlighted data base. Select the Customer File, NWCUST.DBF, from the list of files. dBASE III PLUS will display a list of index files associated with the Customer File. Scroll through the list, and notice the key expressions displayed in the title box. Select first the ACCOUNT and then the ZIP indexes, so that NWCACCT.NDX becomes the master index. Use a DISPLAY STATUS command to verify that the right indexes were opened and in the right order.

This chapter introduces some sophisticated ways to personalize the dBASE III PLUS working environment and create customized views of the information contained in one or more data base files. None of these commands and strategies is essential for working with dBASE III

PLUS, and if you find the details overwhelming, you can experiment with the new concepts later. When you begin to use the techniques presented in this chapter, you will find that the ability to customize the working environment for the requirements of a particular application, task, or user can help you work more productively and comfortably with dBASE III PLUS.

Chapter 13

Exchanging Data with Other Software

Thus far, all the work that you have done with dBASE III PLUS has been carried out entirely within the data base program. Inevitably, however, the time will come when you need to exchange data with other software, perhaps with a program that runs on a completely different type of computer. You may some day need to read data generated by another program into a dBASE III PLUS data base or copy data from a data base file to an external file format.

Although dBASE III PLUS is a highly capable data base manager, it is probably not the only major application running on your computer. As you have undoubtedly realized by now, dBASE III PLUS is less than ideal for calculation-intensive tasks, which are better left to spreadsheet programs and statistics packages. dBASE III PLUS is also lacking in the word processing capabilities that would enable you to produce printed forms that merge information from a data base into a full-page format such as a personalized letter.

One of the ways you can maximize your use of available software resources is to use each application program you own in its area of greatest strength. You might want to use a spreadsheet program to perform calculations on data derived from a dBASE III PLUS data base file or insert the name and address fields from a mailing list data base in personalized letters printed with a word processor.

Although dBASE III PLUS has grown in popularity, and an increasing number of other programs can read a DBF file directly, you cannot assume that the solution to your data interchange problems will be easy, especially if you need to transfer data to or from other types of microcomputers or mainframes. To facilitate data exchange, dBASE III PLUS can read and write a number of *external*, or *foreign*, *file formats*.

This chapter outlines some of the strategies you can use to carry out data transfers in both directions, between dBASE III PLUS and other programs. At times, data exchange can be a tricky proposition. Often it requires far more understanding of how your data is physically stored on disk than does working with the same data within dBASE III PLUS. You may also need to know quite a bit about the requirements and storage formats of the "foreign" program with which you may have little or no experience. Your best line of defense is to arm yourself with as much specific information as possible about the content and format of the data files you will need to read or write.

USING COPY AND APPEND TO CREATE TEXT FILES

As described in Chapter 11, you can use the COPY command to create a new data base containing all or some of the data in a dBASE III PLUS file, and you can combine data base files with APPEND FROM. You can use variations of these commands to COPY data stored in a dBASE III PLUS data base to several external file formats and to APPEND data created by other programs into dBASE III PLUS data bases. To specify that data be read or written in a foreign format rather than as a data base file, you add a TYPE clause to the APPEND or COPY command to identify the type of file you wish to read or write. The syntax is as follows:

COPY TO *file name* TYPE *file type*

or

APPEND FROM *file name* TYPE *file type*

Both of these commands require that the data base that will supply or receive the data be open in the currently selected work area. The *file type* may be any of the following:

- **DELIMITED:** A format in which the fields are separated with commas, and character fields are surrounded (delimited) by punctuation marks
- **SDF:** System Data Format, in which all fields are fixed in length, with no punctuation between fields
- **WKS:** A Lotus worksheet file, which can be read by 1-2-3 and Symphony
- **DIF:** Data Interchange Format, used by VisiCalc and other spreadsheets for data exchange
- **SYLK:** Symbolic Link Format, used by Multiplan and other Microsoft programs for data exchange

When you use the COPY command to write data to an external format, you can determine the order in which records are copied by sorting or indexing the source file before issuing the COPY command, and you can use any combination of a FILTER, scope, FOR, and WHILE clause to specify which records should be copied. You can add a FIELDS clause to specify the fields to be transferred and the order in which to copy them. You cannot copy memo fields, and, as the keyword FIELDS implies, you can copy only whole fields, not expressions such as TRIM(CITY) + ", " + STATE + " " + ZIP.

Two of the standard text file formats—delimited and SDF—can be used to exchange data with a wide variety of other programs, including those running on microcomputers that are incompatible with the IBM PC, and on mini and mainframe computers. In some cases, one of these formats can serve as a transfer medium between two programs when neither can directly read a format that the other can produce. Because of their widespread use, these formats merit special attention, even if using them does not always represent the most direct way to exchange data with other software.

USING THE DELIMITED TEXT FILE FORMAT

A *delimited file* is an ASCII text file in which the fields are separated by commas and character fields are surrounded (delimited) by punctuation marks. The standard delimiter is the double quotation mark ("), but you can specify a different one if you wish. There is a carriage return at the end of every record, so when you use the dBASE III PLUS or DOS TYPE command to display the contents of a delimited file, each record appears to begin on a new line on the screen.

You can read a delimited file into an existing Lotus 1-2-3 spreadsheet (with the / File Import Numbers command sequence). Many word processing programs that have "mail-merge" capabilities, such as WordStar/ MailMerge, Microsoft Word, and Volkswriter, can read this format to produce forms such as personalized letters. In addition, some programs, including WordPerfect, which cannot read delimited files directly, can convert this format to their own unique or proprietary formats.

Figure 13-1 illustrates the delimited file produced by the following command sequence, which copies selected fields from the National Widgets Customer File for those customers who own IBM equipment.

```
USE NWCUST INDEX NWCACCT
COPY TO NWIBM1 TYPE DELIMITED FIELDS CONTACT, COMPANY, ADDRESS,
  CITY, STATE, ZIP, MAIL, LASTORDER, TOTORDERS
  FOR "IBM" $ EQUIPMENT
```

A delimited file contains no field names or other explicit description of the file structure. Programs that read and write delimited files identify the fields by counting commas from the beginning of the record: Field 1 consists of all the characters up to the first comma, Field 2 all the characters between the first and second, and so on. The quotes surrounding character fields are necessary to distinguish embedded commas (as in "J. Thomas Johnson, CPA") from those used as field separators. Similarly, if a field is left blank, the comma that would normally follow this field remains as a place holder, so that the next field is not mistaken for the missing item.

If your data includes embedded quotation marks, or if the program

```
"Judy Barnes","Carol Klein, M.D.","3204 Telegraph Avenue","Oakland","CA","94609",T,19871228,1053.89
"Kathy McDonald","RapidType Secretarial Svc","2457 Union Street","San Francisco","CA","94123",F,19880310,348.52
"Carolyn Sumner","J. Thomas Johnson, CPA","50 California St., #1032","San Francisco","CA","94111",T,19871206,168.42
"Lisa Burns","The Image Makers","1900 Powell St., Ste. 832","Emeryville","CA","94608",T,19871112,389.50
"Gina Aronoff","","601 First Street","Benicia","CA","94510",T,19871214,232.50
```

Figure 13-1 *A delimited file*

with which you need to exchange data requires a different delimiter, you may override the default quotes by specifying your own delimiter character. For example, you could read data into dBASE III PLUS from a delimited file called CUSTOMER.TXT, in which character fields are surrounded by slashes, with the following:

```
APPEND FROM CUSTOMER TYPE DELIMITED WITH /
```

You can eliminate both the delimiters and the field separators (the commas) and instead insert a single blank space between fields by substituting the keyword BLANK for the delimiter character, as in the following:

```
COPY TO NWLETTER TYPE DELIMITED WITH BLANK
```

This format is most useful for copying numeric data (perhaps for transfer to a statistics package for numerical analysis). It is almost always inappropriate for character fields, since any embedded blank spaces would be read as field separators.

When you APPEND a delimited file into a dBASE III PLUS data base, fields from the text file are transferred one by one into the corresponding data base fields. If the delimited file contains extra fields, the data in them will be lost; if it contains fewer fields, the extra fields in the new data base records are simply left blank. If any items in the delimited file are shorter than the matching dBASE III PLUS field width, the entries are padded with blank spaces; if any fields are too long, character data is truncated to fit, and numeric fields are replaced by asterisks to indicate a numeric overflow.

USING THE SDF TEXT FILE FORMAT

SDF is an acronym for System Data Format, a term used by dBASE III PLUS to describe what is more commonly called a *fixed-length record.* In this format (as in the DBF file itself), there are no field separators or delimiters. Each field occupies a fixed number of characters and is identified by its starting position in the record. If a particular item of data requires less than the full field width, it is padded with blank spaces. (Character fields are usually left-justified within the field width, while numeric fields are right-justified.) As in the delimited format, each record ends with a carriage return.

Fixed-length files can be read by some word processors, including Microsoft Word, and are used by many accounting programs and other data bases. In addition, most data downloaded from mainframe data bases and on-line information utilities is in fixed-length format. Figure 13-2 illustrates the SDF file produced by a COPY command similar to the one shown in the previous section:

```
USE NWCUST INDEX NWCACCT
COPY TO NWIBM2 TYPE SDF FIELDS CONTACT, COMPANY, ADDRESS, CITY,
   STATE, ZIP, MAIL, LASTORDER, TOTORDERS FOR "IBM" $ EQUIPMENT
```

Because fields in an SDF file are identified solely by their positions in the record, the sequence and lengths of the fields common to both files must be identical in the dBASE III PLUS data base and the external file. When you APPEND an SDF file into a dBASE III PLUS data base, extra fields in the SDF file are lost, and extra fields in the data base records are left blank.

EXCHANGING DATA WITH SPREADSHEETS

Of the three formats intended for exchanging data with spreadsheets—DIF, SYLK, and WKS—only the Lotus worksheet format is in widespread use today. When you transfer data to or from a spreadsheet format, each row in the spreadsheet corresponds to a record in the data base and each column to a field. If you are not familiar with spreadsheet software, you might think of the spreadsheet display as analogous to the BROWSE screen, with each record laid out horizontally and the fields lined up in columns.

When you use the COPY command to write data to WKS format, dBASE III PLUS creates a new Lotus worksheet file and places the field names in the first row of the spreadsheet as column headers. If you want to add data from a dBASE III PLUS file to a previously created worksheet, you can create a delimited file instead, and use the /**F**ile **I**mport **N**umbers command sequence to read the data into the existing spreadsheet. Alternatively, you could combine the two worksheets with the Lotus /**F**ile **C**ombine command.

```
Judy Barnes        Carol Klein, M.D.        3204 Telegraph Avenue    Oakland          CA94609   T19871228   1053.89
Kathy McDonald     RapidType Secretarial Svc2457 Union Street        San Francisco    CA94123   F19880310    348.52
Carolyn Sumner     J. Thomas Johnson, CPA   50 California St., #1032 San Francisco    CA94111   T19871206    168.42
Lisa Burns         The Image Makers         1900 Powell St., Ste. 832Emeryville       CA94608   T19871112    389.50
Gina Aronoff                                601 First Street         Benicia          CA94510   T19871214    232.50
```

Figure 13-2 *An SDF (fixed-length) file*

When you APPEND FROM a Lotus spreadsheet, dBASE III PLUS assumes that the data begins in the upper left corner of the worksheet area; there are no extra rows above the data and no extra columns to the left. Just as with the two text file formats, data in extra spreadsheet columns is lost, and data base fields with no counterparts in the spreadsheet remain blank.

Note that you can also convert dBASE III PLUS data to Lotus spreadsheet format by using the Lotus Translate utility, which offers one important advantage: The dBASE III PLUS COPY command turns dates into labels, whereas Translate converts them to dates in Lotus spreadsheet format.

COMPENSATING FOR DIFFERENCES IN FILE STRUCTURE

When you exchange data between dBASE III PLUS and other programs, you may have to adjust the data to compensate for differences in the file structures and data storage formats. For example, you may want to load data into an existing dBASE III PLUS data base from an accounting program that stores data in a fixed-length format (an SDF file in dBASE III PLUS terminology). It would be an extraordinary coincidence if the structure of any accounting files matched your dBASE III PLUS file structures, and you cannot alter the accounting files to conform to your existing data bases.

To solve this and similar problems, you can create a temporary dBASE III PLUS data base, the structure of which can be adjusted to precisely match the requirements dictated by the external file format, and use it as an intermediary file. To transfer data into dBASE III PLUS, you could use the following steps:

1. Ensure that the structure of the temporary file exactly matches the external format.

2. APPEND data into the temporary file from the external format.

3. Change the structure and/or data in the temporary file to match your existing dBASE III PLUS file.

4. APPEND data from the temporary file into your data base.

To transfer data from a dBASE III PLUS data base to an external format, you can reverse these steps, as follows:

1. Ensure that the structure of the temporary file matches the existing dBASE III PLUS data base.
2. APPEND data into the temporary file from the dBASE III PLUS data base.
3. Change the structure and/or data in the temporary file to match the external file format.
4. COPY data from the temporary file to the external format.

When you devise a detailed method for implementing a particular data transfer, keep in mind which aspects of the structure are important. None of the external formats identifies fields by name, and in all cases, the dBASE III PLUS fields must be arranged in the same order as the items in the foreign file. (On the other hand, when you APPEND data from one dBASE III PLUS data base into another, the reverse is true—fields are matched up by name and can differ in length, position, and even data file type.) Thus, you could APPEND data from a text file or worksheet into a temporary file in which the fields have the same names as your target data base but occur in the same order as in the external file. You could then APPEND this file into your target data base; in this step, the fields are matched by name and are rearranged in the correct order.

In the delimited format, field widths are unimportant; dBASE III PLUS removes trailing blank spaces when it writes data to a delimited file and adjusts data APPENDed from a delimited file to fit in the field widths defined in the target data base structure. In an SDF file, however, fields are defined by their widths, so the widths of the fields in the data base that receives or supplies the data must match the external file format.

Sometimes you will not only have to adjust the field sequence and widths but also combine or split fields to compensate for differences in file structure. For example, National Widgets might need to copy the name and address fields from the Customer File to a text file for use by a program that expects to find the city, state, and ZIP in a single field. All the variations of the COPY command can copy only whole fields, not complex expressions, so you cannot simply combine these three fields in the COPY command as you would to print them on one line of a mailing label.

To solve this problem, you could create a temporary file that contains all the appropriate fields from the Customer File and one additional field for the combined city, state, and ZIP. The easiest way to create this file is to first copy the selected records from the Customer File:

```
USE NWCUST INDEX NWCACCT
COPY TO NWTEMP FIELDS CONTACT, COMPANY, ADDRESS, CITY, STATE, ZIP
   FOR "IBM" $ EQUIPMENT
```

Next, you would open the temporary file, NWTEMP.DBF, and use MODIFY STRUCTURE to add a new field, perhaps called ADDRESS2, to contain the combination of city, state, and ZIP. You could then fill in this field with a REPLACE command and COPY the data to the appropriate external format:

```
REPLACE ALL ADDRESS2 WITH TRIM(CITY) + ", " + STATE + "  " + ZIP
COPY TO NWIBM3 TYPE SDF FIELDS CONTACT, COMPANY, ADDRESS, ADDRESS2
```

All the variations of the COPY command write dates to the external file format in year/month/day order, with a full four-digit year and no punctuation. For example, the date January 23, 1988 would become 19880123. If you prefer a different style for dates, such as ANSI format (*yy.mm.dd*) or the familiar American (*mm/dd/yy*) format, you must convert the date to a character field. You can do this by copying all or selected records to a temporary file, using a SET DATE command to ensure that dates are displayed in the desired format, and then modify the structure of this file to change the data type of the date field to character.

When you APPEND data from an external file, dates in any format other than *yyyymmdd* format must be read into character fields in a temporary data base. If the external program uses one of the standard dBASE III PLUS date display formats, you can read the data into a character field, use a SET DATE command to select the matching date display format, and modify the structure of the temporary file to convert the character field to a true date.

Logical fields are copied to the external file formats as the single letters T and F. If you prefer a character string, such as "Yes" and "No", you can employ a strategy similar to the one used to combine the CITY, STATE, and ZIP fields to convert the logical values to the more readable character strings. For example, you could copy the appropriate Customer File fields to a temporary file, add an extra field three characters wide, called perhaps MAIL2, to the structure, and REPLACE its contents with "Yes" or "No" by using either an IIF function or two separate REPLACE commands:

```
REPLACE ALL MAIL2 WITH IIF(MAIL, "Yes", "No")
```

or

```
REPLACE ALL MAIL2 WITH "Yes" FOR MAIL
REPLACE ALL MAIL2 WITH "No" FOR .NOT. MAIL
```

When you APPEND data from an external file, you may have to make the opposite conversion. dBASE III PLUS correctly interprets the single letters Y and N as logical values when you read them into a logical field. If the external file contains the longer character strings "Yes" and "No", you can read these values into a character field in a temporary file and fill in the logical field with REPLACE:

```
REPLACE ALL MAIL WITH IIF(MAIL2 = "Yes", .Y., .N.)
```

or

```
REPLACE ALL MAIL WITH .Y. FOR MAIL2 = "Yes"
REPLACE ALL MAIL WITH .N. FOR MAIL2 = "No"
```

You may have to use a combination of all these methods as well as others that are impossible to predict in advance to effect particular data transfer. In some cases, it may be easier to carry out the required changes in the external program, rather than in dBASE III PLUS, especially if you (or your colleagues who need to use the data) are more familiar with that software. For example, you might prefer to copy an entire data base to a Lotus spreadsheet and rearrange the order, widths, and display formats of the columns within 1-2-3, rather than using a temporary dBASE III PLUS data base file.

In some cases, you can use the delimited format as an intermediate exchange medium to transfer data to programs that require a format that dBASE III PLUS cannot create. For example, WordPerfect can convert a delimited file to its own merge file format in which each field begins on a new line and ends with a "Merge Return" code (CTRL-R), and each record ends with an "End of Record" code (Merge E or CTRL-E).

With earlier versions of WordPerfect, you could use a series of search and replace commands to perform the conversion. Make sure that only character fields are copied (using a temporary dBASE III PLUS file if necessary to change data types), so that each field is actually surrounded by the delimiter characters. To accomplish the transformation, you edit the delimited file with WordPerfect and insert the end-of-record markers by searching for the sequence of characters that identifies the end of each record in the delimited file—a quote (the one following the last field in each delimited file record), a hard return, and another quote (the one at the beginning of the next record)—and replacing this sequence with an end-of-record code followed by a hard return.

Next, you search for the sequence of characters that separates fields—quote, comma, quote—and replace this sequence with the end-of-field code followed by a hard return. This leaves you with one extra quote at the very beginning of the file and one at the end, both of which you can delete manually. Variations on this technique can also be applied to other word processors, provided that they permit you to explicitly specify the special codes in search and replace commands.

USING IMPORT AND EXPORT TO EXCHANGE DATA WITH PFS

You can read and write PFS files with the IMPORT and EXPORT commands, which use syntax similar to APPEND FROM and COPY TO.

IMPORT FROM *PFS file name* TYPE PFS

and

EXPORT TO *PFS file name* TYPE PFS

Most of the differences between APPEND and IMPORT, and between COPY and EXPORT, are due to the differences between dBASE III PLUS and PFS. With PFS, designing a data base is inseparable from the process of designing a screen format. Accordingly, the IMPORT command automatically creates not only a dBASE III PLUS data base structure, but also a format file to draw an input screen that resembles the PFS screen layout, and a VIEW file that enables you to open both the data base and the format file at the same time.

Similarly, when you EXPORT data to PFS, you can use a format file to control the structure and screen layout of the resulting PFS file. If no format file is open when you execute the EXPORT command, the PFS file will contain all the fields in the dBASE III PLUS data base except the memo fields, and the screen layout will resemble the default dBASE III PLUS data entry screen drawn by APPEND or EDIT. Note that creating a format file is the only way you can specify which fields should be transferred to PFS, since the EXPORT command does not allow a FIELDS clause. You can, however, control which records are EXPORTed by using any combination of scope, FOR, and WHILE clauses.

If your data base contains a field that is unique, or nearly so, for each record—such as an ID code, an account number, or a part number—make sure that this becomes the first field in the PFS record. Unlike dBASE, PFS permits only one index for a data base file, always based on the first field on the screen. If the unique field does not come first in the dBASE III PLUS file structure, a format file again provides the easiest solution.

If you are not familiar with PFS, you should realize that this program imposes far less structure on its data than dBASE III PLUS. Any type of data may be entered into any field and later treated as either character or numeric when you define record selection criteria. Field lengths are not defined explicitly—the data entry area for a field consists of all the space on the screen between the end of its prompt and the beginning of the next.

When you IMPORT a PFS file into dBASE, all fields become character fields, and the width of each field is set to the number of spaces allocated for the field on the PFS entry screen (or 254 characters, whichever is smaller). In most cases, the resulting dBASE III PLUS fields are much wider than necessary. Any data stored in PFS "Attachment Pages" will be lost; despite the similarity in purpose and usage between Attachment Pages and memo fields, there is no way to transfer data between them, in either direction.

In PFS you do not refer to fields by name, and the screen prompts may be much longer than the ten characters permitted for a dBASE III PLUS field name. dBASE III PLUS resolves these conflicts by assigning the names FIELD01, FIELD02, FIELD03, and so on in a data base created by the IMPORT command and using the PFS screen prompts in the matching format file. For any use except full-screen editing through the automatically generated format file, the "generic" field names are inconvenient.

You can use MODIFY STRUCTURE to correct many of these problems without losing data. You can lengthen or shorten fields, rearrange the order of the fields, change data types, and even assign new field names, provided that you do not try to change field names at the same time as you make any other alterations in the structure.

If you do change field names to facilitate your work at the dot prompt, you can no longer use the format file created by the IMPORT command, which references fields by their original names (FIELD01, FIELD02, and so on). Furthermore, you cannot edit the format file with the menu-driven screen editor invoked with CREATE SCREEN or MODIFY SCREEN, because IMPORT generates only the FMT file used to draw the input screen; it does not provide the SCR file that stores the screen image in a form accessible to the screen editor. Although the FMT file is an ASCII file that you can edit with a word processor or text editor, doing so requires more understanding of the commands it contains (@ . . . SAY . . . GET commands) than you are likely to possess at this stage in your experience with dBASE III PLUS. You may prefer to abandon the format file and define a new one if necessary.

TRANSFERRING dBASE III PLUS DATA TO WORD PROCESSING DOCUMENTS

The examples in this chapter illustrate ways to transfer data between dBASE III PLUS and other applications. At times, you may simply want to create a text file that contains information derived from a dBASE III PLUS data base to be treated as text by another program. For example, you might want to incorporate dBASE III PLUS data into a document produced using a word processor.

Chapter 9 describes a method for "printing" a report or a set of labels to a disk file to help improve the appearance of the printout by editing the resulting file with a word processor and perhaps adding commands to access your printer's special fonts or other print enhancements. You can also export data displayed by commands such as LIST or DISPLAY by using an *ALTERNATE file,* an ASCII text file that contains an exact duplicate of the data displayed on the screen while the file is open. You open an ALTERNATE file with

SET ALTERNATE TO *text file name*

Like other text files produced by dBASE III PLUS, the ALTERNATE file is given the extension TXT unless you explicitly override this default. To begin sending output to the text file, you type

```
SET ALTERNATE ON
```

To temporarily suspend recording in the ALTERNATE file, you use

```
SET ALTERNATE OFF
```

You can SET ALTERNATE ON or OFF as many times as you like during a work session, and when you are finished, you can close the file with

```
CLOSE ALTERNATE
```

Just as when you SET PRINT ON, only sequential output, like the display produced by a LIST command, is copied to the ALTERNATE file; full-screen displays such as the EDIT or BROWSE screens are not. If you intend to enhance the appearance of a report using your word processor and allow the word processor to paginate the listing, it is often more convenient to use an ALTERNATE file than to define a new report and print the report to disk. If you have already defined a report, you might instead add the PLAIN keyword to the REPORT FORM command to suppress the normal headings and page numbers and produce a disk file containing only the raw data.

As you can see from the examples in this chapter, there are no hard and fast rules or standard procedures for exchanging data between applications. The existence of several standard data exchange formats certainly helps, but in all but the most straightforward cases, some experimentation will be required to elucidate the exact sequence of steps that will yield the results you want. Your best strategy is to learn as much as you can about all the standard data formats that can be read and created by dBASE III PLUS and by your other application software so you can choose the optimal combination of conversion steps.

Chapter 14

Writing Simple Programs

When you work with dBASE III PLUS through the ASSIST menus or by typing commands at the dot prompt, you are using the program in an *interactive mode.* You are carrying on a dialog in which you type commands one at a time, and dBASE III PLUS responds to each one by executing the command, displaying an error message and offering help, or prompting you for file names when necessary. Working interactively at the dot prompt offers flexibility and immediacy—you can execute a command as quickly as you can type it, and you can carry out varying ad hoc inquiries with no prior preparation.

The disadvantages of working in interactive mode may become apparent only after you have been using dBASE III PLUS for a while. When an application has matured beyond the testing phase and you have gone through several processing cycles without making major modifications in your procedures, it may seem as if you are repeatedly typing the same command sequences and that dBASE III PLUS is taking longer and longer to do your bidding.

Some of this impatience stems from your own changing frame of reference. As you grow more comfortable with data base concepts and with the dBASE III PLUS command structure, using the program for new tasks will require less effort, and repeatedly retyping the same commands will seem more onerous. Because you may no longer clearly remember how long it took to perform the equivalent operations manually, the computer may not seem as fast as it did the first time you were able to accomplish in two minutes with a SUM command what used to take two hours on a ten-key calculator.

There will probably also be an objective basis for your growing dissatisfaction with the computer's performance. As your files grow larger, operations that used to be virtually instantaneous may take a long time. The time will seem even longer if you sit at the terminal waiting for a command to be completed so that you can type the next one.

You can overcome this frustration by writing dBASE III PLUS programs to automate your work. The dBASE III PLUS language is powerful and sophisticated enough that it can be used to develop complete *turn-key applications*—menu-driven systems that look just like off-the-shelf packages written in languages such as COBOL, Pascal, or C. Not every user has the time, interest, or aptitude to become proficient enough to write a complete menu-driven dBASE III PLUS system, and not every data base application demands this approach. But almost anyone can learn enough about dBASE III PLUS programming to write simple batch-type programs that enable you to realize substantial gains in processing efficiency and make better use of both human and computer time.

DO YOU REALLY WANT TO BECOME A PROGRAMMER?

The term *programming* has arcane and perhaps scary connotations for most people who view their computer hardware and software primarily as tools for getting a job done. At its simplest level, however, a program is nothing more than a set of instructions that directs the computer to carry out a series of operations in a specified order. If you have written a DOS *batch file* (such as the AUTOEXEC.BAT file that is executed every time you boot your computer) or created a *macro* through a spreadsheet, word processor, or RAM-resident macro processing program, you have already ventured into the world of programming.

The transition to using dBASE III PLUS as a programming language can be easy and natural—you can draw on your experience working at the dot prompt. You have already gained a basic familiarity with the syntax of many dBASE III PLUS commands, all of which (along with others that will not be covered in this book) may be incorporated into your programs. Even if you never write programs that do more than what you could accomplish in interactive mode, you can benefit in several important ways. By combining commands that you already know into programs, you can

- Avoid the tedium of having to repeatedly type the same command sequences
- Execute several consecutive commands without having to wait for each one to complete before typing the next
- Reduce the chances that careless errors or omissions in a command sequence will compromise the integrity of your data bases
- Run time-consuming processes unattended at times when the computer is otherwise unoccupied
- Set up procedures that can be run by less experienced users

COMPARING A COMMAND LEVEL PROCEDURE WITH A PROGRAM

A dBASE III PLUS program is an ordinary text file consisting of one or more commands, each one typed just as you would enter it at the dot prompt and each ending with a carriage return. The text file should be given the extension PRG to identify it as a program. To run a program from the dot prompt, you type

DO *program name*

When dBASE III PLUS executes the programs, it reads the lines in the text file one by one and carries out each command in turn. As commands are executed, dBASE III PLUS responds if necessary with the same file name prompts and error messages that it displays in interactive mode.

As a detailed example, recall the method described in Chapter 11 for replacing the PRICE field in new Order File records with the standard prices stored in the Inventory File. To access fields from the Inventory File while reading Order File records, you must have both data bases open in any two work areas, and they must be linked with SET RELATION based on the common fields CATEGORY and PARTNUMBER. At the dot prompt, you could use the following command sequence to open and link the files, read the prices into the new order records, and find any order records for which there was no match in the Inventory File:

```
SELECT 1
USE NWINVENT INDEX NWICATPT ALIAS INVENTORY
SELECT 2
USE NWORDER ALIAS ORDER
SET RELATION TO CATEGORY + PARTNUMBER INTO INVENTORY
REPLACE ALL PRICE WITH INVENTORY->PRICE FOR PRICE = 0
LIST ACCOUNT, CATEGORY, PARTNUMBER FOR PARTNUMBER <>
  INVENTORY->PARTNUMBER
```

These instructions can be combined into a program by creating a text file, perhaps called NWOPRICE.PRG, containing the same seven commands. To run the program, you would type

```
DO NWOPRICE
```

Writing the program, like carrying out the procedure one step at a time from the dot prompt, requires that you understand how to work with multiple data bases, remember the syntax and use of several dBASE III PLUS commands, and know quite a few details of the National Widgets files, including the following:

- The names of the Order and Inventory files
- The syntax of the USE command
- How to select work areas and open more than one data base at a time

- How to assign and use a file alias (this is not essential)
- How to link two files with SET RELATION
- The name of the Inventory File index used as the basis for the linkage
- The names of the common fields used as the basis for the linkage
- How to access fields in an unselected work area by the combination of alias and field name
- The syntax of the REPLACE command
- The names of the fields you want to REPLACE and LIST
- How to test for Order File records for which there are no matching Inventory File records

To run the program, you need only remember its name and the fact that you can run it with a DO command.

NOTATIONAL AND TYPOGRAPHICAL CONVENTIONS

When you write a program, keep in mind that you or one of your co-workers may some day have to add to or modify it. Any measures you take to make your programs more readable and understandable will help a great deal when you edit a program several months later and the details are no longer fresh in your mind.

The command lines in a dBASE III PLUS program, like those you type at the dot prompt, may be entered in any combination of uppercase and lowercase letters. In longer programs, it is advantageous to develop a consistent scheme for identifying file and field names so that they stand out. For example, you could use lowercase letters for dBASE III PLUS command words and uppercase letters for file, field, and memory variable names. Many programmers (and many books on dBASE III PLUS programming) use the equally valid and almost opposite convention.

uppercase letters for dBASE III PLUS keywords and mixed uppercase and lowercase letters for variable names.

Extra spaces are permitted anywhere within a command line, and you may use blank lines to separate groups of commands to identify them (to you, not to dBASE III PLUS) as discrete functional units. Just as when you work at command level, extra spaces can make complex expressions and lists of file or field names easier to read and edit. When a command is too long to fit on one screen line, you may find it helpful to indent the continuation lines to distinguish them from new commands.

Comments are notes included in a program as a kind of internal *documentation* to explain the logic behind a command or group of commands whose purpose might not be self-evident. Comments are ignored by dBASE III PLUS when a program is executed. An entire line may be identified as a comment by beginning the line with either an asterisk (*) or the word NOTE. You may also place a comment after any executable command on the same line by preceding it with two ampersands (&&).

In any program longer than a few lines, it is a good idea to include several comment lines that state the name of the program, a brief description of its purpose, your name, and perhaps the dates on which you wrote the program and last modified it. Including this information in the text of a program ensures that it is always visible when you edit the program or examine a printed copy.

CONTROLLING THE SCREEN DISPLAY DURING PROGRAM EXECUTION

When you run a program, dBASE III PLUS executes the commands as if you had typed each one yourself at the dot prompt and displays exactly the same messages on the screen. For example, a REPLACE command produces a status message that monitors the number of records processed, and a COUNT or SUM command displays the computed values. Figure 14-1 illustrates the appearance of the screen after you run the NWOPRICE.PRG program described earlier in this chapter.

```
. DO NWOPRICE
      6 records replaced
Record#  ACCOUNT    CATEGORY PARTNUMBER
     10  FLOORPLAN  COVER    540-13
     20  KLEIN      PRTWHL   361-12
     22  YORKPUMP   DISK     102-10
     27  FLOORPLAN  COVER    540-13
     32  KLEIN      PRTWHL   361-12
     33  YORKPUMP   DISK     102-10

Command Line  ||<C:>||ORDER            ||Rec: EOF/33      ||Ins  ||  Caps
                         Enter a dBASE III PLUS command.
```

Figure 14-1 *Running the NWOPRICE.PRG program*

In a longer program, or one that contains commands that take a long time to run, such as a program that performs several INDEX, REPLACE, COUNT, or SUM commands on a large data base, the standard messages displayed by dBASE III PLUS may be insufficient to remind you about what the program is doing or inform you how far it has progressed toward completion.

One approach to this problem is to suppress the normal dBASE III PLUS messages with a SET TALK OFF command and substitute your own status displays, but for simple programs like the ones in this chapter, there is a more straightforward solution. You can cause dBASE III PLUS to "echo," or display, each command line to the screen as it is executed with

```
SET ECHO ON
```

When you have SET ECHO ON, comment lines that begin with the keyword NOTE and those that are included on a command line (set off by &&) are echoed to the terminal, whereas separate comments that begin with an asterisk are not.

You can type the SET ECHO command at the dot prompt, but it is more expedient to include it in the program. When ECHO is ON, commands that you type at the dot prompt are also echoed, or repeated, on the next line on the screen, so your program should also include a command at the end to return the system to normal:

```
SET ECHO OFF
```

CONTROLLING A PROGRAM'S ENVIRONMENT

Every dBASE III PLUS program you write, even the shortest, should set up its own working environment and restore the system to normal before returning you to the dot prompt. You, or even someone who knows less than you do about dBASE III PLUS or about the application itself, should be able to run the program without having to type any prior commands and then resume working at the dot prompt in a familiar environment. If a program alters any SET options—for example, if it includes commands such as SET DELETED ON, SET HEADING OFF, or SET STATUS OFF—it should reverse them if necessary to restore the settings that were in effect before the program was run.

A program should open all the data bases it processes and close them afterward so you can leave a program running unattended without worrying that open files will be damaged if a co-worker reboots or turns off the system or that a hardware or power failure will occur after the program has done its work.

Figure 14-2 illustrates a new version of NWOPRICE.PRG that addresses all these issues. The program includes comment lines that explain the FOR clause in the REPLACE command and how the test for missing inventory items works. The program begins with a SET ECHO ON command so that dBASE III PLUS displays the remaining commands on the screen as the program runs, and a SET ECHO OFF command at the end to return the system to normal. The CLOSE DATABASES command closes both open files and selects work area 1, so you can resume your work at the dot prompt with a clean slate.

```
* NWOPRICE.PRG
* PROGRAM TO READ PRICES FROM INVENTORY FILE INTO NEW ORDER RECORDS
* WRITTEN:    6/30/87    M.LISKIN
* REVISED:    7/02/87    M.LISKIN
set echo on

select 1
use NWINVENT index NWICATPT alias INVENTORY
select 2
use NWORDER alias ORDER
set relation to CATEGORY + PARTNUMBER into INVENTORY

* READ PRICE FIELD FROM INVENTORY FILE FOR NEW ORDER RECORDS ONLY
replace all PRICE with INVENTORY->PRICE for PRICE = 0

* PRINT ORDER RECORDS WITH NO MATCH IN INVENTORY FILE
list ACCOUNT, CATEGORY, PARTNUMBER to print;
   for PARTNUMBER <> INVENTORY->PARTNUMBER

close databases
set echo off
```

Figure 14-2 *The revised NWOPRICE.PRG program*

USING THE CREATE/MODIFY COMMAND EDITOR TO WRITE PROGRAMS

dBASE III PLUS provides a rudimentary program editor that is similar to the memo field editor. You invoke the editor by typing

CREATE COMMAND *program name*

or

MODIFY COMMAND *program name*

If you do not include the name of the program, dBASE III PLUS will prompt you to enter it with the message "Enter file name.". The PRG extension is supplied automatically unless you override the default by typing a different one. As with the other full-screen editors, you may use the CREATE and MODIFY variants interchangeably, either to create a new program or to edit an existing file.

The MODIFY COMMAND editor makes use of all the standard dBASE III PLUS full-screen editing commands. The cursor movement and editing command keys and their specific meanings in the program editor are listed in Table 14-1.

The program editor is limited compared with most word processors and text editors. In particular, it cannot handle files longer than 5000 characters, and it lacks many of the cursor movement commands and advanced text editing facilities that would be useful for writing longer, more complex programs. However, it is more than adequate for typing short programs like the ones in this chapter.

Like the memo field editor, the program editor assumes a line length of 65 characters and word wraps longer lines at column 66 by inserting a soft carriage return. (Recall that a dBASE III PLUS command may be up to 254 characters long.) Every command must end with a hard return generated by pressing the ENTER key, and you can always identify a hard return by the < displayed on the right side of the screen.

Defeating the word-wrap feature requires some extra work, but doing so allows you to improve the readability of your programs by splitting command lines at logical breaking points and indenting continuation lines. You can break a line at any point by typing a semicolon (;), pressing ENTER, and continuing the command on the next line. The semicolon prevents dBASE III PLUS from interpreting the hard return as the end of the command.

If the editor wraps a line before you get a chance to split it yourself, you can later delete the soft carriage return (located immediately to the right of the last character on the line, not in column 79) with the DEL key. You can either leave the line extending beyond the right edge of the screen (with a + in column 79 indicating that more text is present) or make sure that you are typing in Insert mode and add a semicolon and a hard return anywhere within the line.

Table 14-1 *Command Keys Used in the Program Editor*

Control Key	Command Key	Function
CTRL-E	UP ARROW	Move the cursor up to the previous line
CTRL-X	DOWN ARROW	Move the cursor down to the next line
CTRL-D	RIGHT ARROW	Move the cursor right one character
CTRL-S	LEFT ARROW	Move the cursor left one character
CTRL-F	END	Move the cursor right one word
CTRL-A	HOME	Move the cursor left one word
CTRL-B	CTRL-RIGHT ARROW	Move the cursor to the end of the line
CTRL-Z	CTRL-LEFT ARROW	Move the cursor to the beginning of the line
CTRL-G	DEL	Delete the character at the cursor position
	BACKSPACE	Delete the character to the left of the cursor
CTRL-T		Delete characters from the cursor to the end of the word
CTRL-Y		Delete the entire line containing the cursor
CTRL-N		Insert a blank line (a hard return)
CTRL-V	INS	Turn Insert mode on (if it is off) or off (if it is on)
CTRL-C	PGDN	Move forward to the next screenful of text
CTRL-R	PGUP	Move backward to the previous screenful of text
CTRL-KB		Reformat the current command line
CTRL-KF		Find a string of characters, searching forward from the cursor position
CTRL-KL		Repeat the previous search
CTRL-KR		Read in the contents of a disk file
CTRL-KW		Write the entire program to another disk file
CTRL-W	CTRL-END	Save the program and return to the dot prompt
CTRL-Q	ESC	Exit without saving the new or changed program
	F1	Turn the help menu on (if it is off) or off (if it is on)

When you use these techniques, remember that any characters appearing to the right of a semicolon on the same screen line will be ignored when the program is executed, so be sure to press ENTER before you continue typing a command. Also, since the command continues with the very first character on the following line, make sure that you do not inadvertently omit any required spaces between the words in a command. For example, the following line would generate an error message because there is no space between PARTNUMBER and FOR.

```
LIST ACCOUNT, CATEGORY, PARTNUMBER;
FOR PARTNUMBER <> INVENTORY->PARTNUMBER
```

This command could be written correctly as follows:

```
LIST ACCOUNT, CATEGORY, PARTNUMBER ;
FOR PARTNUMBER <> INVENTORY->PARTNUMBER
```

or like this:

```
LIST ACCOUNT, CATEGORY, PARTNUMBER;
  FOR PARTNUMBER <> INVENTORY->PARTNUMBER
```

The MODIFY COMMAND editor does not provide a way to print an entire program, but there are two ways to do this from within dBASE III PLUS. For a short program, you can press SHIFT-PRTSC as you create or edit the file to dump the screen image to the printer. You can also use the TYPE command from the dot prompt to print a program (or any other ASCII text file) that is too long to fit on one screen. By default the dBASE III PLUS TYPE command (like its MS-DOS counterpart) displays the file on the screen; to route the output to the printer, you can either toggle the printer on with CTRL-P or add the phrase TO PRINT to the command. Because TYPE does not assume that you are listing a *program,* you must specify the full file name, including the extension, such as in the following command sequence.

```
TYPE NWOPRICE.PRG TO PRINT
```

USING A WORD PROCESSOR TO WRITE PROGRAMS

As mentioned previously, you can use any word processor or text editor that can read and write ASCII text files to create and edit dBASE III PLUS programs. These include editors specifically intended for programming, such as the IBM Personal Editor, Brief, and the Norton Editor, as well as a number of popular word processors, such as WordStar, WordPerfect, Microsoft Word, Volkswriter, and PC-Write.

All the programming editors and some word processors, such as PC-Write, automatically produce ASCII text files as long as you do not insert any formatting codes. Many word processing programs insert "hidden" codes in document files or begin each document with a special header section, which is as indecipherable to dBASE III PLUS (and probably to you) as the dBASE III PLUS file structure information stored at the beginning of a data base file would be to a word processor. Some of the popular word processing programs offer the option of reading and writing ASCII text files. You may have to consult the specific program's user manual to find out how to create a file devoid of special headers, formatting, and command codes. The following are a few examples:

- With WordStar you must open and edit a program in Nondocument mode.
- With Microsoft Word you must select the (F)ormatted (N)o option when you use the (T)ransfer (S)ave command to save a finished program on disk.
- With WordPerfect you must press CTRL-F5 and then select Option 1—"Save current document as a DOS text file"—to save your program.

- With Volkswriter you set the right margin to the maximum value, 250, by entering an asterisk (*) in the ruler line in which you define margins and tabs (the exact method varies with different versions of Volkswriter).

If you are unsure whether a file created by your word processor is an ASCII text file, you can use the DOS or dBASE III PLUS TYPE command to examine the contents. The file should consist entirely of normal printable characters (letters, numbers, and punctuation marks), and you should see only the commands that you have actually typed into the file.

With some programs, primarily those designed to emulate dedicated word processors, producing an ASCII text file is not so convenient. MultiMate and DisplayWrite, for example, require that you use a separate utility program to convert a document file to an ASCII text file, and vice versa. Since the conversion must be repeated every time you edit the program, you may find it easier to stick with the MODIFY COMMAND editor in spite of its limitations.

One of the best choices for a program editor, especially for short programs, is the notepad editor of a RAM-resident utility program like SideKick. These programs can read and write ASCII files, they run faster and offer more power than the dBASE III PLUS MODIFY COMMAND editor, and most are small enough that they do not cause memory conflicts. Furthermore, once the editor is loaded into memory (which is done only once, most likely when you boot your system) and the program you are writing is loaded into the editor, you can call both up to the screen almost instantly from within dBASE III PLUS, make a change, and quickly save the modified program.

ACCESSING A WORD PROCESSOR FROM WITHIN dBASE III PLUS

If you have enough RAM in your computer, you can use the RUN command to access any word processor from within dBASE III PLUS. In addition to the 256K minimum required to run dBASE III PLUS, you will need enough memory to load COMMAND.COM (about 18K under DOS 2 and 24K under DOS 3) and the word processor at the same time. With larger word processors, this may not be practical, especially if you use RAM-resident programs.

To execute the word processor, you type RUN followed by the command that you would use to invoke the program from DOS. For example, if you were using a copy of WordStar called WS.COM, you could run this program with

```
RUN WS
```

If you have a hard disk, check that the word processing software either resides in the same subdirectory as dBASE III PLUS or is accessible through a DOS PATH command. In a floppy disk system, if you cannot place both the word processor and the dBASE III PLUS overlay file (DBASE.OVL) on the same disk because of limited disk capacity or the way your word processor is copy protected, you will have to do some disk swapping. Check that the disk containing COMMAND.COM and the word processor is in the default drive when you type the RUN command; after you exit the word processor, dBASE III PLUS will request the disk with the DBASE.OVL file when it is needed.

When you use a word processor to edit a dBASE III PLUS program, you must specify the PRG file extension. Many word processors supply a different extension by default (often DOC for document), which you must override so that dBASE III PLUS can recognize your file as a program. If you cannot specify the extension, or if you occasionally forget, you can rename the program afterward. For example, if you created a file called NWOPRICE.DOC, you could rename it with the following DOS command:

```
REN NWOPRICE.DOC NWOPRICE.PRG
```

The dBASE III PLUS equivalent would be

```
RENAME NWOPRICE.DOC TO NWOPRICE.PRG
```

If you are sure that you will always want to use an external word processor to edit programs, you can place a TEDIT entry in the CONFIG.DB file to cause the MODIFY COMMAND command to invoke the word processor instead of the dBASE III PLUS program editor:

TEDIT=*program name*

For example, to substitute WordStar for the MODIFY COMMAND editor, you would use the following entry in CONFIG.DB:

```
TEDIT = WS
```

The same memory requirements that govern the use of the RUN command apply to a word processor invoked with TEDIT, and just as with the RUN command, the word processor must be available when you type MODIFY COMMAND. If you specify a file name in the MODIFY COMMAND command (for example, MODIFY COMMAND NWOPRICE), it is passed to the word processor. Of course, if you can save a file without exiting the word processor, you can also edit additional files before returning to dBASE III PLUS.

TYPICAL APPLICATIONS FOR BATCH-TYPE PROGRAMS

When you decide to begin to automate an application by writing some simple batch-type programs, the best way to choose which tasks to automate is to monitor your work at the dot prompt, watching for command sequences that are repeated in the course of a typical processing cycle. The brief summary of the advantages of programming presented earlier in this chapter can serve as a set of informal guidelines to help you identify the operations that would benefit most from combining individual steps into short programs. These might be rephrased as follows:

- Command sequences that are repeated many times during a typical month or year
- Sequences of commands that require little or no user input, especially ones that include several long-running commands

- Complex or lengthy command sequences in which an error or omission could damage the integrity of the data bases
- Procedures that not every user understands how to carry out from the dot prompt

The remainder of this section presents three detailed examples, drawn from the National Widgets system, of the kind of programs that you can write without mastering any new dBASE III PLUS concepts. These programs are longer than the first seven-line version of NWOPRICE.PRG file, but they all consist of commands you have already used at the dot prompt, and they are typical of the types of operations in any application that stand to gain a great deal from automation.

A PROGRAM THAT CALCULATES AND POSTS ORDERS

Any procedure that performs calculations or updates files is a good candidate for a dBASE III PLUS program, especially if it involves lengthy or complex command sequences or commands that take a long time to execute. For example, Chapter 12 described how to use the UPDATE command to post data from a new batch of orders to the year-to-date and total orders fields in the Customer File.

This example was presented to illustrate the UPDATE command, but in a real application, the UPDATE might be only part of a longer sequence of steps. In a typical application, you would enter a batch of new orders, read in the standard prices from the Inventory File, calculate the SUBTOTAL, DISCOUNT, and INVAMOUNT fields, and then perform the UPDATE.

It would also be desirable, since the Order File might grow quite large, to find a better way to identify the "new" order records than to select records in which the PRICE field is zero. A more efficient strategy is to enter new order records into a temporary file. You could open this file for the REPLACE and UPDATE steps, and then APPEND the records into the Order File and empty the temporary file to prepare for the next batch of orders.

Figure 14-3 lists NWOCALC.PRG, a program that performs the order file calculations and then updates the Customer File. The program assumes that the new orders are entered into a temporary file called NWOTEMP.DBF with the same structure as NWORDER.DBF. You could create this file with the following commands:

```
USE NWORDER
COPY STRUCTURE TO NWOTEMP
```

The NWOCALC.PRG program opens the Temporary Order File and the Inventory File and links them with SET RELATION so the PRICE field may be read from the Inventory File into the order records. The temporary file is given the alias ORDER so that command sequences developed using the Order File will work unchanged.

Next, NWOCALC.PRG calculates the SUBTOTAL, DISCOUNT, and INVAMOUNT fields. National Widgets gives discounts based on the dollar value of a purchase; a 10 percent discount is offered on any item for which the SUBTOTAL is more than $50. The program also allows for the use of nonstandard prices and discounts by using a FOR clause in both REPLACE commands to exclude records in which these fields have already been filled in (the values are not zero). When you add records to NWOTEMP.DBF, you could enter a special sale price or discount, which would not be overwritten during subsequent calculation steps.

Notice also that the program cancels the linkage between the Temporary Order File and Inventory File immediately after the only REPLACE command that requires both files to be open (the one that reads the PRICE field from the Inventory File into the order records). Leaving the files linked would not be wrong, but the Temporary Order File calculations do not depend on the inventory data. The program will run a little faster if the RELATION is canceled, because dBASE III PLUS does not have to continue to reposition the record pointer in the Inventory File.

With the order calculations complete, the program opens the Customer File and carries out the UPDATE exactly as you would do from the dot prompt. The "posted" records are then added to the Order File and are deleted from the Temporary Order File.

Notice that only records in which the INVAMOUNT field has a non-zero value are deleted. Although the program prints order records for which no matching Inventory File record was found, it does not pause to allow you to make corrections. In these records, the PRICE

```
* NWOCALC.PRG
* PROGRAM TO PROCESS A NEW BATCH OF ORDERS
* WRITTEN:   6/30/87    M.LISKIN
* REVISED:   7/02/87    M.LISKIN

set echo on

* OPEN DATA BASES FOR ORDER CALCULATIONS
select 1
use NWINVENT index NWICATPT alias INVENTORY
select 2
use NWORDTMP alias ORDER
set relation to CATEGORY + PARTNUMBER into INVENTORY

* CARRY OUT ORDER CALCULATIONS
replace all PRICE with INVENTORY->PRICE for PRICE = 0
list ACCOUNT, CATEGORY, PARTNUMBER to print;
   for PARTNUMBER <> INVENTORY->PARTNUMBER
set relation to
replace all SUBTOTAL with PRICE * QUANTITY
replace all DISCOUNT with SUBTOTAL * .1 for SUBTOTAL >= 50 .and. DISCOUNT = 0
replace all INVAMOUNT with SUBTOTAL - DISCOUNT

* UPDATE CUSTOMER FILE BASED ON ORDER DATA
select 1
use NWCUST index NWCACCT alias CUSTOMER
update on ACCOUNT from ORDER random;
   replace YTDORDERS with YTDORDERS + ORDER->INVAMOUNT,;
   TOTORDERS with TOTORDERS + ORDER->INVAMOUNT

* ADD TEMPORARY ORDER FILE RECORDS INTO ORDER FILE

use NWORDER index NWOACCT
append from ORDER for INVAMOUNT > 0

* DELETE ALL POSTED ORDERS FROM TEMPORARY ORDER FILE
select ORDER
delete for INVAMOUNT > 0
pack

close databases
set echo off
```

Figure 14-3 *NWOCALC.PRG, a program that performs order calculations*

field, and therefore the SUBTOTAL and INVAMOUNT fields, will still have the value 0 when the program completes. These problem records should be left in the Temporary Order File so that you can easily identify them, correct the errors, and process them by rerunning the program NWOCALC.PRG.

Finally, the temporary file is PACKed to permanently remove the deleted records. If you wanted to verify the results of the UPDATE before permanently removing posted records, you could omit the PACK step or make sure to make a backup copy of the temporary file before running the NWOCALC.PRG program.

If this program seems more complicated then carrying out the same steps at the dot prompt, it may be because you are not accustomed to thinking of the the component commands as part of a single procedure. The individual steps were introduced separately, in different chapters in this book, as illustrations of various dBASE III PLUS concepts and commands. In a real application, they would comprise a single logical operation: entering and posting a batch of orders. Nevertheless, some forethought and planning are necessary to make sure that your program includes all the required steps executed in the correct sequence.

A PROGRAM THAT REINDEXES THE DATA BASES

When you work with a data base containing more than a few hundred records, constructing a new index or rebuilding an existing index can be slow, even on a hard disk. In any dBASE III PLUS application, several situations call for building indexes, and they can all be improved by writing programs.

The first, an obvious candidate for automation, is building an index that is not maintained on a daily basis because it is used only to print a report. Although indexing is generally safe to run unattended, it is more risky to print a report with no one physically present. If the paper or ribbon jams, you can lose more than your report—you can burn out the printhead on a dot-matrix printer.

One solution to this problem is to write a program that constructs all the indexes required for a number of reports, run this program overnight, and print the reports the following day. (Of course, if you make further changes to a newly indexed data base before printing one of the reports, you must remember to open the new index so you will not have to rebuild it again.)

Every dBASE III PLUS system should also have, as part of its "disaster recovery" procedures, a program to rebuild all the indexes associated with all the data bases. This program would allow you to return easily to normal operation after you have either inadvertently or intentionally (to save time during high-volume data entry) opened a data base without one or more of its indexes.

The reindexing program can also help if a more drastic hardware or software failure forces you to recover your data bases from a set of backup disks. Since an index can always be recreated from scratch, you can save time by not backing up the index files and just rebuild them when necessary.

The program in Figure 14-4, NWINDEX.PRG, rebuilds all the indexes normally used with the National Widgets system data bases. The program uses the INDEX ON command rather than REINDEX, so that it will run successfully even if some or all of the indexes are damaged or missing.

A PROGRAM THAT COMPILES STATISTICS

The final program presented in this chapter carries out a series of statistical calculations on the Customer File using the SUM and AVERAGE commands first described in Chapter 8. This program, NWCSTATS.PRG, which is listed in Figure 14-5, counts the number of customers who own IBM, Apple, Kaypro, and Compaq computers and accumulates the total and average of the year-to-date and total orders in each group.

As noted in Chapter 8, these statistics represent the kind of management information that is difficult to obtain manually—exactly the type of ad hoc inquiry at which dBASE III PLUS excels. But in a large file, the immediacy of the query process is diminished by the fact that computing the totals can be time-consuming. Every COUNT, SUM, or AVERAGE command causes dBASE III PLUS to read through the entire data base, testing each record against the condition in the FOR clause to determine whether it should be included in the statistics.

You can maximize the efficiency of the commands by using one SUM

```
* NWINDEX.PRG
* PROGRAM TO REBUILD ALL NATIONAL WIDGETS INDEX FILES
* WRITTEN:   6/30/87    M.LISKIN
* REVISED:   7/01/87    M.LISKIN

set echo on

use NWCUST
index on ACCOUNT to NWCACCT
index on ZIP to NWCZIP

use NWORDER
index on ACCOUNT to NWOACCT

use NWINVENT
index on CATEGORY + PARTNUMBER to NWICATPT

use
set echo off
```

Figure 14-4 *NWINDEX.PRG, a program used to rebuild all the indexes for the National Widgets data bases*

or AVERAGE command to process two fields, but even so, accumulating the desired statistics for four types of equipment requires 12 complete passes through the Customer File. Placing the commands in a dBASE III PLUS program enables you to walk away from the computer and return only when all the statistics have been computed. (In this case, you could further speed up the program by omitting the AVERAGE commands entirely, since an average can be calculated by dividing a sum by the matching count.)

In a program like NWOCALC.PRG that contains more than a few calculation steps, the values computed by the first few commands may scroll off the screen before the final statistics have been calculated. The program therefore stores the computed results in memory variables, which can be displayed with DISPLAY MEMORY or printed with LIST MEMORY TO PRINT.

When a dBASE III PLUS program terminates, all memory variables created within the program are automatically RELEASEd (erased from memory). If you think you might want to use the values in a later work

```
* NWCSTATS.PRG
* PROGRAM TO COMPILE CUSTOMER STATISTICS BY TYPE OF EQUIPMENT
* WRITTEN:  06/30/87       M.LISKIN

set echo on
use NWCUST

count to MCOUNTIBM for "IBM" $ UPPER(EQUIPMENT)
sum YTDINV, TOTINV to MYSUMIBM, MTSUMIBM for "IBM" $ UPPER(EQUIPMENT)
average YTDINV, TOTINV to MYAVGIBM, MTAVGIBM for "IBM" $ UPPER(EQUIPMENT)

count to MCOUNTAPP for "APPLE" $ UPPER(EQUIPMENT)
sum YTDINV, TOTINV to MYSUMAP, MTSUMAPP for "APPLE" $ UPPER(EQUIPMENT)
average YTDINV, TOTINV to MYAVGAP, MTAVGAPP for "APPLE" $ UPPER(EQUIPMENT)

count to MCOUNTKAY for "KAYPRO" $ UPPER(EQUIPMENT)
sum YTDINV, TOTINV to MYSUMKAY, MTSUMKAY for "KAYPRO" $ UPPER(EQUIPMENT)
average YTDINV, TOTINV to MYAVGKAY, MTAVGKAY for "KAYPRO" $ UPPER(EQUIPMENT)

count to MCOUNTCOM for "COMPAQ" $ UPPER(EQUIPMENT)
sum YTDINV, TOTINV to MYSUMCOM, MTSUMCOM for "COMPAQ" $ UPPER(EQUIPMENT)
average YTDINV, TOTINV to MYAVGCOM, MTAVGCOM for "COMPAQ" $ UPPER(EQUIPMENT)

save to NWCSTATS
list memory to print
use
set echo off
return
```

Figure 14-5 *NWCSTATS.PRG, a program that computes customer statistics*

session, you must store them in a memory file with a SAVE command. The NWOCALC.PRG program saves the computed statistics in a file called NWCSTATS.MEM; you could load the variables back into memory later with a RESTORE command:

```
RESTORE FROM NWCSTATS
```

Notice that the conditions in the FOR clauses convert the EQUIPMENT field to uppercase letters with the UPPER function to minimize the effect of data entry errors on the accuracy of the statistics. Several people (or the same person at different times) may have entered data into the file using various combinations of uppercase and lowercase letters, such as Kaypro, KAYPRO, and KayPro. If you convert the EQUIPMENT field to uppercase letters and search for all uppercase characters (using the substring operator) within this field, all combinations of uppercase and lowercase characters will be treated the same. Recall that the UPPER function does not change the actual data stored in the Customer File; the EQUIPMENT field is simply converted to uppercase letters for the comparison stated in the FOR clause.

TESTING AND DEBUGGING

Just as it is impossible to work at the dot prompt without making mistakes, no matter how proficient you are and how much experience with dBASE III PLUS you have, you will undoubtedly make errors in the programs you write. Finding the errors, or *bugs* in a program, a process known as *debugging,* can be a frightening prospect at first, because you are one step further removed from the command that caused the problem than when you work interactively.

The most common errors—and the easiest to find and correct—are *syntax errors* similar to the ones you might make at the dot prompt. You may use the wrong command verb, forget an essential phrase or option, use a clause not permitted in the command you are executing, misspell a dBASE III PLUS command word, function name, data base field name, or memory variable name, or combine variables and functions illegally in a complex expression.

When an error occurs within a dBASE III PLUS program, execution pauses and dBASE III PLUS displays the incorrect line along with the same error message that the erroneous command would generate if you had typed it at the dot prompt. Because one program may call another (a capability that is unnecessary in the simple programs in this book), the error listing also traces the chain of programs leading to the one containing the faulty command. For example, an error in the SET RELATION command in NWOCALC.PRG might produce the display illustrated in Figure 14-6.

```
. DO NWOCALC

select 1
use NWINVENT index NWICATPT alias INVENTORY
select 2
use NWORDTMP alias ORDER
set relation to CAGEGORY + PARTNUMBER into INVENTORY
Variable not found.
                          ?
set relation to CAGEGORY + PARTNUMBER into INVENTORY
Called from - C:NWOCALC.prg
Command          ||<C:>||ORDER              ||Rec: None          ||Ins ||    Caps
                 Cancel, Ignore, or Suspend? (C, I, or S)
                        Enter a dBASE III PLUS command.
```

Figure 14-6 *A syntax error in the NWOCALC.PRG program*

Often, a careful examination of the error display will lead you to the source of the problem—in this example, a typographical error in the spelling of the CATEGORY field name. Whenever you run a new program, you should have at hand a printed listing of the program for reference as well as printouts of the structures and contents of any data bases opened by the program, in the appropriate indexed or sequential order. For all but the most obvious errors, seeing the bad command line in context and knowing what data the program was attempting to process when it crashed can be helpful in finding the bug.

Whether or not you have SET HELP OFF, errors in a dBASE III PLUS program do not result in an offer of help. Instead, you are given the choice of three courses of action: "Cancel, Ignore, or Suspend? (C, I, or S)." These selections have the following results:

- **Cancel:** dBASE III PLUS terminates the program and returns you to the dot prompt. Memory variables are RELEASEd, but all data bases remain open, positioned exactly where they were when the error occurred.

- **Ignore:** dBASE III PLUS bypasses the line containing the error and continues execution with the next command in the program.

- **Suspend:** dBASE III PLUS temporarily pauses execution of the program. Memory variables are not RELEASEd, and all data bases remain open, positioned exactly where they were when the error occurred. You can type any commands you wish and then either pick up execution where it was interrupted by typing RESUME or terminate the program by typing CANCEL.

In a simple program in which every step performs some essential processing on a data base file, you would rarely choose to ignore an error, since most commands depend for correct execution on the previous steps in the program. A possible exception is a LIST command, which you might skip the first time you run the program and then correct at your leisure.

If you have made a serious error and you immediately recognize the cause, you can cancel the program, edit it to correct the error, and try running it again. You might also elect to suspend execution, type the corrected line from the dot prompt, and then type RESUME to continue running the program. By using this strategy, you might find several errors in one test run and correct them at once in a single editing session. If you suspend and then continue running a program, you might want to print the screen as a reminder of the changes you must make later.

Unless the cause of an error is immediately evident, the best strategy is to suspend or cancel the program and type commands at the dot prompt to try to track down the bug. When you choose the Suspend option, memory variables remain intact, so if your program creates memory variables (for example, with a COUNT, SUM, or AVERAGE command), it is better to suspend than cancel execution. In either case, all data bases remain positioned exactly where they were when the program crashed, and you can use DISPLAY STATUS, DISPLAY, LIST, or ? commands to answer the questions that might lead you to the source of the problem. Consider the following:

- Have you misspelled a file name, field name, memory variable name, or alias?

- Are the right data base files open?

- Are the right indexes open?
- Is the right index designated the master index?
- Is the right work area selected?
- Is the record pointer positioned correctly in each open file?
- Are files linked correctly with SET RELATION?
- Is the right FILTER condition in effect?
- Do all memory variables named in commands actually exist?

Once you have found the problem, the safest course if you have suspended the program is to CANCEL execution and run the program again rather than use RESUME to pick up where you left off. Knowing that you will start again from scratch, feel free to switch work areas and use commands that reposition the record pointer in your attempts to find the problem.

When you make a syntax error, dBASE III PLUS informs you of that fact in no uncertain terms, but even if a new program runs to completion without generating an error message, you should not assume that it has produced the correct results. You might have stated a condition wrong, failed to position the record pointer correctly before executing a command that uses a WHILE clause, forgotten to cancel a FILTER, or executed a REPLACE command with the wrong data base selected (an error that could go unnoticed if the file contains fields with the same names as the file you intended to process).

Whenever you write a new program, test it on a copy of your data base or a smaller sample file to verify that it correctly manipulates the data. If you use a small test file, make sure that the sample data provides a wide range of input encompassing all the possibilities that exist in the entire data base. For every condition in a FOR or WHILE clause that tests the contents of a particular field, make sure that the test data includes some records in which the field is blank, some that satisfy the condition, and some that do not, even if some of these values "can't" occur in the real system. Devising strategic test conditions is especially important in assessing whether a program can cope with "impossible" values such as negative numbers or finding instances in which you have used the wrong comparison operator in a condition, such as "less than" when you really need "less than or equal to."

Make sure also when you verify a program's performance by carrying out the same operation from the dot prompt that you use a command sequence that is sufficiently different to uncover a potential problem. For example, whenever you use a complex FILTER or condition, be sure to verify the results, not by typing the same condition (which may be syntactically correct but select the wrong records) at the dot prompt, but by using a LIST command that displays the relevant fields from all the records in the data base so you can see that the right records were selected. In some cases, the only way to verify calculations is by performing the same computations on a hand-held calculator based on a printout of the contents of the data bases.

The examples in this chapter barely scratch the surface of what you can do with dBASE III PLUS programs drawing on the commands that you already know how to use at the dot prompt. The programs presented here are necessarily quite detailed and very closely tied to the National Widgets sample system. At the same time, they are typical of the types of operations found in any application that are amenable to automation through simple batch-type programs.

You might try, as a final hands-on practice exercise, creating these or other similar programs and testing them on the National Widgets sample files. If you are working on a real data base, you might instead begin to look for operations in your own application that could benefit from similar treatment. Once you have decided not to allow the prospect of writing programs to intimidate you, you can be on the lookout for command sequences that could be incorporated into short programs to improve the efficiency of your work with dBASE III PLUS.

Appendix A

Command Syntax Notation

This appendix is a key to Appendixes B, C, and D, which provide a concise summary of the dBASE III PLUS commands and functions and the options that may be set in the CONFIG.DB file. These appendixes use the same standard notation as the dBASE III PLUS manual does.

UPPERCASE is used for all dBASE III PLUS keywords (words that are recognized by dBASE III PLUS as part of its command vocabulary), including command verbs; function names; words like FOR, WHILE, and TO, which introduce command clauses; and command options like OFF or DELIMITED. You may always type keywords in any combination of uppercase and lowercase. Command words (but *not* function names) may be abbreviated, provided that the portion of the command word you type is at least four characters long; if you include more than four characters, they must all be correct. For example, DELIMITED may be abbreviated to DELI or DELIM, but not DELIT.

Optional command components are enclosed in square brackets ([]). When you use these options, remember not to type the brackets.

Two options are separated by a slash (/) if one or the other, but not both, may be used in a command. Many of the SET options have two allowable values (in most cases, ON or OFF); the default status of these options is printed in UPPERCASE, with the alternate value in lowercase. For example, the command to turn the terminal's beeper on or off is written as SET BELL ON/off.

Substitutions are printed in *lowercase italics* and enclosed in angle brackets (<>). When you use these commands, remember not to type the brackets or the exact words printed between the brackets; instead, you should make the appropriate substitution. For example, the command to create a new data base is listed as CREATE <*file name*>. To use this command to create the National Widgets Customer File, you would type CREATE NWCUST.

In most cases, dBASE III PLUS command clauses and options may be used in any combination and typed in almost any order. The order used in the command summary in Appendix B was chosen so that the commands would read as much like English sentences as possible.

The following terms are used to describe the substitution items:

alias: An optional alternate name for a data base, which may be up to ten characters long and may contain an embedded underscore (_). The alias is specified in the USE command that opens the file; if you do not assign an alias, dBASE III PLUS assigns the file name as the alias. Some commands require that you use the alias rather than the file name if the two are different.

alias—>field: A field in a data base open in a work area other than the currently selected work area.

character string: Any sequence of characters, enclosed in single quotes ('), double quotes ("), or square brackets ([]).

column: A screen or printer column (horizontal) coordinate. Columns are numbered from left to right, beginning with 0.

condition: A logical expression that evaluates to .T. or .F.

current: Used to describe the disk drive and subdirectory from which dBASE III PLUS was loaded, the selected work area, the data base file open in the selected work area, or the record at the position of the dBASE III PLUS record pointer.

drive: A disk drive designator (A, B, C, and so on), followed by a colon (:) if it forms part of a file name.

exp: Any syntactically valid dBASE III PLUS expression composed of data base fields, memory variables, functions, constants, and operators.

expC: An expression that evaluates to a character string.

expD: An expression that evaluates to a date.

expL: An expression that evaluates to a logical value (.T. or .F.).

expN: An expression that evaluates to a number.

field: The name of a field in the data base open in the currently selected work area.

file name: A valid MS-DOS file name. You must include the disk drive if the file does not reside on the default drive, and specify the full path name if the file is not in the current subdirectory (unless you have used a SET PATH command to specify a search path for files not in the current subdirectory). Any command that manipulates a particular type of file (for example, USE, which opens a data base file, or SAVE, which creates a memory variable file) assumes the standard dBASE III PLUS extension unless you override it by explicitly typing the extension. Commands that may operate on any type of disk file (for example, ERASE or RENAME) must always include the extension. The standard file extensions are

CAT	Catalog data base file
DBF	Data base file
DBT	Data base text file (contains memo field text)
FMT	Format file

FRM	Report form file
LBL	Label form file
MEM	Memory variable file
NDX	Index file
PRG	Program or procedure file
QRY	Query file
SCR	Screen image file
TXT	Text file
VUE	View file

key or *key expression:* The expression used as the basis for indexing or sorting a data base file.

list: One or more items of the same type (fields, files, expressions, indexes, and so on) separated by commas.

memvar: A memory variable.

n: A number.

path: A DOS path name (the path through the subdirectory structure from the current subdirectory to the specified file) followed by a backslash (\).

row: A screen or printer row (vertical) coordinate. Rows are numbered from top to bottom, beginning with 0.

scope: The range of records in a data base to be acted on by a command. The valid scopes are

ALL	The entire file
NEXT <*expN*>	A number of records equal to the value of *expN*, including the current record
RECORD <*expN*>	A single record; its record number is the value of *expN*
REST	All of the records from the current record (including the current record) to the end of the file

In interpreting the *scope*, dBASE III PLUS takes into consideration any factors that affect the sequence or the range of records to be processed, including indexes, FILTERs, and the status of the DELETED option. For example, with a FILTER in effect and DELETED ON,

ALL means all the records that are not marked for deletion and that satisfy the FILTER condition.

skeleton: A pattern of letters and wildcard symbols that a file or variable name must match. The two wildcard characters are ?, which stands for any single character, and *, which substitutes for any combination of characters.

variable: Either a memory variable or a data base field.

Appendix B

dBASE III PLUS Command Syntax Summary

This appendix contains a brief summary of the dBASE III PLUS commands in alphabetical order. This listing is intended to serve as a reference for looking up the exact syntax of a command or for confirming which options are available, not as a learning guide. It does not include usage suggestions or examples for every command, and the use of the full-screen editing commands (such as APPEND and EDIT) and menu-driven commands (such as CREATE/MODIFY REPORT) are not described in detail. Commands that are used primarily in dBASE III PLUS programs are marked with an asterisk (*).

* ?/?? [<*exp list*>]

Displays (if CONSOLE is ON) and/or prints (if PRINT is ON) the expressions in *exp list*, each pair separated by a single space. ? first issues a carriage return and line feed and thus displays or prints the expressions on the next available line. ?? displays the listed expressions beginning at the current cursor position (on the screen) or the current print head position. When no expressions are listed, ? displays or prints a blank line.

* @ <*row*>,<*column*> [[SAY <*exp*>
[PICTURE <*picture*>] [FUNCTION <*function*>]]
[GET <*variable*> [PICTURE <*picture*<][FUNCTION
<*function*>] [RANGE <*exp*>,<*exp*>]]]

* @ <*row*>,<*column*> [CLEAR]

* @ <*row1*>,<*column1*> [CLEAR] TO <*row 2*>,
<*column2*> [DOUBLE]

@...SAY...GET commands are used in format files and in dBASE III PLUS programs to display or print text and data at specific positions on the screen or page. *Row* and *column* may be any valid numeric expressions representing screen or printer coordinates. For the screen, *row* must be between 0 and 24, and *column* must be between 0 and 79. For the printer, both *row* and *column* may range from 0 to 255, provided that lower limits are not imposed by the printer itself.

If a SAY clause is included, the specified expression is displayed on the screen with the *standard* display attributes (if you have SET DEVICE TO SCREEN) or printed (if you have SET DEVICE TO PRINT) at the designated row and column coordinates. Data may be placed on the screen in any order, but printing must proceed from left to right on each line and from top to bottom on each page.

If a GET clause is included, the specified expression is displayed on the screen with the *enhanced* display attributes (if you have SET DEVICE TO SCREEN). If you have SET DEVICE TO PRINT, GET commands are ignored.

If a PICTURE and/or FUNCTION clause are included, the *function* and/or *picture* are used to validate and format data displayed by a SAY clause or collected by a GET clause. See Tables 10-1 and 10-2 for a list of the valid function and template symbols.

If a RANGE clause is included, it specifies the permissible range of values for a numeric or date field. The two *exp*'s in the RANGE clause may be any valid numeric or date expressions (depending on the type of data being collected). The RANGE clause allows the user to press ENTER to leave any existing value unchanged, but if new data is entered, the cursor will not advance to the next item unless the value is within the allowable range.

In a program, one or more @...SAY...GET commands *must* be followed by a READ in order to allow the user to edit the data. Memo fields may be accessed with @...SAY...GET only if the command is part of a format file used with APPEND or EDIT (not activated by a READ).

@ <*row*>,<*column*> erases the specified row, beginning at the specified column.

@ <*row*>,<*column*> CLEAR erases a rectangular area of the screen; the *row* and *column* coordinates specify the upper left corner of the area.

@ <*row1*>,<*column1*> TO <*row2*>,<*column2*> draws a continuous single-line box on the screen, or a double-line box if the keyword DOUBLE is included. The two sets of row and column coordinates specify the upper left and lower right corners of the box. If the two row coordinates are the same, a horizontal line is produced; if the two column coordinates are identical, a vertical line results.

@ <*row1*>,<*column1*> CLEAR TO <*row2*>,<*column2*> erases a rectangular region on the screen; the upper left corner has the coordinates *row1* and *column1*, and the lower right corner has the coordinates *row2* and *column2*.

* ACCEPT [<*expC*>] TO <*memvar*>

Collects input from the user and creates the character string memory variable *memvar* to store the input. If *expC* is included, it is displayed as a prompt. If the user presses ENTER without typing anything else, *memvar* will be a null character string of length zero.

APPEND
* APPEND BLANK
APPEND FROM <*file name*> [FOR <*condition*>] [TYPE DELIMITED [WITH <*delimiter*>/BLANK] /SDF/DIF/SYLK/WKS]

APPEND adds new records to the current data base, using the standard dBASE III PLUS full-screen editing commands. Pressing PGUP allows you to edit existing records; however, these records are displayed in sequential order even if the data base was opened with an index.

APPEND BLANK adds a blank record to the current data base and positions the record pointer to the new record without invoking the full-screen edit mode. Usually, the fields are filled in with REPLACE or GET commands.

APPEND FROM adds records from the named file to the current data base. If a *condition* is specified, it must refer only to fields that are common to both data bases. Unless you have SET DELETED ON, records that have been marked for deletion are APPENDed, and are not marked as deleted in the file that receives the data. Data is transferred between two DBF files by matching identically named fields.

If the SDF ("System Data Format") option is specified, the file from which records are APPENDed is assumed to be a fixed length text file with a carriage return at the end of each record.

If the DELIMITED option is specified, the file from which records are APPENDed is assumed to be a text file in which the fields are separated by commas, with a carriage return at the end of each record. If character fields in the text file are surrounded with any delimiters other than double quotes, the delimiter must be specified in the WITH clause. If DELIMITED WITH BLANK is selected, the fields are assumed to be separated by single spaces.

When dBASE III PLUS APPENDs data from DIF ("Data Interchange Format"), SYLK (Multiplan "Symbolic Link"), or WKS (Lotus Worksheet) files, rows in the spreadsheet become records in the data base, with each column supplying data for a field.

In all variations of the APPEND command, any indexes opened together with the data base are updated to account for the new records.

ASSIST

Invokes a menu-driven mode of operation for dBASE III PLUS.

AVERAGE [<*scope*>] [<*expN list*>] [FOR <*condition*>] [WHILE <*condition*>] [TO <*memvar list*>]

Calculates the average value for each expression in the list for the range of records in the current data base defined by the *scope* and *conditions*. If no expressions are listed, all numeric fields are AVERAGEd. If no *scope* is specified, ALL is assumed. If you have SET TALK ON, the averages are displayed on the screen, and if you have SET HEADING ON, the *expressions* are displayed above the results. If a list of memory variables is included, the named numeric variables are created to store the averages.

BROWSE [FIELDS <*field list*>] [LOCK <*expN*>] [FREEZE <*field*>] [WIDTH <*expN*>] [NOFOLLOW] [NOMENU] [NOAPPEND]

Enters a full-screen edit mode in which records are displayed one per line, with the fields aligned in columns. The first record displayed is the current record. You may not display or edit memo fields using BROWSE. Any data displayed on the screen may be edited, records may be deleted or recalled with CTRL-U, and new records may be added (just as in EDIT) by positioning the record pointer to the last record and then pressing PGDN.

If a FIELDS clause is included, only the named fields are displayed, in the specified order. If the LOCK clause is included, *expN* specifies how many fields remain fixed on the left side of the screen. If the FREEZE option is included, editing is restricted to the specified field, although you may still pan the display left or right to view the entire record. If the WIDTH option is included, *expN* specifies the maximum display width for any field; the data scrolls left and right within this width so you can edit the entire field.

The NOFOLLOW option controls the position of the record pointer after the key field is changed in a data base opened with an index. Normally, the record pointer remains positioned at the same record after you change the index key field, and the screen is redrawn with this record at the top. Since the record has moved in the index, a different set of records will occupy the screen after the change. NOFOLLOW causes the record pointer to be repositioned to the record originally displayed below the one that was changed, so that the screen display remains constant except for the disappearance of the altered record.

The NOAPPEND option prevents you from adding records to a data base from within BROWSE.

LOCK and FREEZE may also be set from the BROWSE option menu invoked by pressing CTRL-HOME. This menu also contains commands to GOTO the TOP or BOTTOM of the file or to a particular record, specified by number, or to carry out a SEEK command if the file was opened with an index; the menu is not accessible if the NOMENU option is included in the BROWSE command.

* CALL <*module name*> [WITH <*expC*>]

Executes a binary program file loaded into memory with the LOAD command. The value of *expC* is passed to the program as a parameter. LOAD and CALL should be used only for subroutines written expressly to be executed this way; COM or EXE files (including most commercial software) should be invoked with the RUN command instead.

* CANCEL

Causes dBASE III PLUS to exit immediately from the currently running program, close all open program files (but not a procedure file, if one is open), and return to the dot prompt.

CHANGE [<*scope*>] [FIELDS <*field list*>] [FOR <*condition*>] [WHILE <*condition*>]

Enters a full-screen mode to edit the specified fields in the range of records defined by the *scope* and *conditions.* If no *scope* is specified, ALL is assumed. CHANGE is identical to EDIT.

CLEAR
CLEAR ALL/FIELDS/GETS/MEMORY/TYPEAHEAD

CLEAR erases the screen, leaving the cursor positioned in the upper left corner and CLEARs all pending GETs.

CLEAR ALL closes all data base files, indexes, format files, and CATALOG files in all of the ten work areas, selects work area 1, and releases all memory variables.

CLEAR FIELDS cancels a field list established with SET FIELDS TO <*field list*>, and turns off the field list as if you had typed SET FIELDS OFF.

* CLEAR GETS cancels all pending GETs, preventing the user from editing any variables that have not yet been collected by a READ. You may not issue more GET commands than specified by the GETS option in CONFIG.DB (128 if you have not changed the default) between CLEAR GETS, CLEAR, or READ commands.

* CLEAR MEMORY releases all memory variables, both PUBLIC and

PRIVATE.

* CLEAR TYPEAHEAD deletes all characters in the typeahead buffer.

CLOSE ALL/ALTERNATE/ DATABASES/FORMAT/INDEX/PROCEDURE

Closes all files of the specified type.

CLOSE ALTERNATE (exactly like SET ALTERNATE[TO]) closes the current alternate file.

CLOSE DATABASES closes all data bases, indexes, and format files in all ten work areas, except a CATALOG file open in work area 10.

CLOSE FORMAT (exactly like SET FORMAT [TO]) closes the format file in the current work area.

CLOSE INDEX (exactly like SET INDEX [TO]) closes all index files in the current work area.

* CLOSE PROCEDURE (exactly like SET PROCEDURE [TO]) closes the current procedure file.

CONTINUE

Searches the current data base, starting with the current record, for the next record that satisfies the condition in the most recent LOCATE command, and leaves the data base positioned at the matching record. If you have SET TALK ON, the record number is displayed. If no matching record is found within the *scope* specified in the LOCATE command, an "End of locate scope" message is displayed.

COPY TO <*file name*> [<*scope*>] [FIELDS <*field list*>] [FOR <*condition*>] [WHILE <*condition*>] [TYPE DELIMITED [WITH <*delimiter*> BLANK] /SDF/ DIF/SYLK/WKS]
COPY FILE <*file 1*> TO <*file 2*>
COPY STRUCTURE TO <*file name*> [FIELDS <*field list*>]
COPY TO <*filename*> STRUCTURE EXTENDED

Copies the range of records from the current data base defined by the *scope* and *condition* to a new file. This file is created by the COPY command or deleted and recreated if it already exists. Records that have been marked for deletion are COPYed unless you have SET DELETED ON. If no *scope* is specified, ALL is assumed. If a *field list* is included, only the named fields are COPYed, in the specified order; otherwise, the new file has the same structure as the original.

If the SDF option is specified, COPY creates a text file consisting of fixed length records with a carriage return at the end of each record instead of a DBF file.

If the DELIMITED option is specified, COPY creates a text file in which the fields are separated by commas, with a carriage return at the end of each record. If a *delimiter* is included, the specified punctuation mark is used to surround character fields instead of the default double quotes. If DELIMITED WITH BLANK is selected, the fields are separated by single spaces, with no punctuation surrounding character fields.

When dBASE III PLUS COPYs data to DIF ("Data Interchange Format"), SYLK (Multiplan "Symbolic Link"), or WKS (Lotus Worksheet) files, records in the data base become rows in the spreadsheet, with each field supplying data for one column and the field names entered into the spreadsheet as column titles.

COPY STRUCTURE creates an empty data base file containing the fields listed in the *field list* in the specified order, or all of the fields in the current file if no *field list* is given.

The STRUCTURE EXTENDED option creates a structure-extended file that describes the structure of the current file (instead of creating a data base with the same structure). The *structure-extended file* is a data base that has one record for each field in the current file, with four fields, named FIELD_NAME, FIELD_TYPE, FIELD_LEN, and FIELD_DEC, that contain the names, types, lengths, and number of decimal places of the fields. This file may be edited with MODIFY STRUCTURE if necessary, and used to create a new data base with the CREATE FROM command.

COPY FILE <*file 1*> TO <*file 2*> creates a copy of *file 1* under the name *file 2*. Any disk file may be copied with this command, so the extension (and path, if the file is not in the current subdirectory) must be included.

COUNT [<*scope*>] [FOR <*condition*>] [WHILE <*condition*>] [TO <*memvar*>]

Counts the number of records in the current data base in the range defined by the *scope* and *condition*. If no *scope* is specified, ALL is assumed. If you have SET TALK ON, the count is displayed on the screen. If a memory variable is included, the named numeric variable is created to store the count.

CREATE <*file name*>
CREATE <*file name*> FROM <*structure-extended file*>

Enters a full-screen mode in which you create a new data base file by defining names, types, lengths, and for numeric fields, number of decimal places, for up to 128 fields, totaling up to 4000 bytes. If you do not specify the *file name,* dBASE III PLUS will prompt you to enter it.

If you include the FROM option, the structure of the new file is determined by the contents of the structure-extended file. This file is a data base that has one record for each field in the structure it describes, with four fields, named FIELD_NAME, FIELD_TYPE, FIELD_LEN, and FIELD_DEC, that contain the names, types, lengths, and number of decimal places of the fields. The file is usually generated with a COPY command using the STRUCTURE EXTENDED option, but it may be defined with CREATE, provided that you adhere to the four standard field names that allow dBASE III PLUS to recognize the data base as a structure-extended file.

CREATE LABEL *<label file name>*

Creates a new label form or edits an existing form in a menu-driven environment. If you do not specify the *file name,* dBASE III PLUS will prompt you to enter it. If no data base is open in the selected work area, you will be prompted to enter it as well. This command is identical to MODIFY LABEL.

To specify the size and shape of the labels, you first select one of five predefined formats. If necessary, you may then change the label width (1-120 characters), label height (1-16 lines), left margin (0-250 characters), number of labels across the page (1-15), lines between labels (0-16 lines), and spaces between labels (0-120 characters) if you are printing more than one across.

For each line on the label, you may specify as the contents any valid dBASE III PLUS expression up to 60 characters long. If more than one data base is open, you may print fields from any open file by referring to all fields in unselected work areas as *alias—>fieldname.*

CREATE QUERY *<query file name>*

Creates a new query file or edits an existing file in a menu-driven environment. If you do not specify the *file name,* dBASE III PLUS will prompt you to enter it. If no data base is open in the selected work area, you will be prompted to enter it as well. This command is identical to MODIFY QUERY.

You may enter up to seven separate conditions linked with the logical operators .AND., .OR., and .NOT. and grouped ("nested") with parentheses. If more than one data base is open, you may include fields from any open file, provided that you have specified the fields to be accessed with a SET FIELDS command or opened a VIEW that includes a field list.

The selection criteria stored in the query file are placed in effect with SET FILTER TO FILE <*query file name*>.

CREATE REPORT <*report file name*>

Creates a new report form or edits an existing form in a menu-driven environment. If you do not specify the *file name*, dBASE III PLUS will prompt you to enter it. If no data base is open in the selected work area, you will be prompted to enter it as well. This command is identical to MODIFY REPORT.

To specify the overall page layout for the report, you may enter up to four page title lines of up to 60 characters each, the page width (1-500 characters), left and right margins, and number of lines per page (1-500). There are options to double space the report, to issue a form feed command to the printer before and/or after printing the report, and to print the report "plain" (without page numbers, date, and page titles).

You may print one or two levels of subtotals, and specify the text to be printed at the beginning of each group of records as a *group* or *subgroup heading*. It is your responsibility to ensure that the data base is sorted or indexed on the same expression that defines the subtotal breaks. You can choose to print a summary-only report that includes only the subtotals and grand totals, with no detail records.

For each column on the report, you may specify as the contents any valid dBASE III PLUS expression up to 254 characters. If more than one data base is open, you may print fields from any open file by referring to all fields in unselected work areas as *alias—>field name*. You may specify up to four lines of column titles, the width of the column, and for numeric fields, the number of decimal places and whether or not to accumulate totals and subtotals for the column.

CREATE SCREEN <*screen file name*>

Creates a new screen form or edits an existing form in a menu-driven environment. If you do not specify the *file name,* dBASE III PLUS will prompt you to enter it. You can select a data base file to provide the fields displayed or collected on the screen, or you can create a data base at the same time you draw the screen image. This command is identical to MODIFY SCREEN.

To define the screen image, you type background text directly on a "blackboard" and define the locations where fields are displayed or collected. For each field, you may also specify a PICTURE, FUNCTION, or RANGE to format and/or validate the data. Boxes and lines consisting of the single- and double-lined graphics characters may also be included on a screen.

The screen image is saved in two ways—an SCR file that stores the screen image for subsequent editing, and an FMT file that draws the input screen for the APPEND, EDIT, CHANGE, and INSERT commands when the format file is invoked with SET FORMAT TO <*format file name*>.

CREATE VIEW <*view file name*> [FROM ENVIRONMENT]

Creates a new view file or edits an existing file in a menu-driven environment. If you do not specify the *file name,* dBASE III PLUS will prompt you to enter it. This command is identical to MODIFY VIEW.

To define the view, you first select one or more data bases, each of which may be opened with one or more indexes. You may also define how to link the files with SET RELATION, specify the list of fields that may be accessed, and optionally, specify a format file and filter condition.

If the FROM ENVIRONMENT clause is included, the view is created based on the files and indexes currently open and the relations, field list, format file, and filter condition currently in effect.

The files are opened and the relationships among them that are defined in the view file are placed in effect with SET VIEW TO <*view file name*>.

DELETE [<*scope*>] [FOR <*condition*>] [WHILE <*condition*>]

Marks for deletion the records in the current data base in the range defined by the *scope* and *conditions.* If no *scope* is specified, only the current record is DELETEd. Records marked for deletion are physically removed from the file and the space they occupy is released only when you PACK the data base. Records marked for deletion may be recovered with the RECALL command until a file is PACKed.

You may SET DELETED ON to cause dBASE III PLUS to ignore deleted records except when explicitly accessed by record number. If you have SET DELETED OFF, deleted records are identified by an asterisk (*) next to the record number in LIST or DISPLAY commands and by the "*Del*" indicator in the Status Bar (or on the top line of the screen if you have SET STATUS OFF) in the full-screen edit modes.

DELETE FILE <*file name*>

This command is identical to ERASE.

DIR[<*drive*>:] [<*path*> \] [<*skeleton*>] [TO PRINT]

Displays a directory of the specified files. If no *drive, path,* or file name *skeleton* is specified, only data base files are listed, and the display includes for each file the number of records, date of last update, and file size. If a *drive, path,* or file name *skeleton* is included, files are displayed four across, much like the listing produced by adding the / W (wide) option to an MS-DOS DIR command. Even with a SET PATH command in effect, only files from the current subdirectory are displayed if no *path* is specified.

DISPLAY [<*scope*>] [<*exp list*>] [FOR <*condition*>] [WHILE <*condition*>] [TO PRINT] [OFF]

Displays the specified expressions for the range of records in the current data base defined by the *scope* and *condition.* If no *scope* is specified, only the current record is displayed; and with no *exp list,* all fields are included. The display pauses every 20 lines to allow you to read the screen; pressing any key displays the next group of 20 lines. If you have SET HEADING ON, the listed *expressions* are displayed as column titles in the same mixture of uppercase and lowercase used in the DISPLAY command.

The contents of memo fields are displayed only if the field names are explicitly included in the *exp list.* TO PRINT causes dBASE III PLUS to echo the screen display to the printer. OFF suppresses the display of the record numbers. The DISPLAY command is similar to LIST, except that LIST assumes a default *scope* of ALL and does not pause every 20 lines.

DISPLAY FILES [LIKE <*skeleton*>] [TO PRINT]

This command is identical to DIR, except that the optional TO PRINT phrase causes dBASE III PLUS to echo the screen display to the printer.

DISPLAY HISTORY [LAST <*expN*>] [TO PRINT]

Displays a list of the commands in history, normally 20 unless you have increased this number with a SET HISTORY command. TO PRINT causes dBASE III PLUS to echo the screen display to the printer. If the LAST clause is included, *expN* specifies the number of commands displayed, which are taken from the bottom of the list. Every 16 lines the display pauses to allow you to read the screen; pressing any key displays the next group of 16 lines.

DISPLAY MEMORY [TO PRINT]

Displays all active memory variables. The display pauses when the screen is full; pressing any key displays the next screenful of variables. TO PRINT causes dBASE III PLUS to echo the screen display to the printer. For each variable the display includes the name, status (PUBLIC or PRIVATE), data type, stored value, the program (if any) that created the variable, and for numeric variables, the display value (which may include fewer decimal places than the stored value).

At the end of the display, dBASE III PLUS summarizes the number of variables defined, the number of bytes they occupy, the number of remaining variables (256 minus the number already defined), and the number of bytes remaining (the value of MVARSIZ, which is 6000 bytes unless you have increased it with an entry in CONFIG.DB, minus the number already used). This command is similar to LIST MEMORY, except for the pause after filling the screen.

DISPLAY STATUS [TO PRINT]

Displays the current status of the working environment, with a pause between screens to allow you to read the display. TO PRINT causes dBASE III PLUS to echo the screen display to the printer.

For each currently active work area, dBASE III PLUS displays the open data base, all index file names and index key expressions, the file alias, the name of the DBT file if the data base contains memo fields, the name of any open format file, the FILTER condition if one is in effect, and any RELATION used to link the file to another data base. In a network environment, the display includes any file locks currently in effect and a list of any records currently locked.

The display also includes the file search path, default disk drive, selected printer port, left margin for printouts, the currently selected work area, the status of most of the options controlled by SET commands, and the function key assignments. This command is similar to LIST STATUS, except for the pauses between screens.

DISPLAY STRUCTURE [TO PRINT]

Displays the structure of the current data base file. The display pauses after every 16 fields; pressing any key displays the next 16 fields. TO PRINT causes dBASE III PLUS to echo the screen display to the printer. For each field the display includes the name, data type, length, and for numeric fields, number of decimal places. If a field list is in effect, the fields specified in the SET FIELDS commands are marked with a ">". dBASE III PLUS also displays the number of records in the file, the date of last update, and the total record length (the sum of the field lengths plus the one character used for the deletion marker). This command is similar to LIST STRUCTURE, except for the pause every 16 fields.

DISPLAY USERS

In a network environment, displays a list of the network workstation names of the users currently logged onto dBASE III PLUS, with the currently logged user marked with a "<".

DO <*program name*> [WITH <*parameter list*>]

Runs the specified dBASE III PLUS program or calls the named procedure, if a procedure file is open. (If a procedure in the open procedure file has the same name as a program, the procedure will be executed.) When the program or procedure terminates, control returns to the line in the calling program that follows the DO command or to the dot prompt if the DO command was executed from the dot prompt.

If a *parameter list* is included, the listed expressions are passed to the called program, which must contain a PARAMETERS command with the same number of parameters. The correspondence between the parameters in the DO command in the calling program and the PARAMETERS command in the called program or procedure is established by the order in which they are listed. The parameters may include any valid dBASE III PLUS expressions, but if fields are passed as parameters, the file alias must be specified, even for fields in the currently selected work area. All changes made to the values of any parameters specified as memory variables in the calling program are passed back to the calling program.

* DO CASE...ENDCASE

This program structure selects one out of a number of possibilities. The general form of this structure is

```
DO CASE
  CASE <condition 1>
    <program statements>
  [CASE <condition 2>
    <program statements>]
  [CASE <condition 3>
    <program statements>]
  [<more cases>]
  [OTHERWISE
    <program statements>]
ENDCASE
```

Any number of statements may be included in a CASE. dBASE III PLUS assumes that only one of the *conditions* in the CASE statements is true, and if more than one is true, only the statements following the first will be executed. If the optional OTHERWISE clause is included, it must follow all of the other CASES; the statements following OTHERWISE are executed if none of the conditions in the preceding CASE statements is true. If none of the conditions is true and no OTHERWISE clause is included, no action is taken.

* DO WHILE...ENDDO

This program structure repeats execution of a group of program statements as long as a specified condition remains true. The general form of this structure is

```
DO WHILE <condition>
  <program statements>
ENDDO
```

If the *condition* is never true, the statements within the loop are not executed even once; if the condition never becomes false, the loop will run forever. dBASE III PLUS checks the condition only once on each pass through the loop, so if the condition becomes false midway through, the remaining statements are still executed unless you exit the loop with EXIT or return to the DO WHILE statement with LOOP to force dBASE III PLUS to reevaluate the condition immediately. If the *condition* contains a macro, it is evaluated only once, on the first pass through the loop, so you cannot use a macro if the value of the variable expanded as a macro is changed within the loop.

EDIT [<*scope*>] [FIELDS <*field list*>] [FOR <*condition*>] [WHILE <*condition*>]

Enters a full-screen mode to edit the specified fields in the range of records defined by the *scope* and *conditions*. If no *scope* is specified, ALL is assumed. EDIT is identical to CHANGE.

EJECT

Ejects the paper in the printer to the top of the next page.

ERASE <*file name*>

Erases the specified file from the disk. Any disk file may be ERASEd with this command, so the extension (and path, if the file is not in the current subdirectory) must be included. Only one file at a time may be ERASEd, and you may not ERASE any file that is currently open.

* EXIT

Causes dBASE III PLUS to EXIT immediately from the currently running DO WHILE loop and resume execution with the first command following the ENDDO statement.

EXPORT TO <*file name*> TYPE PFS

Exports data to a PFS file from the data base open in the currently selected work area. If a format file is open, it is used as a model for the PFS screen layout; if not, the PFS screen will resemble the standard dBASE III PLUS data entry screen.

FIND <*character string*>/<*n*>

Searches the first index named in the USE command that opened the current data base for the specified record. If the index is based on a character string, a literal search string need not be enclosed in quotation marks unless it includes leading blank spaces. When you search for a character string stored in a memory variable, the variable name must be preceded by the macro symbol (&) so that dBASE III PLUS searches for the value of the variable rather than the characters that make up its name. If the index is based on a numeric field, you must specify the key value as a numeric constant, not by storing it in a memory variable. In every other respect, FIND works like SEEK.

GO/GOTO <*expN*>/BOTTOM/TOP

Positions the current data base to the specified record. GOTO BOTTOM positions the data base to the last record in the file or, with an index open, to the last record in indexed order. GOTO TOP positions the data base to the first record in the file or, with an index open, to the first record in indexed order. If you have used SET DELETED ON or SET FILTER to limit the range of records being processed, GO TOP and GO BOTTOM position the data base to the first or last record that satisfies all of the specified conditions; however, you may still GOTO any record by number.

HELP [<*keyword*>]

Displays a screen of help text summarizing the syntax and usage of the specified keyword. HELP with no keyword calls up the first screen in the menu-driven help system.

* IF...ELSE...ENDIF

This program structure selects one of two alternatives. The general form of the structure is

IF <*condition*>
<*program statements*>
[ELSE
<*program statements*>]
ENDIF

If the *condition* is true, the statements following IF (which may include another IF loop) are executed. If the condition is false and the optional ELSE is included, the statements between ELSE and ENDIF are executed. With no ELSE clause, no action is taken.

IMPORT FROM <*file name*> TYPE PFS

Imports data from a PFS file and creates a data base file, a format file that matches the PFS screen layout, and a view file that enables you to open the data base and format file together (with a SET VIEW command).

INDEX ON <*key expression*> TO <*index file name*> [UNIQUE]

Builds an index for the current data base based on the specified *key expression.* If the *key expression* or *file name* are omitted, dBASE III PLUS will prompt you to enter them. The *key expression* may be up to 100 characters long. When the INDEX command completes, dBASE III PLUS leaves the new index open (and closes any other indexes open previously) with the record pointer positioned at the end-of-file.

An index may be based on a single character, numeric, or date field, resulting in alphabetical, ascending numeric, and ascending calendar date order, respectively. If fields of different data types are combined to form the key expression, all must be converted to character strings (using the DTOC function for dates and the STR function for numeric fields).

If the UNIQUE keyword is included, only the first record in a group that share the same value for the *key expression* is included in the index. Thereafter, whenever the file is opened with this index, it will appear to contain unique index keys.

* INPUT [<*expC*>] TO <*memvar*>

Collects input from the user and creates the memory variable *memvar* to store the input. If *expC* is included, it is displayed as a prompt. The data type of the memory variable is determined by the data type of the user's entry, which may be any valid dBASE III PLUS expression. If a syntactically incorrect expression is entered, an error message is displayed and the prompt is repeated. If the user presses ENTER or types only blank spaces, dBASE III PLUS repeats the prompt.

INSERT [BEFORE]
* INSERT BLANK

INSERT adds a new record to the current data base, using the standard dBASE III PLUS full-screen edit commands. If BEFORE is included, the new record is placed before the current record; otherwise, it is inserted after the current record. In either case, all of the remaining records are moved down to make room for the new entry, which can be very slow in a large data base. If you have SET CARRY ON, the fields take their default values from the current record, or from the previous record if you have specified the BEFORE option.

An alternative is to use an index to access the file in the desired order and allow new records to be APPENDed to the end of the file. dBASE III PLUS does this automatically if INSERT is used with an index open.

INSERT BLANK adds a blank record to the current data base and positions the record pointer to the new record without invoking the full-screen edit mode. Usually, the fields are filled in with REPLACE or GET commands.

JOIN WITH <*alias*> TO <*file name*> FOR <*condition*> [FIELDS <*field list*>]

Creates a new data base file based on the contents of the current data base and a second file, which is open in another work area and is specified by its *alias*. The two files are matched up record by record, and dBASE III PLUS adds a record to the new data base for each pair of records from the two files that satisfies the *condition*.

If a *field list* is included, it defines the structure of the new file. Otherwise, this file contains all of the fields from the current file plus as many fields from the second as permitted by the 128-field limit, except for memo fields, which are ignored by the JOIN command. No field names will be duplicated even if both files contain fields of the same name. Because dBASE III PLUS reads through the entire second file for each record in the current file, this command can be very time-consuming.

LABEL FORM <*label format file*> [<*scope*>] [FOR <*condition*>] [WHILE <*condition*>] [TO PRINT] [TO FILE <*file name*>] [SAMPLE]

Prints labels from the current data base, using the specified label format file, for the range of records defined by the *scope* and *conditions*. If no *scope* is specified, ALL is assumed. If the label form references fields from more than one data base, all of the necessary data base and index files must be open and the files must be linked with SET RELATION.

TO PRINT causes dBASE III PLUS to print the labels as well as display them on the screen. TO FILE creates a disk file that contains an exact image of the printed labels. SAMPLE causes dBASE III PLUS to print rows of asterisks that occupy the same amount of space as a label to enable you to align the label stock in the printer.

LIST [<*scope*>] [<*exp list*>] [FOR <*condition*>] [WHILE <*condition*>] [TO PRINT] [OFF]

Displays the specified expressions for the range of records in the current data base defined by the *scope* and *conditions*. If no *scope* is specified, ALL is assumed, and with no *exp list*, all fields are included. If you have SET HEADING ON, the listed expressions are displayed as column titles, in the same mixture of uppercase and lowercase used in the LIST command.

The contents of memo fields are displayed only if the field names are explicitly included in the *exp list*. TO PRINT causes dBASE III PLUS to echo the screen display to the printer. OFF suppresses the display of the record numbers. The LIST command is similar to DISPLAY, except that DISPLAY assumes a default *scope* of one record and pauses the display every 20 lines.

LIST FILES [LIKE <*skeleton*>]

This command is identical to DISPLAY FILES, except that the display does not pause when the screen is full, making the LIST version better for printing the listing.

LIST HISTORY [LAST <*expN*>] [TO PRINT]

This command is identical to DISPLAY HISTORY, except that the display does not pause when the screen is full, making the LIST version better for printing the listing.

LIST MEMORY [TO PRINT]

This command is identical to DISPLAY MEMORY, except that the display does not pause when the screen is full, making the LIST version better for printing the listing.

LIST STATUS [TO PRINT]

This command is identical to DISPLAY STATUS, except that the display does not pause when the screen is full, making the LIST version better for printing the listing.

LIST STRUCTURE [TO PRINT]

This command is identical to DISPLAY STRUCTURE, except that the display does not pause when the screen is full, making the LIST version better for printing the listing.

* LOAD <*binary file name*>

Loads a binary file into memory for execution with CALL. Five modules may be LOADed into memory at once. LOAD and CALL should be used only for subroutines written expressly to be executed this way; COM or EXE files (including most commercial software) should be invoked with the RUN command instead.

LOCATE [<*scope*>] [FOR <*condition*>] [WHILE <*condition*>]

Searches the range of records in the current data base defined by the *scope* and WHILE clause for the first record that matches the specified *conditions.* If no *scope* is specified, ALL is assumed. If a matching record is found, the data base is left positioned at this record; if you have SET TALK ON, the record number is displayed. The CONTINUE command may be used to search for additional records that satisfy the same *conditions.* If no matching record is found, an "End of locate scope" message is displayed, and the FOUND() function assumes the value .F.

LOGOUT

In a data base with a PROTECT security system, closes all open files and presents a new log-in screen, exactly as if you had QUIT and reentered dBASE III PLUS.

* LOOP

Causes dBASE III PLUS to bypass the remaining steps in a DO WHILE loop and return immediately to the DO WHILE statement to reevaluate the condition.

MODIFY COMMAND [<*file name*>]
MODIFY FILE [<*file name*>]

Invokes the dBASE III PLUS editor to create or edit a text file, usually a dBASE III PLUS program or format file. If you do not specify the *file name,* dBASE III PLUS will prompt you to enter it. If the file already exists, it is loaded into the editor; if not, a new file is created. The MODIFY COMMAND editor can handle a file up to 5000 characters long. You can use the TEDIT option in CONFIG.DB (TEDIT = <*program name*>) to substitute another editor or word processor for the dBASE III PLUS editor so that the external program is invoked by MODIFY COMMAND.

The MODIFY FILE variant does not assume that the file to be created or edited is a program file, so you must specify the extension.

MODIFY LABEL <*label file name*>

This command is identical to CREATE LABEL.

MODIFY QUERY <*label file name*>

This command is identical to CREATE QUERY.

MODIFY REPORT <*report file name*>

This command is identical to CREATE REPORT.

MODIFY SCREEN *<label file name>*

This command is identical to CREATE SCREEN.

MODIFY STRUCTURE *<file name>*

Changes the structure of the current data base file and adjusts existing records to match the new structure. dBASE III PLUS creates a temporary copy of the file structure to which you make your changes; the data is then appended from the original file and this file is renamed with a BAK (backup) extension.

The same rules that govern the APPEND FROM *<file name>* command apply to transferring data from the backup file to the new structure. You may change field lengths, add or delete fields, or change the data type of a field without losing data (provided that the contents of the field are consistent with the new type). If a character field is shortened, the contents are truncated to fit; numeric data that is too long is replaced with asterisks. If a field is deleted, the data is lost; and if a field is added, it will be blank in every record. You may change field names, provided that you do not make any other changes at the same time. All indexes must be rebuilt after a file structure is modified.

MODIFY VIEW *<label file name>*

This command is identical to CREATE VIEW.

* NOTE/*

Identifies a statement as a comment (nonexecutable) line in a dBASE III PLUS program. You can also include a comment on the same line as a program statement by preceding the comment with &&.

* ON ERROR/ESC/KEY *<command>*

Specifies a command to be executed under one of three conditions: when an error occurs, when the ESC key is pressed, or when any key is pressed.

The *command* may be any valid dBASE III PLUS command, but it is usually a DO command that invokes another program or procedure, which takes corrective action in response to an error or process the user's request to interrupt the currently running program. The three ON commands may be used in any combination; with both ON ESCAPE and ON KEY in effect, pressing ESC activates the ON ESCAPE command rather than the ON KEY command.

PACK

Permanently removes from the current data base all records previously marked for deletion and rebuilds any indexes opened with the data base in the USE command. After a file is PACKed, there is no way to recover the deleted records. PACK reclaims the disk space formerly occupied by the deleted records, but the new file size and number of records are updated on the disk (and therefore reported correctly by the DIR command) only after the file is closed.

* PARAMETERS <*exp list*>

Creates local memory variables corresponding to the values passed to a program or procedure in a DO command. If present, the PARAMETERS command must be the first executable (non-comment) line in the program or procedure. The correspondence between the parameters in the DO command and the PARAMETERS command is established by the order in which they are listed. The parameters may be any valid dBASE III PLUS expressions, but if fields are passed as parameters, the file alias must be specified, even for fields in the currently selected work area. All changes made to the values of any parameters specified as memory variables in the calling program are passed back to the calling program.

* PRIVATE [ALL [LIKE <*skeleton*>]]/[<*memvar list*>]

Declares the specified memory variables private to the program that created them, so that local variables may be given the same names as PUBLIC variables or variables in a program higher in a chain of programs that call each other.

* PROCEDURE *<procedure name>*

Used to identify the individual procedures in a procedure file. A procedure name may be up to eight characters long. Each procedure must begin with a PROCEDURE command and should end with a RETURN.

* PUBLIC *<memvar list>*

Makes the memory variables in the *memvar list* available to all programs in a system. A variable must be declared PUBLIC before it is initialized. Within a program PUBLIC variables may be erased from memory by naming them explicitly in a RELEASE command or by using CLEAR MEMORY or CLEAR ALL, but not RELEASE ALL.

QUIT

Closes all open disk files and exits from dBASE III PLUS to the operating system.

* READ [SAVE]

Allows editing of the variables displayed by all of the @ . . . SAY . . . GET commands issued since the last READ, CLEAR GETS, or CLEAR command. The cursor is positioned initially in the first variable, and the user may edit the data by using the standard full-screen cursor movement and editing commands.

If the SAVE option is included, the READ command does not also CLEAR the GETs, so that a subsequent READ may collect the same set of fields again. It is up to you to ensure that you do not allow too many GETs between READ commands. By default, dBASE III PLUS permits 128, but you can increase this to 1023 with an entry in CONFIG.DB.

RECALL [<*scope*>] [FOR <*condition*>] [WHILE <*condition*>]

Recovers ("undeletes") all of the records marked for deletion in the current data base in the range of records defined by the *scope* and *conditions.* If no *scope* is specified, only the current record is RECALLed.

REINDEX

Rebuilds all of the index files that are open in the current work area, based on the original key expression(s), which are stored in the index file(s). If the original index was created after a SET UNIQUE ON command or if the UNIQUE keyword was specified in the INDEX command, the new index file will also have this attribute. If an index file is damaged, dBASE III PLUS may not be able to read the key expression, and you must use the INDEX command instead.

RELEASE [ALL [LIKE/EXCEPT <*skeleton*>]]/ [<*memvar list*>]
* RELEASE MODULE

Erases from memory the specified variables and frees the space for defining additional variables. When used in a program, RELEASE ALL erases only variables created within the program.

RELEASE MODULE unloads a binary file placed in memory by the LOAD command.

RENAME <*old file name*> TO <*new file name*>

Renames the specified file. Since you may use this command to rename any disk file, the file extension (or full path name, if the file is not in the current subdirectory) must be specified. If you RENAME a DBF file that contains memo fields, you must also remember to RENAME the corresponding DBT file. Only one file at a time may be renamed, and you may not rename a file that is currently open.

REPLACE [<*scope*>] <*field*> WITH <*exp*> [,<*field2*> WITH <*exp2*> . . .] [FOR <*condition*>] [WHILE <*condition*>]

Substitutes the results of evaluating the listed expressions for the current values of the specified fields, for the range of records in the current data base defined by the *scope* and *conditions.* If no *scope* is specified, only fields in the current record are REPLACEd.

If you REPLACE the values of the key fields in a data base opened with one or more indexes, the indexes are automatically updated. This also means that the index entry for the record is immediately moved to its new location in the index, and the "next" record will not be the same one as before the REPLACE; this type of REPLACEment should therefore not be performed on an indexed file.

REPORT FORM <*report form file*> [<*scope*>] [FOR <*condition*>] [WHILE <*condition*>] [NOEJECT] [PLAIN] [SUMMARY] [HEADING <*expC*>] [TO PRINT] [TO FILE <*file name*>]

Prints a report, using the specified report form file, for the range of records from the current data base defined by the *scope* and *conditions.* If no *scope* is specified, ALL is assumed. If the report form references fields from more than one data base, all of the necessary data base and index files must be open and the files must be linked with SET RELATION.

TO PRINT causes dBASE III PLUS to print the report as well as display it on the screen. TO FILE creates a disk file that contains an exact image of the printed report. The HEADING clause may be used to specify an optional extra heading line that is printed on the first line of each page, centered above the page title.

The NOEJECT, PLAIN, and SUMMARY keywords may be used to override the values for the corresponding parameters defined in the report form. NOEJECT suppresses the page eject normally sent to the printer before beginning the report. PLAIN causes dBASE III PLUS to print the report with no date or page numbers, and to print the page title and column headings only once, on the first page. SUMMARY produces a report that includes only subtotals, subsubtotals, and totals, with no detail records.

RESTORE FROM <*file name*> [ADDITIVE]

Loads the variables in the specified memory file into memory. Without the ADDITIVE option, any existing variables are first RELEASEd. If the command was issued from within a program, the newly loaded variables become PRIVATE; if it was typed from the dot prompt, they are PUBLIC. If the ADDITIVE option is included, the variables in the memory file are *added* to the ones currently in memory. With the ADDITIVE option, variables stored as PUBLIC become PUBLIC again, provided that you declare them PUBLIC prior to the RESTORE command.

RESUME

Continues to execute a program previously interrupted with the ESC key and suspended (rather than canceled). Execution resumes with the command following the one interrupted by the ESC key.

* RETRY

Returns control from the currently running program to the calling program. Execution resumes with the command that caused the second program to be called instead of the next one. This command is often used in a network environment to attempt to lock a file or record that might be locked by another user, and in error-handling procedures to allow the user to correct the error condition, after which the program retries the operation that caused the error.

* RETURN [TO MASTER]

Causes dBASE III PLUS to exit from the current program or procedure and return control to the calling program or procedure or to the dot prompt if the program was invoked from the dot prompt. Execution resumes with the command following the DO command that called the second program. ENTER TO MASTER jumps to the highest-level dBASE III PLUS program (the user's first entry point into the system) instead of to the calling program. A RETURN command may occur anywhere within a program. If there is no RETURN command, a program terminates after the last statement is executed.

RUN <*command*>
!<*command*>

Executes the specified MS-DOS command, batch file, or program. COMMAND.COM must be available, either in the root directory of the disk from which the system was booted or, under DOS 3, in any subdirectory identified to DOS with a SET COMSPEC command. You must have enough additional memory in your computer beyond the 256K required by dBASE III PLUS to load COMMAND.COM and the external program into RAM along with dBASE III PLUS.

SAVE TO <*file name*> [ALL LIKE/EXCEPT <*skeleton*>]

Saves the specified memory variables on disk in the named memory variable file. If you include an ALL LIKE or ALL EXCEPT clause, only memory variables with names that match the *skeleton* are SAVEd.

SEEK <*exp*>

Searches the index named first in the USE command that opened the current data base for data matching the specified expression. You may search on less than the full index key value, but the portion you specify must begin at the start of the field. SEEK is similar to FIND, except that FIND can accept only a single numeric or character string constant as its object, whereas SEEK can accept any valid expression.

If the search succeeds, the data base is positioned at the first record in which the index key matches the value of the *expression*. The FOUND()

function has the value .T., and EOF() is .F. If there is no matching record, dBASE III PLUS displays the message "No Find", positions the data base at the end-of-file, and sets the EOF() function to .T. and FOUND() to .F.

SELECT <*work area/alias*>

Switches to the specified work area. A work area may always be selected by number (1-10) or by letter (A-J), and any work area in which a data base is open may also be selected by the file's alias. When you SELECT a work area, any data bases open in other work areas remain positioned exactly where they were. Fields from these files may be specified for display or for use in calculations using the notation *<alias>—><field name>*.

SET

Invokes a menu-driven, full-screen mode for viewing and changing many of the SET options. The options are described individually. Note that the default values of options with two or more alternate values are indicated in uppercase.

SET ALTERNATE TO [<*file name*>]
SET ALTERNATE on/OFF

SET ALTERNATE TO *<file name>* opens the specified text file. Once the file is open, SET ALTERNATE ON causes dBASE III PLUS to echo all sequential screen output (all text except that displayed by the full-screen commands) to the text file. SET ALTERNATE OFF suspends recording in the ALTERNATE file. You may SET ALTERNATE ON and OFF as many times as necessary during a work session. To close the text file, use CLOSE ALTERNATE or SET ALTERNATE TO after the last SET ALTERNATE OFF command.

SET BELL ON/off

Determines whether or not dBASE III PLUS sounds the computer's bell (usually a beeper) when the user's entry completely fills a field or when a data entry error is made (for example, typing an invalid date or entering characters into a numeric field).

SET CARRY on/OFF

Determines whether or not the data entered into each new record APPENDed to a data base serves as the default field values for the next record entered. The status of the CARRY option affects only records added with the full-screen APPEND or INSERT commands; even if you SET CARRY ON, all of the fields in a record added with APPEND BLANK or INSERT BLANK remain blank.

SET CATALOG TO [<*catalog file name*>]
SET CATALOG on/OFF

SET CATALOG TO <*catalog file name*> opens the specified catalog data base in work area 10, or creates it if it does not exist. A CATALOG is a normal dBASE III PLUS data base file with the extension CAT instead of DBF, which may be displayed and updated from the dot prompt as long as you do not change the structure.

The CATALOG records all files used in an application and their associations. With a CATALOG open, the file lists displayed by the ASSIST menus include only files in the CATALOG, and a CATALOG query clause—substituting a "?" where dBASE III PLUS expects a file name—may be used in any command issued from the dot prompt to call up a list of available files of the correct type and, where appropriate, associated with the specified data base.

When a CATALOG is open, it is updated when files are created, renamed, or deleted. When a new file is added to the CATALOG, if you have SET TITLE ON, dBASE III PLUS will prompt you to enter an

80-character title, which is then displayed along with the file name in response to a CATALOG query clause. You can temporarily disable the CATALOG update process with SET CATALOG OFF and reactivate it with SET CATALOG ON.

SET CENTURY on/OFF

Determines whether dates are displayed and entered with four-digit years. With CENTURY OFF, the century is assumed to be 1900 and the year is always displayed as two digits; nevertheless, if a calculation creates a value for a date field in another century, the century is stored and used in subsequent calculations. With CENTURY ON, all dates are displayed and entered with four-digit years.

SET COLOR TO [<*standard foreground/standard background*>] [, <*enhanced foreground/enhanced background*>] [, <*border*>]
SET COLOR on/off

SET COLOR TO determines the colors or monochrome display attributes used for information displayed by dBASE III PLUS (the *Standard* display), data entered by the user (the *Enhanced* display), and the *Border* (the area of the screen outside the 24-line by 80-column display area). If any of the five values are omitted, the defaults are used: white letters on a black background for the standard area, black letters on a white background for the enhanced area, and black for the border. The attributes are entered using the following codes:

Color	Low Intensity	High Intensity
Black	N	
Blue	B	B+
Green	G	G+
Cyan	BG	BG+
Red	R	R+
Magenta	RB	RB+
Brown	GR	
Yellow		GR+
White	W	W+
Blank	X	

Monochrome Attribute	**Low Intensity**	**High Intensity**
Light	W	W+
Dark	N	
Inverse	I	I+
Underlined	U	U+

SET COLOR ON/OFF selects between color and monochrome displays if both are present. The default value matches the monitor in use when dBASE III PLUS was loaded.

SET CONFIRM on/OFF

Determines whether the operator must confirm each field or memory variable entry by pressing ENTER. If you SET CONFIRM ON, the cursor does not advance automatically to the next item when the data entry area is filled completely—the user must press ENTER.

* SET CONSOLE ON/off

Determines whether sequential output appears on the console (the screen). Data displayed in the full-screen edit modes is not affected by the status of this setting. SET CONSOLE OFF may be used to prevent data printed by REPORT, LABEL, or ? commands from also appearing on the screen. Even if you SET CONSOLE OFF, input may be entered by the operator, although it is not echoed to the screen, and all dBASE III PLUS error messages are displayed.

SET DATE AMERICAN/ansi/british/italian/ french/german

Establishes the display format for date fields and memory variables. No matter which display format is in effect, dBASE III PLUS can carry out date arithmetic and date comparisons, and it can SORT or INDEX on a single date field in correct chronological order. These are the formats:

AMERICAN	MM/DD/YY
ANSI	YY.MM.DD

BRITISH	DD/MM/YY
ITALIAN	DD-MM-YY
FRENCH	DD.MM.YY
GERMAN	DD.MM.YY

* SET DEBUG on/OFF

Determines whether the command lines echoed by SET ECHO ON are displayed on the screen or printed on the printer. If you SET DEBUG ON, the output of the ECHO option is routed to the printer so that formatted screens are not disrupted by the echoed program lines.

SET DECIMALS TO <*expN*>

Determines the number of decimal places displayed when an expression involving division or the SQRT, LOG, or EXP function is evaluated. The default is 2, and you may specify any value between 0 and 15. If you also SET FIXED ON, the SET DECIMALS option controls the display of all numeric variables and calculations, not just those involving division, SQRT, LOG, or EXP. In calculations involving multiplication, the number of decimal places in the result is equal to the sum of the number of decimal places in the two quantities multiplied. Otherwise, it is the same as in the quantity with the most decimal places.

SET DEFAULT TO <*drive*>

Establishes the default disk drive to be used by dBASE III PLUS to read and write all disk files unless a different drive is explicitly included with the file name.

SET DELETED on/OFF

Determines whether dBASE III PLUS processes records that have been marked for deletion. If you SET DELETED ON, deleted records are ignored in all commands, except when the record number is specified explicitly (for example, in an explicit GOTO command or a command with a *scope* of a single record). If SET DELETED ON is issued with a file already open, it does not automatically reposition the record pointer to the first non-deleted record; you can use GOTO TOP for this purpose.

SET DELIMITERS TO [<*delimiter(s)*>] [DEFAULT]
SET DELIMITERS on/OFF

SET DELIMITERS ON/OFF determines whether fields displayed by GET commands are surrounded by delimiters. SET DELIMITERS TO <*delimiters*> designates the actual delimiter character(s). You may specify either one or two characters, enclosed in quotes. If you specify one character, it is used as both the beginning and ending delimiter; if you specify two, the first is used as the beginning delimiter and the second as the ending delimiter. If you SET DELIMITERS ON without assigning delimiters, a colon (:) is used. The DEFAULT option restores this default delimiter after a previous SET DELIMITERS TO command.

* SET DEVICE TO printer/SCREEN

Determines whether the output of @ ... SAY commands is routed to the printer or to the screen. When you have SET DEVICE TO PRINTER, all GET clauses are ignored.

* SET DOHISTORY on/OFF

Determines whether commands executed from dBASE III PLUS programs are recorded in the history list, along with the commands you type from the dot prompt. This option is most often used as a debugging aid, to enable you to retrace execution of a program after a test run. If you SET DOHISTORY ON, you will usually want to increase the number of commands retained in history (from the default 20) with SET HISTORY TO.

* SET ECHO on/OFF

Determines whether command lines in programs are echoed to the screen as they are executed. This option is most frequently used to monitor the progress of a program or to trace execution for debugging purposes. If you also SET DEBUG ON, the echoed command lines are routed to the printer instead of the console so that formatted screen displays are not disrupted.

SET ENCRYPTION ON/off

In a data base with a PROTECT security system in effect, determines whether new files created by copying existing data bases (with commands such as COPY or SORT) are encrypted. The status of this option does not affect files defined with the CREATE command; these must be encrypted through the PROTECT program. ENCRYPTION must be OFF in order to COPY or EXPORT a data base file to one of the external formats supported by dBASE III PLUS—DELIMITED, SDF, DIF, SYLK, WKS, and PFS.

* SET ESCAPE ON/off

Determines whether dBASE III PLUS responds when the user presses the ESC key. If you SET ESCAPE OFF, a dBASE III PLUS command or program can be interrupted only by rebooting or turning off the computer.

SET EXACT on/OFF

Determines whether character strings are compared using the full length of both strings. If you SET EXACT OFF, dBASE III PLUS examines only the number of characters in the string on the right side of the equal sign if this string is shorter. If you SET EXACT ON, the two strings are considered equal only if they are the same length and have the same value.

SET EXCLUSIVE ON/off

In a network environment, determines whether files are opened in exclusive or shared mode. The file open mode is determined by the status of the EXCLUSIVE option at the time a file is opened, even if you subsequently reset the EXCLUSIVE option. Any file opened with EXCLUSIVE OFF can only be accessed by one user at a time. If a file is opened in shared mode, a file or record-locking system should be implemented to prevent damage caused by multiple simultaneous updates. A file may also be opened for exclusive use by including the EXCLUSIVE keyword in the USE command.

SET FIELDS TO [<*field list*>/ALL]
SET FIELDS on/OFF

SET FIELDS TO *field list* specifies the fields from one or more open data base that are accessible to most dBASE III PLUS commands. SET FIELDS ON activates the field list defined with SET FIELDS commands, and SET FIELDS OFF temporarily disables the field list. Regardless of the order in which the fields are named in the SET FIELDS command, they are presented in the full-screen edit modes in the order they occur in the file structure(s).

Successive SET FIELDS commands add to the field list, so you are not limited by the 254-character command length limit. However, the ALL option sets the field list to all fields in the current data base, and no others. To access all fields from the current data base, together with selected fields from other work areas, the SET FIELDS TO ALL command must therefore precede the other SET FIELDS commands. To access fields from more than one file in a meaningful way, the files must share a common key and they must be linked with SET RELATION; usually this means that for each record in the selected data base, there is only one matching record in the file accessed through the RELATION.

SET FILTER TO [<*condition*>]/[FILE <*query file name*>]

Establishes a condition that determines which records are processed by all dBASE III PLUS commands. With a FILTER in effect, records that do not pass the condition in the filter are ignored, except when the record number is specified explicitly (for example, in an explicit GOTO command, or with a *scope* of a single record). SET FILTER TO FILE reads a condition previously stored in a query file constructed with CREATE QUERY.

All commands that position the data base act relative to the FILTER, but the SET FILTER command itself does not reposition the record pointer, even if the current record does not pass the FILTER *condition*; you can use GOTO TOP for this purpose. A separate FILTER may be in effect in each active work area, but with any work area selected, only the FILTER in this area is recognized by dBASE III PLUS. A FILTER may also reference fields in data bases open in other work areas, but this usually makes sense only if the files are linked with SET RELATION.

SET FILTER TO, with no *condition,* cancels the FILTER in the current work area. If a FILTER depends on fields in more than one file, you must be sure to cancel the FILTER if any of the files involved are closed.

SET FIXED on/OFF

Determines whether dBASE III PLUS displays all numeric expressions with a fixed number of decimal places. If you SET FIXED ON, the SET DECIMALS option determines the number of decimals displayed for all numeric variables; otherwise, SET DECIMALS affects only the results of calculations involving division, SQRT, LOG, or EXP.

SET FORMAT TO [<*format file name*>]

Opens a format file that draws a formatted data entry screen for the full-screen APPEND, EDIT, CHANGE, and INSERT commands. SET FORMAT TO, with no file name, or CLOSE FORMAT closes the format file open in the current work area.

SET FUNCTION <*exp*> TO <*expC*>

Assigns a new meaning to one of the programmable function keys. On most IBM and compatible computers, there are 10 or 12 function keys, referred to by the numbers 2 through 10 or 12 (or numeric expressions that evaluate to these values). You may not assign a new value to the Help key (usually F1), which is reserved for invoking the dBASE III PLUS menu-driven help system. Each of the other function keys may be assigned any arbitrary sequence of characters. In this string, pressing ENTER may be symbolized by a semicolon (;).

SET HEADING ON/off

Determines whether dBASE III PLUS displays column headings in LIST, DISPLAY, SUM, COUNT, and AVERAGE commands. If you SET HEADING ON, the field names, variable names, or expressions are displayed as column headings, in the same mixture of uppercase and lowercase used in the command. The width of each column of data on the screen is the width of the quantity displayed or the column heading, whichever is greater.

SET HELP ON/off

Determines whether dBASE III PLUS displays the message "Do you want some help? (Y/N)" when a syntax error is made in a command typed at the dot prompt.

SET HISTORY TO <*expN*>
SET HISTORY ON/off

SET HISTORY determines the number of commands that are retained in the history list. SET HISTORY OFF temporarily disables the history feature, and SET HISTORY ON turns it back on. The default is 20, and you may specify any value between 0 and 16,000.

SET INDEX TO [<*index file list*>]

Opens the specified index file(s) together with the current data base. You may open up to seven indexes for each data base, all of which are updated to reflect new entries and changes made to the key fields. The index named first in the *index file list* is the *master index,* which determines the order in which records are displayed or printed; this is the only index that may be used to retrieve records with FIND or SEEK. The SET INDEX command positions the data base to the record that matches the first index entry. SET INDEX TO, with no list of index files, or CLOSE INDEX closes all indexes in the current work area.

SET INTENSITY ON/off

Determines whether the *standard* display colors or monochrome attributes used for data displayed by dBASE III PLUS are the same as the *enhanced* display colors used for data entered by the user. SET INTENSITY OFF eliminates the difference between these two areas and uses the same colors for the *enhanced* area that were SET for the *standard* area.

SET MARGIN TO <*expN*>

Establishes the left margin used for all printed output, including reports and the output of LIST TO PRINT and DISPLAY TO PRINT commands. The default is 0. For reports and labels, this value is added to the margin specified in the report or label form.

SET MEMOWIDTH TO <*expN*>

Determines the display width for memo fields in LIST, DISPLAY, and ? commands. The default is 50.

SET MENUS on/OFF

Determines whether a help menu listing the cursor movement and editing commands is displayed by default in the full-screen edit modes. Regardless of the status of this setting, you may always toggle the menu on or off by pressing F1.

SET MESSAGE TO [<*expC*>]

Defines a character string up to 79 characters long that is displayed on line 24 of the screen. The message is only displayed if you have also SET STATUS ON, but it is replaced by the standard dBASE III PLUS messages in menu-driven commands such as ASSIST or any of the full-screen CREATE/ MODIFY editors.

SET ODOMETER TO [<*expN*>]

Determines how frequently dBASE III PLUS updates the display of the number of records processed by such commands as APPEND, COPY, and COUNT. The display is updated every *expN* records; higher values for ODOMETER will result in slightly faster command execution. The default is 1.

SET ORDER TO [<*expN*>]

Determines which of the indexes opened with the data base in the current work area is the master index (the one that controls the order in which records are processed and the one used for FIND and SEEK commands). The *expN* evaluates to a number that corresponds to the position of the index in the index file list in the command (USE or SET INDEX [TO]) that originally opened the indexes. SET INDEX TO 0 causes dBASE III PLUS to process the file in sequential order, as if no indexes were open. SET ORDER is a faster way to switch indexes than SET INDEX, since no files are actually opened or closed.

SET PATH TO [<*path name list*>]

Establishes the search path used by dBASE III PLUS to find disk files not present in the current subdirectory. APPEND FROM, the CREATE/ MODIFY editors, DO, LABEL, REPORT, RESTORE, SET PROCEDURE, TYPE, and USE all use the search path. The COPY, CREATE, INDEX, JOIN, SAVE, and SORT commands, which also create files, search the specified path for files of the same name if you have SET SAFETY ON. However, all new files created by any dBASE III PLUS commands are written in the current subdirectory if you do not specify a full path name.

Regardless of the PATH, DIR (with no path name included), DELETE FILE, ERASE, RENAME, and SET ALTERNATE TO act only on files in the current subdirectory unless a full path name is specified. SET PATH TO behaves much like the MS-DOS PATH command. It does *not* have the same effect as the MS-DOS CHDIR (change directory) command (the way SET DEFAULT TO <*drive*> is equivalent to switching the currently logged disk drive). SET PATH TO, with no path names listed, cancels any previously established search path.

SET PRINT on/OFF

Determines whether sequential output (all text except that displayed by the full-screen commands) sent to the console is also echoed to the printer.

SET PRINTER TO [<*DOS device name*>]
SET PRINTER TO [\\SPOOLER/<*computer name*> \<*printer name*>=<*DOS device name*>]

SET PRINTER TO *DOS device name* selects the local printer, specified by the DOS name of the output port (for example, LPT1: or COM1:), to be used for printed output. The default is LPT1:. This command is equivalent to the MS-DOS MODE command for redirecting printer output, which may be used instead, either before you load DBASE III PLUS or with a RUN command. If output is redirected to a serial printer, the baud rate and other communications parameters must first be set with a MODE command.

In a network environment, SET PRINTER TO *computer name* \ *printer name*=*DOS device name* routes output to a network printer via the network print spooler. This printer is identified by the network computer and printer names in an IBM network, or as SPOOLER in a Novell network.

SET PRINTER TO redirects printed output to the default printer assigned at the operating system level. In a network environment, it also empties the print spooling file.

* SET PROCEDURE TO [<*procedure file name*>]

Opens the specified procedure file, which may contain up to 32 separate procedures. SET PROCEDURE TO, with no procedure file name listed, or CLOSE PROCEDURE closes the current procedure file.

SET RELATION TO [<*key expression*> /RECNO()/<*expN*> INTO <*alias*>]

Establishes a relationship between the currently open data base and a data base open in another work area, which is specified by its alias. Only one RELATION may be SET from any given work area, but multiple RELATIONS may be SET into the same work area from two or more other data bases. The files may be linked by record number or based on a common field or fields.

To link the files by record number, you must open the second file with no index. If the RECNO() option is included, or no TO clause is specified, the files are linked so that the record pointer in the second file is always positioned to the same record number as the first file. If a numeric expression is specified in a TO clause, moving the record pointer in the first file automatically positions the second file to the record number specified by *expN*.

To link two files by a common key, the *key expression* must be present in both files (although the component fields need not have the same names), and the second file must be indexed by this expression. With the RELATION in effect, moving the record pointer in the first file automatically positions the second file to the record with the matching value of the key expression, exactly as if you had executed a FIND or SEEK command.

In either case, if dBASE III PLUS fails to find a matching record, the second file is positioned at the end-of-file, the EOF( ) function is .T., and FOUND( ) is .F. in the second work area. SET RELATION TO, with no RELATION specified, cancels the RELATION SET from the current work area.

SET SAFETY ON/off

Determines whether dBASE III PLUS displays a warning message and requests confirmation before executing any command (such as COPY, INDEX, or SORT) that would overwrite an existing disk file.

SET SCOREBOARD ON/off

Determines whether or not dBASE III PLUS displays status indicators (such as *Del* and *Ins*) and error messages (for example, when an invalid date is entered) on the top line of the screen. If you have SET STATUS ON, these messages are displayed in the Status Bar, and error messages appear on line 24; with STATUS OFF, all the scoreboard information is displayed on line 0. If you SET STATUS OFF and also SET SCOREBOARD OFF the error messages are not displayed, but dBASE III PLUS still refuses to allow the cursor to advance beyond a field that contains invalid data until the entry is corrected.

SET STATUS ON/off

Determines whether dBASE III PLUS uses the last three lines on the screen for a status display. The *Status Bar* on line 22 displays the current disk drive, data base if one is open, current record or command, whether the current record is deleted, and the status of the INS, NUMLOCK, and CAPSLOCK keys. In a network environment, the Status Bar also informs you whether the current file was opened for exclusive or read-only use, and whether the current file or record is locked. Line 23 is used for a *Navigation Line* that describes how to choose among available command options, and line 24 contains a message (which you may customize with SET MESSAGE) describing your options. Even if you have

SET STATUS OFF, the status display is always present in menu-driven commands such as ASSIST and the CREATE/ MODIFY editors. A format file designed for use with STATUS ON should not display data on lines 22 through 24.

* SET STEP on/OFF

Determines whether dBASE III PLUS runs programs in single-step mode. If you SET STEP ON, dBASE III PLUS pauses after executing each program line. Pressing ESC cancels the program, S suspends execution, and pressing the space bar causes dBASE III PLUS to execute the next command. SET STEP ON is usually used, together with SET TALK ON and SET ECHO ON (which displays each command line as it is executed), to debug dBASE III PLUS programs.

SET TALK ON/off

Determines whether dBASE III PLUS displays the results of the actions taken in response to your commands—for example, the values STOREd to memory variables, the record number of the new current record after a SKIP or LOCATE command, and the status messages that monitor the progress of commands that process entire data bases (such as INDEX, DELETE, COPY, COUNT, and REPLACE).

SET TITLE ON/off

Determines whether dBASE III PLUS prompts you for a title, or description, for each new file created when a CATALOG is open. If you SET TITLE OFF, files are still added to the CATALOG, but the TITLE field is left blank.

SET TYPEAHEAD TO <*expN*>

Specifies the size of the typeahead buffer. The default is 20, and you may specify any value between 0 (which disables the typeahead buffer) and 32,000. The buffer is also disabled if you SET ESCAPE OFF. If you SET

TYPEAHEAD TO 0, commands and functions that depend on the typeahead buffer (ON KEY and INKEY()) will no longer work.

SET UNIQUE on/OFF

Determines whether an index can contain duplicate key entries. If you SET UNIQUE ON and then build an index, it will contain only one entry for any given key value. This option may be used to determine if the data base itself contains any duplicate key values (by checking to see if the number of records indexed equals the number of records in the file) or to prepare a list of all of the possible key values (by COPYing all or some of the fields with the index open). Since such an index may not contain pointers to all of the records, it should *not* be used to access the data base for adding new records or editing existing data.

SET VIEW TO *<view file name>*

Opens all the files specified in the *view file,* including data bases, indexes, and the optional format file if one is included in the view, and selects the work area specified when the view was defined. If the view includes RELATIONs, a FILTER condition, or a field list, these are also placed in effect.

SKIP [*<expN>*]

Moves the record pointer forward (if *expN* is positive) or backward (if *expN* is negative) the specified number of records; a SKIP command with no *expN* moves the pointer forward one record. If an index is open, dBASE III PLUS moves forward or backward in the index *expN* entries and then repositions the record pointer to the corresponding record. If you have SET DELETED ON or if you have SET a FILTER, only records that satisfy all the selection criteria are counted.

If you SKIP past the last record in a file, the data base is positioned at a blank record (which is *not* actually added to the file), and the EOF() function is set to .T. If you SKIP backward past the first record in the file, the record pointer remains positioned at the first record in the file and the BOF() function is set to .T.

SORT TO <*new file name*> ON <*field1*> [/A]/[/D] [/C] [, <*field2*> [/A]/[/D] . . .] [<*scope*>] [FOR <*condition*>] [WHILE <*condition*>]

Creates a new data base file containing the range of records from the current data base defined by the *scope* and *conditions.* You may SORT on up to ten fields. The first field determines the major sort order, within which records are sorted according to the second field, and so on.

The sort order may be qualified by three optional parameters: /A (or the keyword ASCENDING) specifies ascending (low-to-high) order (the default), /D (or DESCENDING) specifies descending (high-to-low) order, and /C specifies *case-independence,* which treats uppercase and lowercase versions of a letter as equivalent. (Normally, the sort order parallels the sequence of the ASCII character codes, and all of the uppercase letters precede all of the lowercase letters.) If you combine the A or D options with the C option, only one slash is required—for example, /AC.

You may SORT on any combination of numeric, character, and date fields (not logical or memo fields), but the sort keys must be whole fields. To create a file sorted on a more complex expression, you can build an index based on the desired expression and then COPY the file with the index open.

STORE <*exp*> to <*memvar list*>
<memvar>=<*exp*>

STORE creates the named variables and assigns them the initial values and data types specified by the *expression.* If you use the equal sign syntax, only one memory variable at a time may be created.

SUM [<*scope*>] [<*expN list*>] [FOR <*condition*>] [WHILE <*condition*>] [TO <*memvar list*>]

Calculates the sum for each expression in the list for the range of records defined by the *scope* and *conditions.* If no expressions are listed, all numeric fields in the current data base are SUMmed. If no scope is specified, ALL is assumed. If you have SET TALK ON, the sums are displayed on the screen; and if you have SET HEADING ON, the listed expressions are displayed above the results. If a list of memory variables is included, the named numeric variables are created to store the sums.

* SUSPEND

Temporarily suspends execution of a program and returns control to the dot prompt without closing any files or RELEASEing memory variables. This is equivalent to choosing the Suspend option after pressing ESC to interrupt the currently running program. SUSPEND is used primarily for debugging purposes, to pause a program at a specific point. While the program is suspended, you can type any commands at the dot prompt and then use the RESUME command to continue from the point of interruption or the CANCEL command to cancel the program and return to the dot prompt.

* TEXT...ENDTEXT

A program structure used to display or print a block of text. The text between TEXT and ENDTEXT is displayed (if you have SET CONSOLE ON) or printed (if you have SET PRINT ON) without processing or interpretation by dBASE III PLUS.

TOTAL ON <*key field*> TO <*file name*> [<*scope*>] [FIELDS <*field list*>] [FOR <*condition*>] [WHILE <*condition*>]

Creates a new data base containing summarized data for the specified numeric fields in the current data base for the range of records defined by the *scope* and *conditions*. If no *field list* is included, all numeric fields are TOTALed. The new file has the same structure as the current data base, except that memo fields are not included. Each record in the new file contains totals for a group of records in the current file with the same value in the *key field*. The current file must be either sorted or indexed on the *key field,* and the numeric fields must be large enough to accommodate the totals.

TYPE <*file name*> [TO PRINT]

Displays the contents of the specified file on the screen. TO PRINT causes dBASE III PLUS to print the file as well as displaying it on the screen.

* UNLOCK [ALL]

In a network environment, releases the most recent lock placed on the file in the currently selected work area. This may be a file lock placed in effect by a call to the FLOCK( ) function, or a record lock effected by a call to the LOCK( ) or RLOCK( ) function. If the ALL keyword is included, all locks in all work areas are released.

UPDATE ON <*key field*> FROM <*alias*> REPLACE <*field1*> WITH <*exp1*> [, <*field2*> WITH <*exp2*>. . .] [RANDOM]

Updates the current data base based on information contained in a second file, which is open in another work area and is specified by its *alias.* Records are matched up based on the content of the *key field,* which must be present in both files. The current file must be either sorted or indexed on the common key field. If the second file is not also sorted or indexed on this field, the RANDOM keyword must be included in the command, and the current file must be indexed, *not* sorted on the common key (this is the most efficient way to use the UPDATE command), so that dBASE III PLUS may use an internal SEEK to find the right record to UPDATE. For each record in the second file, the designated *fields* in the matching record in the current file are replaced with the specified *expressions,* which may reference any fields from both files.

USE [<*file name*>] [INDEX <*index file list*>] [ALIAS <*alias*>] [EXCLUSIVE]

Opens the specified data base in the currently selected work area, together with up to seven indexes. If you do not specify an alias, dBASE III PLUS automatically assigns the file name as the alias. If an alias is specified, it must be used in place of the file name in the standard *alias—>field name* notation for referring to fields in work areas other than the currently selected area.

If no indexes are listed, the USE command leaves the data base positioned at the first record. If one or more indexes are opened with the file, the data base is positioned to the record corresponding to the first entry in the first index named (the master index).

In a network environment, if the keyword EXCLUSIVE is included, the file is opened for exclusive rather than shared use, and only one work station at a time may access the file. This is equivalent to issuing a SET EXCLUSIVE ON command prior to opening the file. A file must be opened for exclusive use in order to use commands that affect the entire data base, including INSERT, MODIFY STRUCTURE, PACK, REINDEX, and ZAP.

USE, with no file name, closes the data base and all associated index and format files in the current work area.

* WAIT [<*expC*>] [TO <*memvar*>]

Pauses execution of the current program until a key is pressed. If *expC* is included, it is displayed as a prompt; otherwise, dBASE III PLUS displays its default prompt, "Press any key to continue..." If a TO clause is included, a character memory variable with the specified name is created to store the operator's keystroke. If the operator presses ENTER, *memvar* will become a null string of length zero.

ZAP

Empties the current data base of all records. This command is equivalent to DELETE ALL, followed by PACK. ZAP operates much faster because it does not actually process all of the records, but instead moves the end-of-file marker and resets the record count to 0. Any indexes opened with the data base in the USE command are adjusted to match the new empty file.

Appendix C
dBASE III PLUS Functions

All dBASE III PLUS functions are expressed as the name of the function followed by the function's input(s) (also referred to as "arguments") in parentheses. Even if the function requires no explicit input, parentheses are used to distinguish the function from a field or memory variable with the same name. A function is considered to have the data type of the output it produces, and it may be used anywhere that an expression of that type is permitted. Functions that are used primarily in dBASE III PLUS programs are marked with an asterisk (*).

&<*character variable*>

Substitute the *value* of the named variable for the variable name. The macro can be used to provide variable input in contexts in which dBASE III PLUS expects a field name or condition.

Example:

```
. STORE "FOR 'IBM' $ UPPER(EQUIPMENT)" TO MCONDITION
. LIST &MCONDITION
```

ABS(<*number*>)

Input: Numeric expression
Output: Number

Evaluates to the absolute value of the numeric expression. The absolute value of a negative number is the positive number with the same magnitude; the absolute value of a positive number is identical to the number itself.

* ACCESS( )

Input: None
Output: Number

Evaluates to the access level of the last user to log onto a multi-user system, or to 0 in a single-user system. This function may be used to control access to a menu option, or to allow a single option to call two or more different programs, depending on which user requests the option.

ASC(<*character string*>)

Input: Character string expression
Output: Number

Evaluates to the decimal ASCII code of the first character in the character string expression.

Examples:

```
. ? ASC("ABCPLUMB")
  65
. ? ACCOUNT
ABCPLUMB
. ? ASC(ACCOUNT)
  65
```

AT(<*character string 1*>, <*character string 2*>)

Inputs: Character string expression, character string expression
Output: Number

Evaluates to the starting position of character string 1 in character string 2, or 0 if the first string is not found anywhere within the second.

Example:

```
. ? ACCOUNT
ABCPLUMB
. ? AT("PLUMB", ACCOUNT)
  4
```

* BOF( )

Input: None
Output: Logical value

Evaluates to .T. when you attempt to move the record pointer backward past the beginning-of-file by executing a SKIP −*n* command. If the data base is opened without any indexes, the beginning-of-file is the first record. With an index open, it is the record corresponding to the first index entry. After the SKIP −*n* command, the data base remains positioned at the first record.

CDOW(<*expD*>)

Input: Date expression
Output: Character string

Evaluates to a character string containing the name of the day of the week corresponding to the specified date.

Examples:

```
. ? LASTORDER
01/20/88
. ? CDOW(LASTORDER)
Wednesday
. ? CDOW(LASTORDER + 30)
Friday
```

CHR(<*number*>)

Input: Numeric expression
Output: Character

Evaluates to a character string consisting of the single character specified by the decimal ASCII code represented by the numeric expression.

Example:

```
. ? CHR(65)
A
```

CMONTH(<*date*>)

Input: Date expression
Output: Character string

Evaluates to a character string containing the name of the month corresponding to the specified date.

Example:

```
. ? LASTORDER
01/20/88
. ? CMONTH(LASTORDER)
January
```

* COL( )

Input: None
Output: Number

Evaluates to a number representing the current cursor column (horizontal) position on the screen. This function may be used to display data immediately following the last item displayed or a fixed number of columns away from the last item, without reference to the absolute cursor position.

CTOD(<*character expression*>)

Input: Character expression
Output: Date

Evaluates to a true date matching the character string representation of the date supplied as input. This function is the only way to express a constant date in dBASE III PLUS, and it must be used anywhere a constant date is required, for example, to initialize a date memory variable, REPLACE a date field with a constant value, or compare a date variable with a constant date.

Examples:

```
. STORE CTOD("  ") TO MDATE
```

```
. REPLACE LASTORDER WITH CTOD("09/01/87")
```

```
. LIST FOR LASTORDER <= CTOD("12/31/86")
```

DATE( )

Input: None
Output: Date

The system date as obtained from the operating system.

DAY(<*date*>)

Input: Date expression
Output: Number

Evaluates to a number representing the day of the month in the specified date.

Example:

```
. ? LASTORDER
01/20/88
. ? DAY(LASTORDER)
 20
```

* DBF( )

Input: None
Output: Character string

Evaluates to a character string consisting of the full name (or path name, if the file is not in the current subdirectory) of the data base open in the current work area, or a null string if no data base is open.

Example:

```
. USE NWCUST INDEX NWCACCT, NWCZIP
. ? DBF()
C:NWCUST.dbf
```

DELETED( )

Input: None
Output: Logical value

Evaluates to .T. if the current record is marked for deletion, or .F. if it is not.

DISKSPACE( )

Input: None
Output: Number

Evaluates to the number of bytes of free space remaining on the disk in the currently logged drive. This function may be used to test whether enough space remains before beginning a SORT or COPY command. To determine the disk space remaining on a drive other than the current drive, you may reset the default drive with the SET DEFAULT command.

Example:

```
. USE NWINVENT
. SET DEFAULT TO A:
. ? DISKSPACE()
    101584
. SET DEFAULT TO C:
. RUN COPY NWINVENT.DBF A:
```

DOW(<*date*>)

Input: Date expression
Output: Number

Evaluates to a number representing the day of the week in the specified date.

Example:

```
. ? LASTORDER
01/20/88
. ? DOW(LASTORDER)
 4
```

DTOC(<*date*>)

Input: Date expression
Output: Character string

Evaluates to a character string representation of the date expression supplied as input. This function is often used to convert a date to a character string so that it may be concatenated with another character string for display or printing, or for use in an index key expression.

Examples:

```
. ? "Last order date: " + DTOC(LASTORDER)
Last order date: 01/20/88

. USE NWTXN
. INDEX ON ACCOUNT + DTOC(LASTORDER) TO NWTACCDT
```

* EOF( )

Input: None
Output: Logical value

Evaluates to .T. when you attempt to move the record pointer past the end-of-file by executing a SKIP *n* command. If the data base is open without any indexes, the end-of-file is the last record. With an index it is the record corresponding to the last index entry. After the SKIP *n* command, the data base is not positioned at any valid record; the RECNO( ) function evaluates to a number 1 greater than the number of records in the file, and all fields have been values. EOF( ) is also set to .T. if a FIND or SEEK command fails to find the specified record or if a data base accessed through a SET RELATION command has no record that matches the key expression on which the RELATION is based.

* ERROR( )

Input: None
Output: Number

Evaluates to a number corresponding to the error that has just occurred. This function always returns 0 unless an error-trapping routine has been established with the ON ERROR command. The ERROR( ) function may be used to detect and respond to certain recoverable error conditions, such as a missing file, or, in a network environment, an attempt to lock a record currently being modified by another user.

EXP(<*number*>)

Input: Numeric expression
Output: Number

Evaluates to the result of raising *e* (the base for natural logarithms) to the power specified by the numeric expression.

* FIELD(<*number*>)

Input: Numeric expression
Output: Character string

Evaluates to a character string containing the name of the field specified by number in the data base open in the current work area, or a null string if there is no corresponding field in the current data base. This function may be used to determine the number of fields in a data base or to handle a series of fields as an array.

* FILE(<*file name*>)

Input : Character expression
Output: Logical value

Evaluates to .T. if the specified file is present on the disk. If the file name is a literal character string (not a memory variable), it must be enclosed in quotation marks. This function may be used to test for the existence of a file before attempting to use it, so that a program may take the appropriate corrective action (creating the file or informing the user) if the file is missing.

* FKLABEL(<*number*>)

Input: Numeric expression
Output: Character string

Evaluates to a character string containing the name of the programmable function key specified by number. Unless the keyboard has a separate Help key, the meaning of the first function key (usually labeled F1) cannot be reassigned, and FKLABEL(1) returns the name of the second function key. This function may be used to change the meanings of the function keys without having to know their names.

Examples:

```
. ? FKLABEL(1)
F2

. SET FUNCTION FKLABEL(4) TO "USE NWCUST INDEX NWCACCT,NWCZIP;"
```

* FKMAX( )

Input: None
Output: Number

Evaluates to the number of programmable function keys on the keyboard. Unless the keyboard has a separate Help key, FKMAX( ) evaluates to a number 1 smaller than the actual number of keys. This function may be used to test for the existence of certain function keys before attempting to reassign their meanings.

* FLOCK( )

Input: None
Output: Logical value

Evaluates to .T. if it is possible to lock the file that is open in the currently selected work area, or .F. if the attempt fails because the file is already locked by another user. This function simultaneously tests the status and attempts to lock the file. Once locked, the file may be unlocked with the UNLOCK command, by closing the file, or by exiting from dBASE III PLUS. A file is generally locked for operations that affect the entire file or update many records.

* FOUND( )

Input: None
Output: Logical value

Evaluates to .T. when a FIND, SEEK, LOCATE, or CONTINUE command positions the record pointer at a valid record in the data base in the current work area, or when the record pointer is repositioned automatically to a valid record in a data base in another work area linked to the current file with SET RELATION. In general, when EOF( ) is .T., FOUND( ) is .F. dBASE III PLUS keeps track of the value of the FOUND( ) function separately in each work area, but a work area must be selected to display or operate on this value.

* GETENV(<*character string*>)

Input: Character string expression
Output: Character string

Evaluates to a character string containing the operating system environment parameter specified as input, or a null string if the parameter has not been set.

Examples:

```
. ? GETENV("COMSPEC")
C:\COMMAND.COM

STORE "PATH" TO MFILEPATH
. ? GETENV(MFILEPATH)
C:\;C:\UTILITY
```

IIF(<*condition*>, <*expression 1*>, <*expression 2*>)

Inputs: Logical expression, expression, expression
Output: Same data type as expressions 1 and 2

Evaluates to expression 1 if the condition is .T., or expression 2 if the condition is .F. The two expressions may be of any data type, but they must be of the same data type. This function is most useful for displaying fields conditionally at the dot prompt and printing fields conditionally in reports and labels.

Example:

```
. ? MAIL
.T.
. ? IIF(MAIL, "Yes", "No")
Yes
```

* INKEY( )

Input: None
Output: Number

Evaluates to a number corresponding to the key pressed by the operator, or the first key in the keyboard buffer if there is more than 1. Unlike the WAIT command, using the INKEY( ) function does not pause the currently running program. Since the function returns a value of 0 unless a key is pressed at the instant it is evaluated, it is generally used within a DO WHILE loop that monitors the keyboard and registers the user's keypress.

INT(<*number*>)

Input: Numeric expression
Output: Number

Evaluates to the integer portion of the number represented by the numeric expression (the result of dropping any digits beyond the decimal point). To round off a number to the nearest integer, use the ROUND function instead.

Example:

```
. ? YTDORDERS
    366.81
. ? INT(YTDORDERS)
       366
```

* ISALPHA(<*character string*>)

Input: Character string expression
Output: Logical value

Evaluates to .T. if the first character of the expression providing the input is a letter of the alphabet, or .F. if it is not.

Examples:

```
. ? ISALPHA("ABC Plumbing")
.T.
. ? ADDRESS1
1850 University Avenue
. ? ISALPHA(ADDRESS1)
.F.
```

* ISCOLOR( )

Input: None
Output: Logical value

Evaluates to .T. if the system is using a color/graphics monitor, or .F. if the display is a monochrome screen. This function may be used to detect which type of monitor is present and set the display attributes accordingly. The color selections should be made with caution, however, since not every color/graphics system can actually display colors. For example, the COMPAQ display returns a .T. value.

* ISLOWER(<*character string*>)

Input: Character string expression
Output: Logical value

Evaluates to .T. if the first character of the expression providing the input is a lowercase letter of the alphabet, or .F. if it is not.

Examples:

```
. ? ISLOWER("ABC Plumbing")
.F.
. ? ADDRESS1
1850 University Avenue
. ? ISLOWER(ADDRESS1)
.F.
```

* ISUPPER(<*character string*>)

Input: Character string expression
Output: Logical value

Evaluates to .T. if the first character of the expression providing the input is an uppercase letter of the alphabet, or .F. if it is not.

Examples:

```
. ? ISUPPER("ABC Plumbing")
.T.
```

```
. ? ADDRESS1
1850 University Avenue
. ? ISUPPER(ADDRESS1)
.F.
```

LEFT(<*character string*>, <*length*>)

Inputs: Character string expression, numeric expression
Output: Character string

Evaluates to a substring (part of a string) of the character string represented by the expression providing the input. The substring begins with the first (leftmost) character and the length is specified by the numeric expression. If the requested length exceeds the length of the original character string, the substring consists of the full string.

Example:

```
. ? COMPANY
ABC Plumbing
. ? LEFT(COMPANY, 9)
ABC Plumb
```

* LEN(<*character string*>)

Input: Character string expression
Output: Number

Evaluates to the length of the character string represented by the character string expression. The length of a data base field is always the full field width. The TRIM function may be used to eliminate trailing blanks.

Examples:

```
. ? TRIM(COMPANY)
ABC Plumbing
. ? LEN(COMPANY)
        25
. ? LEN(TRIM(COMPANY))
        12
```

* LOCK( ) or RLOCK( )

Input: None
Output: Logical value

Evaluates to .T. if it is possible to lock the current record in the data base open in the current work area, or .F. if the record is already locked by another user. This function simultaneously tests the status and attempts to lock the record. Once locked, the record may be unlocked with the UNLOCK command. This function is generally used for operations that involve updating records one at a time, so that multiple users may access the same file, but not the same record, at the same time.

LOG(<*number*>)

Input: Numeric expression
Output: Number

Evaluates to the natural (base *e*) logarithm of the number represented by the numeric expression.

LOWER(<*character string*>)

Input: Character string expression
Output: Character string

Evaluates to the result of converting the character string represented by the character string expression to all lowercase. This function may be used to convert a character string entered in various mixtures of uppercase and lowercase to a consistent format for comparison to another variable or constant.

Examples:

```
. ? EQUIPMENT
Kaypro 10, Brother
. ? "kaypro" $ EQUIPMENT
.F.
. ? "kaypro" $ lower(EQUIPMENT)
.T.
```

LTRIM(<*character string*>)

Input: Character string expression
Output: Character string

Evaluates to a character string consisting of the result of evaluating the specified character string expression, with all leading blanks removed. This function is useful for removing leading blanks created when a numeric expression is converted to a character string with the STR function.

Example:

```
. ? "Year-to-date Orders: $" + LTRIM(STR(YTDORDERS, 10, 2))
Year-to-date Orders: $366.81
```

* LUPDATE( )

Input: None
Output: Date

Evaluates to the date on which the data base in the current work area was last updated by adding, changing, or deleting data.

MAX(<*numeric expression*>, <*numeric expression*>)

Inputs: Numeric expression, numeric expression
Output: Number

Evaluates to the number represented by the greater of the two numeric expressions. This function is useful for displaying fields conditionally at the dot prompt and printing fields conditionally in reports and labels.

Example:

```
. REPLACE ALL DISCOUNT WITH MAX(PRICE * .15, 5.00)
```

* MESSAGE( )

Input: None
Output: Character string

Evaluates to a character string containing the error message normally displayed by dBASE III PLUS in response to the error that has just occurred. This function always returns 0 unless an error-trapping routine has been established with the ON ERROR command.

MIN(<*numeric expression*>, <*numeric expression*>)

Inputs: Numeric expression, numeric expression
Output: Number

Evaluates to the number represented by the smaller of the two numeric expressions. This function is useful for displaying fields conditionally at the dot prompt and printing fields conditionally in reports and labels.

Example:

```
. REPLACE ALL DISCOUNT WITH MIN(PRICE * .15, 10.00)
```

MOD(<*numeric expression*>, <*numeric expression*>)

Input: Numeric expression, numeric expression
Output: Number

Evaluates to the remainder that results from dividing the first numeric expression by the second.

Example:

```
. STORE DATE() - LASTORDER TO MTIME
       372
. STORE INT(MTIME / 365) TO MYEARS
```

```
              1
. STORE MOD(MTIME, 365) TO MDAYS
              7
. ? "Last order: " + str(MYEARS, 1) + " year(s), " + str(MDAYS, 3)
  + " days"
Last order: 1 year(s),   7 days ago
```

MONTH(<*date*>)

Input: Date expression
Output: Number

Evaluates to a number representing the month in the specified date.

Example:

```
. ? LASTORDER
01/20/88
. ? MONTH(LASTORDER)
  1
```

* NDX(<*numeric expression*>)

Input: Numeric expression
Output: Character string

Evaluates to a character string consisting of the full name (or path name, if the file is not in the current subdirectory) of the index file whose position in the index file list specified in the USE command that opened the data base in the current work area corresponds to the value of the numeric expression. NDX evaluates to a null string if no such index is open.

Example:

```
. USE NWCUST INDEX NWCACCT, NWCZIP
. ? NDX(2)
C:NWCACCT.ndx
. ? NDX(3)

.
```

* OS( )

Input: None
Output: Character string

Evaluates to a character string containing the name of the operating system currently running. This function may be used to determine which operating system is active before using the RUN command to run an external command or program specific to a particular operating system.

* PCOL( )

Input: None
Output: Number

Evaluates to a number representing the current printhead column position. This function may be used to print data immediately following the last item printed or a fixed number of columns to the right of the last item, without reference to the absolute printhead position.

* PROW( )

Input: None
Output: Number

Evaluates to a number representing the current printhead row position. This function may be used to print data on the next available row (line) on the page or a fixed number of rows below this row, without reference to the absolute printhead position.

* READKEY( )

Input: None
Output: Number

Evaluates to a number corresponding to the key pressed by the operator to exit from any full-screen edit mode, including a series of @...SAY...GET commands followed by a READ. Each key can generate two possible values, depending on whether or not data was changed during the full-screen edit process.

RECCOUNT( )

Input: None
Output: Number

Evaluates to the number of records in the data base open in the currently selected work area.

RECNO( )

Input: None
Output: Number

Evaluates to the record number at the position of the record pointer in the data base open in the currently selected work area. If the data base is positioned past the end-of-file, RECNO( ) evaluates to 1 greater than the number of records in the file. This means that if the data base is empty, RECNO( ) has the value 1.

RECSIZE( )

Input: None
Output: Number

Evaluates to the record length of the data base in the currently selected work area. This function may be combined with the RECCOUNT( ) function to calculate the approximate size of a data base (not including the space occupied by the file header).

REPLICATE(<*character string*>, <*number*>

Inputs: Character string expression, numeric expression
Output: Character string

Evaluates to a character string consisting of the character string specified as input, repeated a number of times equal to the value of the numeric expression.

Examples:

```
.? REPLICATE("=", 25)
=========================
. ? REPLICATE("-*", 10)
-*-*-*-*-*-*-*-*-*-*
```

RIGHT(<*character string*>, <*length*>)

Inputs: Character string expression, numeric expression
Output: Character string

Evaluates to a substring (part of a string) of the character string represented by the expression providing the input. The length of the substring is specified by the numeric expression, and the substring is taken from the right side of the original string. If the requested length exceeds the length of the original character string, the substring consists of the full string.

Example:

```
. ? COMPANY
ABC Plumbing
. ? RIGHT(trim(COMPANY), 8)
Plumbing
```

* RLOCK( ) or LOCK( )

Input: None
Output: Logical value

RLOCK( ) is identical to LOCK( ) and is provided for parity with the FLOCK( ) function.

ROUND(<*number*>, <*decimals*>)

Inputs: Numeric expression, numeric expression
Output: Number

The result of rounding off the number represented by the first numeric expression to the number of decimal places specified by the second. If *decimals* is a negative number, the specified number of digits to the *left* of the decimal point is rounded off.

Examples:

```
. ? YTDORDERS
    366.81
. ? ROUND(YTDORDERS, 1)
     366.80
. ? ROUND(YTDORDERS, 0)
     367.00
. ? ROUND(YTDORDERS, -2)
     400.00
```

* ROW( )

Input: None
Output: Number

Evaluates to a number representing the current cursor row position on the screen. This function may be used to display data on the next available row (line) on the screen or a fixed number of rows away from this row, without reference to the absolute cursor position.

RTRIM(<*character string*>)

Input: Character string expression
Output: Character string

RTRIM is identical to TRIM and is provided for parity with the LTRIM function.

SPACE(<*number*>)

Input: Numeric expression
Output: Character string

Evaluates to a character string consisting of the number of blank spaces specified by the numeric expression. This function is often used to initialize a blank character memory variable without having to count spaces.

SQRT(<*number*>)

Input: Numeric expression
Output: Number

Evaluates to the square root of the number represented by the numeric expression.

STR(<*number*> [,<*length*>] [,<*decimals*>])

Inputs: Numeric expression, numeric expression, numeric expression
Output: Character string

Evaluates to a character string representation of the number specified by the first numeric expression. The length of the string is specified by the second expression, and the number of decimal places by the third. If the length is omitted, it is assumed to be 10. If you do not specify the number of decimal places, 0 is assumed. This function may be used to convert a number to a character string so that it may be concatenated with another character string for display, printing, or use in an index key expression.

Examples:

```
. ? "Balance: " + STR(BALANCE,10,2)
Balance:       143.57

. USE NWTXN
. INDEX ON ACCOUNT + STR(INVAMOUNT,10,2) TO NWTACCIN
```

* STUFF(<*character string 1*>, <*starting position*>, <*length*>, <*character string 2*>)

Inputs: Character string expression, numeric expression, numeric expression, character string
Output: Character string

Evaluates to a character string consisting of the string represented by character string 1, with a substring of the specified length and starting at the indicated starting position removed and replaced by character string 2. If the length is 0, no characters are removed before the substitution is made; and if character string 2 is a null string, no replacement is made.

Example:

```
. ? EQUIPMENT
IBM PC, NEC7710
. ? STUFF(EQUIPMENT, AT("PC", EQUIPMENT), 2, "PS/2")
IBM PS/2, NEC7710
```

SUBSTR(<*character string*>, <*starting position*> [,<*length*>])

Inputs: Character string expression, numeric expression, numeric expression
Output: Character string

Evaluates to the substring (part of a string) of the specified character string that begins at the position represented by the first numeric expression. If a second numeric expression is included, it specifies the length of the substring. If the length is omitted, the substring begins at the designated starting position and includes all of the remaining characters in the original string.

Examples:

```
. ? COMPANY
ABC Plumbing
. ? SUBSTR(COMPANY,5,4)
Plum
. ? SUBSTR(COMPANY,5)
Plumbing
```

TIME( )

Input: None
Output: Character string

Evaluates to a character string representation of the current system time.

TRANSFORM(<*expression*>, <*picture*>)

Inputs: Expression, character string expression
Output: Same data type as expression

Evaluates to the result of formatting the expression with the specified PICTURE. This function may be used to format fields displayed from the dot prompt and to print formatted data in reports and labels. The data type of the output is the same as the data type of the original expression; however, you cannot accumulate column totals and subtotals in a report printed by the built-in report generator for any numeric fields formatted with this function.

Examples:

```
. ? COMPANY
ABC Plumbing
. ? TRANSFORM(COMPANY, "@!")
ABC PLUMBING

. ? TOTORDERS
   1Ø53.89
. ? TRANSFORM(TOTORDERS, "@CX 9,999,999.99")
    1,Ø53.89 CR
```

TRIM(<*character string*>)

Input: Character string expression
Output: Character string

Evaluates to a character string consisting of the result of evaluating the specified character string expression, with all trailing blanks removed. This function is identical to RTRIM.

* TYPE(<*expression*>)

Input: Any expression
Output: Character

Evaluates to a single character representing the data type of the specified expression, for a character (C), numeric (N), logical (L), or memo (M) expression (date type expressions are not permitted as input). If a variable does not exist or if the expression is not syntactically correct, the function evaluates to U (undefined). To use this function to test for the existence of a variable, the variable name supplied as input must be enclosed in quotation marks; otherwise, the *contents* of the variable are evaluated, not the variable itself.

UPPER(<*character string*>)

Input: Character string expression
Output: Character string

Evaluates to the result of converting the specified character string expression to all uppercase. This function may be used to convert a character string entered in various mixtures of uppercase and lowercase to a consistent format for comparison to another variable or constant.

Examples:

```
. ? EQUIPMENT
Kaypro 10, Brother
. ? "KAYPRO" $ EQUIPMENT
.F.
. ? "KAYPRO" $ upper(EQUIPMENT)
.T.
```

VAL(<*character string*>)

Input: Character string expression
Output: Number

Evaluates to a true number matching the character string representation of the number supplied as input.

* VERSION( )

Input: None
Output: Character string

Evaluates to a character string containing the name of the version of dBASE III PLUS that is running. This function may be used to test the version of dBASE III PLUS before issuing a command or using a function not present in an older version.

YEAR(<*date*>)

Input: Date expression
Output: Number

Evaluates to a four-digit number representing the year in the specified date.

Example:

```
. ? LASTORDER
01/20/88
. ? YEAR(LASTORDER)
 1988
```

Appendix D
The CONFIG.DB File

The CONFIG.DB file may be used to customize the status of the dBASE III PLUS working environment to suit your personal preferences. CONFIG.DB is an ASCII text file consisting of one or more command lines, each of which controls one option. If this file is present in the subdirectory from which you load dBASE III PLUS, or a subdirectory specified in a DOS PATH command, the settings it contains are automatically placed in effect when you start up the program.

Most of the options you may specify in CONFIG.DB may also be established with SET commands either from the dot prompt or from a dBASE III PLUS program. The eight options that may *not* be SET from the dot prompt govern the use of external word processors and the allocation of RAM for memory buffers, which must be known to dBASE III PLUS when the program is first loaded. These options are marked with an asterisk (*) and explained in this appendix.

There are also some SET commands that have no CONFIG.DB equivalents. These include all of the commands that require a data base to be open, such as SET FIELDS and SET FILTER, as well as several others: SET DATE, SET DOHISTORY, SET FIXED, SET MESSAGE, SET PRINTER, and SET TITLE.

The syntax used in CONFIG.DB is different from the syntax of the corresponding SET options. The general format for a CONFIG.DB entry is

<option> = *<value>*

instead of

SET *<option>* *<value>*

or

SET *<option>* TO *<value>*

The syntax for the CONFIG.DB entries that have SET equivalents is listed here without further explanation, except for several minor differences that are noted below the commands. See Appendix B for a more complete explanation of all of the SET commands. As in the descriptions of the SET options in Appendix B, the default values of options with two or more alternate values (for example, ON or OFF) are indicated in uppercase.

ALTERNATE = *<file name>*

This command is equivalent to the two SET commands

SET ALTERNATE TO *<file name>*
SET ALTERNATE ON

BELL = ON/off

* BUCKET = *<number>*

This option specifies the amount of memory (expressed in kilobytes) reserved by dBASE III PLUS for PICTURE, FUNCTION, and RANGE clauses in @...SAY...GET commands. The default is 2, and you may specify any number between 1 and 31. This number should be increased if you experience inexplicable problems with @...SAY...GET commands.

CARRY = on/OFF

CATALOG = <*file name*>

CENTURY = on/OFF

COLOR = <*standard foreground/standard background*>, <*enhanced foreground/enhanced background*>, <*border*>

* COMMAND = <*command*>

The specified command is run automatically when you first load dBASE III PLUS. The default CONFIG.DB file provided with dBASE III PLUS contains the line COMMAND = ASSIST so that the program starts up in ASSIST mode. The COMMAND command is often used to run the main menu program in a dBASE III PLUS application. If the user invokes a different command file when loading dBASE III PLUS by typing DBASE <*program name*>, it overrides the CONFIG.DB entry.

CONFIRM = on/OFF

CONSOLE = ON/off

DEBUG = on/OFF

DECIMALS = <*number*>

DEFAULT = <*disk drive*>

DELETED = on/OFF

DELIMITERS = <*delimiter character(s)*>
DELIMITERS = on/OFF

Note: The delimiter characters must *not* be enclosed in quotes, as they are in the equivalent SET command.

DEVICE = SCREEN/print

ECHO = on/OFF

ENCRYPTION = ON/off

ESCAPE = ON/off

EXACT = on/OFF

EXCLUSIVE = ON/off

F<*number*> = <*character string*>

Note: This is equivalent to SET FUNCTION.

FIXED = on/OFF

* GETS = <*number*>

This option determines the number of GETs that may be collected between READ, CLEAR GETS, or CLEAR commands. The default is 128, and you may specify any number between 35 and 1023.

HEADING = ON/off

HELP = ON/off

HISTORY = <*number*>

INTENSITY = ON/off

MARGIN = <*number*>

* MAXMEM = <*number*>

This option determines the amount of memory (expressed in kilobytes) that is not released by dBASE III PLUS to an external application executed with a RUN command. The default value is 256, and you may specify any number between 200 and 720. MAXMEM should be raised if you have increased the amount of memory used by dBASE III PLUS by increasing the values of MVARSIZ, GETS, or BUCKET, so that these necessary memory buffers are not overwritten when external programs or commands are executed.

MEMOWIDTH = <*number*>

MENUS = ON/off

* MVARSIZ = <*number*>

This option specifies the amount of memory (expressed in kilobytes) reserved by dBASE III PLUS for memory variables. The default is 6, and you may specify any number between 1 and 31.

PATH = <*path name list*>

PRINT = on/OFF

PRINTER = <*DOS device name*>

* PROMPT = <*character string*>

This option changes the dBASE III PLUS command prompt from the standard dot (.) to the specified character string.

SAFETY = ON/off

SCOREBOARD = ON/off

STATUS = ON/off

STEP = on/OFF

TALK = ON/off

* TEDIT = <*file name*>

This option specifies an external text editor or word processing program that is substituted for the standard dBASE III PLUS MODIFY COMMAND editor. The file name should be entered exactly as you would type it at the MS-DOS prompt to invoke the editor (it must not include an extension).

TYPEAHEAD = <*number*>

UNIQUE = on/OFF

VIEW = <*file name*>

* WP = <*file name*>

This option specifies an external text editor or word processing program that is substituted for the standard dBASE III PLUS memo field editor. The file name should be entered exactly as you would type it at the MS-DOS prompt to invoke the editor (it must not include an extension).

Appendix E
Error Messages

This appendix lists in alphabetical order the messages displayed by dBASE III PLUS in response to errors encountered at the dot prompt or from within programs, together with the most common causes of the errors and, where appropriate, suggested remedies. Warning messages, informational messages, and most of the messages displayed in the ASSIST menu and the full-screen editors are not included, because for the most part these messages are self-explanatory.

A DBF file in view is not in current directory.

A data base file referenced in a VIEW that you have attempted to open with SET VIEW TO or MODIFY VIEW cannot be found either in the current subdirectory or in any of the subdirectories accessed through a SET PATH TO command.

ALIAS name already in use.

The alias specified in a USE command has already been assigned to a data base open in one of the ten work areas. This can occur if you try to assign the same alias name to two different data base files or if you try to open the same file in two work areas. The error may also occur if you assign one of the single letters A through J as a data base file name or alias (these letters are reserved for referring to the ten work areas).

ALIAS not found.

The alias specified in a SELECT command cannot be found, usually because you have forgotten which data base files are open or because you have misspelled the alias.

ALTERNATE could not be opened.

The ALTERNATE file named in an ALTERNATE=*filename* entry in CONFIG.DB could not be opened, because the disk directory was full or because an invalid file name was specified.

Beginning of file encountered.

A SKIP −*n* command was executed with the BOF function already set to .T. This will occur on the second consecutive attempt to SKIP backward beyond the beginning-of-file. (The first SKIP −*n* simply sets the BOF function to .T., leaving the data base positioned at the first, or first indexed, record.)

Cannot erase a file which is open.

An ERASE or DELETE FILE command was issued without first closing the specified file with the appropriate USE or CLOSE command (depending on which type of file you are erasing). CLEAR ALL may be used to close all open files.

Cannot JOIN a file with itself.

The file named in the WITH clause in a JOIN command was the same file that is open in the selected work area.

Cannot select requested database.

A SELECT command requested by number a work area higher than 10.

Cannot write to read only file.

An attempt was made to write to a file assigned the "Read-Only" attribute at the operating system level.

CONTINUE without LOCATE.

A CONTINUE command was executed without a prior LOCATE command. CONTINUE is used only to search for the next record that matches the condition specified in a previous LOCATE command.

Cyclic relation.

A SET RELATION command was issued to link the current data base to another data base from which a RELATION affecting the current file was already SET. This may be direct; for example:

```
SELECT 1
USE NWCUST INDEX NWCACCT
SELECT 2
USE NWORDER INDEX NWOACCT
SET RELATION TO ACCOUNT INTO NWCUST
SELECT 1
SET RELATION TO ACCOUNT INTO NWORDER
```

It may also occur in a chain of more than two files. For example:

```
SELECT 1
USE NWORDER INDEX NWOINVC
SELECT 2
USE NWTXN INDEX NWTACCT
SELECT 3
USE NWCUST INDEX NWCACCT

SELECT NWCUST
SET RELATION TO ACCOUNT INTO NWTXN
SELECT NWTXN
SET RELATION TO INVOICE INTO NWORDER
SELECT NWORDER
SET RELATION TO ACCOUNT INTO NWCUST
```

Database is encrypted.

An attempt was made to use a data base file encrypted by the PROTECT utility either from a single-user version of dBASE III PLUS or by an unauthorized user in a multi-user system.

Database is not indexed

A FIND or SEEK command was issued with no index open for the current data base, or you have attempted to SET RELATION TO a data base opened with no index.

Data Catalog has not been established.

An attempt was made to use a catalog query clause (entering a "?" where dBASE III PLUS expects a file name) to list the available files of a given type, but with no CATALOG file open.

Data type mismatch.

Data types were mixed incorrectly in an algebraic expression or condition, or a data type was used that does not match the type required by the context of the command. This can occur if you attempt to REPLACE a field with data of a different type, if the object of a SEEK does not match the data type of the index key expression, or if you attempt to SORT on a logical or memo field.

.DBT file cannot be opened.

An attempt was made to open a data base file containing memo fields for which the DBT file was not available. This can occur if you copy or rename a DBF file using the DOS COPY or REN commands or the dBASE III PLUS COPY FILE or RENAME equivalents, and forget to also copy or rename the DBT file.

Directory is full

An attempt was made to create a new file on a disk that already has the maximum number of directory entries permitted by the MS-DOS operating system.

Disk full when writing file - <*file name*>
Abort, Ignore or Delete old files (A, I, or D)?

An attempt was made to write to a disk that has no space remaining. If you choose A (abort), dBASE III PLUS asks you to confirm your intention to interrupt the command with the message, "** WARNING ** Data will probably be lost. Confirm (Y/N)."

If you answer Y, dBASE III PLUS returns to the dot prompt, leaving the output file incomplete. If you answer N, dBASE III PLUS repeats the "Abort, Ignore, or Delete" message. If you choose I (ignore), dBASE III PLUS will retry the write operation, find the disk still full, and repeat the "Abort, Ignore, or Delete" message. If you choose D (delete old files), dBASE III PLUS confirms your selection with the message, "Delete obsolete files to provide disk space. . .(Esc to abort)."

The program then presents the names of the files on the disk, one by one, and allows you to delete each file or to go on to the next one. dBASE III PLUS resumes the operation in progress when all file names have been displayed or when you press ESC to interrupt. If you are able to delete enough unneeded files to make room for the file being written, the original command that generated the error will complete normally.

DO's nested too deep.

An attempt was made to nest programs (allow one program to call another) more than the maximum of 20 levels (20 programs) deep.

End of file encountered.

A SKIP command was executed with the EOF function already set to .T. This will occur on the second consecutive attempt to SKIP beyond the end-of-file. (The first SKIP simply sets the EOF function to .T., leaving the data base positioned at an empty record beyond the end-of-file.)

This error can also occur if a data base is opened with an index that does not match the data base (perhaps because it was created with a different number of records in the file), so that a record referenced by the index does not exist in the file. It can also occur under certain conditions if an index file, data base file, or report or label format file is damaged by a disk error.

End-of-file or error on keyboard input.

A file specified in a DOS SET ENVIRONMENT command to replace keyboard input was damaged by a disk error.

Exclusive use on database is required.

In a network environment, an attempt was made to execute a command that requires exclusive use of a data base file, with EXCLUSIVE set OFF.

*** Execution error on + : concatenated string too large.

*** Execution error on − : concatenated string too large.

An attempt was made to concatenate two or more character strings with + or − to create a string longer than 254 characters. The resulting string will contain the first 254 characters of the combination.

*** Execution error on ^ or ** : negative base, fractional exponent.

An expression contains a negative number raised to a power between 0 and 1. (This is the equivalent of extracting a root, such as a square root, of a negative number, which cannot be done.)

*** Execution error on CHR( ) : Out of range.

The input provided to a CHR function was less than 0 or greater than 255, the range of ASCII character codes.

*** Execution error on LOG( ) : Zero or negative.

The input provided to a LOG function was zero or negative. (Since the logarithm of a number is the power to which *e*, the base of natural logarithms, must be raised to yield the number and *e* is a positive number, there can be no zero or negative logarithms.)

*** Execution error on NDX( ) : Invalid index number.

The input provided to the NDX function (which returns the name of the index file opened in the specified position in the index list in the USE command) was not within the allowable range of 1 to 7.

*** Execution error on REPLICATE( ): String too large.

An attempt was made to create a character string longer than 254 characters with the REPLICATE function.

*** Execution error on SPACE( ): Negative.

*** Execution error on SPACE( ): Too large.

The input provided to the SPACE function to specify the length of the string of blank spaces to create was not within the allowable range of 1 to 254.

*** Execution error on SQRT( ): Negative.

The input provided to a SQRT function was a negative number. (You cannot take the square root of a negative number.)

*** Execution error on STORE( ): String too large.

An attempt was made to create a character-string memory variable longer than 254 characters with the STORE function.

*** Execution error on STR( ): Out of range.

One of the two numeric inputs to the STR function was incorrect. Either the length of the desired character string was less than 0 or greater than 19, or you specified more decimal places than the length can accommodate.

*** Execution error on STUFF( ): String too large.

An attempt was made to create a character string longer than 254 characters by using the STUFF function to substitute a longer string for a portion of the original string.

*** Execution error on SUBSTR( ) : Start point out of range.

The starting point for the substring specified in a SUBSTR function was greater than the total length of the character string.

^ ^Expected ON or OFF

One of the SET options in CONFIG.DB that must be either ON or OFF was given some other value.

Field not found.

A field name that does not exist in the data base structure was specified in the FREEZE option of the BROWSE command.

File already exists.

An attempt was made to RENAME a file with the name of another existing disk file.

File does not exist.

An attempt was made to access a file that cannot be found on the disk either in the current subdirectory or in any of the subdirectories specified in the search path established with SET PATH.

File is already open.

An attempt was made to open a disk file that was already open or to perform an operation not permitted on an open file. This error can occur if you try to open a file, such as an index or report form file, that is already open in another work area. (Attempting to open a data base file in two work areas yields the "ALIAS name already in use" error message.) The error can also occur if you attempt to COPY, SORT, ERASE, RENAME, TYPE, or edit (with MODIFY COMMAND) an open file, or if you try to SORT a file to itself (specify the current file name to receive the sorted output) or to a file that is open in another work area.

File is in use by another.

An attempt was made to open a file in a multi-user application, when the file has already been opened for EXCLUSIVE use at another workstation.

File is not accessible.

An illegal character (one of the prohibited punctuation marks +, “, <, >, ?, *, [, or]) was used in a file name, or an attempt was made to open a file with the disk directory already full.

File too large—some data may be lost

An attempt was made to edit a text file or memo field larger than 5000 bytes with the MODIFY COMMAND editor or the memo field editor. If you make this error, you should exit immediately from the editor by pressing ESC to avoid truncating the file.

File was not LOADed.

An attempt was made to place a binary file in memory with the LOAD command, but the file is not available. This error can also occur if a CALL or RELEASE MODULE command references a binary file not found at the specified memory location.

Illegal character data length.—detected on field <*n*>
Illegal decimal length.—detected on field <*n*>
Illegal field name.—detected on field <*n*>
Illegal field type.—detected on field <*n*>
Illegal numeric data length.—detected on field <*n*>
Maximum record length exceeded.—detected on field <*n*>

One or more of the records in a structure-extended file contains an illegal field name, length, type, or number of decimal places, or the total record length is greater than 4000 characters. The invalid field is field number *n* in the data base structure described by the structure-extended file and therefore record *n* in this file. Since a structure-extended file is created from an existing data base, this error can only occur if you have edited the resulting file and entered incorrect data into one or more of the records. Any values entered for the length or number of decimals for a date or memo field are ignored, without generating an error.

Improper data type in subsubtotal expression.
Improper data type in subtotal expression.

Either a logical expression or memo field was specified as the basis for accumulating subtotals or subsubtotals in a report form. The error message appears only when you try to run the report, not when you are creating or editing the form.

Index damaged. REINDEX should be done before using data.

An attempt was made to open an index file that was damaged, usually by interrupting an INDEX or REINDEX command with ESC.

Index expression is too big (220 char maximum).

An attempt was made to build an index based on a key expression longer than 220 characters. Note that it is the expression that specifies the index key, which may be 220 characters long; the combination of fields that make up the key itself may not exceed 100 characters.

Index file does not match database.

The index opened with the data base in a USE command was based on a key expression that contains one or more fields not present in the data base. This can occur if you open an index with the wrong data base, or if you change the field names or types and forget to reconstruct the index afterward.

Index interrupted. Index will be deleted if not completed. Abort indexing? (Y/N)

An INDEX or REINDEX command was interrupted with ESC. You are given the choice to continue building the index or abort the process, in which case the partially constructed index file is deleted.

Index is too big (100 char maximum).

The fields that form the index key specified in an INDEX command exceed 100 characters in combined length. Note that the expression that specifies the index key may be 220 characters long.

Insert impossible (Press SPACE)

An attempt was made to insert a new column into a report form, using CREATE REPORT or MODIFY REPORT, when the report already contains 24 columns.

Insufficient memory

An attempt was made to load dBASE III PLUS, access an external operating system command or program with a RUN command, or LOAD a binary module without enough RAM available. This error will occur if you do not have enough memory to load an external editor you have designated to replace the MODIFY COMMAND editor or the memo field editor with the TEDIT or WP entries in CONFIG.DB. This error may also occur if you specify more consecutive GETs between READ, CLEAR, or CLEAR GETS commands than are allowed (the default is 128), or if you try to RUN an external command that causes you to exceed the limit of 20 open DOS files (which will happen if you have many files already open within dBASE III PLUS and then try to load COMMAND.COM, your external program, and whatever files it requires).

Internal error: CMDSET( ):

Internal error: Illegal opcode

Internal error: Unknown command code

Records do not balance (program error).

Too many merge steps.

Unassigned file no.

Unknown SCEDIT( ) return code:

These messages all report errors that theoretically "can't happen." Usually, they mean that the dBASE III PLUS program files have been damaged. If your version of dBASE III PLUS is not copy-protected, you should make a new working copy of the program. With a copy-protected version, you can try recopying the non-copy-protected files from the master disk, or uninstalling and then reinstalling the program.

Internal error: EVAL work area overflow

An attempt was made to use an expression too complex for dBASE III PLUS to evaluate.

Invalid date. (press SPACE)

An attempt was made to enter an impossible date, such as 13/44/87, into a date variable. Pressing the space bar gives you another chance to enter the date correctly.

Invalid DIF Character.
Invalid DIF File Header.
Invalid DIF Type Indicator.

An attempt was made to APPEND data from a DIF file that contains an invalid character (such as a non-ASCII character), a corrupted file header, or an invalid data type indicator. These problems can occur if the DIF file is damaged by a disk error or by a problem with the program that produced the DIF file.

Invalid DOS SET option.

An attempt was made to SET a DOS option that does not exist.

Invalid function argument.

One of the expressions entered as an argument (input) to a dBASE III PLUS function is the wrong data type or outside of the allowable range.

Invalid function name.

An attempt was made to use a function name not recognized by dBASE III PLUS. This error rather than "Syntax error" can also occur if you construct an incorrect expression using variable names and parentheses in such a way that dBASE III interprets the name of a variable as an intended function name (because it is followed by a pair of parentheses with one or more "inputs" in between).

Invalid index number.

An attempt was made to specify an index number in a SET ORDER command that is outside the permissible range of 0 to 7 or higher than the actual number of indexes opened with the data base.

Invalid operator.

An attempt was made to use an operator in a way that is not permitted, for example, with inappropriate data types.

Invalid printer port.

An attempt was made to redirect output to a nonexistent printer port with a SET PRINTER TO command, either in a single-user system or to select a local printer from a network workstation.

Invalid printer redirection.

An attempt was made to redirect output to a nonexistent network printer with a SET PRINTER TO \ \ command.

Invalid SYLK File Dimension Bounds.
Invalid SYLK File Format.
Invalid SYLK File Header.

An attempt was made to APPEND data from a SYLK file that contains data that is outside the boundaries of the file, has an unrecognizable data format, or has a corrupted file header. These problems can occur if the SYLK file is damaged by a disk error or by a problem with the program that produced the SYLK file.

^ — Keyword not found.

A word not recognized by dBASE III PLUS was used in one of the entries in CONFIG.DB.

Label file invalid.

dBASE III PLUS cannot read the specified label form file, possibly because the disk has been damaged, or because you have named a file in your command that is not a dBASE III PLUS label form file.

Line exceeds maximum of 254 characters.

A command line more than 254 characters long was entered into a program or format file.

Master catalog is empty.

A CATALOG query clause was used in a SET CATALOG TO command (SET CATALOG TO ?), but the list of valid CATALOG files could not be displayed because the master catalog file, CATALOG.CAT, contained no records.

Maximum path length exceeded.

The file search path in a SET PATH command exceeded the maximum permissible length of 60 characters.

Maximum record length exceeded.

Using either CREATE or MODIFY STRUCTURE, an attempt was made to add a new field to a data base structure or lengthen an existing field so that the total record length would exceed the maximum permissible length of 4000 characters.

Maximum record length exceeded.—detected on field <*n*>

See description of the "Illegal data length" messages.

Memory Variable file is invalid.

dBASE III PLUS cannot read the specified memory variable file, possibly because the disk has been damaged, or because you have named a file in your command that is not a dBASE III PLUS memory variable file.

Mismatched DO WHILE and ENDDO.

An ENDDO line was found in a program with no matching DO WHILE statement.

Network is busy.

In a network system running under the dBASE Administrator, more tasks were initiated than the file server can handle. Under these circumstances, you may also get other seemingly unrelated or unreasonable error messages. If this error occurs, try to close any open data bases before you exit from dBASE III PLUS to minimize the chance that data will be lost.

No database is in USE. Enter file name:

An attempt was made to execute a command that requires an open data base file with no data base open in the currently selected work area. You may enter the file name and the command will resume; but you may not open an index with the file this way. You can also press ESC to cancel the command, open the data base and index(es) with USE and/or SET INDEX, and then type the original command again (or retrieve it from HISTORY and resubmit it).

No fields to process.

An attempt was made to use the SUM or AVERAGE commands from the ASSIST menus on a data base with no numeric fields. This error also occurs if you execute a command that displays fields after establishing a field list (with SET FIELDS) that does not include any fields from the currently selected data base.

No fields were found to copy.

A COPY command was executed with a FIELD list in effect (established with the SET FIELDS command) that does not include any fields from the currently selected data base.

No find.

The index key value specified in a FIND or SEEK command was not found in the index. When a FIND or SEEK command fails to find the specified record, the EOF function is set to .T. and FOUND becomes .F.

No PARAMETER statement found.

An attempt was made to pass parameters to a program or procedure that does not contain a PARAMETERS statement.

Not a character expression.
Not a Logical expression.
Not a numeric expression.

An attempt was made to use an expression of the wrong data type where the data type *must* be character, logical, or numeric, for example, attempting to SUM a character field.

Not a dBASE database.

The file specified in a USE command was not recognized as a dBASE III PLUS data base file, possibly because the disk has been damaged, or because you have named a file in the command that is not a dBASE III PLUS data base file.

Not a valid PFS file.

The file specified in an IMPORT command was not recognized as a PFS data base file, possibly because the disk has been damaged, or because you have named a file in the command that was not created by PFS.

Not a valid QUERY file.

The file specified in a SET FILTER TO FILE command was not recognized as a query file, possibly because the disk has been damaged, or because you have named a file in the command that is not a dBASE III PLUS query file.

Not a valid VIEW file.

The file specified in a SET VIEW TO FILE command was not recognized as a view file, possibly because the disk has been damaged, or because you have named a file in the command that is not a dBASE III PLUS view file.

Not enough disk space for SORT.

The specified disk drive does not have room to accommodate both the temporary file used by the SORT command and the final sorted file. (This amounts to the size of the original file plus the size of the final sorted file.)

Not enough records to SORT.

The file specified in a SORT command does not have at least two records.

** Not Found **

The index key value specified in the FIND option of the BROWSE command was not found in the index. In this case, both the EOF and FOUND functions retain their previous values and the same set of records remains on the screen.

not readable

A DIR command was used to list the data base files on a disk, and dBASE III PLUS was unable to read one of the files, possibly because the file was damaged by a disk error.

Not suspended.

A RESUME command was issued when no command file was interrupted and suspended.

Numeric overflow (data was lost).

An attempt was made to give a numeric field a value too large for the field to accommodate. When this occurs, dBASE III PLUS may display the field in exponential notation (although it cannot be edited in this form) or replace the contents of the field with asterisks. This error can occur if you try to REPLACE a field with too large a value, or if the sums accumulated by a TOTAL command are too large to fit in the fields.

Operation with Logical field invalid.

Operation with Memo field invalid.

An attempt was made to perform an operation that is not permitted for the specified field type. For example, you cannot INDEX or SORT on a memo or logical field or use the value of a memo field in any expression (for example, testing the value in a condition in a FOR or WHILE clause).

Out of memory variable memory.

An attempt was made to create a new memory variable when the existing variables already exceed the amount of space allocated for memory variables (the default is 6000 bytes, which you may change with the MVARSIZ entry in CONFIG.DB).

Out of memory variable slots.

An attempt was made to create more than a total of 256 memory variables.

^—Out of range

Too large a value was specified for one of the options in CONFIG.DB (for example, a number greater than 31 for MVARSIZ, the number of kilobytes of memory allocated for memory variables).

Position is off the screen.

An attempt was made to use a row coordinate outside of the range 0 to 24 or a column coordinate outside of the range 0 to 79 in an @...SAY...GET command, with output routed to the screen. This error commonly occurs if you use or adapt a program or format file designed to print a report on paper to display data on the screen.

Printer is either not connected or turned off.

An output port was specified in a SET PRINTER TO command, with no peripheral device assigned to that port.

Printer not ready.

An attempt was made to send output to the printer with the printer not turned on or off. This error may occur if you do not redirect output to the correct port in a system with more than one printer. It also occurs if you try to print to a serial printer with dBASE III PLUS version 1.0.

Query not valid for this environment.

The query file named in a SET FILTER TO FILE command contained references to fields not present in the data base(s) currently open. Usually, this is because the query file was created for use with a different data base or set of data bases.

Record is in use by another.

In a network environment, an attempt was made to access a record that is currently locked by another user.

Record is not in index.

A record number that is not present in the index file was used in a command (for example, GOTO, or a command with RECORD *n* as the scope). This can occur if records were added to a data base without opening the index in the USE command and the index was not rebuilt afterward.

Record is not locked.

In a network environment, an attempt was made to update a record that was not first locked.

Record is out of range.

A record number used in a command (an explicit GOTO or a command with RECORD *n* as the scope) is not present in the data base file. This error can occur when an index does not match the data base file and dBASE III PLUS attempts to position the record pointer at the non-existent record corresponding to an index entry. These problems are commonly caused by rebooting or turning off the system without closing a data base file (and thereby updating the record count) after new records have been appended.

Record not inserted.

This warning message is displayed if you exit from an INSERT command with ESC, and the record is not added to the file.

Records do not balance (program error).

See description of the "Internal error" messages.

Relation record is in use by others.

In a network system, one workstation has opened two files and linked them with SET RELATION, a second workstation has used the RLOCK function to lock a record in the file accessed through the RELATION, and the first workstation has attempted to use a GOTO or SEEK command to position the record pointer in the main data base to the record linked to the locked record.

Report file invalid.

dBASE III PLUS cannot read a report form file, possibly because the disk has been damaged, or because you have specified a file that is not a dBASE III PLUS report form file.

Structure invalid.

An attempt was made to use the CREATE FROM command to create a new data base from an invalid structure-extended file. This can occur if the file was damaged by a disk error or if you have used MODIFY STRUCTURE to change the field names or types in the structure-extended file.

Syntax error.

An expression or part of a command is constructed incorrectly.

Syntax error in contents expression
Syntax error in field expression
Syntax error in group expression
Syntax error in subgroup expression

One of the expressions used to specify the contents of a line in a label form, a column in a report form, or the field(s) on which to base the subtotal or subsubtotal breaks in a report is incorrect. Because CREATE/MODIFY LABEL/REPORT check for syntax errors as you create or edit a report or label form, these errors can only occur if the form was created or modified outside of dBASE III PLUS; if a field name or type was changed in the data base structure so that a formerly correct expression is no longer valid; or if a label or report form is used with a different data base that is missing one of the fields specified in the label form or that has a field with the same name but a different type than the one for which the form was designed.

Table is full.

An attempt was made to place more than five binary modules into memory with the LOAD command.

Too many characters in REPORT.

An attempt was made to define a report form so complex that more than the maximum of 1440 bytes was required to store the form.

Too many files are open.

An attempt was made to open more than the number of files permitted by the operating system. With no FILES entry in CONFIG.SYS, the default number of files is 8 (of which 3 are available to you); this may be increased to 20 (leaving 15 for you) by including the command FILES = 20 in the CONFIG.SYS file present in the root directory of the disk from which the system is booted. The maximum refers to disk files of all types, not just data base files.

Too many indices.

More than the maximum of seven index files were named in a USE or SET INDEX command.

Too many merge steps.

See description of the "Internal error" messages.

Too many sort key fields.

More than the maximum of ten fields were named in a SORT command.

^—Truncated

A file name specified in CONFIG.DB (for example, in the TEDIT or WP options) is more than eight characters long. dBASE III PLUS truncates the name to the first eight characters.

Unable to load COMMAND.COM.

An attempt was made to execute an external program or command using RUN or to use an external word processor assigned to substitute for the standard dBASE III PLUS editor with a TEDIT or WP entry in CONFIG.DB, but COMMAND.COM was not available. COMMAND.COM must be present in the root directory of the disk used to boot the system or in a subdirectory identified to the operating system with the MS-DOS SET COMSPEC command.

Unable to Lock.

In a network environment, an attempt was made to lock a record using CTRL-O in one of the full-screen edit modes, but the record was already locked by another user.

Unable to Skip.

In a network environment, an attempt was made to SKIP to a record that was locked by another user.

Unassigned file no.

See description of the "Internal error" messages.

Unauthorized access level.

In a dBASE III PLUS system with a PROTECT security system in effect, an attempt was made to access a field or file by a user with an access level that does not have permission to carry out the requested operation on the specified data.

Unauthorized login.

Three successive unsuccessful attempts were made to log into dBASE III PLUS with a PROTECT security system in effect.

Unbalanced parentheses.

An expression does not have the same number of left and right parentheses. This error will also occur if you do not specify the same number of Start and End conditions in the Nest option of CREATE/MODIFY QUERY, since this command creates an expression containing parentheses.

Unknown function key.

A function key name or number that does not exist on the keyboard was specified in a SET FUNCTION command.

Unknown SCEDIT() return code:

See description of the "Internal error" messages.

*** Unrecognized command verb.

The first word in a command line is not one of the verbs recognized by dBASE III PLUS.

Unrecognized phrase/keyword in command.

One of the clauses in a command begins with a word not recognized by dBASE III PLUS. This may occur when you leave out a required keyword (like FIELDS or WITH), so that the following word (often a field name) occurs where dBASE III PLUS expects the keyword that normally introduces the clause.

Unsupported path given.

An attempt was made to specify the subdirectory one level up from the current subdirectory as ". . \" in a CREATE command. This notation is permitted in other dBASE III PLUS commands.

Unterminated string.

The ending delimiter for a character string was omitted.

Valid only in programs.

An attempt was made to use a command at the dot prompt that is permitted only in dBASE III PLUS programs, such as SUSPEND, DO CASE, DO WHILE, or any of the other components of the dBASE III PLUS programming structures.

Variable not found.

A command specified a field name not found in the current data base or a memory variable name that is not one of the currently active memory variables.

** WARNING ** Data will probably be lost. Confirm (Y/N)

The "Abort" option was selected when a command generated a "Disk full when writing file" error message. See description of the "Disk full" error message.

Wrong number of parameters.

The number of parameters specified in the DO command that called a program or procedure did not match the number specified in the PARAMETERS statement in the called program or procedure.

Trademarks

Apple®	Apple Computer, Inc.
AT®	International Business Machines Corporation
BRIEF™	UnderWare™, Inc.
COMPAQ®	COMPAQ Computer Corporation
dBASE®	Ashton-Tate
dBASE III®	Ashton-Tate
dBASE III PLUS™	Ashton-Tate
Epson®	Seiko Epson Corporation
Framework II™	Ashton-Tate
IBM®	International Business Machines Corporation
Kaypro™	Kaypro Corp.
Lotus®	Lotus Development Corporation
Microsoft®	Microsoft Corporation
MS-DOS®	Microsoft Corporation
MultiMate®	MultiMate International Corporation
Multiplan™	Microsoft Corporation
Norton®	Peter Norton Computing
Novell™	Novell Corp.
1-2-3®	Lotus Development Corporation

PC-File III®	ButtonWare, Inc.
PC-Write®	Quicksoft, Inc.
PFS®	Software Publishing Corp.
PS/2™	International Business Machines Corporation
Rolodex™	Zephyr American Corporation
SideKick®	Borland International, Inc.
SuperCalc®	Computer Associates International, Inc.
SuperLoc™	Softguard Systems, Inc.
Symphony®	Lotus Development Corporation
WordPerfect®	WordPerfect Corporation
WordStar®	MicroPro International Corporation
VisiCalc®	Lotus Development Corporation
Volkswriter®	Lifetree Software, Inc.
XT™	International Business Machines Corporation

Index

E

The manuscript for this book was prepared and submitted to Osborne/McGraw-Hill in electronic form. The acquisitions editor for this project was Nancy Carlston, the technical reviewer was Lisa Biow, and Fran Haselsteiner was the project editor.

Cover art by Bay Graphics Design Associates. Color separation by Colour Image. Cover supplier, Phoenix Color Corp. Book printed and bound by R.R. Donnelley & Sons Company, Crawfordsville, Indiana.

WordPerfect® Made Easy

by Mella Mincberg

Here's the book that makes learning WordPerfect® quick, easy ... even enjoyable. With Mincberg's follow-along lessons, this IBM® PC compatible word processing software will be at your command in just a couple of hours. Edit text, save and print a document, set tabs, format pages. You'll become a skillful WordPerfect user as you work through practical applications. When you're ready to explore more sophisticated WordPerfect features, Mincberg is there with detailed instructions to help you run WordPerfect's spell checker and mail merge, manage files, create macros, and use special enhancements like windows and line numbering. Mincberg, author of the ever-so-useful *WordPerfect®: Secrets, Solutions, Shortcuts*, draws on her years of computer training experience to help you become an assured, savvy WordPerfect user. (Includes quick-reference command card.)

$18.95 p

0-07-881297-6, 400 pp., 7³/₈ x 9¹/₄

Microsoft® Word Made Easy, Second Edition

by Paul Hoffman

Hoffman's top-selling *Microsoft® Word Made Easy* has been revised to cover Microsoft's latest version of this widely used word processing software. Both beginning and experienced users will find a clear presentation of Word's new features, "made easy" for immediate application. Hoffman covers text outlining, spelling correction, hyphenation, creating indexes and tables of contents, and laser printers. Word's new functions, style sheets, windows, and glossaries are described in depth, and you'll find extra tips for using the mail-merge function. In the tradition of Osborne's "Made Easy" series, all techniques are explained with practical hands-on examples and are illustrated with helpful screen displays.

$16.95 p

0-07-881248-8, 300 pp., 7³/₈ x 9¹/₄

Your IBM® PC Made Easy (Includes IBM PC (DOS 2.0) And PC-XT)

by Jonathan Sachs

"In one word, OUTSTANDING! Perfect for beginning and advanced users, an excellent tutorial/reference. A very thorough guide to most facets of your IBM PC, from PC-DOS, hardware, software, resources supplies, batch files, etc. Rating: A" (Computer Book Review)

$14.95 p

0-07-881112-0, 250 pp., 7¹/₂ x 9¹/₄

C Made Easy

by Herbert Schildt

With Osborne/McGraw-Hill's popular "Made Easy" format, you can learn C programming in no time. Start with the fundamentals and work through the text at your own speed. Schildt begins with general concepts, then introduces functions, libraries, and disk input/output, and finally advanced concepts affecting the C programming environment and UNIX™ operating system. Each chapter covers commands that you can learn to use immediately in the hands-on exercises that follow. If you already know BASIC, you'll find that Schildt's C equivalents will shorten your learning time. *C Made Easy* is a step-by-step tutorial for all beginning C programmers.

$18.95 p

0-07-881178-3, 350 pp., 7³/₈ x 9¹/₄

Using dBASE III® PLUS™

by Edward Jones

Osborne's top-selling title, *Using dBASE III,®* by Edward Jones, has now been updated to include Ashton-Tate's new upgrade, dBASE III® PLUS.™ With Jones' expertise you'll be in full command of all the new features of this powerful database software. Learn to design, create, and display a dBASE III PLUS database, devise entry forms with the dBASE III PLUS screen painter, generate reports, use Query files, and plug into dBASE III PLUS networking. In addition, you'll find out how to install dBASE III PLUS on a hard disk, conduct data searches, and manipulate assistant pull-down menus. *Using dBASE III® PLUS™* is a thorough and practical handbook for both beginning and experienced dBASE III users.

$18.95

0-07-881252-6, 350 pp., 7³/₈ x 9¹/₄

Advanced dBASE III PLUS™: Programming and Techniques

by Miriam Liskin

Liskin's enormously successful *Advanced dBASE III*® has been completely revised to offer comprehensive coverage of dBASE III PLUS™. Expand your dBASE® skills as you learn programming techniques that let you design and implement more effective dBASE III PLUS business applications. Nationally known columnist and consultant Miriam Liskin addresses the "real world" business environment so you can make the most of dBASE III PLUS modes of operation. Liskin's discussion of new features offers you greater convenience when you work with multiple files at the dot prompt. You'll learn how to write portable, hardware-independent systems and use new error-trapping capabilities so you can work with more flexible on-line help systems. You'll also find out how to benefit from file- and record-locking features that enable you to design a multiuser data base system that can be especially important in networking.

$21.95 p

0-07-881249-6, 816 pp., 7³/₈ x 9¹/₄

The Osborne/McGraw-Hill Guide to Using Lotus™ 1-2-3,™ Second Edition, Covers Release 2

by Edward M. Baras

Your investment in Lotus™ 1-2-3™ can yield the most productive returns possible with the tips and practical information in *The Osborne/McGraw-Hill Guide to Using Lotus™ 1-2-3.™* Now the second edition of this acclaimed bestseller helps you take full advantage of Lotus' new 1-2-3 upgrade, Release 2. This comprehensive guide offers a thorough presentation of the worksheet, database, and graphics functions. In addition, the revised text shows you how to create and use macros, string functions, and many other sophisticated 1-2-3 features. Step by step, you'll learn to implement 1-2-3 techniques as you follow application models for financial forecasting, stock portfolio tracking, and forms-oriented database management. For both beginners and experienced users, this tutorial quickly progresses from fundamental procedures to advanced applications.

$18.95 p

0-07-881230-5, 432 pp., 7³/₈ x 9¹/₄

The Advanced Guide to Lotus™ 1-2-3™

by Edward M. Baras

Edward Baras, Lotus expert and author of *The Symphony™ Book, Symphony™ Master,* and *The Jazz™ Book,* now has a sequel to his best-selling *Osborne/McGraw-Hill Guide to Using Lotus™ 1-2-3.™* For experienced users, *The Advanced Guide to Lotus 1-2-3* delves into more powerful and complex techniques using the newest software upgrade, Release 2. Added enhancements to 1-2-3's macro language, as well as many new functions and commands, are described and thoroughly illustrated in business applications. Baras shows you how to take advantage of Release 2's macro capabilities by programming 1-2-3 to simulate Symphony's keystroke-recording features and by processing ASCII files automatically. You'll also learn to set up your own command menus; use depreciation functions, matric manipulation, and regression analysis; and convert text files to the 1-2-3 worksheet format.

$18.95 p

0-07-881237-2, 325 pp., 7³/₈ x 9¹/₄

dBASE III PLUS™: The Complete Reference

by Joseph-David Carrabis

This indispensable dBASE III PLUS™ reference will undoubtedly be the most frequently used book in your dBASE III® library. *dBASE III PLUS™: The Complete Reference* is a comprehensive resource to every dBASE III and dBASE III PLUS command, function, and feature. Each chapter covers a specific task so you can quickly pinpoint information on installing the program, designing databases, creating files, manipulating data, and many other subjects. Chapters also contain an alphabetical reference section that describes all the commands and functions you need to know and provides clear examples of each. Carrabis, author of several acclaimed dBASE books, discusses the lastest features of dBASE III PLUS, including networking capabilities; the Assistant, a menu-driven interface; and the Applications Generator, a short-cut feature for creating database files and applications without programming. *dBASE III PLUS™: The Complete Reference* also includes a glossary and handy appendixes that cover error messages, converting from dBASE II to dBASE III PLUS, and add-on utilities.

$25.95 p, Hardcover Edition

0-07-881315-x, 600 pp., 7³/₈ x 9¹/₄

$22.95 p, Paperback Edition

0-07-881012-4, 600 pp., 7³/₈ x 9¹/₄

1-2-3®: The Complete Reference

by Mary Campbell

1-2-3®: The Complete Reference is the authoritative desktop companion for every Lotus® 1-2-3® user. All commands, functions, and procedures are explained in detail and are demonstrated in practical "real-world" business applications. Conventionally organized according to task, this essential reference makes it easy to locate information on topics such as printing, macros, graphics production, and data mangement. Each chapter thoroughly describes a 1-2-3 task and all the procedures it requires, followed by an alphabetical listing of every command or function applied. Special emphasis is placed on compatible software packages, including Report Writer™, Reflex™ and others, that you can use to extend 1-2-3's capabilities. Campbell, a consultant and writer whose magazine columns appear monthly in *IBM PC UPDATE*, *Absolute Reference*, and *CPA Journal*, draws on her years of 1-2-3 expertise to provide you with this outstanding, comprehensive resource.

$25.95 p, Hardcover Edition
0-07-881288-7, 928 pp., 7³/₈ x 9¹/₄

$22.95 p, Paperback Edition
0-07-881005-1, 928 pp., 7³/₈ x 9¹/₄

C: The Complete Reference

by Herbert Schildt

Once again Osborne's master C programmer and author Herb Schildt, shares his insight and expertise with all C programmers in his latest book, *C: The Complete Reference.* Designed for both beginning and advanced C programmers, this is an encyclopedia for C terms, functions, codes, applications, and more. *C: The Complete Reference* is divided into five parts, each covering an important aspect of C. Part one covers review material and discusses key words in C. Part two presents an extensive summary of C libraries by category. Part three concentrates on various algorithms and C applications and includes information on random number generators as well as artificial intelligence and graphics. Part four addresses interfacing efficiency, porting, and debugging. Finally, part five is for serious programmers who are interested in C++, C's latest direction. The book also includes complete information on the proposed ANSI standard

$27.95 p, Hardcover Edition
0-07-881313-1, 740 pp., 7³/₈ x 9¹/₄

$24.95 p, Paperback Edition
0-07-881263-1, 740 pp., 7³/₈ x 9¹/₄

DOS: The Complete Reference

by Kris Jamsa

Why waste computing time over a baffling PC-DOS™ command or an elusive MS-DOS® function? *DOS: The Complete Reference* has the answers to all of your questions on DOS through version 3.X. This essential resource is for every PC- and MS-DOS user, whether you need an overview of the disk operating system or a reference for advanced programming and disk management techniques. Each chapter begins with a discussion of specific applications followed by a list of commands used in each. All commands are presented in the same clear, concise format: description, syntax, discussion of arguments or options, and examples. For comprehensive coverage, *DOS: The Complete Reference* discusses Microsoft® Windows and EDLIN, and provides two special appendixes covering the ASCII chart and DOS error messages. A ready resource, *DOS: The Complete Reference* is the only DOS consultant you'll need.

$27.95 p, Hardcover Edition
0-07-881314-x, 840 pp., 7³/₈ x 9¹/₄

$24.95 p, Paperback Edition
0-07-881259-3, 840 pp., 7³/₈ x 9¹/₄

WordPerfect®: The Complete Reference

by Karen L. Acerson

Osborne's highly successful Complete Reference series has a new addition, *WordPerfect®: The Complete Reference*. Every WordPerfect feature, key, menu, prompt, and error message is explained in simple terms for new users, and with sophisticated technical information supplied for those with experience. Acerson, an early member of WordPerfect Corporation who has been helping WordPerfect users get the most from their software since 1983, discusses the techniques for integrating WordPerfect with Lotus® 1-2-3®, dBASE® III, and other widely used software. Here's another ideal desktop companion to add to your collection.

$27.95 p, Hardcover Edition
0-07-881312-3, 675 pp., 7³/₈ x 9¹/₄

$24.95 p, Paperback Edition
0-07-881266-6, 675 pp., 7³/₈ x 9¹/₄

Available at fine bookstores and computer stores everywhere.

For a complimentary catalog of all our current publications contact:
Osborne/ McGraw-Hill, 2600 Tenth Street, Berkeley, CA 94710

Phone inquiries may be made using our toll-free number.
Call 800-227-0900 or 800-772-2531 (in California). TWX 910-366-7277.

Prices subject to change without notice.

Full-Screen Editing Commands

Control Key	Keypad Key	Function
CTRL-E	UP ARROW	Move the cursor up one line
CTRL-X	DOWN ARROW	Move the cursor down one line
CTRL-D	RIGHT ARROW	Move the cursor right one character
CTRL-S	LEFT ARROW	Move the cursor left one character
CTRL-F	END	Move the cursor right one field, column, or word
CTRL-A	HOME	Move the cursor left one field, column, or word
CTRL-C	PGDN	Move forward to the next screen
CTRL-R	PGUP	Move backward to the previous screen
	CTRL-PGUP or CTRL-PGDN or CTRL-HOME	Enter the memo editor
	CTRL-PGUP or CTRL-END	Save the current memo field and exit the memo editor
CTRL-B	CTRL-RIGHT ARROW	BROWSE: Pan the display right to display the next group of fields Memo/Program Editors: Move the cursor to the end of the line
CTRL-Z	CTRL-LEFT ARROW	BROWSE: Pan the display left to display the previous group of fields Memo/Program Editors: Move the cursor to the beginning of the line
CTRL-G	DEL	Delete the character at the cursor position
	BACKSPACE	Delete the character to the left of the cursor
CTRL-T		Delete characters from the cursor to the end of the word
CTRL-Y		Delete characters from the cursor to the end of the line Memo/Program Editors: Delete the line containing the cursor
CTRL-U		Mark the current record for deletion CREATE/MODIFY Editors: Delete the current field
CTRL-V	INS	Turn Insert mode on (if it is off) or off (if it is on)
CTRL-N		Insert a new line or field
CTRL-KB		Reformat the command or paragraph containing the cursor
CTRL-KF		Find a string of characters, searching forward from the cursor
CTRL-KL		Repeat the previous search
CTRL-KR		Read a disk file into the current memo field or program
CTRL-KW		Write the current memo field or program to another disk file
CTRL-W	CTRL-END	Save changes and exit
CTRL-Q	ESC	Exit without saving changes
	F1	Turn help menu on (if it is off) or off (if it is on)
	CTRL-HOME	Access special option menus

Commands

APPEND [BLANK]

APPEND FROM <*file name*> [FOR <*condition*>] [TYPE DELIMITED [WITH <*delimiter*> /BLANK]/SDF/DIF/SYLK/WKS]

ASSIST

AVERAGE [<*scope*>] [<*expN list*>] [FOR <*condition*>] [WHILE <*condition*>] [TO <*memvar list*>]

BROWSE [FIELDS <*field list*>] [LOCK <*expN*>] [FREEZE <*field*>] [WIDTH <*expN*>] [NOFOLLOW] [NOMENU] [NOAPPEND]

CHANGE [<*scope*>] [FIELDS <*field list*>] [FOR <*condition*>] [WHILE <*condition*>]

CLEAR

CLEAR ALL/FIELDS/GETS/MEMORY/TYPEAHEAD

CLOSE ALL/ALTERNATE/DATABASES/FORMAT/INDEX/PROCEDURE

CONTINUE

Note: This reference does not include commands and functions that are used primarily for programming in dBASE III PLUS.

Commands

COPY TO <*file name*> [<*scope*>] [FIELDS <*field list*>] [FOR <*condition*>] [WHILE <*condition*>] [TYPE DELIMITED [WITH <*delimiter*>/BLANK]/SDF/DIF/SYLK/WKS]

COPY FILE <*file 1*> TO <*file 2*>

COPY STRUCTURE TO <*file name*> [FIELDS <*field list*>]

COPY TO <*filename*> STRUCTURE EXTENDED

COUNT [<*scope*>] [FOR <*condition*>] [WHILE <*condition*>] [TO <*memvar*>]

CREATE <*file name*>

CREATE <*file name*> FROM <*structure-extended file*>

CREATE LABEL <*label file name*>

CREATE QUERY <*query file name*>

CREATE REPORT <*report file name*>

CREATE SCREEN <*screen file name*>

CREATE VIEW <*view file name*> [FROM ENVIRONMENT]

DELETE [<*scope*>] [FOR <*condition*>] [WHILE <*condition*>]

DELETE FILE <*file name*>

DIR [<*drive*>:] [<*path*>\] [<*skeleton*>] [TO PRINT]

DISPLAY [<*scope*>] [<*exp list*>] [FOR <*condition*>] [WHILE <*condition*>] [TO PRINT] [OFF]

DISPLAY FILES [LIKE <*skeleton*>] [TO PRINT]

DISPLAY HISTORY [LAST <*expN*>] [TO PRINT]

DISPLAY MEMORY [TO PRINT]

DISPLAY STATUS [TO PRINT]

DISPLAY STRUCTURE [TO PRINT]

DISPLAY USERS

DO <*program name*> [WITH <*parameter list*>]

EDIT [<*scope*>] [FIELDS <*field list*>] [FOR <*condition*>] [WHILE <*condition*>]

EJECT

ERASE <*file name*>

EXPORT TO <*file name*> TYPE PFS

FIND <*character string*>/<*n*>

GO/GOTO <*expN*>/BOTTOM/TOP

HELP [<*keyword*>]

IMPORT FROM <*file name*> TYPE PFS

INDEX ON <*key expression*> TO <*index file name*> [UNIQUE]

INSERT [BLANK] [BEFORE]

JOIN WITH <*alias*> TO <*file name*> FOR <*condition*> [FIELDS <*field list*>]

LABEL FORM <*label format file*> [<*scope*>] [FOR <*condition*>] [WHILE <*condition*>] [TO PRINT] [TO FILE <*file name*>] [SAMPLE]

LIST [<*scope*>] [<*exp list*<] [FOR <*condition*>] [WHILE <*condition*>] [TO PRINT] [OFF]

LIST FILES [LIKE <*skeleton*>]

LIST HISTORY [LAST <*expN*>] [TO PRINT]

LIST MEMORY [TO PRINT]

LIST STATUS [TO PRINT]

LIST STRUCTURE [TO PRINT]

LOCATE [<*scope*>] [FOR <*condition*>] [WHILE <*condition*>]

LOGOUT

MODIFY COMMMAND [<*file name*>]

MODIFY FILE [<*file name*>]

MODIFY LABEL <*label file name*>

MODIFY QUERY <*label file name*>

MODIFY REPORT <*report file name*>

MODIFY SCREEN <*label file name*>

MODIFY STRUCTURE <*file name*>

MODIFY VIEW <*label file name*>

PACK

QUIT

RECALL [<*scope*>] [FOR <*condition*>] [WHILE <*condition*>]

REINDEX

RELEASE [ALL [LIKE/EXCEPT <*skeleton*>]]/[<*memvar list*>]

RENAME <*old file name*> TO <*new file name*>

REPLACE [<*scope*>] <*field*> WITH <*exp*> [,<*field2*> WITH <*exp2*>. . .] [FOR <*condition*>] [WHILE <*condition*>]

Note: This reference does not include commands and functions that are used primarily for programming in dBASE III PLUS.

Commands

REPORT FORM <*report form file*> [<*scope*>] [FOR <*condition*>]
[WHILE <*condition*>]
[NOEJECT] [PLAIN] [SUMMARY] [HEADING <*expC*>] [TO PRINT]
[TO FILE <*file name*>]

RESTORE FROM <*file name*> [ADDITIVE]

RESUME

RUN <*command*> / !<*command*>

SAVE TO <*file name*> [ALL LIKE/EXCEPT <*skeleton*>]

SEEK <*exp*>

SELECT <*work area/alias*>

SET

SET ALTERNATE TO [<*file name*>]

SET ALTERNATE on/OFF

SET BELL ON/off

SET CARRY on/OFF

SET CATALOG TO [<*catalog file name*>]

SET CATALOG on/OFF

SET CENTURY on/OFF

SET COLOR TO [<*standard foreground/standard background*>]
[, <*enhanced foreground/enhanced background*>] [, <*border*>]

SET COLOR on/off

SET CONFIRM on/OFF

SET DATE AMERICAN/ansi/british/italian/french/german

SET DECIMALS TO <*expN*>

SET DEFAULT TO <*drive*>

SET DELETED on/OFF

SET DELIMITERS TO [<*delimiter(s)*>] [DEFAULT]

SET DELIMITERS on/OFF

SET ENCRYPTION ON/off

SET EXACT on/OFF

SET EXCLUSIVE ON/off

SET FIELDS TO [<*field list*>/ALL]

SET FIELDS on/OFF

SET FILTER TO [<*condition*>]/[FILE <*query file name*>]

SET FIXED on/OFF

SET FORMAT TO [<*format file name*>]

SET FUNCTION <*exp*> TO <*expC*>

SET HEADING ON/off

SET HELP ON/off

SET HISTORY TO <*expN*>

SET HISTORY ON/off

SET INDEX TO [<*index file list*>]

SET INTENSITY ON/off

SET MARGIN TO <*expN*>

SET MEMOWIDTH TO <*expN*>

SET MENUS on/OFF

SET MESSAGE TO [<*expC*>]

SET ODOMETER TO [<*expN*>]

SET ORDER TO [<*expN*>]

SET PATH TO [<*path name list*>]

SET PRINT on/OFF

SET PRINTER TO [<*DOS device name*>]

SET PRINTER TO [\ \SPOOLER/<*computer name*> \<*printer name*>=
<*DOS device name*>]

SET RELATION TO [<*key expression*>/RECNO( )/<*expN*> INTO
<*alias*>]

SET SAFETY ON/off

SET SCOREBOARD ON/off

SET STATUS ON/off

SET TALK ON/off

SET TITLE ON/off

SET TYPEAHEAD TO <*expN*>

SET UNIQUE on/OFF

SET VIEW TO <*view file name*>

SKIP [<*expN*>]

SORT TO <*new file name*> ON <*field1*> [/A]/[/D] [/C] [, <*field2*>
[/A]/[/D]. . .]
[<*scope*>] [FOR <*condition*>] [WHILE <*condition*>]

STORE <*exp*> to <*memvar list*> / <*memvar*>=<*exp*>

Note: This reference does not include commands and functions that are used primarily for programming in dBASE III PLUS.

Commands

SUM [<*scope*>] [<*expN list*>] [FOR <*condition*>] [WHILE <*condition*>] [TO <*memvar list*>]

TOTAL ON <*key field*> TO <*file name*> [<*scope*>] [FIELDS <*field list*>] [FOR <*condition*>] [WHILE <*condition*>]

TYPE <*file name*> [TO PRINT]

UPDATE ON <*key field*> FROM <*alias*> REPLACE <*field1*> WITH <*exp1*> [, <*field2*> WITH <*exp2*>. . .] [RANDOM]

USE [<*file name*>] [INDEX <*index file list*>] [ALIAS <*alias*>] [EXCLUSIVE]

ZAP

Functions

&<*character variable*>

ABS(<*number*>)
Input: Numeric expression
Output: Number

ASC(<*character string*>)
Input: Character string expression
Output: Number

AT(<*character string 1*>, <*character string 2*>)
Inputs: Character string expression, character string expression
Output: Number

CDOW(<*expD*>)
Input: Date expression
Output: Character string

CHR(<*number*>)
Input: Numeric expression
Output: Character

CMONTH(<*date*>)
Input: Date expression
Output: Character string

CTOD(<*character expression*>)
Input: Character expression
Output: Date

DATE()
Input: None
Output: Date

DAY(<*date*>)
Input: Date expression
Output: Number

DELETED()
Input: None
Output: Logical value

DISKSPACE()
Input: None
Output: Number

DOW(<*date*>)
Input: Date expression
Output: Number

DTOC(<*date*>)
Input: Date expression
Output: Character string

EXP(<*number*>)
Input: Numeric expression
Output: Number

IIF(<*condition*>, <*expression 1*>, <*expression 2*>)
Inputs: Logical expression, expression, expression
Output: Same data type as expressions 1 and 2

INT(<*number*>)
Input: Numeric expression
Output: Number

LEFT(<*character string*>, <*length*>)
Inputs: Character string expression, numeric expression
Output: Character string

LOG(<*number*>)
Input: Numeric expression
Output: Number

LOWER(<*character string*>)
Input: Character string expression
Output: Character string

LTRIM(<*character string*>)
Input: Character string expression
Output: Character string

MAX(<*numeric expression*>, <*numeric expression*>)
Inputs: Numeric expression, numeric expression
Output: Number

Note: This reference does not include commands and functions that are used primarily for programming in dBASE III PLUS.

Functions

MIN(<*numeric expression*>, <*numeric expression*>)
- Inputs: Numeric expression, numeric expression
- Output: Number

MONTH(<*date*>)
- Input: Date expression
- Output: Number

RECCOUNT()
- Input: None
- Output: Number

RECNO()
- Input: None
- Output: Number

RECSIZE()
- Input: None
- Output: Number

REPLICATE(<*character string*>, <*number*>)
- Inputs: Character string expression, numeric expression
- Output: Character string

RIGHT(<*character string*>, <*length*>)
- Inputs: Character string expression, numeric expression
- Output: Character string

ROUND(<*number*>, <*decimals*>)
- Inputs: Numeric expression, numeric expression
- Output: Number

RTRIM(<*character string*>)
- Input: Character string expression
- Output: Character string

SPACE(<*number*>)
- Input: Numeric expression
- Output: Character string

SQRT(<*number*>)
- Input: Numeric expression
- Output: Number

STR(<*number*> [,<*length*>] [,<*decimals*>]
- Inputs: Numeric expression, numeric expression, numeric expression
- Output: Character string

SUBSTR(<*character string*>, <*starting position*> [,<*length*>])
- Inputs: Character string expression, numeric expression, numeric expression
- Output: Character string

TIME()
- Input: None
- Output: Character string

TRANSFORM(<*expression*>, <*picture*>)
- Inputs: Expression, character string expression
- Output: Same data type as expression

TRIM(<*character string*>)
- Input: Character string expression
- Output: Character string

UPPER(<*character string*>)
- Input: Character string expression
- Output: Character string

VAL(<*character string*>)
- Input: Character string expression
- Output: Number

YEAR(<*date*>)
- Input: Date expression
- Output: Number

Note: This reference does not include commands and functions that are used primarily for programming in dBASE III PLUS.

IF YOU ENJOYED THIS BOOK . . .

help us stay in touch with your needs and interests by filling out and returning the survey card below. Your opinions are important, and will help us to continue to publish the kinds of books you need, when you need them.

What brand of computer(s) do you own or use? ____________

Where do you use your computer the most? ☐ At work ☐ At school ☐ At home

What topics would you like to see covered in future books by Osborne/McGraw-Hill?

____

How many other computer books do you own? ____________

Why did you choose this book?

- ☐ Best coverage of the subject.
- ☐ Recognized the author from previous work.
- ☐ Liked the price.
- ☐ Other

Where did you hear about this book?

- ☐ Book review.
- ☐ Osborne catalog.
- ☐ Advertisement in: ____________
- ☐ Found by browsing in store.
- ☐ Found/recommended in library
- ☐ Other

Where did you find this book?

- ☐ Bookstore
- ☐ Computer/software store
- ☐ Department store
- ☐ Advertisement
- ☐ Catalog
- ☐ Required textbook
- ☐ Library
- ☐ Gift
- ☐ Other

Where should we send your FREE catalog?

NAME ____________

ADDRESS ____________

294-1 CITY ____________ STATE ____________ ZIP ____________